Woman Walking Ahead

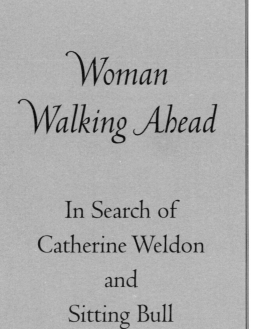

Woman Walking Ahead

In Search of Catherine Weldon and Sitting Bull

Eileen Pollack

UNIVERSITY OF NEW MEXICO PRESS

ALBUQUERQUE

UNIVERSITY OF NEW MEXICO PRESS

ALBUQUERQUE

© 2002 by Eileen Pollack

All rights reserved.

First edition

Library of Congress Cataloging-in-Publication Data

Pollack, Eileen.

Woman walking ahead : in search of Catherine Weldon and Sitting Bull /
Eileen Pollack.—1st ed.

p. cm.

Includes bibliographical references and index.

ISBN 0-8263-2844-x (cloth : alk. paper)

1. Weldon, Catherine.   2. Sitting Bull, 1834?–1890.   3. Women social reformers—
United States—Biography.   4. Ghost dance.   5. Dakota Indians—Biography.
6. Hunkpapa Indians—Biography.   I. Title.

E99.D1 W386 2002

978.004´9752—dc21

2002000357

For James Alan McPherson
teacher, friend

Look, Catherine! There are no more demons outside the door.

The white wolf drags its shawled tail into the high snow

through the pine lances, the blood dried round its jaw;

it is satisfied. Come, come to the crusted window,

blind as it is with the ice, through the pane's cataract;

see, it's finished. It's over, Catherine, you have been saved.

Derek Walcott
Omeros

Contents

Part 1

1

Leaving Brooklyn

~ *Y*ears ago, in graduate school, one of my professors suggested I write a book about a mysterious white woman who lived with Sitting Bull during the last years of his life. This woman and her son took a train to the Dakotas and moved in with Sitting Bull. She read him stories about Napoleon, painted his portrait, and gave him advice about how to fight the government. He proposed marriage, and that upset her. She left the reservation. Her son died. No one knew what became of her after Sitting Bull was killed.

My professor couldn't recall the woman's name or the book in which he found her. All he knew was that she made an authentic gesture of friendship toward someone unlike herself at a time when such gestures were rare. My professor, who is black, grew up in Savannah, Georgia, fatherless and poor, before desegregation. Unexpected gestures of friendship helped him stay alive, as his own gifts to his friends and students helped us get by. I was touched by his generosity, his faith in my ability to unearth the buried shards of this forgotten woman's story. But I was reluctant to start a project so outside my expertise.

Months went by. Years. One snowy afternoon I was wandering the stacks of the Boston Public Library when I came across a biography of Sitting Bull published in 1932 by a writer named Stanley Vestal. Chapter 34 was called "Sitting Bull's 'White Squaw.'"

Catherine Weldon was a representative of the National Indian Defense Association, who had come all the way from Brooklyn, New York, to see [Sitting Bull]. . . . She was a lady, well dressed, and not bad looking, indeed overdressed, with many showy rings and brooches, and fashionable clothes. Her hair was graying, for she was nearing, if she had not already reached, that age at which some women suffer a change and do unaccountable things. A strange apparition at Standing Rock.

In another of Vestal's books, I found copies of three letters Weldon wrote to Sitting Bull, along with a letter she wrote to Red Cloud, chief of the Oglala Sioux at Pine Ridge, and five notes she sent the agent in charge of Standing Rock, the reservation where Sitting Bull lived. Also included in Vestal's book were fragments from the journal Weldon kept at Standing Rock and the text of a speech she delivered to Sitting Bull's warriors to convince them that their belief in an Indian messiah was "misguided." Her voice was flighty, temperamental, manipulative, brash.

I kept rereading those few letters. They provided all anyone seemed to know about Weldon's life. As far as I could tell, she traveled out to Standing Rock in June 1889 to help Sitting Bull and his tribe withstand the government's coercion to sell great portions of their land. Sitting Bull, who was then in his fifties, lived forty miles from the agency, at a remote site on the Grand River. Bitter and despairing, he was recovering from a nearly fatal bout of pneumonia. Yet he roused himself from his sickbed and drove all that way to meet her.

If Vestal's account is to be believed, Sitting Bull found an attractive, middle-aged widow in fashionable but ostentatious clothes that set her apart from the drab wives of the soldiers at nearby Fort Yates. Her aggressive behavior baffled him, but she treated him as a great leader, enjoyed confronting the agent on his behalf, and seemed dedicated to helping his people keep their land. And if Weldon's own version of their meeting is reliable, Sitting Bull welcomed her offer to act as his lobbyist, translator, and adviser. With the help of the small Indian-rights organization to which she belonged, she supplied him with maps and lists of fair prices for his land. So vociferously did she campaign for Sitting Bull's rights that the agent in charge of Standing Rock ordered her to leave. ("SHE LOVES SITTING BULL" ran the headlines. "A New Jersey Widow falls victim to Sitting Bull's Charms.")

In Weldon's absence, a panel of commissioners from Washington held a meeting from which Sitting Bull was barred and bullied his followers into signing away their land. With the cession now law, Weldon returned to Brooklyn. But she couldn't forget Sitting Bull or the beauty of the Plains. The following spring, she wrote a letter to James McLaughlin, the agent in charge of Standing Rock, begging to be allowed to return.

Strangely, he granted her request, and in May 1890, Weldon traveled back to Standing Rock. A few weeks later, she sent for her son. At first, they lived with two mixed-race women, Alma Parkin and Louise Van Solen, on the prosperous Parkin Ranch just north of the reservation. Then Weldon took Christie and moved to Sitting Bull's camp, where they lived with his two wives and their children and two hundred members of their band, the Hunkpapa Sioux. Weldon joined the women in their chores and kept her friends alive during the ferocious drought that year by selling her possessions. *Toka heya mani win*, they named her, Woman Walking Ahead. If one credits Weldon's diary, Sitting Bull considered her a friend. He even proposed marriage, but Weldon grew insulted and turned him down. Afterward they had a more serious fight. A religious ceremony called the Ghost Dance found its way to Standing Rock. The Indians believed that if they performed this dance, a messiah would appear, wipe out all the whites, and bring back the dead Indians, along with herds of buffalo, fresh grass, and vanished game. Weldon scoffed at the possibility. She told Sitting Bull that the army would use this talk as an excuse to attack the dancers and get rid of him.

But Sitting Bull wouldn't listen. Angry and afraid—many of her former friends saw her as a traitor—Weldon took Christie and left the reservation. The new religion spread. The white settlers grew frantic. The government sent in troops. The Sioux "uprising" of 1890–91 was the last significant Indian war; the aftermath included the murder of Sitting Bull, his young son Crow Foot, and six Hunkpapa warriors, as well as the massacre of two hundred Sioux at Wounded Knee, among them twenty or thirty refugees from Sitting Bull's camp.

The press held Weldon responsible. Reporters claimed that she had stirred Sitting Bull's "martial ardor" by providing him with gifts and throwing feasts for his people to restore his standing in their eyes. In a way, the charge was true. Although Weldon repeatedly told Sitting Bull that the messiah would never come, she did revive his spirits when he was ill. Her gifts helped to feed his followers. Sitting Bull's resistance to breaking up the reservation into privately owned allotments kept alive the ideal that Indians should live as Indians and hold their land in common.

Although Weldon on her own would have left little trace on history, by befriending Sitting Bull she threw a much larger shadow. How many women besides Helen of Troy have been held responsible for a war? In her own day, Weldon's name would have been as recognizable to her contemporaries as Jane Fonda's or Patty Hearst's name is to us. At the least, she was guilty of supporting a leader whom few other whites would recognize as great for decades to come. She traveled to a reservation and lived among the Indians, not to study or convert them or transform them into whites, but to help them live as Indians. She painted four portraits of Sitting Bull, apparently from life, at Grand River, yet all but one seemed lost. She barely is mentioned in the most up-to-date biography of Sitting Bull. Here was a woman who walked ahead of the most radical white Indian-rights activists of her century. She abandoned safety and sense, her possessions, her beloved son, and, for all her efforts, history abandoned her.

I wanted to follow Weldon's shadow and see where it might lead. But writing such a book would require that I scour archives throughout the East and Midwest. I would need to visit Standing Rock, whose inhabitants, I had heard, were still hostile to most white outsiders. Weldon followed her vocation across rigid ethnic lines, an activity to which society still objects, though for different reasons now. In writing a book about a white woman who traveled to the Dakotas and foisted her "help" on Sitting Bull, moved into his house, then burst out in indignation because he asked her to marry him, a woman who claimed to be the Indians' friend but grew so exasperated with their "backward" notions of religion that she dismissed them as "poor mis-guided beings . . . groping blindly for the true light & not finding it," I would betray my own prejudices. I would offend every Indian I interviewed (did one even call them "Indians"?).

If you are a white liberal who yearns to do good among those of another culture, you needn't hunt far for excuses to stay at home. If you are a mother, that's the best excuse. No one wants to be like Mrs. Jellyby, that lady of very remarkable strength who spends every moment Dickens allots her in *Bleak House* worrying about the unfortunate natives of Borrioboola-Gha while her own unkempt children go bouncing down flights of stairs. Weldon was a mother. She left her son in Brooklyn the first time she traveled west, and the press accused her of deserting him. When she moved to Standing Rock for good, she sent for her son, and her relatives accused her of disregarding his welfare in favor of "dirty-blanket Indians," thereby exposing him to the dangers that led to his death. If I traipsed around the country following Weldon's tracks, I would be abandoning my own son, who was then only three. Year after year, I kept putting off my search.

Once, as a sort of substitute, I tried to write a play in which Weldon and Sitting Bull acted out their tragedy on a stage devoid of scenery, relieving me of the need to describe a reservation I had never seen. But understanding Weldon and Sitting Bull turned out to be impossible without a knowledge of the world they lived in. I put away my notes, but every so often I took them out and read them. Who was Catherine Weldon? Wasn't she aware that moving in with Sitting Bull would open her to scandal? Her support for a Lakota chief still viewed by most Americans as Custer's savage killer would incur the government's rage. Yet she followed her eccentric vision. And, when my son seemed old enough, I finally followed mine.

~⌒

It was the sort of sparkling autumn day when New York is its best. I descended to the subway with a plastic map of Brooklyn and two destinations: the Historical Society, where I would try to turn up clues to Weldon's life before she went to Standing Rock in June 1889, and the address "16 Liberty Street," which she inscribed on her letter to the agent the following spring, begging permission to come back. The only glitch was that no Liberty Street appears on any modern map of Brooklyn. Liberty Avenue divides Bedford-Stuyvesant from Crown Heights. Maybe Weldon had been careless in writing her address and she meant Liberty Avenue. My plan was to spend the morning at the Historical Society, determining whether a Liberty Street had once existed or Weldon had really lived on Liberty Avenue. Armed with this information, I would hire a cab and find her house.

Ascending in Brooklyn, I was relieved to find myself on a broad, sunny square in front of the State Supreme Court Building. The plaza stretched north, row after row of peddlers' booths manned by merchants from Peru, Africa, India, Korea, and Puerto Rico. *Look, lady, look!* They hawked statues of the Virgin Mary, hairy alpaca sweaters, rip-offs of designer watches, bathroom fixtures, socks. The shoppers, like the peddlers, belonged to every ethnic group identifiable, and some I couldn't identify. I turned west and passed the Gap, Banana Republic, and Barnes & Noble, dead ending on a promenade overlooking the East River and the iridescent Manhattan skyline.

The Historical Society, its brick facade embellished with the heads of famous people I didn't recognize and Latin words I couldn't translate, seemed as comforting as home. Unfortunately, it wasn't open. My guidebook had promised that the museum would open at ten, but a sign notified patrons that the archives would remain closed until noon. If I waited that long to do my research, I wouldn't have time to find Weldon's house before dark. I saw no choice but to take a taxi to Liberty Avenue before I knew for sure if Weldon ever lived there.

Half an hour passed. Why were there no taxis? Everyone seemed too busy to ask, except a pudgy, dimpled man sitting in the driver's seat of an ambulance, licking sprinkles from a doughnut. "Excuse me," I said. "Is there something special I have to do to get a cab in Brooklyn?"

"Yeah. There's this special little dance. Here, I'll show you." He swung open the ambulance door and climbed out. I must have seemed startled.

"Don't worry, sweetheart." He climbed back in the ambulance. "You just flag one down. They're not yellow, like in Manhattan. They have these little cardboard 'car for hire' signs on the dash."

I walked back to the corner and, now that I knew what to look for, saw an unmarked car with a hand-lettered FOR HIRE sign. I slid into the backseat, but the absence of a meter and driver ID unnerved me. Years before, in London, I had been kidnapped and robbed by two con men masquerading as cabbies. "Are you sure this is a regular taxi?" I asked.

"Sure, sure, where you go?"

"Liberty Avenue."

The driver glared at me. I am very small and short and even in my forties appear to be sixteen. "That very bad neighborhood," he said, by which of course he meant that everyone there was black. "Why girl like you go there and come right back again, this bad neighborhood?" He narrowed his eyes as if I might be headed to Bed-Stuy to buy drugs.

"I'm writing a book about a woman who used to live there."

"Very far," he grumbled. "Cost a lot of money. Thirty dollar each way."

"That's ridiculous! Isn't there a bus?"

"No bus. Very bad neighborhood, girl like you." He swiveled around and studied me. He was young, with a sparse mustache, a delicate mouth, and smooth, tan cheeks. He was from India, I guessed, from his accent and his hair, black and shiny as his vinyl jacket. The cab smelled of cardamom and too-fruity cologne. He wore an oversized, shiny gold ring on his right hand and no ring at all on his left. "Okay, sweetheart, I take you there and back, thirty dollar. You want to look around a few minute, I get out with you, make sure you stay safe."

"Thirty dollars round-trip?"

"Sure, sure." He smiled a crooked smile, then floored the gas, bouncing us down a potholed alley behind the courthouse. He seemed to know where he was taking me; the alley linked up with Atlantic Avenue. The stores were saggy and run-down. A hairless dog trotted along the curb with what appeared to be a telephone receiver in its mouth. One magnificent old building—a civic center? an opera house?—had had its roof blown off. But what really would have happened if I had taken a bus through Bed-Stuy, then gotten out and walked around?

"So, this woman you visit," the cabby said, "where you know her from? She a friend of yours?"

"Oh, no," I said, "she lived there a hundred years ago. She's dead now."

"Why you want to go there, then, this woman is dead!"

"I'm writing a book about her," I repeated.

"Book? That's what you do, you write book?"

"Well, I teach, too. I write books and teach."

"Who you teach, little children?"

"Older people. College."

"What is college?" he asked.

His English was fluent; it was the concept of a college education he lacked. He had stopped attending school as a "little child," he said. I asked what country he was born in. "I come from Pakistan," he mumbled, as if the truth might be dangerous. Then he changed his mind. I wanted to know? He would tell me. As the eldest son, he was saving his money to bring his brother to America. That's what family members did in his country. Not like here, one person doesn't care about the other one. He flapped his hand. "In Pakistan, even if a man is all grown up, his father wants to give him licks, the son takes the licks, he does what the father says. Your parents, they give birth to you, they grow you up, they still lick you. Even if they are eighty, even if you are all grown up, you say nothing, you take licks. There, in my country, I see my younger brother on the street, he is doing something he should not be doing, I give him licks. He says nothing, it is what he expects from older brother. Here, a man I know, he hits his son, just one lick, the boy calls 911!" He glanced in the rearview mirror. "You think that is right?"

Of course the boy was right. Children don't deserve to be beaten. But it seemed elitist and Eurocentric to find fault with a different culture. And so I said and did what I usually say and do when someone from another culture says or does something that upsets me. I said and did nothing.

"You have husband? He doesn't mind you travel this way, alone?"

I did have a husband. But I was using this trip—I only saw this now—to escape the silences between us. Like Weldon, I was looking for something more exciting than domestic life. "Yes," I said. "I'm married. My husband doesn't mind."

"You have child?"

That was easy. "Yes. I have a little boy. He's seven."

"Boy! That is good. In my country, all the parents want boy. In your country, the parents want girl more." He shook his head—crazy.

"Some parents here prefer boys, some prefer girls. Some people don't care."

His turn to say nothing. What sort of parent wouldn't care about the gender of his child? He pulled off the main road and drove a block south. "Liberty Ave.," the sign read. The neighborhood consisted of rubble-strewn lots, monstrous brick apartments—public housing, I guessed—and three lusterless brick homes that once had stood upright, a house to each side, but now, with no support, seemed sway walled and so vulnerable a good punch might wreck them. In the garage of one house a man bent beneath a car hood.

"You!" the cabby yelled. The man withdrew his head. He looked around, puzzled. He was an older black man with hair the color of iron filings. His neck was permanently kinked from working under car hoods. Like his house, he seemed someone who would have been happier with a neighborhood around him. The cabby motioned roughly for him to join us. "You know where is number sixteen?"

The man, already bent, leaned his head inside the window. "No sixteen anywhere around here. Who you looking for?"

"Never mind," I said quickly, before the driver could insult him, "I was just looking for the house of someone who used to live here. We didn't mean to bother you."

The man pulled back his head; he was prepared to help, but not if his help wasn't wanted. Without straightening, he ambled back to his garage and stuck his head beneath the car hood. I told the cabby to pull up to the lot ahead, where a fence protected a stack of tires. Two gutted Barcaloungers faced the sidewalk, as if to provide a prime viewing spot for a parade. "She must have lived right here," I said with false confidence. "This lot would have been number sixteen. A hundred years ago, the whole neighborhood would have looked different. This would have been the country." The image seemed plausible—a bucolic Brooklyn neighborhood of stately homes and white children like Christie Weldon playing ball in the open fields where those ugly apartments now stood. I told the driver we could go.

"That's all? You drive out here, write a few words on paper, pay me so much?"

"I saw what I needed."

He headed us back the way we had come. "Where you live?" he asked. "Where you go home to?"

I lived in Ann Arbor, but home still felt like Boston, where I had lived for fifteen years, or the Catskills, where I had grown up. I loved the mountains, and the sea. I had only moved to Michigan because my husband got a job there. I forced myself to say it. "Michigan. Near Detroit."

"You need to fly there in plane?"

Yes, I said, Michigan—the Midwest—was in the middle of the country.

"What middle?"

"You know how New York is on this coast and California is on the west coast?"

He shook his head. "What is coast?"

"The ocean? You know, New York is on the Atlantic Ocean, and California is on the Pacific Ocean?"

He lifted his hands from the wheel. "I don't know about oceans."

"Well, the Midwest is midway between the two coasts."

"I never see map of this country," he admitted, and I tried to imagine living in a country without having any idea of where anything was. But then, I knew nothing about Pakistan. Until my son was born—Noah, who so loves puzzles and maps—I couldn't have filled in a third of the states in my own country. Truth be told, I still got confused by some of those states out west.

He pulled up beside the courthouse.

"What's your name?" I asked. It suddenly seemed important.

"Why you want to know?"

"I want to put you in my book."

One side of his mouth jerked up. "In your book, you call me Sam."

"Is Sam your real name?"

"You just put down 'Sam.' In your country, I am only Sam."

I handed him two twenties. He pocketed the bills and didn't offer to give me change. I couldn't bring myself to ask. I was paying him for his help in finding Weldon's house. I wanted to help him bring his brother to America. And I was giving him a tip for forcing me to admit what I already knew: that Catherine Weldon, long before her falling-out with Sitting Bull, thought him backward and superstitious, even as she believed in his right to keep his land. Like most liberals—like me—she was a victim of the fallacy that she could accept anything and anyone as long as she remained well-intentioned enough.

By now the Historical Society was open. I climbed the polished stairs to an unsettling collection of the musty and cybernetic—card catalogs and computer terminals, genealogies, dusty ledgers, and microfiche readers. A harried librarian with a skein of auburn hair unraveling down her back stood behind a counter, answering a patron's questions on the phone while sorting clippings with latex-gloved hands. "Try the death and marriage notices first," she mouthed to me, pointing with ghoulish fingers toward a shelf of obituaries and marriage announcements culled from the *Brooklyn Daily Eagle* in the mid-1800s.

The lists had been carefully typed on a manual typewriter, crinkly page after crinkly page. I spent an hour learning that plenty of Weldons had been married in Brooklyn in the mid-1800s, but not one of them was named Catherine. Plenty of Weldons had died, but again, not a Catherine. Perhaps Weldon and her husband lived across the river and she only moved to Brooklyn when, a new widow, she couldn't afford Manhattan rents.

I tried the city directory, a sort of phone book for people who lived in an age before phones, and cranked the spool of film covering May 1889 to May 1890 through the viewer. I tweaked the focus knob and saw "Weldon Catherine—

wid. h. 68 Box" leap into view. I whooped, and the librarian looked up at me and smiled. I could see the next years of my life unscroll before my eyes. One clue would lead to the next, then the next, then the next. I didn't need any special qualifications to hunt for Catherine Weldon. All I needed to do was look.

I found no listing for Catherine Weldon for 1888, but the listings the year before showed "Weldon Catharine, wid. Richard, h. 68 Box." I whooped again—Richard! No one had known her husband's name. Box Street was in an industrial neighborhood along the East River. In an earlier directory, I found a Richard Weldon living near Box. He was listed as a "joiner." It seemed odd that a woman who always was described as cultured and overdressed should be married to a carpenter. Then I saw my error. I found listings for *both* "Catharine, wid. Richard" at 68 Box and a "Weldon Richard, joiner" on a street nearby. The Richard who was a carpenter wasn't Catherine's husband. Maybe it was a coincidence that she lived so near his flat. Or this other Richard Weldon was her dead husband's father or his uncle or some other relative. (In the 1888 directory, a Patrick Weldon, driver, is listed at 68 Box, supporting the hypothesis that Weldon, as a widow, was living with her in-laws, who helped to raise her son.)

So Weldon was a widow living on Box Street before she went to Standing Rock in 1889. She returned to Brooklyn not long after, rented a new apartment, and spent the winter there before she moved back to the reservation in the spring of 1890. I found a blurry map of Brooklyn from the 1890s, and yes, there it was, Liberty *Street,* intersecting Nassau, Fulton, and Sprague, a few blocks from where I sat. My trip with Sam the Cabby had been a wild-goose chase. The neighborhood in which Liberty Street once lay was now covered by something called "Cadman Plaza." I asked the librarian what that was.

She scowled. "Cadman Plaza was one of Robert Moses's projects. He tore down a beautiful old neighborhood. Walt Whitman used to live there. He printed *Leaves of Grass* in a building at the corner of Fulton and Cranberry. People think Moses was a great man, but he did some awful things."

In a computer file I found a photo of a horse and carriage trotting down Liberty Street, circa 1890. The neighborhood was clean but plain—cobblestones, a fountain, stores or stables at street level, modest apartments above. Four jaunty men in vests crowded the doorway of Aschner's Cigar Store, which sold Gail and Ax's Little Joker Tobacco. Weldon must have passed the saluting wooden chief in front of the cigar store on her way to mail her letters to Sitting Bull.

The "fruit" streets east of Liberty—Cranberry, Pineapple, Orange—remained a refuge for bohemians from Weldon's time until the late 1930s, with such illustrious residents as Truman Capote, W. H. Auden, Carson McCullers, Benjamin Britten, Gypsy Rose Lee, Paul and Jane Bowles, and Richard Wright.

Then, in the 1940s, Robert Moses leveled the brownstones to make room for the Brooklyn-Queens Expressway. Reality bore little resemblance to the vision of a lost Brooklyn I had evoked to Sam the Cabby, a pastoral utopia in which everyone was white and genteel until impoverished blacks took over. The real transformation of the city had already come in Weldon's time. From 1880 to 1890, Brooklyn's population jumped a quarter of a million people. The lush, shaded avenues of mansions and row houses gave way to slums, shantytowns, and factories. The apartments on Liberty Avenue, where Sam the Cabby accosted the mechanic, were more likely to have housed struggling Jewish immigrants and working-class blacks than cultured whites like Weldon. Blacks had been living in Brooklyn since the early 1800s. As soon as a black family saved enough money, they fled Manhattan for Brooklyn, where the living conditions were a little more pleasant and the bigotry less pronounced. Nearly eleven thousand blacks lived in Weldon's Brooklyn, many successful enough to own their own homes and cottages at the shore. Weldon needn't have traveled to the Dakotas to find oppressed minorities, any more than I needed to travel to the reservation to test my claims to liberal tolerance. The quaint bohemian neighborhood in which Catherine Weldon lived was destroyed not by blacks but by a white urban reformer.

I checked an index of wills from the 1880s. No Richard Weldon. The librarian suggested I try the courthouse. Better hurry, she warned. It was nearly four o'clock and the courthouse closed at five.

Back the way I had come, past Starbucks and Banana Republic, up the courthouse steps, down to the grubby basement, past scaffolds, mops, and ladders. I entered room 109 and found a man behind the counter, so gray he seemed coated with plaster from the renovations in the hall. I asked to see a will.

"You have the number?" he said.

I didn't. He motioned to the gray metal cabinets that stretched across the room. I found the *W*'s. No Richard. But there, a Catherine Weldon, with the date of death given as Feb. 10, 1939. The clerk had disappeared. "Hello?" I said. "Hello?"

He shuffled from behind the door. The clock said 4:20. A three-day weekend would start at five. I offered him the number and date of Weldon's file. He shook his head. "No more wills today. Takes too long. You'll have to wait until Tuesday."

"But I can't come back Tuesday. I'm leaving town tomorrow."

He shrugged.

"Couldn't someone mail me a copy?"

"Maybe. If you pay."

Was he fishing for a bribe? "Where should I arrange it?"

"Upstairs. The cashier's office."

I sprinted up the steps and raced past dejected men sprawled on marble benches outside various courtrooms into the cashier's office, where a portly man was sitting with his feet up on his desk, waiting for the holiday. I asked to see a will.

"You can't see these wills," he said.

"But the man downstairs—"

"These wills are here for safekeeping. You can't see these wills unless you have a certificate to prove that the person who wrote the will you want is deceased."

"A certificate? The woman I'm interested in died sixty years ago."

"Then what are you doing up here? These are only current wills."

I explained what I was doing.

"Oh yeah," he said. "You give us seventy dollars, we look up the will and send you a photocopy. Even if we don't find the will, it's seventy bucks."

I told him to forget it. With the forty bucks I had wasted on the cab, I didn't want to waste another seventy. I didn't even know if I had the right will.

I pushed open the courthouse doors and stepped into the muted gold late-afternoon light. I passed the peddlers, who were now shouting about their incense and bathroom fixtures to the people hurrying home from work, and, on the other side of the square, came to a narrow park that ran between two streets. CADMAN PLAZA, said a plaque. The sun zebraed the walk with the shadows of iron palings. A shabby older man walked a shabby mutt. Two drunks lay curled around each other on a bench. A woman washed her car with a pink washcloth and water from a child's beach bucket. I hurried past a cluster of dreary sixties-era brick apartments called Whitman Close to the upscale shops at the corner of Cranberry and Henry Streets. The silhouettes of branches swayed against the brownstones. Catherine Weldon once lived here. She left her safe, peaceful home to help an Indian she had never met. She stood here, where I was standing, then turned west to face the sun, as I was turning now to face it. What must she have thought? *I am going to Dakota Territory. It is very far away. I am not certain what will happen. But I am going to go there anyway. I will leave tomorrow.*

And she went.

2

A Strange Apparition

I knew from the start that unless I uncovered a trunk of Weldon's diaries, I would never be able to write a conventional biography about her. Little of what extraordinary people do can be explained by a few facts from their childhoods. Most of any person's inner life necessarily must elude us. But the gaps in Weldon's story can never be filled in for reasons distinct to her. Anyone who aligns herself with a tribe slated for extinction must be made to vanish with it. If Hitler had won his war, we would know nothing of those few Germans and Poles who risked their lives to save the Jews.

As little as I wanted my search for Weldon's story to compete with what I found, I couldn't leave myself out. The importance of any gesture lies in its ability to inspire others to do the same. Weldon walked ahead of most whites. But I had the unshakable impression that she was looking back to see if anyone was following. She wanted to be the only white woman who was friends with Sitting Bull, yet she wanted other whites to see him as she described him in her biography and portrayed him in her paintings. Society tried to erase her tracks. But I wondered if Weldon herself might have taken care to leave as few tracks as possible. Maybe she was so bruised by the consequences of her actions and the opprobrium of white society that she erased herself.

At the very least, if I were to follow Weldon's trail, I would need to know what she looked like. In 1964, a pseudohistorian named David Humphreys Miller published an article about Weldon in *Montana Magazine*. He cadged most of his material from Vestal's biography of Sitting Bull and invented the rest.

The illustration for the story ("Sitting Bull's White Squaw: The overdressed zealot from Brooklyn who braved dishonor to befriend the recalcitrant old chief") shows a dejected Sitting Bull seated before his tipi, cupping his face in one hand and staring into space as if he wants to be anywhere except posing for this photo. He slumps on the ground between his younger wife, Four Robes, and a sour-faced white woman sitting stiff backed on a chair. She wears a long pleated skirt, a severely tailored jacket, a blouse bowed at the throat, and a misshapen hat. "AGING SITTING BULL huddles with his family outside his lodge in this picture, taken by Stanley Morrow," the caption reads. "Although it cannot be documented, it is believed possible that the white woman seated at his left is Mrs. Weldon who joined his household. On the chief's right is his youngest wife (No. 9) with her one-year-old baby on her back. Her twins, aged 5 years, are seated on either side of a white child."

But Sitting Bull had stopped living in a tipi long before he met Weldon. The mounted soldier behind the tent makes it likely that the photo was taken in 1882, when Sitting Bull was held prisoner at Fort Randall. The five-year-old twins are Crow Foot and Run Away From, who were adolescents when Weldon lived with the chief. Weldon mentions in a letter that her own son was thirteen when she brought him to the reservation; the white child in Miller's photo—it might even be a girl—is no older than six. The woman is charmless, in her fifties, hardly in keeping with Miller's own description of Weldon as possessing "great physical attractiveness." The careful language of the caption indicates that Miller knew the woman couldn't be Weldon. Not to mention that the photo he credits—I found it in the archives of the Historical Society of South Dakota—is clipped to a note to the effect that the white woman is "Miss Sallie Battles," an army officer's niece who took an interest in Sitting Bull while he was a prisoner at Fort Randall.

Vestal never met Weldon. He based his description on the testimony of Indians who had known her forty years earlier. How discerning could aging warriors have been about a society lady from New York? Maybe she was only overdressed in comparison to the drab wives of the soldiers. She wasn't gaudy so much as stylish. She came from Brooklyn, after all, and thought herself an artist.

Not only did no one know what Weldon looked like, no one knew how old she was. According to Vestal, she was "nearing that age at which some women suffer a change and do unaccountable things." But women, like men, do unaccountable things at many ages. I had a hunch that Vestal was blaming Weldon's impulsive journey on menopause, which might put her in her late forties or fifties, although many men make jokes about hot flashes and temper tantrums in women in their thirties. I did a little reading—Vestal was a colorful enough

1. Sitting Bull and his family outside their tipi while he was a prisoner of war at Fort Randall in 1882. The white woman seated on the chair, often misidentified as Catherine Weldon, is an army officer's niece named Sallie Battles, who befriended Sitting Bull's daughter Standing Holy. Courtesy of the State Historical Society of North Dakota, Fiske 7169.

character that several biographies have been written about him—and found out that his wife left him when she was forty. Filing for divorce, she blamed her discontent on the debts her husband had incurred in carrying out his research, the months he left her with their daughters while he traveled around the West gathering material for his books, his behavior when he drank, the shabby house they lived in, and her hatred of the Oklahoma town in which he forced her to live so he could teach at the university and of the other faculty wives, whom she called "those Norman bitches." In her younger years, Isabel Vestal had published a few short stories, but her career shriveled as his prospered. She wanted to regain her health and devote herself to literature. "I am an artist, not a household slave!" she insisted. Vestal granted that she had a point—but only about his debts. The rest of her objections he blamed on her "psychotic condition" brought about by "menopause and anemia."

Deep in the boxes of Vestal's collected papers at the University of Oklahoma are notes from an interview that Vestal conducted with a Lakota warrior named Little Soldier, who claimed that Weldon was thirty-seven years old when she lived with Sitting Bull. The very specificity of this number led me to believe it. Why would Little Soldier invent an age of thirty-seven instead of, say, thirty-eight? But I had to wonder how he got that number. Did he walk up to her and ask? How did he know the English words for thirty-seven?

My confusion grew as I unearthed newspaper accounts from Weldon's time. Many reporters gave her age as "early thirties" and described her as "attractive." But these same reporters repeatedly called her an "old crank." All I could say for sure was that a widow with a son in his early teens couldn't have been much younger than thirty or much older than fifty-three.

Nor was I able to turn up clues to Weldon's early life. In none of her letters does she mention her childhood. The only relatives she discusses are a nephew and niece who lived in Kansas City. She never mentions her husband. When I started my search, I found only one hint as to what her life was like before she met Sitting Bull. In 1964, a writer named Charles Handleman published an article in *The West* nearly identical to the story published a few months earlier by David Humphreys Miller—down to the mislabeled photo of Sallie Battles. Just one tidbit seems new. A "present-day informant, Mrs. Ann Harding Mordock, 'Princess Sun Tama,' of New York's surviving Matinecoc tribe," told Handleman that "[Mrs. Weldon] made several visits with her brush and palette to the remnant Indian groups of the Eastern Seaboard" before she went to Standing Rock. "Matinecoc" is an ambiguous name for a group of Indians who lived on Long Island. Weldon seems to have confined herself to painting whatever Indians she could find within a short distance of her home while her husband was alive. After his death, she left Christie in New York and traveled west to meet some Indians whose traditions hadn't yet been corrupted by whites. In this light, her husband's death seems less a misfortune than a liberation. She didn't care if she remarried. Maybe she didn't like men. Or she resented the restraints of Victorian marriage.

Weldon enters history only when she travels west and helps Sitting Bull fight the government's policy of allotment. It wouldn't be much of an exaggeration to say that the only whites in America who actively opposed the opening of the Great Sioux Reservation to white settlers were Catherine Weldon and her friends, Thomas and Cora Bland, who ran the Indian-rights association to which she belonged. Bad enough that the Lakota tribes had been confined for twenty years to the Great Sioux Reservation, a tract of land that, though a fraction of the size of the territory the tribes originally inhabited, comprised more than half of what is now South Dakota. In 1888, Congress tried to pass a bill that would chop this enormous expanse of land into six smaller reservations—Standing Rock, Cheyenne River, Lower Brule, Crow Creek, Rosebud, and Pine Ridge. The sum of these smaller reservations would be far less than the whole. On each reservation, each Indian family would be allotted 160 acres. The total of these plots would be smaller than the expanse the tribe had held in common. The "extra" nine million acres would be sold to white homesteaders for fifty cents an acre.

Naturally, this scheme pleased those whites who chafed at so many Indians living in their midst on land they wanted for themselves. But it also fit the agenda of liberal politicians like Senator Henry Dawes, who believed that the Indians' best hope for survival was to assimilate and farm, gain citizenship, and vote. Year after year, Dawes and his allies championed the act that came to bear his name. The only Americans—left or right—who opposed the Dawes Act besides Weldon and her compatriots were the Indians, who thought farming a dull, cowardly occupation and resisted the very notion of owning private land.

Luckily, the treaty that established the Great Sioux Reservation in 1868 stipulated that three-fourths of the adult males of each tribe must approve any future changes to the agreement. Richard Henry Pratt, director of the Carlisle School in Pennsylvania, which the Indians despised for stealing their children and returning them as adults unable to live happily among either whites or Indians, headed the commission whose purpose was to travel to each of the Lakota agencies and gather the needed signatures.

On July 23, 1888, the commissioners showed up at Standing Rock. Sitting Bull refused to see them. Days dragged on. Weeks. The commissioners wouldn't let the Indians return to their farms to tend their livestock and crops. Sitting Bull and his fellow chiefs refused to buckle to the commissioners. Pratt got angry

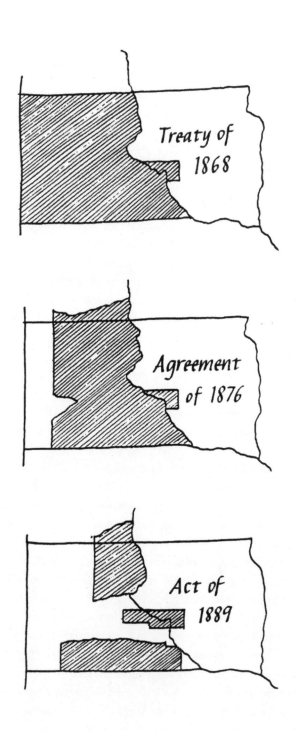

2. Reduction of the Great Sioux Reservation, 1868–89.

and went home. He recommended that Congress put the agreement into force without the Indians' signatures, since they were too ignorant to know what was in their own best interest. But the Indians' supporters in Washington raised such a fuss that they prevented Pratt's plan.

In October, the government brought Sitting Bull and sixty chiefs to the nation's capital to work out a new agreement. The Indians stayed at the Belvedere Hotel, visited the Smithsonian, admired George Catlin's paintings of the West, and smoked their first cigarettes. Then the secretary of the interior presented the chiefs with a new offer—a dollar an acre—and Sitting Bull surprised everyone by responding. Previously he had refused to consider any price for his land. Now he delivered a two-hour speech in which he pushed for $1.25 an acre. Maybe he figured that the whites were going to get the land no matter what. Or his price was so high that the whites would never pay it. By speaking in favor of the deal he could appear to be agreeable, get the commissioners off his back, and go home. Let Congress nix the price. Certainly the secretary of the interior thought $1.25 an acre absurdly high.

This was when Catherine Weldon struck up a correspondence with Sitting Bull. Perhaps she was responding to a request from Thomas Bland. Or she read about the cession bill in the newspapers and took the initiative herself. When Sitting Bull got back to Standing Rock, Weldon sent him letters from Brooklyn. These haven't survived, but she mentions elsewhere that they contained details of the commissioners' deliberations in Washington, lists of fair prices for Dakota land, and maps of the scheme to carve up the reservation. Showing the Indians maps was no small act of subversion. The whites counted on the Indians not to understand exactly how much land their tribe would lose if the big reservation were divided into smaller ones, each smaller reservation divided among its members, and the rest sold off to whites. Like the cabby I met in Brooklyn, Sitting Bull had only a vague idea of how enormous his holdings were. The maps Weldon sent him gave a dimension to his loss. He was willing to sell his autograph for a dollar or two to curiosity seekers at Bill Cody's Wild West Show, but he wasn't about to sign away half his reservation. Even if each family got a few acres now, more Indians would be born. What land would their children live on?

But once-unreasonable demands can become a small price to pay for what a nation now wants. In 1889, the Dakotas were granted statehood, homesteaders clamored for more land, and the government decided that $1.25 per acre wasn't so absurd (after the first three years, the price would fall to seventy-five cents per acre and fifty cents after that). In June, a new commission set out to gather the signatures of those chiefs who had proposed the higher price. But now the Indians refused to sign. The commissioners traveled from agency to agency, saving

Standing Rock for last. Their plan was to intimidate the weaker chiefs into signing, forcing Sitting Bull to fall into line. Weldon showed up at Standing Rock while the commissioners were browbeating the chiefs at the lower agencies. Her plan was to take a message from Sitting Bull to the chiefs at those other agencies to strengthen their resistance. This wasn't an easy task. The agency at Standing Rock sits just above the line that divides North and South Dakota. The Cheyenne River Agency lies a hundred miles south, at the intersection of the Missouri and Cheyenne Rivers. Crow Creek and Lower Brule lie southeast, below Pierre, and Rosebud farther south, with Pine Ridge to the southwest, sitting neatly on the border with Nebraska. The distances were daunting. Barely any roads crossed this vast expanse, and no outsiders were allowed to enter the reservation without permission from the agents, who ran their fiefdoms like kings.

When Weldon went to Standing Rock, she didn't think that she would encounter trouble from the agent. Of all the bureaucrats who ran the Indians' lives (the agents' duties included disbursing food and clothes, administering the schools, keeping track of every Indian enrolled in every tribe, and generally encouraging the "hostiles" to give up their tribal ways), James McLaughlin was the most competent and honest. He had been trying for years to break Sitting Bull's power, but he hadn't favored the earlier proposal to chop up the reservation and sell the "surplus" land. He knew that the Indians were being cheated, and, by his own lights, James McLaughlin always protected "his" Sioux.

In his own way, McLaughlin was as complicated as Weldon and Sitting Bull. A short, hot-tempered Irishman, he augmented the ferocity of his appearance by wearing excessively tall bowler hats, thick-soled boots, and an impressive array of facial hair. Early in his career he had married a pretty, round-faced woman named Marie Louise Buisson, who was a quarter Santee Sioux. He liked his Indian charges—as long as they did what he told them—and devoted his career to their interests—or what he assumed these to be. Soldiers usually despised agents as do-gooders who didn't understand that the best way to get Indians to do what you wanted was to kill them, but McLaughlin got along with the officers at the fort that protected his agency. Most settlers distrusted Catholics, but the homesteaders around Standing Rock and the citizens of Mandan and Bismarck to the north were confident of McLaughlin's ability to control "his" Indians. The Indian bureaucracy in Washington was run by missionaries who had split up the reservations according to which church wanted what. The Catholics had been given Standing Rock—with all its hostile Sioux, the Protestants didn't want it—and since McLaughlin and his wife were upstanding Catholics, he had everyone's support. Even Thomas Bland supported James McLaughlin—until Weldon took him on.

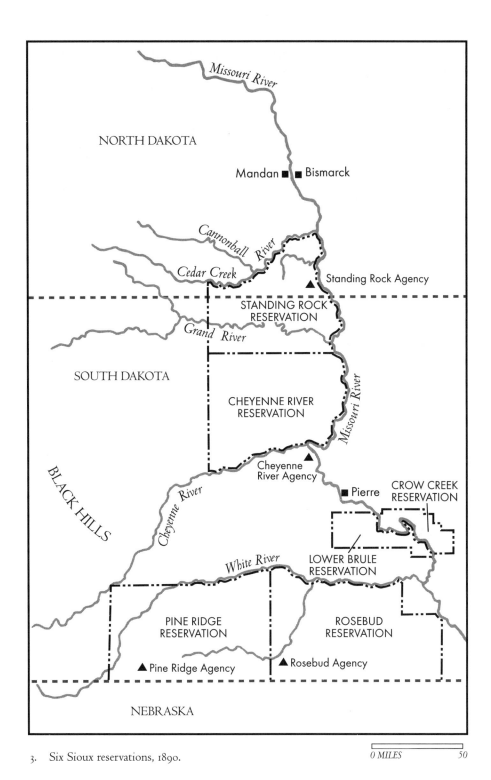

NORTH DAKOTA

Missouri River

Mandan ■ ■ Bismarck

Cannonball River

Cedar Creek

▲ Standing Rock Agency

STANDING ROCK
RESERVATION

Grand River

SOUTH DAKOTA

CHEYENNE RIVER
RESERVATION

Missouri River

BLACK HILLS

Cheyenne River

▲ Cheyenne
River Agency

■ Pierre

CROW CREEK
RESERVATION

LOWER BRULE
RESERVATION

White River

PINE RIDGE
RESERVATION

ROSEBUD
RESERVATION

▲ Pine Ridge Agency

▲ Rosebud Agency

NEBRASKA

0 MILES   50

3.   Six Sioux reservations, 1890.

4. James McLaughlin and Standing Rock agency staff, circa 1899. Left to right: Joe Primeau, storekeeper; George Faribault, farmer; E. S. Hart, physician; James McLaughlin, agent; Bird M. Robinson, secretary; Jim Merrill, issue clerk. Courtesy of the State Historical Society of North Dakota, Fiske B0102.

On her way south from Bismarck, Weldon stopped at a small settlement eight miles below the Cannonball River, which formed the northern border of the reservation. From a previous journey west, she knew several Indians who lived there. "I had long ago contemplated a visit to Dakota, to visit some Indian friends," she wrote later to Red Cloud, chief of the Oglala Sioux at Pine Ridge. "Some are at Cannon Ball now, some at Standing Rock and some at the Yankton Agency. I was glad to get away from the busy world to breathe air of Dakota once more & to see the faces I liked to look upon." Sitting Bull, she learned, "was almost dyeing at the time & was reported even dead." She asked around the settlement to find out how he was but heard nothing for days and remained "ignorant as to whether he was alive or dead & much worried about him."

The whites heard the same news and made bets on what day "the old troublemaker" would kick off. "The report that Sitting Bull is dying of pneumonia at Standing Rock agency is not generally received with sorrow throughout Dakota," sneered the *Yankton Daily Press*. On June 15, 1889, the *Bismarck Weekly Tribune* reported that D. F. Barry, a local photographer, had paid a call on Sitting Bull at his camp on the Grand River, where the chief was recovering from a nearly fatal disease. The verbal portrait Barry paints is of a tired, sick old man who fears that the whites will harangue him into signing yet another agreement he can't read. But he hasn't given up. "Sitting Bull is confined to his tent," Barry reported, "but is able to sit up, and although he has failed perceptibly during his illness he is still defiant, outspoken and resolute."

Sitting Bull wanted to keep fighting, Barry said, but he felt impaired by his lack of an adviser he could trust who spoke and read English. "The white is wise in books," Sitting Bull told the photographer. "He can read and write and we cannot. We know nothing about books, and the whites have fooled us. Now we are approached with another treaty, but us old men will not sign it. We are not able to deal with your people, but in a few years our young men will know how to handle papers. They are going to school and will soon know how to trade with the government." Little wonder that Sitting Bull responded favorably to an offer of help from a sympathetic white woman who was even then waiting to see him.

Eventually Sitting Bull recovered enough to send Weldon a welcoming message via the photographer and McLaughlin's eldest son, Harry, who had led Barry to the camp. It seems foolish to send a message to your ally via your enemy's son. But Weldon and McLaughlin hadn't yet engaged in the verbal warfare that came to mark their acquaintance. And if you wanted to send a message forty miles through the wilderness, you had little choice but to send it with anyone traveling that way. Weldon learned of the letter's existence two weeks later, from Sitting Bull, but she never received it; Harry McLaughlin had delivered it to his dad. The chief sent another message. That, too, was intercepted; Weldon received the letter five days after it should have reached her. By then, she had learned from an Indian messenger that Sitting Bull wished to speak to her but was too ill to travel. While she waited for him to grow stronger, McLaughlin galloped up to the Cannonball to have a word with this intruder.

She couldn't have been hard to pick out. The settlement on the north bank of the river, just off the reservation, consisted of the Parkin Ranch, a post office, and a store. Passengers traveling on the stage from Bismarck to Standing Rock or Fort Yates stayed overnight at a small hotel on the ranch, but there weren't exactly dozens of fancy New York ladies hanging around the premises. The settlement south of the river consisted solely of Indians, and McLaughlin knew every one of them. No matter whether Weldon was staying at the ranch or among the Indians, the agent would have spotted her right away.

And she would have spotted him, a short, mustachioed white man riding into town in a long, formal coat, a tightly buttoned vest, straight-cuffed trousers, and heavy boots. He must have looked around until he saw a white woman he didn't recognize, then swung down from his saddle and walked over to greet her. Weldon didn't wait for his approach but strode forth to greet him. She described their conversation in her letter to Red Cloud. The agent, she said, acted in a suspiciously friendly way. Apropos of nothing, he began to speak of Sitting Bull.

He is a coward, you know. He is a selfish man, no one's friend but his own. He thinks he is a great chief, but he is not the least bit important. He is just a backslider, an obstructionist. He is a heavy burden on the younger men, who are more progressive.

Oh? Weldon said. Really?

And your friend Dr. Bland is absolutely without influence on this reservation, McLaughlin told her. The National Indian Defence Association hasn't the slightest foothold at Standing Rock.

Weldon guessed that the agent's uncanny knowledge of her motives came from the letters he had intercepted, but for once she refused the bait for a fight. ("I did not answer," she wrote Red Cloud, "& I do not *know* whether he was aware that I am a member, but I think he is else he would not have spoken of the N.I.D. Asso.") She sensed that if she pushed McLaughlin too far, he would toss her off the reservation, as had happened to her friend Thomas Bland a few years earlier when he traveled to Pine Ridge to stick up for Red Cloud and ended up in a confrontation with the agent there, a tyrannical martinet named Valentine T. McGillicuddy.

And McLaughlin backed down. Weldon doesn't record their parting words, but he seems to have told her that she was welcome to stay on the Parkin Ranch for as long as they might have her or she might visit the agency, provided she made no trouble among the Indians. *And now, if you will excuse me, Mrs. Weldon, I have responsibilities to attend.* And he mounted his horse and rode off.

If Valentine T. McGillicuddy was a corrupt tyrant at Pine Ridge, James McLaughlin was an honest tyrant at Standing Rock. He was then what he would be until the last day of his life, the loyal representative of a bureaucracy whose mission was to solve the "Indian problem" by turning the Indians into whites. To this end, he needed to stamp out the Indians' traditional practices and break up the communal life of each tribe. Some of the younger Indians were willing to live as whites. But Sitting Bull thought Lakota ways superior—for Lakotas, at least—and he was determined to fight for his tribe's survival. McLaughlin saw no choice but to oppose him.

After her unsettling encounter with the agent at the Cannonball, Weldon traveled south to the agency to see what she could determine about Sitting Bull's health. The commissioners were already at the lower agencies, intimidating the chiefs into signing the cession agreement, and Weldon's trip to Standing Rock was part of an NIDA campaign to keep them from succeeding. When the Indians at Rosebud shouted down the commissioners, the *Yankton Daily Press* expressed the certainty that a letter from Thomas Bland was to blame. On June 13, the paper was outraged to report "evidence of an effort on the part of the defense association to neutralize in advance the work of the commission. Documents signed by the officers of the defense association were circulated among the Indians with the design of prejudicing them against the congressional act for the cession of a portion of the reservation. These documents have been preserved. If they are sufficient to break the influence of the defense association they will prove of genuine benefit to the Indians." The whites apparently thought it fair that they pressure the Indians into signing the bill, but it was treason to urge them not to.

Despite letters from the NIDA and the resistance of the Sioux themselves, the commissioners gained the required signatures at Rosebud and headed triumphantly to Pine Ridge. Even the Yankton paper acknowledged that the commissioners would find succeeding there much harder. Although Red Cloud had been one of the earliest Sioux chiefs to surrender, that had only given him longer to be angry at his treatment. Among other humiliations, the government had confiscated a large herd of ponies from Red Cloud's people, and the Oglalas were still hoping to get them back. Red Cloud had long been a member of the NIDA, a fact that led the Yankton paper to charge that he was under the influence of "Indian defense association cranks" who had put the notion to oppose the cession into "the wily old red skin's brain" during a recent trip to Washington.

At Standing Rock, Sitting Bull was now healthy enough to be interviewed. When a reporter told him how many Sioux at the lower reservations were signing the treaty, "he would not believe it. He said he had Indians at the lower conference who reported to him, and he knew that no such number as reported have signed." Sitting Bull deemed it more likely that the commissioners were lying in an attempt to scare the Indians at the upper agencies into signing. In truth, the Yankton paper reported that Red Cloud had come out in fervent opposition to the treaty. "His hostility is based entirely upon the teachings of the Indian rights association and its organ, Dr. Bland's paper, the Council Fire." The paper tried to discredit Bland by charging that he intended to keep nearly half the reimbursement for the ponies he was helping Red Cloud get back.

As reports trickled into Standing Rock that the Oglalas were signing, Weldon became impatient to put forward her plan. And Sitting Bull roused himself from his sickbed to travel to the fort to see her; the importance he gave their meeting is obvious from his agreeing to drive forty miles in a rickety wagon over dusty roads in the oppressive June heat, having just recovered from pneumonia.

If I picture that first meeting, what I see is Sitting Bull, haggard and wan, in raggedy leggings and a dusty shirt, driving his wagon onto the agency grounds. Coughing, he leans down and asks one of the agency Indians where he can find the white woman who has come from New York. Someone runs and fetches her. *Sitting Bull is here! He asks you to come and meet him!*

Weldon rises from the stone wall above the river where she has been trying to find some shade and escape the surveillance of the agency employees and their wives, the off-duty soldiers and their wives, the traders and their wives, not to mention the Indians and their wives. Brooklyn might be monstrous in the summer heat, but at least in a city one could go about one's business in relative anonymity. Here she is the prime subject of every conversation. At this very moment, she knows, they are discussing her manners, face, and dress, the outrageousness of her wearing so small a bustle and so loose a corset and going about the country unaccompanied even by another woman, let alone a man. She shakes her head. The whites think her arrogant, but they are the arrogant ones, dismissing her ability to understand "the Indian question"—as if it is a question how to treat your fellow human creatures humanely—simply because she has been living in New York for the past several years. They know nothing about her, and they would rather invent fantasies than speak to her in person, as any civilized person would do.

If only Sitting Bull had been healthy when she arrived, she wouldn't have had to waste so many weeks. She has a limited time before she must return to New York and relieve her husband's relatives from caring for her son. There is nothing here to see, nothing to do, and nowhere to go without being told not to go there. Yesterday she stopped by the agency school and sat at the back of the room to observe what teaching methods the schoolmistress was using. But she caused such a turning of heads and outburst of whispering that she took her leave before the schoolmistress could ask.

Now her wait is over. Sitting Bull is here. He has come many miles to meet her. She mustn't keep him waiting. She smoothes her skirt, adjusts her bustle. If she takes pains with her appearance, it is not because she cares whether or not he finds her attractive, but only because this is what she would do if meeting the president of the United States, or the pope, or the king of Siam.

She ties her bonnet and tugs the brim—the sun and wind are fierce—then crosses the hard-packed yard to the agency. Everyone is watching; she feels them staring from the trading post, from the schoolhouse, from the windows of Major McLaughlin's office. She feels like an actress on a stage. *The stage of history,* she thinks, and she, for one, is not shy to play her role. Let the other whites see the way an Indian like Sitting Bull ought to be treated, the way he would be treated in any capital in Europe, as the great general and political leader he is.

Shielding her eyes, she looks up. Sitting Bull climbs down from his wagon and shuffles closer, hand moving from hat to heart, then to an outstretched position, then back to his head, as if he is trying to remember whether it is more appropriate when meeting a white lady to shake her hand or remove his hat. He is shorter and less imposing than she pictured him, but how silly to expect that he would wear a headdress. And he is very pale for an Indian, so clearly in the grasp of a lingering disease. Just think if she had missed him by a day because he had expired from pneumonia!

She smiles and moves closer. He nods and offers his hand, awkwardly, as if holding out a hoe. She grasps it in her own gloved hand and shakes it firmly, then greets him in Lakota, just a few words she learned during her time among her friends: *Hau Mitakuyepi, Tatanka Iyotanka! Niye it kokim wan.* Greetings, Sitting Bull, to meet you I have come.

And, as she hoped, Sitting Bull seems relieved to find out she speaks his language. A broad, alluring smile spreads across his face. How especially gratifying it is to make a man smile if he isn't prone to smiling, if he has recently been ill, if he distrusts most others of one's race.

Hello! he shouts in English, gripping her hand again, remembering the few words he learned with the Wild West show. Hello, Missus Weldon! I am Seeda Boo!

The question remains who this Sitting Bull was—not as a figure in a Wild West show or an icon on a poster, but as a man, a human being. From his birth in the early 1830s to the years of his adolescence, the only whites Sitting Bull met were the traders who sold him guns with which to fight his enemies the Crows. Of the seven Sioux tribes, the Lakota were the fiercest. The Lakota themselves were split into seven smaller tribes—the Oglala, Brule, Miniconjou, Two Kettle, Sans Arc, Blackfeet, and Hunkpapa. Sitting Bull came of age when Lakota culture was at full strength, and even then, among his own people, the Hunkpapas, legends grew around his exploits. He killed his first buffalo at ten. Proud of his hunting, he was even prouder of his generosity. He gave away his game to the poorest members of his band. As he boasted later to reporters: I was considered a good man even then.

At fourteen, he insisted on accompanying his father and several other warriors on a raid against the Crows. Sitting Bull—who at that age was called Slow, not because he couldn't run fast, but because he was so deliberate in his actions—rushed ahead of the grown-ups and counted first coup, smacking a

5. Sitting Bull. Courtesy of the State Historical Society of North Dakota, Barry C0436-02.

Crow warrior so hard that the man fell from his horse. In the victory ceremony that night, his father put Sitting Bull on a beautiful pony, presented him with a shield he had made himself, then led Sitting Bull around the camp and sponsored a feast in his honor.

In his pictorial autobiography, Sitting Bull shows himself in his twenties triumphing against a dozen Crows and Assiniboines. His fellow warriors inducted him into the Strong Heart Society as one of their two sash-wearers, men who inspired courage by rushing ahead of their fellow warriors, staking their sashes to the ground, and refusing to retreat until their comrades ran up and freed them. Sitting Bull rode into battle with a seven-foot lance at the lead of a band of warriors who terrified their enemies by screaming: *Tatanka Iyotanka tahoksila!* We are Sitting Bull's boys!

As ferocious as he could be, he had a forgiving nature. One day he came upon a party of Hunkpapa warriors who had just slaughtered a family of Assiniboines. Only the thirteen-year-old son remained alive. The boy was firing arrows at the older men, who rode in a circle, taunting him. They admired his bravery, but they would have killed the boy anyway—an enemy was an enemy—if he hadn't looked up and seen something in Sitting Bull's face that caused him to throw his arms around the older man's legs and call out: *Help me, older brother!* Maybe the boy felt more warmly toward Sitting Bull than he did toward the other Hunkpapas because Sitting Bull had arrived too late to massacre his family. But Sitting Bull did have a special look about him—you can see it in his photos, a sort of soulfulness or compassion—and the boy might have been responding to that. Sitting Bull adopted the boy—Little Assiniboine, he was called, Little Hohe, *Hohecikana*—because Sitting Bull had no brother by blood and had recently lost his first son. The rest of the Hunkpapas were touched by this gesture. The Assiniboine boy must have seen more than self-serving reasons to love his protector—the Hunkpapas had obliterated his family, yet even after Sitting Bull offered him a chance to go home, he chose to stay. Years later, when Catherine Weldon moved in with Sitting Bull at Grand River, Hohecikana was still living with the chief. He remained there until the last moment of Sitting Bull's life. Then he died beside him.

The devotion of this adopted brother set Sitting Bull on a pattern of saving captives. When Crow warriors killed Sitting Bull's father, the Hunkpapas took as prisoner several Crow women and a child. Don't sacrifice them for my sake, Sitting Bull said. My father was an old man. He suffered from a toothache and was almost eager to be killed. He died honorably, as did the Crow warrior who killed him. (Sitting Bull himself had struck down his father's killer.) The tribe relented and showed mercy, and Sitting Bull sent the captives home.

His generosity and bravery helped to make Sitting Bull attractive as a husband. He limped from several war wounds and stood only five-foot ten, but he was muscular and wide chested, with a large head, long, soft braids, a strong chin, and eyes that seemed mournful or angry or wise, depending on his mood. He liked and respected women. They could tell he liked them—by the attention he paid, by the way he softened his voice and raised its pitch when he spoke to them. His first wife, Light Hair, died in 1857, giving birth to their son (the boy died four years later). Sitting Bull grieved for her, but he soon brought home a new wife, Red Woman, and another wife, Snow on Her. This second wife argued all the time with Red Woman. Night after night she insisted on sleeping on the same pallet as Sitting Bull and Red Woman. Sitting Bull had to lie on his back between them, each woman gripping one arm so he wouldn't roll toward the other, a position that aggravated his war injuries. Snow on Her spread rumors that Red Woman had been unfaithful. But Red Woman called together the camp and swore that her body had been enjoyed only by Sitting Bull. Did any man say otherwise? When none did, Sitting Bull sent Snow on Her home to her parents, although he kept their two girls.

In 1871, Red Woman died, leaving Sitting Bull to raise their son, plus the daughters by his banished wife, Snow on Her. His mother, Her Holy Door, and his sister, Pretty Feather, helped care for these children, as well as Pretty Feather's son One Bull, whom Sitting Bull adopted, but Sitting Bull felt the need to take another wife, Four Robes, and yet another wife, Seen by the Nation, who was Four Robes's older sister. It was Four Robes herself who asked Sitting Bull to marry her sister, since Seen by the Nation was a widow with two young sons, one of them a deaf-mute. Unlike Red Woman and Snow on Her, the sisters got along. The Indians told Vestal later that these two wives never objected to all the entertaining they had to do or their husband's habit of giving away their horses, buffalo robes, and food. Vestal's informants were male. Maybe they overestimated the women's good nature. But there was no greater honor among Sioux women than to be the wife of a rich and generous chief, so Sitting Bull's wives probably were happy to entertain on his behalf.

Some sources say that Sitting Bull had as many as nine wives in his lifetime, but only these five have been documented. Four Robes and Seen by the Nation remained with Sitting Bull until his death, bearing children in their forties. His mother continued to live with him for many years. She was proud of his bravery, although as he got older and came to carry more responsibility for his family, she asked him to take fewer risks and hang back a little in battle. Why do you always need to be the one to pull the most dangerous stunts? she asked. When she died, just after he surrendered and came in to the reservation, he mourned and mourned.

To many Americans, the name "Sitting Bull" evokes a taciturn Indian who pulled off a military upset that wiped out Custer's troops, then crossed his arms and refused to say another word. In reality, he was a gifted and complex man— a visionary whose dreams had a habit of coming true, a medicine man who could predict the weather with eerie accuracy, a composer whose songs gave his people strength, and a war chief so successful that several white generals seriously believed he had attended West Point. McLaughlin repeatedly told reporters that Sitting Bull was a coward, but among his own people Sitting Bull held a reputation for bravery. Once, to prove to the younger warriors that his decision to quit a battle was based on wisdom rather than cowardice, Sitting Bull walked into an open valley within range of the soldiers' guns, sat down, filled his pipe, smoked calmly as bullets pinged around him, then walked back to his people.

Sitting Bull would have been the Hunkpapas' chief even if whites had never entered the Plains. But they did come, in such numbers that Sitting Bull's uncle, Four Horns, proposed a radical plan. Those Indians who wished to have nothing to do with the whites would relinquish their independence and place themselves under a single war chief. Until then, no chief had ruled more than his own band. None presumed to control all seven Lakota tribes, plus their allies the Yanktonais. Lakota chiefs ruled by consent. If the people consented to Four Horns's plan, it was partly from desperation and partly from respect for Sitting Bull. When you tell us to fight, we will fight, Four Horns told his nephew. When you tell us to make peace, we shall make peace.

The Lakota tribes under Red Cloud and Spotted Tail went to live on reservations. The rest followed Sitting Bull and Crazy Horse through ten years of misery, avoiding battles when they could, attacking when they had no choice, hunting buffalo when they could find buffalo, slipping into reservations and helping themselves to rations, then returning to the Plains. In his pictorial autobiography, Sitting Bull shows himself winning honor by counting coup on white soldiers. Who they are isn't clear, since he was asked to explain the pictures while he was a prisoner of war because he reputedly had killed Custer. This last charge isn't true—directly. But then, Custer might have won if it hadn't been for Sitting Bull's talents as a leader.

That spring of 1876, the army was intent on killing any Indians who refused to settle on reservations, and Sitting Bull and Crazy Horse were determined not to lose what little freedom they had. For protection, Sitting Bull pulled together as many bands as possible. By mid-May he had attracted hundreds of lodges of his own Hunkpapas, plus the Oglalas under Crazy Horse, the Miniconjous, the Sans Arcs, the Blackfeet, and the Yanktonais, about three thousand Indians, of whom eight hundred were warriors. They were searching for buffalo, but they knew they might encounter white soldiers, who kept hounding them no matter what they did or where they went.

Seeking a vision of what such a meeting might bring, Sitting Bull organized a Sun Dance in the valley of the Rosebud. After purifying himself in a sweat lodge, he entered the sacred circle and performed the pipe ceremony. Then he sat against the sacred tree while Hohecikana poked an awl beneath the skin on Sitting Bull's left arm, gouged a nub of flesh, then sliced the flesh free. Hohecikana worked his way up from Sitting Bull's wrist until he had taken fifty pieces. Then he did the right arm. Blood flowing, Sitting Bull cried out in prayer.

Then he started dancing. He didn't pierce his chest or drag buffalo skulls that day, as he had done in previous years, but he danced around the sacred tree, blood congealing on both arms. He danced all that afternoon, not stopping to eat or drink, then kept dancing all that night and all the next morning. At noon he seemed to faint. He didn't fall. He just stood in one spot, staring at the sun and wobbling. His friends eased him to the ground and sprinkled water on his face. He opened his eyes and described the vision he had been granted of soldiers and horses "as numerous as grasshoppers" falling upside down into an Indian camp. The soldiers' heads were pointed toward the earth and their hats were coming off. A voice told Sitting Bull that the soldiers had no ears to listen to reason, so all of them would die, but the Indians weren't supposed to mutilate the bodies because the soldiers were gifts from God. That seemed a good sign. In the next few days, thousands more Indians deserted their reservations and joined Sitting Bull's traveling city. That seemed an even better sign.

When Custer and his soldiers stumbled into this massive encampment and started shooting, Sitting Bull's first concern was for his family. This was no small group—it consisted of his wives, his mother, his two teenage daughters by Snow on Her, his young son by Red Woman, his two stepsons (their mother was Seen by the Nation), his sister, Pretty Feather, and the twins Crow Foot and Run Away From, to whom Four Robes had given birth three weeks earlier. Once he got his relatives to the hills, Sitting Bull rode back to cheer on his warriors. No one knows exactly which brave killed Custer, but it wasn't Sitting Bull. Several other Indians claimed the honor, and not a soul would testify to seeing Sitting Bull near Custer. He had earned enough glory. Better to let the young men satisfy their lust for honor and revenge.

Later Sitting Bull rode among his warriors, urging them to put out of their minds all the depredations the soldiers had inflicted on them and let the survivors go. These last few soldiers will tell their commanders how strong we are, he said, so they won't launch another attack. If we kill every single soldier, the whites will go crazy with anger and come after us. More soldiers are probably on their way. (They were.) Let's leave the survivors. And don't loot the bodies, he told the women, who moved through the battlefield mutilating the corpses and stripping their possessions. This had been part of his vision at the Sun Dance, that his people must leave the soldiers untouched. One Bull said later that Sitting Bull told the Sioux they should not set their hearts on anything the white people had or it would be a curse to them. No one listened. The Indians were furious at the whites for marching into their camp and for all the past atrocities the soldiers had visited on the Indians' own dead and wounded (the soldiers had been known to slit open the wombs of pregnant women or make purses of the private parts of girls). They looted the soldiers' bodies. Sitting Bull reputedly urged compassion for a dying black man named Isaiah Dorman, who, though married to a Hunkpapa woman, had signed on with Custer as an interpreter. Surrounded by Hunkpapa warriors and their wives, Dorman begged to be killed quickly. Some of the Indians said later that Sitting Bull rode up, gave Dorman a drink of water, and ordered the warriors to spare him. But the people were too angry. They saw Dorman as a traitor, and as soon as Sitting Bull rode off, they killed him and cut off his penis and stuffed it in his mouth.

Even if Sitting Bull didn't kill Custer, he helped to join the tribes into an alliance so powerful that the soldiers couldn't win. So he was a fitting target for the nation's retribution. Custer was dead, and 263 American soldiers had died with him. Congress gave the army everything it demanded to chase Sitting Bull. The huge city had split up, unable to find game for so many mouths. The last few free tribes followed the last few buffalo north. The soldiers burned any Indian villages they could find, destroying stockpiles of meat and skins. That winter was frigid. Children died. The old people despaired and grew ill. Band after band gave up and went to live at the agencies. On May 6, 1877, Crazy Horse and his Oglalas surrendered. That same week, Sitting Bull and a thousand of his Lakotas straggled into Canada. The news that soldiers had stabbed Crazy Horse in the back while leading him to jail confirmed Sitting Bull's fears of what would happen to him if he returned to his native land.

The Canadians told Sitting Bull that he could stay in their country as long as he obeyed the queen's laws and didn't get into fights with Canada's own tribes. James Walsh, the Mountie in charge of Sitting Bull's camp, treated the chief so fairly that the two became friends. But the government didn't want to be responsible for feeding a bunch of Indians the Americans should be feeding or giving them a reservation. Some of the younger warriors defied Sitting Bull by slipping back into the United States to steal horses. Why should Canada be held responsible for the damages? More Indians straggled north. The Sioux couldn't battle the Canadian tribes for the last remaining buffalo. They couldn't follow the herds south. Walsh was replaced with a hard-liner who hadn't made promises to Sitting Bull that the government didn't want to keep.

Band by band, the Sioux allowed themselves to be shipped down the Missouri River to Standing Rock. Among them went Sitting Bull's eldest daughter, Many Horses, who had eloped with a suitor her father didn't like. Sitting Bull feared that the whites would mistreat his daughter to get even with him. Starving and poorly clothed, he and his last few hundred followers turned themselves in. He gave his rifle to Crow Foot and told the five-year-old boy to hand it to Major Brotherton. I surrender this rifle to you through my young son, Sitting Bull said in Lakota. I wish him to learn in this way that he has become a friend of the Americans. I wish him to learn the habits of the whites and to be educated as their sons are educated. I wish it to be remembered that I was the last man of my tribe to surrender my rifle. This boy has given it to you, and he now wants to know how he is going to make a living.

From his treatment those first days, Sitting Bull might have decided that the only way his people could earn a living was by letting tourists gawk at them. When their boat docked in Bismarck, hundreds of whites surged forward to glimpse "Custer's killer." They saw a middle-aged Indian in a shabby shirt and tattered pants wearing strips of red flannel around his braids and a pair of green goggles some kindly soul had given him to protect his infected eyes from the sun. Through those sunglasses, Sitting Bull saw his first railroad car, which he declined to enter. He visited his first white city and was treated to dinner at a hotel, where he ate with a knife and fork and tasted his first bowl of ice cream. He also earned his first money, signing autographs for as much as five dollars apiece.

Back aboard the boat, Sitting Bull traveled south to Standing Rock, where he was reunited with those followers who had surrendered earlier. His daughter already had been deserted by her husband, and she rejoined her father's camp. Sitting Bull gave interviews and allowed photographers to take his portrait. The government promised that he would be allowed to live out his life at Standing Rock, but after three weeks the army declared him a dangerous prisoner of war and ordered him shipped to Fort Randall. I won't go, Sitting Bull said. I would rather fight and die here. Let them stab me in the back, the way they killed Crazy Horse. Some of the warriors began to talk of resisting. But before anything could happen, the soldiers surrounded Sitting Bull, and when the next steamboat docked—it was the *Sherman*, bringing James McLaughlin to his new post as agent—the soldiers forced Sitting Bull and 167 of his followers up the gangplank at bayonet point.

At Fort Randall, Sitting Bull and his people put up tipis above the river and sat around doing nothing. The enforced idleness drove Sitting Bull crazy. All right, he said, I give in, I promise I will act peaceably and obey the rules. Just send me back to Standing Rock. But the government detained him another year and a half. He put on weight, played with his children, suffered a stream of visitors, and allowed his photo to be taken with Miss Sallie Battles.

By the time the government pardoned him and sent him back to Standing Rock, McLaughlin had taken over. He had sprinkled the chief's warriors across the reservation, urging them to give up their lodges for cabins, fence their plots, and start farming. When Sitting Bull asked to be treated as the representative of his tribe, McLaughlin informed him that he would be treated exactly like any other Indian. To reporters eager to romanticize the chief, McLaughlin characterized Sitting Bull as "an Indian of very mediocre ability, rather dull. . . . He is pompous, vain, and boastful, and considers himself a very important personage." Seeing that he would get nowhere with the agent, Sitting Bull moved forty miles southwest of the agency, to a plot on the Grand River not far from his birthplace. He farmed, raised horses, cows, and chickens, and built a root cellar, sheds, haystacks, and a second, smaller cabin.

Twelve miles away, a Congregationalist missionary named Mary Collins put up a two-room house—without the tribe's consent—and became the first white woman with whom Sitting Bull was to have sustained contact. Not that he hurried to dignify her presence with a visit. But his young people started venturing to her house. Anyone who stopped by the mission got food. Collins could speak Lakota, which few missionaries could, and she was able to read the young people stories and sing them hymns in their own language. When she convinced twelve young men to join a Bible-study club, Sitting Bull grew furious. He had only two hundred people at his camp; he couldn't afford to lose so many young men. He proposed a compromise: the young men could attend services at Collins's house on Sundays if she would stop interfering with their attendance at the Indians' dances the other days. But Collins hated the dances. Not only did they prevent the young men from coming to her house, they interfered with her campaign to convince the Indians to give up their pagan ways.

Sitting Bull went to Collins's house to see if he could persuade her to change her mind. He called to her from her fence. Wenonah! (This was the name the Indians called Collins, a name that means "Princess," although it's not clear whether the Indians bestowed the name on her or she bestowed it on herself.) Wenonah! he called again.

Collins—what follows is her own account—chose not to answer.

Wenonah! he called a third time.

Again she didn't answer. He walked up to her door and knocked. He was angry, Collins said. He told her in Lakota: Wenonah, I called you—didn't you hear me?

Yes, she said, I heard you.

Well, why didn't you answer me or come out to see what I wanted?

Sitting Bull, she lectured, ladies never go out to the fence to speak to gentlemen; gentlemen always come in to speak to ladies.

Sitting Bull mumbled an apology. Oh, I didn't know that. Ashamed, he went away.

The next time, he came with twelve warriors. Sitting Bull sat on one chair, Collins sat on the other, and the rest of the men gathered around them on the floor. Sitting Bull took out his pipe and offered it to his friends, at which Collins announced that she never permitted smoking in her house. Sitting Bull put away his pipe, but he wasn't about to apologize again. He demanded to know if Collins intended to remain living on Sioux land and arguing with Sioux traditions.

Yes, she certainly did intend to stay and keep up her missionary work.

Were her horses going to keep on eating their grass and drinking their water?

Oh, she said, is the grass yours?

Sitting Bull nodded.

Is the water yours, too?

He nodded again.

Well, then, Collins told him, your water is ruining my garden, and you should make your rain stop doing that!

For a moment, the chiefs looked at her as if she were insane. Then, Collins says, "a smile broke over their faces and they laughed."

Whether Sitting Bull actually found humor in Mary Collins's jokes or she only thought he did, he gave up trying to convince her to leave. She was fearless. She spoke Lakota. She offered medical care to the Sioux and served food to her guests, which other whites were too stingy to offer. When she sent a teacher to open a school in Sitting Bull's camp, Sitting Bull at first ignored him, then gave in and allowed five of his children to attend the school. Sitting Bull never counted Collins as his friend, as he later counted Weldon. And he resented her attempts to convert him. (When Collins and the other missionaries erected crosses on his land, Sitting Bull put up a prayer tree with a buffalo skull on top. The whites say it isn't right for Indians to worship the skulls of buffaloes who gave us the meat of their bodies, he scoffed, but they want us to worship the statues of whites who never gave our ancestors anything.) But he trusted Mary Collins enough to let her nurse his children and teach them to read.

To the end of his life, Sitting Bull retained the ability to judge each white person on his or her own merits, remarkable considering that nearly every

6. Mary Collins, a Congregationalist missionary who built a house and church on Sitting
Bull's land, shown here visiting the Indians in her wagon. Courtesy of the State
Historical Society of North Dakota, A2930.

white person he met lied to him or tricked him. A mail carrier named Frank
Grouard fell into the hands of the Hunkpapas and was about to be executed
when Sitting Bull saved him. Years later, Grouard signed on with the army and
led the soldiers to Lakota villages no other white scout could have found.

And then there was Big Leggins Bruguier. He rode into Sitting Bull's camp
and asked—in Lakota—for asylum from the whites, since he had killed a white
man in a brawl at Standing Rock. Sitting Bull gave Bruguier a horse and took
him in. Bruguier served as the chief's interpreter. Later, in return for clemency
and an army paycheck, he turned scout and told the soldiers exactly where to
find the chief's camp. They just missed him.

Still, Sitting Bull considered several whites his friends. He respected the bravery and honesty of a Jesuit priest named Pierre-Jean de Smet, who traveled into
his camp in the middle of a war to tell the Sioux about Christianity and persuade them to discuss peace. And he trusted Major Walsh, in Canada. After he

surrendered, Sitting Bull received bundles of hate mail. But he also received fan mail. Tourists who attended the Wild West shows in which Sitting Bull appeared sometimes jeered or spat, but many whites gazed at him with awe and begged for his autograph.

At the start of September 1883, a few weeks after the government released Sitting Bull from Fort Randall, the politicians of Dakota Territory asked McLaughlin to bring the chief to Bismarck to celebrate the laying of the cornerstone of the new capitol. McLaughlin had mixed feelings. He disliked the chief for presuming to know what was best for his people, and the last thing he wanted was for Sitting Bull to become more puffed up than he already was. But the more Sitting Bull saw of white cities, the more impressed he might be, and the more he would long for the comforts of civilization. (Touring white cities was exactly what reformers prescribed for curing Indians of their "savagery." Merrill E. Gates, who served on the Board of Indian Commissioners from 1884 to 1922, claimed that the only way to bring the Indian from savagery to citizenship was to make him "more intelligently selfish. . . . We need to *awaken in him wants.* In his dull savagery he must be touched by the wings of the divine angel of discontent. . . . Discontent with the teepee and the starving rations of the Indian camp in winter is needed to get the Indian out of the blanket and into trousers,—and trousers with a pocket in them, and with a *pocket that aches to be filled with dollars!*") If anyone was to get the credit for turning a savage into a parade mascot in a few weeks' time, it ought to be his agent.

McLaughlin escorted three hundred Indians to Bismarck. The warriors and their families camped along the railroad tracks, while Sitting Bull stayed with the other VIPs at the Sheridan House, a hotel named for the general who had given the country its most enduring definition of a good Indian. (Custer's wife stayed there after her husband's death, waiting for a train to take her east.) Tired after a day's traveling, Sitting Bull and his wife (history doesn't record which one) lay down on the floor beside the exceptionally high bed in their room. In the adjoining room, McLaughlin slept with his own wife, presumably *in* the bed.

The next morning, Sitting Bull rode to the fairgrounds with the governor of Dakota Territory and the former and current secretaries of the interior. He mounted a scaffold and sat beside a visiting British nobleman. Henry Villard, president of the Northern Pacific Railroad, spoke first, followed by President Grant. Then Sitting Bull delivered a short oration, which McLaughlin translated. The chief consented to ride a train and pronounced himself "half-civilized," this barely a month after his arrival at Standing Rock. Who could take credit for the chief's exemplary behavior if not James McLaughlin?

What a strange relation the two men had. Six months after that parade,

McLaughlin told Sitting Bull that he needed to travel to St. Paul on business. Sitting Bull asked to go with him, on the grounds that he wanted to see more of how whites lived. Why, yes, McLaughlin said, it could only do you good. One of Sitting Bull's wives went along on the trip (the railroad donated the tickets but couldn't condone polygamy), as did McLaughlin's wife and One Bull. The group stayed at a hotel and toured the city's banks and factories, a grocery store, the post office, and the fire department, where Sitting Bull was allowed to touch off the signal that sent the firemen sliding down their poles. The trip didn't make Sitting Bull covet white luxuries, but he seems to have enjoyed himself.

When various showmen asked McLaughlin to be allowed to take Sitting Bull on tour, the agent bragged of his ability to handle the chief and offered his wife and son as interpreters. Vestal characterizes the McLaughlins as social climbers, sensitive to the stigma of Marie's Indian blood; accompanying Sitting Bull on tours seemed a good way to gain entrance to society. Maybe that was true. Or McLaughlin wanted to get the chief off the reservation so he couldn't influence the other Indians. He consented to Sitting Bull and several companions going on a tour to New York and Philadelphia, staging scenes of Sioux life. The summer after that, Sitting Bull signed a contract with Bill Cody to appear in his Wild West show for four months, earning $50 a week, plus a bonus of $125 and all the proceeds from selling his autograph. Why would a man supremely conscious of his dignity allow himself to be paraded before whites in a spectacle one newspaper described as "A Group of Howling Savages Pursu[ing] a Defenseless Stage Coach"? For one thing, Sitting Bull never actually appeared in the shows. His duties were to ride in the opening parade and talk to any whites who visited his lodge. Cody made sure to introduce his star as "head chief of all the Sioux," a title Sitting Bull enjoyed flinging back at McLaughlin. When Sitting Bull mentioned that he liked the trained gray circus horse he rode in the parades, Cody gave him the horse and paid to send it back to Standing Rock. Cody treated Sitting Bull fairly, and he allowed him to escape the stifling tensions of the reservation—a prison, really, with McLaughlin as jailer—to see the larger world, which was more amazing, terrifying, and depressing than anything Sitting Bull had imagined. He was grieved but not surprised by all the poor people on the streets. Sioux warriors gained honor by killing their enemies. But any Indian who ate well and slept in a fine lodge while members of his tribe suffered hunger was a monster. Sitting Bull sent home most of his earnings to feed his family, but he gave away the rest to starving beggars and newsboys.

Along with a bundle of cash, Sitting Bull took back to the reservation a distrust for white society and the respect of many whites. McLaughlin couldn't call him a nobody when the whites' own newspapers kept praising him as the greatest leader of his people. McLaughlin was torn between his wish to keep Sitting Bull under his control and his desire to be rid of him. In 1887, when Cody arranged to take his show to England and perform at Queen Victoria's jubilee, McLaughlin refused to let Sitting Bull go, charging that the chief was "a consummate liar and too vain and obstinate to be benefitted by what he sees, and makes no good use of the money he thus earns." Perhaps Sitting Bull was disappointed not to meet the queen. But he sensed that he was needed more at home. Already he was hearing more talk of the whites taking his people's lands.

～○

This, then, was the Sitting Bull whom Catherine Weldon met that afternoon when he drove his dusty wagon onto agency grounds. For all that he had spent time with white women, for all that she had spent time with Indians, their first encounter must have been a shock for them both. He was frail and poorly dressed. She was healthily robust, in the heavy skirt and bustle, frilly, tailored shirtwaist, ornate bonnet, and gloves Victorian women always wore. Sitting Bull had been born into a society in which the horse was a relatively recent innovation and the rifle the most advanced form of technology, a society in which a man proved his worth by killing his enemies in face-to-face combat and bringing home the man's scalp so his mother or sister could brandish it in triumph in her victory dance. Until recently, Weldon had been living in a bohemian neighborhood in Brooklyn, where the only Indian she saw on a regular basis was that statue in front of the cigar store. Sitting Bull was a devout believer in his Indian religion. Weldon, by her own confession, was an impious woman who had not been true to Christ, "not worshipped him, not obeyed him." He was the husband of two wives, the widower of several others, the devoted and ever watchful father of many children. She was the widow of a brief marriage to a man she didn't love, the mother of an only child who lived much of his life with relatives or at boarding school. Sitting Bull was a conservative who preferred tradition. Weldon, a liberal artist, detested superstition and was agog at modern science (in her speech to the warriors at the Ghost Dance, she would brag about the white man's ability to use electricity to cure "rheumatism & many other diseases" and execute murderers).

Yet they got on. Each liked and admired the other. Vestal thinks the admiration reached the point of infatuation on Weldon's side, and, though he mocks what he takes to be Weldon's hysteria, he probably is right that her admiration for Sitting Bull can be attributed to his representing a freedom and authenticity denied to most Victorian women.

She was an artist, and being an artist, had no use for shams. And yet, in that pallid imitation of Europe which then passed for American culture, she herself, as an artist, could only be a sham. Her talent was a curse, fit to drive her to absurdities in that world to which it had, and could have, no authentic relation. Added to that baffling, smothering wet blanket was the damning fact that she was a female. . . .

When Sitting Bull arrived, the old man's charm immediately swept Mrs. Weldon off her feet. She had come to see a great man and was not disappointed. In him she saw the integrity, the wholeness that her baffled heart looked for in vain in that travesty of culture which had frittered away her talents. To her he seemed a rock in a weltering sea.

The wild, run-on sentences in Weldon's letters reveal that she did have an enthusiastic nature. But Vestal's insinuation that "the old man's charm" allowed him to sweep Weldon off her feet—with all the erotic associations that phrase implies—reads like speculation. The truth, I would guess, is that Weldon was overwhelmed by Sitting Bull's charisma and all he symbolized as the most powerful chief of the most powerful tribe on the Plains. What woman—or man— wouldn't have felt stirred by Sitting Bull's presence? A woman of another race only ten or twenty years his junior might well have been conscious of the sexual possibilities between them. But the pleasure a woman gets from such a meeting comes precisely from her status as the only woman who would be taken seriously by such a man, not as a potential bedmate, but as a partner, an adviser. Even as a woman takes satisfaction in knowing that she could be the romantic object of such a leader, if she is to be taken seriously she must discourage any idea that she might actually be an object of pursuit.

Weldon herself took care to describe their meeting in businesslike terms. "I saw Sitting Bull at Yates," she wrote to Red Cloud, "he had come up 40 miles, ill as he was to meet me. He was glad to see me for he had many things to tell me. He has become a member of the N.I.D. Association, also Thunder Hawk, Hohecikana, Bears Rib, Wakinyanduta, Circling Bear, Matowaoynpa, Ceya Apapi (Strike Kettle), Black Shield, Wasicun Maza Wizi Hansku & Tasmka Duta. Many more would have joined but I had no time, nor chance to see them, but Sitting Bull said he knew they would join, but he wanted their own word for it." Here, as in her other descriptions of Sitting Bull, we hear the voice of a woman who is conscious that other whites and Indians might attribute her desire to meet the chief to the sexual frustration of a widow and is therefore trying to allay that interpretation.

And Sitting Bull? How did he interpret her actions? He left no written record.

But he probably found her helpful. She had sent him those maps and land lists. And he must have considered her unusual, even for a white woman. She did not treat him with disdain, and her fine dress and jewelry made her seem richer and more important than the other whites at Standing Rock. Most of all she was courageous, willing to travel alone from New York to the wildest Sioux reservation and stand up to the agent, which even Sitting Bull's warriors wouldn't always do. Sitting Bull enjoyed reading the NIDA's magazine, the *Council Fire*—or rather, he listened as someone read it aloud in Lakota—and, at Weldon's invitation, he joined the NIDA and persuaded ten of his friends to join.

According to Weldon, she told the chief she wished she had more time to recruit supporters, but she was anxious to proceed to the other agencies. Judging by her letter to Red Cloud, it seems that Sitting Bull not only approved of Weldon's plan, he wanted to go with her. If she would be willing to wait until he had grown strong enough to travel, he would escort her to the Cheyenne River Reservation himself. We will take my wagon, he said. It is a comfortable way to travel, and several members of my family can come along. The trip will seem proper. We can tell the agent that we are going to visit my relatives at Cheyenne River.

That is a wonderful idea, Weldon said. I am grateful for your offer to accompany me. With you there in person, the other chiefs will never sign the treaty.

Sitting Bull returned home to rest and prepare for the trip while Weldon passed the time at Standing Rock trying to endure the stares and cutting remarks of the other whites and the tedium of life in a place that didn't welcome visitors. The settlement lay on a treeless plain west of the Missouri. The fort was a collection of low wood buildings around a dusty parade ground—when it rained, the dust turned to a gluey mud called gumbo—while the agency, within walking distance to the north, consisted of McLaughlin's office, a trading post, a store, a school with a bit of grass around it, and a stone pedestal topped with a rock in the shape of an Indian woman with a child on her back, which gave the agency its name. (Three years earlier, Sitting Bull and McLaughlin had presided over the rock's removal from its original location on a hill to the pedestal by the agency. A photo gives the impression that the Indians have been allowed out of jail for the day and the whites would as gladly shoot them as smile. If the dour women are typical of the soldiers' wives, Weldon wouldn't have needed much in the way of good looks to stand out.)

There was no hotel at the agency, but visitors must have been frequent, and someone put them up. While Weldon was waiting for Sitting Bull, she met a woman she describes to Red Cloud as "[a] relative of Sitting Bull, Mrs. Van Solen." Mary Louise Picotte Van Solen was a half-blooded Sioux who lived on

In the photo: Fort Yates in its prime © by F.B. Fiske

7. Fort Yates, Dakota Territory, "in its prime." Courtesy of the State Historical Society of North Dakota, Fiske A1095.

her sister's ranch north of the Cannonball. On Weldon's return the following spring, she and her son lived on that ranch. Maybe, on this trip, she already knew the sisters; they might have been among the "mixed-race friends" she stopped to see on her way to Standing Rock. Maybe Louise Van Solen had driven Weldon south from the ranch to the agency. But Weldon's bland reference to "Mrs. Van Solen" as a relative of Sitting Bull indicates that they weren't yet close friends.

Still, Weldon told Van Solen about her plans. Part Sioux herself, Van Solen would have applauded Weldon's efforts. But she wouldn't have wanted Sitting Bull to get arrested. Indians, she reminded Weldon, could leave the reservation only with a pass. And the only person with the authority to issue a pass was the agent. Weldon was suspicious of McLaughlin from their encounter on the Cannonball and his derogatory remarks about Sitting Bull and the NIDA, but she went to his office ("reluctantly," she told Red Cloud) and asked him to issue one.

Was she insane? McLaughlin said. How could he let Sitting Bull leave Standing Rock when the commissioners were expected any day? How could he allow the most militant Indian in the country to travel to the reservations where the commissioners were trying to persuade the chiefs to sign? Furthermore, Weldon would not be permitted to travel through the reservation on her way to the lower agencies.

Come now, Weldon chided (her account of the quarrel jives with McLaughlin's own). Are you afraid of a woman and a woman's influence?

Woman or not, McLaughlin said, you have no business meddling in affairs about which you know nothing.

I am a United States citizen! You cannot prevent me from traveling where I want to go and speaking to whomever I please.

You may travel on any public road you wish. But not on the roads of the reservation.

Weldon threatened to report the agent to her friends in Washington. But McLaughlin didn't respond well to threats. "High words passed between us both," she wrote to Red Cloud, "& I rose indignantly & left the office."

An article about the altercation ran in the *Bismarck Daily Tribune* on July 2 and was reprinted across the country.

SHE LOVES SITTING BULL

A new Jersey [*sic*] Widow falls victim to Sitting Bull's Charms.

A sensation is reported from the Standing Rock Agency, the chief participants being Mrs. C. Wilder, of Newark, New Jersey, and Sitting Bull, the notorious old chief. Sitting Bull has many admirers, and among them is numbered Mrs. Wilder. During Bull's recent illness she visited him at his camp, and when he recovered sufficiently to travel she made arrangements with him to convey her in his wagon from Standing Rock to the Rosebud Agency. It is against the rules to leave their reservation without permission. A person to whom Mrs. Wilder told of her contract with Sitting Bull suggested that she had better see Agent McLaughlin. She acted upon the suggestion and the Major informed her that he could not permit Sitting Bull to go about from one agency to another and positively refused to have the wily old chief accompany her to Rosebud.

No sooner had the agent refused than Mrs. Wilder flew into a rage, and declared her intention to see her political friends in Washington and secure Major McLaughlin's removal. Those who came from Standing Rock state that she used the most scathing and abusive language to the Major and accused him of using the Indians as prisoners. So abusive and threatening was her language that the agent politely ordered her to leave the reservation.

"Those who came from Standing Rock" had to mean McLaughlin, since he was the only source of news from his agency. That a gentlewoman would curse a gentleman, especially a gentleman representing the Church, justified to most readers that he would order her to leave. "Mrs. Wilder is a widow and is visiting the reservation," the article went on. "She is a great admirer of Sitting Bull, and it is gossip among the people in the vicinity of the Agency that she is actually in love with the cunning old warrior." Whatever the state of "Mrs. Wilder's" affections, the reporter expressed his approval of McLaughlin's politics. "Agent McLaughlin's position in the matter is unquestionably right, especially at this time, as Sitting Bull would surely prove a disturbing element at the lower Agencies during the conference of the Commission of the question of opening the reservation to settlement."

To be fair, McLaughlin did not order Weldon to leave. He simply wouldn't let her travel the most direct route from Standing Rock to Cheyenne River across the reservation's roads. And he didn't believe the rumor that she was in love with Sitting Bull. After the article was printed, the agent received a letter from a Dr. Alexander Wilder of Newark, New Jersey, demanding that McLaughlin apologize for slandering his wife. McLaughlin begged the doctor's pardon and corrected the reporter's error. "The woman referred to is named Mrs. C. Weldon (not Wilder) and I understand that her home is in Brooklyn, New York." He expressed the opinion that even though Mrs. Weldon was "considerably 'off' on the Indian question," she was undoubtedly sincere. And he told the doctor she wasn't really having an affair with Sitting Bull. She was only his "great admirer, looking upon him as a model of all that is perfect."

Weldon, meanwhile, was writing letters to Thomas Bland and the Commissioner of Indian Affairs, calling for McLaughlin's removal. She also sent a messenger to Grand River to tell the chief to forget their trip. Sitting Bull was so indignant that he returned to the agency anyway to ask McLaughlin for the permit on his own behalf. In Weldon's letter to Red Cloud, she relates that McLaughlin declined to see the chief, leaving the discussion to a crony named Louis Faribault, who walked Sitting Bull to the guardhouse and insinuated that he wanted the pass so he could carry off Weldon and rape her. If you take her anywhere in that wagon of yours, Faribault said, you will end up in the penitentiary.

"The old chief was so much surprised and pained that his heart ached when he heard these vile insinuations," Weldon wrote. "He told Farrabault [sic] how he looked upon me as upon his own daughter and would have shielded & protected me from all harm."

For her part, Weldon "felt much disappointed & pained" and "resolved to leave Yates at once" to spare her friend further trouble. In a chivalrous gesture that would also give them a chance to talk, Sitting Bull offered to drive Weldon and her luggage the short distance from Fort Yates to the Missouri River so she could take the ferry to Winona, the tiny town on the eastern shore where the public roads began. It was also the town where the soldiers went to gamble, drink, and buy sex. Perhaps in an oblique, stilted way, Sitting Bull and Weldon talked about Winona and how it did the Indian men no good to have a place so near where they could go to buy liquor. It was scandalous that the white and Indian prostitutes who lived there did such an open business. Such behavior never would have been tolerated from a Lakota woman in the old days. Perhaps Sitting Bull gave McLaughlin credit for prohibiting the white drifters around the agency from "marrying" Lakota women to take advantage of their rations and forbidding the soldiers from the fort to visit Lakota villages for sex.

But Weldon and Sitting Bull probably spent most of that very short ride making plans for Weldon's trip to the other agencies and discussing what she needed to do in New York and Washington to further Lakota interests. We will see each other again, she promised. What traveler who has been befriended by the famous leader of a distant people wouldn't think of coming back?

At the ferry, Sitting Bull clambered wearily from his wagon, helped his passenger dismount, then lifted down her trunk. The soldiers and female travelers waiting at the landing would have made comments about the spectacle of Sitting Bull acting the squire to an attractive white lady from out east. *Look at that, Old Bull has gone courting a rich white squaw! I wonder if that's the fashion in New York, to promenade yourself with a filthy savage. Isn't she afraid of being alone with him? Even if he doesn't take his way with her, she'll pick up some terrible disease just from sitting in his wagon.*

Weldon and Sitting Bull shook hands. *Good-bye! Good-bye! I'll write to you soon. Don't give in to the commissioners!* As the ferry was pulling out, he waved one final time, then climbed aboard his wagon and drove back to the agency, taking the opportunity to pick up a few supplies before starting the grueling ride home.

Even that brief journey led to scandal. As Weldon complained in her letter to Red Cloud, Sitting Bull's "polite attentions & friendly words were heard & seen & straightway a romantic story was printed in the Sioux City Journal of July 2nd. A story full of the vilest falsehoods, stating that I had told Sheriff McGee of Emmons County that I purposely came from New York to marry Sitting Bull, that the Agent tried to prevent a meeting, but that Sitting Bull succeeded in seeing me. I never saw nor spoke to this man to my knowledge, in fact do not know who he is & he dares to circulate such atrocious untruths. All this is the Agents work. He fears Sitting Bull's influence among his people and therefore pretends to his face that not politics were his motives for refusing the pass, but my welfare & he took this opportunity to humble the old chief & make his heart more than sad.

"In order to lessen my influence as a member of the N.I.D.A. he makes me ridiculous by having the story printed, in which it is stated that I should have said that I came all the way from N. York to marry Sitting Bull. Red Cloud, is there no protection for defenceless women?"

Although McLaughlin didn't start the rumors about Weldon's "affair" with Sitting Bull, he couldn't resist feeding them. There probably seemed no better way of discrediting the NIDA than by slandering its representative. And nothing could be easier than slandering a woman who traveled on her own and met with Indians unescorted. But was Weldon right in claiming she was "defenceless" against such attacks? The return address on her letter indicates that she sent it from the Yankton Agency, downriver from Cheyenne River, Lower Brule, and Crow Creek, proving that, despite McLaughlin's efforts to prevent her, she did reach these lower agencies. And the postscript she wrote to Red Cloud proves that McLaughlin was right to fear her influence with the chiefs at those agencies. "I forgot to mention that Sitting Bull would have liked to see you & that he says he will never sign nor will his followers, but that he is afraid some of the other chiefs may sign in order to become popular." That the army, in the end, maintained all the power is proved by the letter's failure to reach Red Cloud. W. F. Godfrey, the postmaster at Pine Ridge, encountered Weldon's letter and passed it back to a Major Roberts at Fort Yates, with the comment: "I herewith inclose you a fair specimen of a letter from a female crank; and if it but provokes a smile, after perusal, its mission will have been accomplished." The letter ended up in McLaughlin's possession, so it is more likely that the agent read Weldon's complaints against him than that Red Cloud saw the letter.

The likelihood that Weldon, prohibited from traveling the reservation roads, took the steamboat south from Winona and spent the next few weeks working against the commissioners at the lower agencies is supported by an article in the Yankton paper dated July 10, 1889. The correspondent noted General Crook's complaint that the Indians at Crow Creek "have been tampered with by Dr. Bland's Indian Defense association, and I know they listen to him rather than to those they should know as their truest friends." Maybe Weldon did the tampering, circulating a letter from Bland among the Indians. If so, she kept her name out of the papers by remaining off the reservation and meeting in secret with representatives of the tribe.

In any event, her efforts failed. The Indians at the lower agencies had been nearly unanimous in their opposition to the cession, but the commissioners managed to sign up thousands of warriors, dividing faction against faction,

enemy against enemy, meeting with this man in secret, promising that man anything he demanded, soothing any grievance. If only a few men could be flustered
into signing, the rest would rush to sign—"stampeding," the strategy was
called—since those who didn't sign feared the act would pass anyway and they
would be left with nothing. By the end of July, Weldon must have given up and
taken the train back to Brooklyn.

At Standing Rock, everyone had called a brief truce to travel up to Bismarck
for the big Fourth of July celebration in honor of the state's first constitutional
convention. Even as the settlers were trying to do away with the Indians, they
asked McLaughlin to bring a contingent of warriors to help celebrate the holiday. Once again, the agent escorted Sitting Bull to Bismarck—the chief wore
a black Prince Albert coat—and he and his warriors attracted the most applause
of anyone in the parade. Everyone had a good holiday, then they traveled back
to Standing Rock to resume their fight.

Sitting Bull, for his part, went about the reservation trying to line up the
other chiefs behind him. Let us stand as one family as we did before the white
people led us astray, he told his warrior society, the Silent Eaters. Don't worry,
they assured him. We will never sign that piece of paper. We would be crazy to
give the whites even one more acre of our land.

Confident from their recent triumphs at the lower agencies, the commissioners arrived at Standing Rock. McLaughlin, who favored this treaty as he
had not favored the less generous one, was informed by his superiors that he
must help them swing the deal or lose his job. Days passed and the commission made no progress. McLaughlin became desperate and asked his wife to
throw a party. While the gala was in full swing and all the commissioners and
soldiers were enjoying themselves on the dance floor, the agent and his translator slipped away and met secretly in a deserted stable with one of the lesser
chiefs, John Grass. There, in the dark, McLaughlin threatened and sweet-talked
John Grass into switching sides. Then he went around to the other chiefs and
played off one against the other (*John Grass has signed—you wouldn't want him to get
his share of the money while you are left with none*). McLaughlin wrote speeches for the
chiefs to read to explain to their people why they were now supporting the treaty.
He stationed his Indian police around the council so Sitting Bull wouldn't scare
the lesser chiefs out of doing what they had promised.

Sitting Bull didn't learn about this meeting until after it had started. He and
his Silent Eaters rode up on horseback and tried to force their way past the tribal
police, but only Sitting Bull was allowed in. When the Indians saw him, they got
nervous. General Crook assured them that no one would be hurt. "You need
not be alarmed, because no one will be allowed to interfere with you. And if any

8.   Sitting Bull addressing Indians and government commissioners at Fort Yates in 1889. James McLaughlin and his wife are seated at the table. Courtesy of the State Historical Society of North Dakota, Barry C1424.

damage or injury is done those who have signed, we will ask to have it paid for from the rations of those who do not sign. So there must be no trouble. Now the tables will be moved down here and those who want to sign can do so."

Sitting Bull jumped up. I would like to tell you something, he said through the interpreter. Unless you object to my speaking. If you do, I will not speak. No one has told us of this council today, and we just got here.

Crook asked McLaughlin if Sitting Bull had been told about the council.

"Yes, sir," McLaughlin said. "Everybody knew about it."

The commissioners hustled John Grass and his followers toward the tables. Sitting Bull's men tried to force their way inside, but the police blocked them. Everyone—even One Bull—hurriedly signed. Sitting Bull stomped out and rode off. As the commissioners were leaving, a clueless reporter asked Sitting Bull what the Indians thought of the cession.

Don't talk to me about Indians! the chief shot back. There are no Indians left! Except my band of Hunkpapas, they are all dead, and those wearing the clothing of warriors are women.

3

In the World Celestial

*G*iven Sitting Bull's illness, the urgency of the fight on the lower reservations, and Weldon's wish to spare her new friend any difficulties her attentions might create, she didn't have long to get to know him before he drove her to the ferry. She couldn't have spent more than a few weeks agitating against the land bill at Cheyenne River and visiting her mixed-race friends at Yankton before she returned to Brooklyn—not to the apartment at 68 Box Street in Greenpoint, but the more bohemian brownstone on Liberty Street.

There she passed the winter of 1889–90, trying to figure out what to do next. In 1852, a doctor named Thomas Williamson and the Reverend Stephen Return Riggs published the first *Dakota Grammar and Dictionary*, an expanded edition of which was being prepared by the Bureau of American Ethnology even as Weldon sat in her apartment studying the older version. No doubt she used what she learned when she wrote to Sitting Bull. She spent time caring for her son and telling him of the wonders and inequities she had seen on the reservation. She must have communicated regularly with Thomas and Cora Bland. The Blands often went on tour, and there was a New York chapter of their association, so it's likely that Weldon met them that winter, if they hadn't met before. She introduced them to Christie; in a letter she wrote later to Sitting Bull, she intimates that the Blands knew Christie and mourned his death. But most of the time, I think, she paced her gloomy flat, considering the possibility of returning to live with her Indian friends for good.

Sitting Bull spent those same winter months hunkered down at Grand River, brooding on the passage of the bill he opposed and wondering how his people would survive. He also devoted time to dictating his replies to Weldon's letters. These must have been barely comprehensible; the only members of his camp who were even minimally literate in English were the older children who had returned from Carlisle or were studying at the day school Mary Collins had established.

I left Weldon pacing her Brooklyn flat and Sitting Bull brooding in his cabin while I tried to learn everything I could learn about Weldon's few white friends and the founders of the political group in whose name she did her work. I discovered as much about Weldon by comparing her to other Indian-rights activists of her day as I did by finding traces of her own life. And I felt that I had uncovered the stories of people, who, like Weldon herself, deserved more attention than they had gotten.

~~

Most Victorian women who lived among the Sioux wrote copiously about their childhoods. As a child in Iowa, Mary Collins attended Sunday school at her church. The pastor's wife wanted her own daughter to become a missionary, but the little girl died. The disappointed mother informed her class that God meant one of them to serve as her daughter's replacement. In her memoir, Collins says that she knew she was the chosen girl, but she tried to avoid her destiny by engaging in "frivolous" pursuits such as riding horses and socializing. Every sermon stung her with the knowledge that she wasn't living as God intended. Finally she asked the Board of Missionaries to send her to Micronesia. The board judged her lungs too weak and ordered her to set up a mission among the Sioux. Reluctant to live among "those horrid Indians," as she called them then, she nonetheless went where God sent her and lived most of her life at Standing Rock, converting enough of Sitting Bull's tribe that she was able to consider her time well spent.

Elaine Goodale, who volunteered to teach Oglala children at Pine Ridge during the same period as Weldon lived at Standing Rock (later, as superintendent of education, she inspected the schools at Standing Rock and gave James McLaughlin high marks for running them), wrote a book about her life. Born into a genteel New England family, she was raised on a farm in the Berkshires and educated by a fastidious, high-strung mother who spoke constantly of "'the beauty of service,' 'plain living and high thinking,' 'our own duties and others' rights.'" The "ultra-modern theories" that governed her education, Goodale said, stressed "individual self-expression at a considerable risk of faulty adjustment to society." She read Shakespeare, Dickens, and George Eliot, studied Greek from a local clergyman, played the piano, and wrote poetry.

9a.   Elaine Goodale at the White River mission on the Lower Brule Reservation, January
1887. Goodale is standing in front of the door. The woman to Goodale's right
is Laura Tileston, a missionary, and the woman to Tileston's right is Goodale's
housekeeper. Goodale's Lakota neighbors pose to her left. Courtesy of the family
of Elaine Goodale Eastman.

9b.   Elaine Goodale with her traveling outfit and driver, 1890–91. Courtesy of the family of
Elaine Goodale Eastman.

Goodale wanted to go to Radcliffe, but she couldn't afford the tuition. Hiring herself out as a governess struck her as loathsome. But a suggestion from a family friend, the dashing Civil War commander General Samuel Chapman Armstrong, saved her from that fate. Armstrong had led a Negro brigade in the war, then started a vocational school for blacks at Hampton Roads, Virginia. "His shining countenance and rapid speech, overflowing with enthusiasm for humanity and bubbling with wit, proved irresistible," Goodale wrote, and she decided that she would rather teach free blacks at Hampton than work as a governess for a wealthy family in New York.

As an experiment, a few Indians had been sent to Hampton. Goodale's ingenuity in inventing methods for teaching Indians made her class a success, at least in Goodale's eyes, and she determined to take her skills where they were needed most. She gave in to entreaties that she travel with a companion, but most of her acquaintances still were horrified. "In view of the much stricter conventions of the eighteen-eighties, it is not to be wondered at that our families and older women friends strongly disapproved of the plan," Goodale wrote. "'Young ladies' in that era rarely ventured far from the beaten track, and a missionary school in Virginia was quite unconventional enough! Dire consequences were freely predicted in case we persisted, ranging from attacks by the savages to the cut direct from 'Society' on our return to civilization."

Given that both women risked censure, why did Goodale write about her experiences and Weldon did not? Both women needed money. Religious and educational journals were eager to print anything about the Indians; they were "a live issue," Goodale said. My guess is that Weldon's experiences were too painful for her to dwell on. Weldon's trips to Standing Rock and the nebulous tasks she performed on Sitting Bull's behalf weren't sanctioned by the government, as was Goodale's teaching at Pine Ridge. Charles Eastman, the Indian who proposed to Elaine Goodale, was a young, single doctor who had been educated in Boston and wrote eloquent books about his childhood on the Plains. Their marriage was repugnant to many whites, but at least Goodale didn't live as a single woman in an isolated cabin with a polygamous old renegade. She earned the public's admiration for nursing the victims at Wounded Knee, while Weldon was castigated for causing the war that led to the massacre. Weldon blamed herself for the misfortunes that befell her son and Sitting Bull. She wouldn't have wanted to bring back such distressing memories. And she was a painter, not a writer. Her scenes of Indian life and her portraits of Sitting Bull were the only record of her experience she meant to leave behind. And no one bothered to save them.

Weldon's lack of an official mission separates her from the other Victorian women remembered today for living among the Indians. This might make her seem a dilettante. But it also absolves her, in hindsight, of many of the blunders her compatriots committed. Unlike Mary Collins, Weldon harbored no desire to convert the Indians to Christianity. Teachers like Elaine Goodale saw it as a virtue that their pupils grow up to speak and write English as opposed to their native tongues; as late as 1937, she was still trying to convince John Collier, the progressive new Commissioner of Indian Affairs, "that Indian religions are non-ethical and are based on fear and the propitiation of supposed malicious spirits or deities!" But Weldon never espoused assimilation. She proposed teaching domestic science to the Hunkpapa women only because she needed to justify her presence at Grand River and because the conditions under which the Hunkpapas were forced to live made such new skills vital.

In a small way, Weldon was a muckraker, trying to explain the Indians' discontent to the readers of eastern papers. But writing extensive exposés of reservation politics was never Weldon's goal, as was true of Helen Hunt Jackson, the author of *Century of Dishonor*, or Helen Pierce Grey, a freelance journalist arrested for investigating rumors of corruption at the Crow Agency in Montana. Writers like Grey and Jackson brought the Indians' abuse to the attention of many whites. But spending a few months in a library or a few weeks on a reservation before returning to white society to write a book and give lectures is a different endeavor entirely from taking your only child and retiring among your Indian friends because you admire how they live.

Still, as curious as Weldon was about Lakota culture, she wasn't an anthropologist. She had no training as a scientist and didn't seem interested in recording a vanishing way of life, perhaps because she didn't see that way of life as something that necessarily must vanish. Alice Fletcher, the most respected female anthropologist of the nineteenth century and one of the foremost Victorian scientists of either sex, contributed an enormous fund of information to white understanding of Indian culture. But her position of authority, combined with her certainty that she knew what was best for the people she was studying, led her to become the government's primary agent for carrying out allotment and destroying the communal structures of tribes across the land. Only much later did Fletcher admit the truth—quietly, in private—that allotment had been a terrible mistake for most of the tribes she had hoped to help.

What saved Weldon from absorbing the ideas that led nearly every other liberal of her time to advocate allotment and assimilation was that she accepted no one's counsel. Helen Hunt Jackson, Elaine Goodale, Alice Fletcher, and Mary Collins moved in the same reformers' circles. Jackson, who grew up in Amherst and was one of Emily Dickinson's earliest friends and champions, started life as a poet; as such, she was introduced to a very young Elaine Goodale, who had garnered precocious fame by publishing a book of poems. Alice Fletcher was converted to the Indian cause at a lecture delivered in Boston in 1879 by a journalist named Thomas Tibbles and a young Ponca woman named Susette La Flesche, who later became his wife. Two years after the lecture, Fletcher took her first camping tour among the Sioux in the company of these newlyweds. While visiting La Flesche's family on the Omaha Reservation, Fletcher met Susette's brother, Francis, with whom she shared the remainder of her life in a relationship that still defies categorization (he was nineteen years her junior and became her adopted son, but he acted as Fletcher's escort, her scientific colleague, and her emotional partner as well). Jackson, whose revulsion for female lecturers was initially weakened by a talk by Anna Leonowens, the English governess whose fanciful account of her years in the court of the king of Siam set at least a few Victorian women dreaming of life as an adviser to a charismatic "barbarian" prince, was incited to write *Century of Dishonor* by the same Tibbles–La Flesche lecture that so inspired Alice Fletcher. Jackson died in 1885, two years before the Dawes Act. But the other women reformers mingled frequently, listening to each other's speeches and validating each other's endorsement of allotment and assimilation as the Indians' brightest hope.

Of all the Victorian women who lived among the Indians, only Catherine Weldon remained apart from these ideas. She didn't get her inspiration from a parent or family friend, as was true of Elaine Goodale, or from God, like Mary Collins, or from her husband, whom she never credits with inspiring her to do anything. Perhaps any calling is irrational. How could I explain why I was spending so much time trying to uncover clues about a woman I had never met who lived a century earlier in a place I had never been? Still, I felt sure that if only I kept searching, I might find a clue to the source of Weldon's views.

The only white friends Weldon mentions in her letters are Thomas and Cora Bland, who led the tiny Indian-rights society to which she belonged. The National Indian Defence Association was the most extreme of the East Coast groups lobbying for Indian rights. Like other white liberals, they believed that the Indians' best chance for survival was to learn to read and write English, win citizenship, and vote. But the Blands didn't see why this meant that the Indians needed to give up their tribal land, their religions, language, or culture. If they were going to convert to Christianity, it ought to be because Christians acted in such a way that a sensible person wanted to be one. Not surprisingly, the NIDA was the only Indian-rights organization with more than a few Indian members.

I tried for months to obtain a complete set of the NIDA's journal, the *Council*

10. Thomas Bland, from the frontispiece of his self-help book, *How to Get Well and How to Keep Well.*

Fire, believing that the Blands might have told their readers about Weldon's adventures with Sitting Bull. She might have contributed articles. They might have printed her picture. The Smithsonian claimed to own the entire set, even the eleventh volume, which I hadn't been able to find anywhere else, so I hopped a plane to Washington, that city to which the government brought the chiefs of every major tribe to see how futile it would be to resist the powers of democracy and continue living as they wished.

~⌐

After a drab Michigan winter, I was stunned by the magnificence of the nation's capital in May. The sky was the throbbing blue of the field of stars on the flag. Every tree along the Mall seemed giddy pink with blossoms. Bare-legged black women in powder-blue silk dresses, red suits, and yellow shifts walked with unhurried grace toward the offices they worked in, entering the FBI or Supreme Court beneath mottoes that proclaimed everyone equal before the law. The new Museum of the American Indian wasn't due to open for another few years, on a site between the National Air and Space Museum and the Capitol, as if Native Americans would at last find a home between the technology that displaced their culture and the government that made it official policy to kill them. Unfortunately, the old Museum of Natural History didn't hold much information about Sitting Bull. All I really found were photos of his signatures, one differing from the next like the signatures of a child trying on identities, although by the time Sitting Bull returned from the Wild West show his autograph was fixed.

Frustrated, I wandered the museum with the other members of the public. There, in a display case, I came across the Winchester rifle Sitting Bull surrendered at Fort Buford in 1881. It was a beautiful gun. The polished wood stock was studded with shiny tacks in the pattern of a cross. After all the months I had spent scrolling through blurry microfilm, this was the first three-dimensional object associated with Sitting Bull that I had seen. He held this rifle to his shoulder, took aim, and shot Crow warriors, white soldiers, deer, and buffalo. He handed this rifle to his son and prompted him to ask how the Sioux would earn their living now that their old ways were gone.

In another wing, a computerized catalog of the National Anthropological Archives listed a monograph titled *A Brief History of the Late Military Invasion of the Home of the Sioux,* published by Thomas Bland in 1891. The likelihood that a report about the Ghost Dance written by Thomas Bland would contain information about Catherine Weldon made it all I could do not to follow the librarian into the stacks. When she returned and admitted that the pamphlet wasn't there, I kicked her desk and cursed.

At least the archives held copies of the *Council Fire,* every volume except the elusive eleventh, which I learned didn't exist; the Blands had run low on strength that year and taken a vacation. The Smithsonian owned real copies of the magazine. I slid them from their sheaths and sat holding the very tabloids Catherine Weldon might have held.

The *Council Fire* was founded in 1878 by a man named Alfred Meacham, one of those Americans who make us wonder if people weren't braver and more eloquent in pioneer times.

Meacham was born in Indiana in 1826 to parents who had left North Carolina to demonstrate their abhorrence of slavery. Meacham's father lost his money, and the family moved to Iowa. When Alfred was twenty-four, he and his brother, Harvey, traveled west to dig for gold. Unlike the other miners, neither Meacham drank. In Bland's account of his hero's story, Alfred Meacham's temperance so enraged a gang of rowdies in a San Francisco bar that they demanded he choose between a beating and a drink. Mounting a whiskey barrel, Alfred orated "in eloquent and pathetic language" the story of his mother begging him on her deathbed that he never drink or gamble. "The rough miners . . . were deeply affected, and tears coursed down cheeks . . . and when the speaker closed by asking, 'Would you have me break that promise?' 'No, no, no,' came up as a response."

The Meacham brothers lived sober, industrious lives, but they didn't strike it rich. They returned to Iowa to marry their sweethearts. Then both couples traveled to Oregon to run a farm and a hotel. In his spare time, Alfred developed careers as a temperance orator, a politician, and a lawyer. His most famous case involved a stranger about to be hanged by vigilantes for horse stealing. Drawing a revolver, Meacham placed himself beside the prisoner and vowed that he would defend the man's right to a legal trial with his life. At last a witness rode up, his testimony vindicating the accused man, who proved to be a preacher.

Meacham's integrity won the Indians' confidence. When his beloved brother was killed by a falling tree, Alfred sat in his house crying so piteously that the local Indians paid a call. "Your religion is not good," one Indian said, "or you would not grieve for your dead brother. His spirit is here; it cannot go away and be happy while you cry," and in this Alfred found consolation.

The most momentous event in Meacham's life—and the event that later affected Weldon—came when President Grant appointed him Superintendent of Indian Affairs for Oregon. Dutifully, Meacham inspected every agency and made peace with Captain Jack, the whites' nickname for the Modoc chief, Kintpuash. Not that this required much persuading. Captain Jack wanted to make peace. Meacham's virtue lay in his being one of the few whites Captain Jack trusted. At Meacham's urging, Captain Jack agreed to leave his land along the Tule River and settle on the Klamath reservation.

11. Portrait of Alfred Meacham from the frontispiece to his book *Wigwam and War-path*.

But the Klamath didn't want the Modoc living on their land and treated them badly. In 1872, the humiliated Modoc left the reservation to settle in a beautiful valley along the Lost River. The army wasn't amused. You couldn't have Indians wandering away from a reservation and settling where they pleased. War followed, with bloodshed on both sides. Pursued by soldiers, fifty-one Modoc warriors and their families took refuge in the Lava Beds—as rocky and burned out as they sound. How could the whites object? Who else would want to live there? But the government demanded that Captain Jack give up a band of Modocs who had killed a dozen settlers, several of whom had been Captain Jack's friends.

Meacham by now held no post in the Indian bureaucracy, but Grant begged him to travel to the Lava Beds and make peace with his old friend. Meacham agreed, only to be told that he could offer no concessions without the consent of Edward Canby, commander of all the troops in the Pacific Northwest. Hampered by Canby, Meacham found it impossible to negotiate. Soldiers kept arriving and surrounding the Modoc refuge. The Modoc warriors, furious with their chief's pacifism, came up with a plan to assassinate Canby. When Captain Jack refused, they threw a shawl around his shoulders, called him a fish-hearted woman, and threatened to expel him from the tribe. The best he could do was convince them to allow Canby one last chance to remove his soldiers. If Canby refused, each warrior would open fire at a delegate of the peace commission.

The peace party's interpreter, a Modoc woman named Wi-ne-ma, who was Captain Jack's cousin and the wife of a white settler named Toby Riddle, warned Meacham not to return to the Modoc camp. Meacham begged Canby to listen, but the general summoned a clergyman named Eleazar Thomas and the two men set off. Meacham saw no honorable alternative but to follow. When Wi-ne-ma realized she couldn't stop him, she said good-bye to her son, grabbed her husband, and went after him.

Captain Jack's warriors greeted the delegates with insincere cordiality—not to mention guns—and Meacham sensed danger. He could have galloped off— what follows is Meacham's own account—but he chose to sit with the other delegates around the council fire. Captain Jack asked Canby: Will you remove your soldiers from the Lava Beds? Canby said no. The chief asked again. Meacham signaled Canby to agree, if only to gain their safety, but Canby "firmly pronounced his own death sentence, as well as that of Dr. Thomas, by saying that the 'soldiers could not be withdrawn.'"

At that point, Reverend Thomas flung himself on his knees and began praying for peace. Captain Jack leaned forward and touched Meacham's arm. *Peace will come only if the soldiers are withdrawn.* A Modoc warrior named Schonchin sprang up and repeated the ultimatum: *All the soldiers must leave!* The warriors burst out with a battle cry, and Captain Jack shot Canby in the face. Canby ran, but another Indian killed him. Reverend Thomas received a shot and was allowed to stagger a few yards, "his murderers taunting him with not believing Wi-ne-ma, jeering him, and ridiculing his religion and the failure of his prayers. Pushing him down, they shot him through the head, stripped him and . . . gathered up the dripping garments and joined the other murderers at the council fire."

Two delegates escaped. But Schonchin drew a pistol and fired at Meacham. The bullet tore through his collar. As Meacham describes his own ordeal, "Before the next shot, Wi-ne-ma was between [Schonchin] and his victim, grasping his arms and pleading for my life. I walked backwards forty yards, while my heroic defender struggled to save me. Shacknasty Jim joined Schonchin in the attack, while Wi-ne-ma, running from one to the other, continued to turn aside the pistols aimed at me, until I went down. After I fell I raised my head above the rock over which I had fallen, and at the instant Schonchin aimed at me so correctly that this shot struck me between the eyes, and glanced out over the left eye, which was blinded. A shot from Shacknasty Jim struck me on the right side of the head, over the ear, which stunned me, and I became unconscious."

Meacham later learned that while he lay in a faint Shacknasty Jim began pulling off his clothes. Another Modoc was about to fire into Meacham's head, but Shacknasty Jim pushed away the gun and told him not to waste his powder. Having taken Meacham's coat, pants, and vest, the two Modocs left the body to Wi-ne-ma. *Take care of your white brother!* they taunted. And Wi-ne-ma did take care of him, wiping the blood from his face and straightening his limbs, believing as she did that her friend Meacham was dead.

A Modoc named Boston Charley, who also believed Meacham to be dead, began, in Meacham's words, "the difficult task of scalping a bald-headed man," a task made harder by the dullness of the knife and Wi-ne-ma's strong arms, which kept pulling him away. Boston Charley smacked her with his gun. "Wi-ne-ma, dazed by the blow for a moment, in half-bewilderment saw the dull blade cutting down to the bone, while Boston, enraged and impatient, set one foot upon the back of my neck, and muttering curses in broken English, succeeded in cutting a circle almost around the upper part of my head, and had already so far lifted the scalp that he had inserted the fingers of his left hand beneath it preparatory to tearing it off, when Wi-ne-ma, recovering her presence of mind, resorted to strategy, shouting exultingly, 'Kap-ko Bostee-na-soldier!' (soldiers coming,) and Boston left his work unfinished."

An hour later, the soldiers found Wi-ne-ma still kneeling by her friend and Meacham insisting that he was dead. "By strong arms I was borne to the

Hospital," he wrote later. "My wounds were dressed, and the surgeons gave the opinion that since I was a *strictly temperance man* I '*might* survive.'"

Captain Jack eventually was betrayed by the same warriors who had mocked him for not wanting to murder Canby. A trial was held. The renegades got off. Captain Jack refused to tell his side of the story. "Why bother," he told Meacham. "I am already convicted." When the chief was led back to his cell to await hanging, Meacham walked beside him. "Every step the rattle of the chains upon his limbs reported his coming doom," Meacham said, "and when the iron door swung open to receive him, and I standing upon its threshold beside him, gave him my hand for the last time, he besought me, in most beseeching tone, 'His-wox-us-dit-che sti-noz, Kem-kan-ha nu-tocks.' (Chief with a straight tongue, tell my side of the story.) There, in that dark hour of that man's life, I promised him with 'Ku-moo-kum-choocks' (the Great Spirit) as my witness, that 'with malice toward none, and charity for all,' 'with fear of none but God, I would declare the right as God gave me to see the right.'"

Debilitated by his wounds, Meacham nevertheless traveled around the country, giving lectures that fulfilled his promise. "My right to tell 'the other side' is certified to by Modoc bullets in my maimed hands and mutilated face," Meacham prefaced each talk. When asked how he who had suffered such pain at the hands of the Indian could plead for the race, Meacham answered that he wasn't pleading for the Indian, he was pleading for Humanity.

No wonder that when Thomas Bland met Meacham walking on the Boston Common in June 1875, Bland took to him so quickly that he immediately persuaded Meacham to come live with him in New York. "My wife and myself, both being physicians, as well as friends," Bland wrote in his biography of Meacham, "it was but natural that he should come to our home. For months he lay on the border-line that divides the transient world of visible shadows from that invisible realm of eternal realities." But Meacham regained enough vigor to deliver an average of five lectures a week for the next two years. The Blands were drawn into Meacham's work, helping him plan the first number of the *Council Fire*, which was published in Philadelphia on January 1, 1878 (the frontispiece portrays the bald, mutton-chopped, mustachioed founder). When Meacham decided that his journal would be more widely read if it were printed in Washington, he moved to that city, at which the Blands, "being much pleased with the capital, resolved also to move there."

The Indian Bureau sent Meacham around the country to arbitrate disputes with various tribes, and the job of publishing the *Council Fire* fell to the Blands. Meacham depleted his remaining strength, and one evening, as he sat editing the *Council Fire*, he surrendered to a stroke. Just before he ceased to breathe, Bland tells us, Meacham's face was illuminated "as though his vision had caught a glimpse of Heaven's transcendent scenery, and his soul was being ravished by songs angelic." The description sounds like hollow Victorian rhetoric until one discovers that Bland later became famous not only for his books about medicine, but his scientific proof of the existence of ghosts.

Although they both carried out full schedules as physicians, Thomas and Cora Bland obeyed their friend's wish that they continue publishing his journal. As I browsed through the *Council Fire* from its debut under Meacham to the final issue by the Blands, I caught repeated sightings of Catherine Weldon's enemies and friends. And yes, toward the end, I caught a glimpse of Weldon herself.

~~~

"After years of repeated importunities by the friends of the Indian," Meacham started that first issue, "I have consented to establish a journal devoted to his interest, assured that my own race are willing to do right whenever convinced of the right, and that the other stands to bury the tomahawk and scalping knife forever, whenever justice is guaranteed to them. . . ." With this explanation, Meacham wrote, we light

THE COUNCIL FIRE.
    May it burn until every Indian on the continent of America has been recognized as a man . . . ; until he has been admitted to citizenship . . . ; and until the last savage council fire in America shall have died out forever.

Evil as he thought the government's policies to be, Meacham made a point of supporting the officials who carried them out. This accounts for the initial loyalty of agents like James McLaughlin, who, I was startled to discover, was one of the *Council Fire*'s earliest supporters. The man who later became Sitting Bull and Catherine Weldon's greatest foe was, at the start, Meacham's biggest fan. But then, the *Council Fire* under Meacham wasn't the extremist publication it became under the Blands. In 1878, as the young agent in charge of the reservation at Devils Lake, Dakota, McLaughlin sent in his dollar so he could receive the magazine. He had read the March issue and was "very much pleased with it. My sentiments coincide with those expressed in the Council Fire, and I heartily endorse your views on the Indian question." He sent another dollar to obtain a copy of Meacham's monograph "Wi-ne-ma and her People," complaining that the greatest difficulty the friends of the Indian must contend with was the press. "[W]henever an error or a wrong has been committed by agents of the government, or the Indians, the same has always been exaggerated, and the majority of newspaper men have been ever ready to write up every rumor and sensational article detrimental to the Indian," a charge that seems farcical given his later practice of feeding scandals about Sitting Bull and Weldon to the press.

McLaughlin's initial enthusiasm was inspired by Meacham's support for a system in which agents reported to their churches rather than to the army, as many politicians wished. And he appreciated the journal's delicate position on the practice of white men taking Indian wives. Married to a Sioux woman he loved dearly, McLaughlin felt the sting of opprobrium heaped on those "squaw men" who hung around the agencies and lived off the rations of their Indian "wives." A columnist who signed his letters "Wigwam Writer" maintained that he could give the names of scores of army officers who lived with Indian women, then deserted their offspring, an act of abandonment no Indian would be brute enough to consider. But not every man with an Indian wife was dissipated, the columnist said. Some were married lawfully to Indian women; they loved their children and took care of them. "Our wives and children are as dear to us as other men's families are to them," Wigwam Writer concluded.

McLaughlin railed against the "squaw men" at his own agency. But the *Council Fire's* ability to make distinctions between the white vagrant who shacked up with an Indian woman to take advantage of her rations and that rarer man who was devoted to his wife must have impressed an agent who was a rare specimen himself.

In March 1880, McLaughlin mailed in eight dollars to renew his own subscription and bestow the *Council Fire* on seven friends. He was sending the money, he told Meacham, because "you need something more tangible than words of encouragement in your present work. Your advocation of the Indian cause commends you to all lovers of justice as well as the friends of the Indian, and I regret that I cannot assist you in a more substantial manner. . . ." McLaughlin's salary was only about $1200 that year, but he sent Cora Bland an additional $5, begging her to add it to the fund for procuring a steel-plate portrait of Colonel Meacham. A year later, he sent the staggering sum of $14, with the request that the editor renew those earlier subscriptions and send the magazine to still more of his friends. He was, McLaughlin wrote, "pleased to see the steady progress of THE COUNCIL FIRE, whose glow is being generally felt, and the fagots from the pen of its fearless editor is illuminating the Indian question so that it is better known and understood throughout the country than in the past. . . . Colonel Meacham, you have selected the right place for a thankless but useful work, which, sooner or later, must be appreciated and bring its reward. Wishing you renewed energy, I remain, very sincerely, JAMES McLAUGHLIN, U.S. Indian Agent."

McLaughlin's love of writing—he kept up a staggering correspondence—is obvious from his delight in such flourishes as those fagots lit by the pen of THE COUNCIL FIRE's fearless editor. Meacham could have had him for a columnist, although one wonders what McLaughlin's contributions would have been after Sitting Bull's arrival at Standing Rock.

Under Meacham's leadership, the *Council Fire* offered a multitude of voices—Indians and agents, army officers, "squaw men," clergymen, politicians. Women contributed as often as men. Cora Bland, like her husband, traveled west several times to find out about the Indians' needs. "Being a physician of that class which seeks to solve the problem of disease, and find and apply rational remedies, and having long since accepted the idea . . . that the state of the mind has more influence than physical surroundings over the health of the body," Cora wrote, "I resolved during my recent and somewhat extended visit to the Indian Territory [in September 1879] to study the problem of Indian civilization from the standpoint of this theory." Her conclusion? The Indians were dying of nostalgia and a sickness of the soul.

Virtually nothing is known about Cora Bland, but she must have been a strong model for Weldon, who mentions her several times. Cora Bland taught and practiced medicine in the nation's capital, helped to found the American Red Cross, and presided over the Women's National Health Association, but the presence of her name on the *Council Fire* masthead was enough to taint the journal as a refuge for "sentimental" and "womanish" ideas. When the much larger and more mainstream Indian Rights Association considered buying the *Council Fire*, the would-be editor declared himself receptive only if he could wrest the magazine "from the Cora Bland atmosphere and surroundings."

Cora was too tough-minded to warrant such attacks, but the writings of women like Fanny Kelly did give the *Council Fire* a saccharine tone. Kelly was the sort of woman Weldon could have been but wasn't. Kelly grew up in the West, suffered at the hands of real Indians—as Weldon never did—then capitalized on her contact with the Sioux by writing a book.

Kelly's story proves that turning one's misfortunes into a ticket on the celebrity tour is no modern invention. But then, Kelly had little capital but misfortune. While her family was emigrating to Kansas, her father died of cholera. Her mother went on and tried to farm amid border wars, drought, and locust infestations; Fanny's teenage years were harsh, and she married at an early age, joining her fortunes to those of a Civil War veteran fifteen years her senior and setting off to Idaho. They traveled with Fanny's niece, seven-year-old Mary, whom Fanny had adopted, as well as two Negro servants, another white family named Larimer, and several tagalong single men.

On July 12, 1864, Fanny and her niece and Sarah Larimer and her son were taken captive by a band of Oglala Sioux. Kelly's husband and one Negro servant escaped; the other men were killed. After two days, Sarah Larimer managed to escape with her son. Fanny tried to flee but got caught. One night, she lowered Mary from their horse and told her to hide until daybreak, when she should find her way back to the trail. Kelly's act seems irrational—the child's scalped remains were found a few days later by members of another wagon train—but it proves how scared she was about what would happen to the little girl if she remained with the Sioux.

Terrified of her captors, repulsed by the buffalo meat they fed her ("most filthy, being covered with grass and the excrement of the buffalo"), Kelly avoided abuse by working even harder than the warriors' wives. She learned enough Lakota to converse with the women, nursed the sick, taught the Indians a little English. She was helpful and meek (not to mention pretty—she was in her early twenties, with curly dark hair and a pleasing face), and a Hunkpapa named Brings Plenty bought her from the Oglalas, renamed her "Real Woman," and took her as a wife—or rather, as a servant, since Kelly insisted later that no Indian man ever touched her "unchastely."

At one point, this band of Hunkpapas, which included Sitting Bull, ran into a wagon train. In the fight that followed, Sitting Bull was shot. The settlers circled their wagons and threw up ramparts. Frustrated, the Sioux forced Kelly to write a message to the settlers, asking them to ransom her. The whites tried to buy her back, but the Indians demanded more horses and food than their leader felt comfortable giving, especially since Kelly had encoded a warning in her message to the effect that the Indians would attack no matter what the whites did. The whites declined to bargain. The Indians grew bored and left. Sitting Bull, who spent the next few weeks lying around the camp convalescing from his wound, noticed that the whites kept sending emissaries to buy Real Woman. He also noticed that her submission was the product of fear rather than affection.

Why don't you feed her up? he told Brings Plenty. Why don't you take better care of her? Traders will be coming. We must take this woman back and make a good showing.

Mind your own business, Brings Plenty snapped.

A Blackfeet Sioux named Crawler, who had come on a rescue mission from the whites, offered Brings Plenty a string of horses if he would give back Real Woman. But Brings Plenty said he preferred Real Woman to horses. Some of the Hunkpapas supported Sitting Bull and Crawler. Others supported Brings

Plenty; after all, a warrior had the right to do what he wanted with his captive, and they didn't appreciate an outsider's interference.

Sitting Bull tried to patch things over. Friends, he said, this woman is out of our path. You can see in her face that she is homesick and unhappy here. So I am going to send her back.

In the meantime, Crawler went into Brings Plenty's lodge. A knife and gun were drawn, but Crawler emerged with Kelly. Although Sitting Bull and the other Sioux who accompanied Kelly to Fort Sully tried to show their good intentions, Kelly warned the soldiers that the Indians planned to use her as an excuse to infiltrate the fort. As soon as she was inside, the soldiers slammed shut the gates, keeping Sitting Bull and his insulted followers outside.

Reunited with her husband, Kelly went to live in Ellsworth, Kansas, a town so new that she was its first female resident. But bad luck followed her to Ellsworth. The army destroyed an Indian camp nearby, and Kelly and the other settlers had to hide in a dugout to escape retribution. They were saved by Negro troops from the South. But these soldiers brought with them a plague of cholera that killed many of their own number and many whites, including Kelly's husband. Pregnant and alone, she fled to another town, but the residents there feared the plague and wouldn't let her in. Kelly gave birth to her son in an abandoned cabin, then fell ill herself. The doctor who nursed her back to health returned with her to Ellsworth—maybe he wanted to marry her—but he died as well.

Destitute, Kelly traveled to Wyoming to collaborate with Sarah Larimer on a book about their captivity. A year later, as the manuscript was nearing completion, Larimer ran off to Philadelphia and published the book under her own name. Kelly sued and won. The case was settled out of court for a small sum, plus Kelly's legal fees and the requirement that Larimer destroy the unsold copies of her book.

Still without a livelihood, Kelly traveled to Washington to petition the Indian Bureau for $5000 for the "valuable services" she claimed she had performed in warning the wagon train and the soldiers at Fort Sully of her captors' intended treachery. She ran into Red Cloud, chief of the Oglalas, who was in Washington with his own petitions. A few of his warriors recognized Kelly from the days she had been their captive "and seemed quite rejoiced at the meeting," Kelly wrote later. So desirous was the chief of showing his good will that he told the Indian Bureau to pay Kelly the sum she needed from the Oglalas' own funds. Red Cloud's generosity must have had something to do with Kelly's decision to speak well of the Oglalas from then on. A revised version of her memoir was published in 1871, under her own name. (Larimer published another version of *her* ordeal, but it didn't find many readers since she had had the good luck to escape after two days.)

As a friend to the Sioux, Kelly became a frequent visitor at the Blands' house in Washington. Meacham saw in Kelly someone whose suffering gave her the same validation as a peacemaker that he claimed for himself. Kelly, for her part, used the *Council Fire* to advise Indians that they mustn't give in to hating whites. Just don't accept the white man's whiskey, she warned, and don't allow white men to take your women, no matter what they promise. She hinted that she was planning to establish a home for the abandoned children of mixed-race marriages between Indians and whites—"the connecting links of the two races," she called these outcasts, with the sort of euphemistic do-gooding that infuriated more conservative reformers.

Kelly never did establish such a home. She settled in the capital, invested in real estate, and sent her son to private schools. In 1880, this notice appeared in the *Council Fire:* "MARRIED . . . Wm. F. Gordon, of Kansas, to Mrs. Fanny Kelly, of Washington, D.C. Mrs. Gordon *nee* Kelly, assures her Indian friends that though she has taken a brave into her teepee, she will not forget her Indian friends wherever there is an opportunity to plead for them. Her husband is also a worker in the good cause, and with hearts and hands united we hope to see them glide along the path of duty. . . ."

Coy and not-so-coy references to intimate relations between Indians and whites appeared often in the *Council Fire*, especially in its early days, when Meacham shared with other liberals the surety that the Indians' best hope lay in assimilation. At first, the *Council Fire* made little mention of Sitting Bull, a mysterious figure who had defeated Custer and fled to Canada. Only when the soldiers made Sitting Bull's people miserable enough that they started to surrender did reporters offer more than wild theories as to who Sitting Bull was.

In 1881, the *Council Fire* printed an account by an unnamed female correspondent describing the arrival at Standing Rock of three boatloads of Sitting Bull's followers. Everyone thronged the river to watch the landing, this author wrote, with several hundred of the agency Sioux there to greet their relatives. The great warrior Gall, who later became one of Sitting Bull's rivals, was on the first boat. His elderly mother was in the camp, and, upon seeing her, Gall "cried one large tear," which so moved the officer guarding him that he uncovered his head and turned away, muttering, "I can't witness that, it is so painfully interesting."

In a passage that indicates the repugnance Weldon provoked in whites by living among the Sioux, the anonymous female writer describes getting out of her carriage and mingling with the Indians, "somewhat to the disgust of some of our party, who object strongly to what they call 'Indian filth.' But I was curious; and had been used to cleanliness all my life. Taking a papoose in my arms, I patted its pretty beaded covering, and pressed it to my breast, and made signs that I would like to have it. The squaw was evidently flattered by my admiration of the baby and its ornaments, but was by no means willing to part with it."

Properly escorted by a certain "Lieutenant R., of the seventh cavalry," the author went to visit Crow King, a boyhood friend of Sitting Bull. She entered the warrior's lodge, sat beside him on his robe, and shook his hand; his "neat and fine appearance" impressed her. Crow King told the writer he was glad to see a "white squaw" in his lodge. This visit was such a success she paid a call on Sitting Bull's daughter, "but she had gone to a dance; so I was not presented. She is said to be quite pretty, as beauty goes with the Sioux, and recently eloped with a dusky swain, whom her father disapproved."

Sitting Bull did not arrive in Bismarck until August. A reporter from St. Paul gained an interview, which the *Council Fire* reprinted. That interview throws light on the regard Sitting Bull might have held for a white woman like Catherine Weldon, although how much of this sentiment is real and how much calculated to win the approval of his audience—or tease them—is hard to know. Through an interpreter, the reporter asked Sitting Bull where and when he was born.

I don't know where I was born and cannot remember, Sitting Bull told him in Lakota. I know that I *was* born, or I would not be here now. I was born of a woman—I know this is a fact because I exist.

The reporter asked a harder question: How many wives and children did he have?

Sitting Bull counted on his fingers. I have nine children and two living wives, and one wife who has gone to the Great Spirit. I have two pairs of twins.

A lieutenant observing the interview chimed in, "Tell Sitting Bull he is more fortunate than I am. I can't get one wife."

Spurred by the chief's laughter, the reporter asked Sitting Bull which wife was his favorite.

I think as much of one as the other, he said. If I did not, I would not keep them. I think if I had a white wife, I would think more of her than the other two.

Maybe this is evidence that he later asked Weldon to marry him because he preferred a white wife. Or he was making a joke. Few readers of the time would have heard the humor in Sitting Bull's replies to the reporter's nosy questions. Few readers of the time would have expected Sitting Bull to have a sense of humor.

Even then, the *Council Fire* didn't allot much space to Sitting Bull. The Blands were more interested in Valentine T. McGillicuddy, the agent at Pine Ridge, and his treachery in trying to depose Red Cloud as chief of the Oglalas. "Agent McGillicuddy is an epicurean in his habits of diet, a fop in dress and manners, and a petty tyrant in character," Bland ranted. McLaughlin, by comparison, was engaged in a campaign to force the army to stop cutting timber on the reservation. He wanted the fort closed: not only were the soldiers destroying the woods, but their influence on the Indian women was injurious, and the sight of soldiers living idly set a bad example for the men. How could the Blands not support an agent as superior as McLaughlin when McGillicuddy was stealing thousands of dollars' worth of supplies from his charges at Pine Ridge, mistreating the Blands' friend Red Cloud, and threatening to kill him?

And Red Cloud was a much earlier member of the Blands' circle than Sitting Bull. Having been presented with a subscription to the *Council Fire* by Fanny Kelly, Red Cloud reported that he liked to read the journal and put it away for his children to read. Sitting Bull didn't join the NIDA until Weldon's first visit to Standing Rock in 1889, while Red Cloud and his men were already subscribing generously in the early 1880s. On Christmas Day 1882, Red Cloud appeared at a literary reception in the Blands' parlor in Washington, with piano music provided by Miss Fannie Friend of Boston and a "short but flattering" introduction by Bland. Red Cloud spoke for ten minutes, "confining himself to remarks about the kind treatment he had received in Washington, and his wish and that of his people to become like his friends who were present."

Red Cloud traveled often to the capital to plead for the removal of his agent, and Bland traveled west at least once to help Red Cloud. Although Bland's destination was Pine Ridge rather than Standing Rock, his journey gives us some idea of what Weldon's trips were like—and where she got the idea of going. Bland started for Sioux country on June 13, 1884, arriving in Valentine, Nebraska, the terminus of the Sioux City and Pacific Railroad, four days later. He hoped to be met at the station, but Red Cloud hadn't received his note; possibly McGillicuddy intercepted the message, as McLaughlin later intercepted Weldon's messages to Sitting Bull. After waiting three days, Bland accepted a ride in the wagon of a white man with an Indian wife headed toward Pine Ridge. The entire agency—the bureaucratic nerve center from which McGillicuddy ran the lives of Red Cloud's people—consisted of a few tents, several dirt-floor cabins, and Cooper's Hotel, where Bland took a bath and changed his linen in preparation for meeting McGillicuddy.

Before leaving Washington, Bland had armed himself with a letter from the secretary of the interior authorizing him to "visit his friends among the Indians." When McGillicuddy read this letter, he broke up laughing. "You are not in the United States now," he said, "but on an Indian reservation, where I am in supreme command."

Bland dared to talk back. "Even on an Indian reservation, a citizen has his rights!"

12. Red Cloud, chief of the Oglala Sioux at Pine Ridge. Courtesy of the Nebraska State Historical Society, W938-119-48D/RG2185: 119-97.

In reply, McGillicuddy issued ammunition to his Indian police and ordered them to toss Bland in a carriage—clean underwear and all—and drive him to the no-man's-land beyond the reservation. On a farm across the border, Bland pinned a map to a tree and explained to some Indians what would happen to their land if they signed the treaty they were being asked to sign. The seditious nature of smuggling maps to the Indians, as Weldon later smuggled maps to Sitting Bull, is demonstrated by the response of an Oglala warrior named No Water, who told the doctor that even though he couldn't read, he sure could figure out "that map you show us ain't right; the line ought to be straight in the west side, and not cut into our land as it does on the map." All this Bland delighted in describing to his readers, among them Weldon and McLaughlin, who, when they had their shouting match at Standing Rock five years later, must have had memories of Bland's fight with McGillicuddy in their heads. Weldon would have been trying to avoid getting tossed off the reservation, as had happened to Bland. And McLaughlin would have been trying to act more reasonably than his counterpart at Pine Ridge. After all, McLaughlin still counted himself a supporter of Alfred Meacham, and it must have cost him a fair amount to know that he would be seen as an enemy by people he once considered allies.

On and on went the battle, with Red Cloud undertaking his eighth trip to Washington in 1885 to testify against McGillicuddy, and Bland providing evidence that the agent had been skimming money from the funds he was allotted to buy food and supplies for the Oglalas. By comparison, the Blands' contact with Sitting Bull was brief. When the Wild West show came to Washington in June of that year, Thomas and Cora visited Sitting Bull at his hotel. The chief was in his fifties, Thomas wrote, "of medium height, compact build, head above average in size, and quite well developed in the intellectual and moral regions, but with a large back head, and great width between the ears." Sitting Bull greeted both Blands warmly. I have heard of you as a friend of the Indians, and I am glad to see you and shake hands with you, he said through an interpreter. The Blands made no reference to his military career, "but we talked freely with him about other matters of interest. He said: 'I am learning to live like a white man—I have farmed three times now'—meaning that he had been engaged in farming three years. 'I want to learn about how the white people live, and that is why I came with Mr. Cody. I wanted to see the big cities and the Great Father, so I could learn how white men do, and tell my people.'" Thomas showed Sitting Bull a portrait of Red Cloud, and a smile lit the chief's face. He knew all about Red Cloud's difficulties with McGillicuddy. When Bland asked if Sitting Bull wanted his children to go to school, the chief said, "Yes. They must live like white people, so they must learn all that white people know." Sitting Bull, Bland said, retained his dignity by refusing to take part in Cody's show "except to be introduced to the people in a public speech by Mr. Cody."

Only in the mid-1880s did the Blands divert their attention from the right of Indians to live without being robbed by their agents to their right to continue living as Indians. As they had been killed or rounded up, the public had come to favor a just policy toward the vanquished. The question was no longer whether the Indians should be allowed to live, Bland wrote, but whether the best course was "a policy that shall have for its outcome the civilization of the remnants of the native tribes and their preservation as a distinct people, or their absorption into the conglomerate mass of the body politic." To gain the Indians' possessions without provoking public outcry, the Indians' enemies now pretended to be their friends. Allotment was nothing more than a clandestine attempt to break up the reservations, give a small homestead to each Indian family, and sell the rest cheaply to whites. In 1885, Bland started the NIDA to give voice to the unpopular opinion that dissolving tribal relations and granting individuals their own land would harm the Indians in the long run.

Lyman Abbott, a liberal Christian reformer, defended the Dawes Act in such rational terms that it is easy to imagine why most good-hearted white liberals thought the Blands crazy to oppose it. "We want to break down the reservation system, and put the Indian in the midst of civilization, wisely, honestly, and with full regard to the essential rights of the Indian as a man. If any one can tell me where is a good place to put a boil on a body, I can tell where is a good place to put an Indian reservation. It is a sore. No one wants to live next to an Indian reservation. We want the Indians treated as the negroes were. We want them given homes, implements of industry, education, the rights and protection of citizenship, and then we want to say, We will not feed or clothe or pauperize you any more. You must take care of yourself and confront the civilization of the nineteenth century."

But Abbott's optimistic view of forced assimilation incensed the Blands. They believed that the Indians' only hope lay in a policy that would give them titles to their reservations, "to be occupied by them in common, or divided, in severalty, as they may prefer; protect them in their right to local self-government till they shall be prepared to become citizens of the United States. . . ." By advocating the Indians' right to continue to living as Indians until they chose to live as whites, the Blands were, in effect, guaranteeing them the opportunity to live as Indians forever. When an exasperated President Cleveland asked Charles Painter, a representative of the more "reasonable" Indian Rights Association, if his organization could *please* try to get along with the NIDA, Painter said: "No Sir! . . . We are entirely opposed to the ideas of that Association. It seems to me as if they are defending the Indian's right to be an Indian and would perpetuate the conditions which must force him to remain an Indian."

Debating Bland's ideas in the *Springfield Republican,* Senator Dawes denounced Bland as "a very strange man . . . wild in his ideas and his attempts to state the facts." Dawes supported McGillicuddy, as did Herbert Welsh, who ran the IRA. Welsh used IRA funds to distribute thousands of copies of Dawes's attack on Bland. Then Bland blasted Welsh for misappropriating IRA money. Eventually Bland triumphed. Gloating, he reported in an 1886 issue of the *Council Fire* that Valentine T. McGillicuddy had at last been removed from office.

Bland was less successful in opposing the Dawes Act. Although Bishop William Hare, the Episcopalian missionary to the Sioux, fumed that copies of the *Council Fire* were circulating among the Indians and inciting them to oppose the cession, Bland couldn't overcome the power of Senator Dawes and his liberal white allies back east. "The Friends of the Indian," as they called themselves, owed their position to President Grant's peace policy of the early 1870s, by which the government resolved to treat the Indians with "kindness and justice" rather than brutality. Grant's policy, which led to the formation of the supervisory Board of Indian Commissioners and the apportionment of Indian agencies among various church groups, allowed the involvement of reformers who had long advocated fair dealings with the Indians. The Modocs' assassination of Canby might have sabotaged this new policy if not for Meacham's remarkable decision to hit the lecture trail in Captain Jack's defense.

But Meacham's disciple, Thomas Bland, couldn't compete with the rise of assimilationist groups like the IRA and its female counterpart, the Women's National Indian Association. Not only were the Friends of the Indian more numerous, they could flaunt the advantage of a beautiful mountaintop retreat just north of New York, an ornate resort called Lake Mohonk, operated by a pair of Quaker brothers with the Dickensian names of Albert and Alfred Smiley. Here the Friends of the Indian met every year from 1883 through 1916, with such luminous speakers as Lyman Abbott, Henry Dawes, Alice Fletcher, Merrill Gates, Herbert Welsh, Samuel Armstrong, Thomas J. Morgan, and Amelia Quinton and such assimilated Indian stars as Charles Eastman—Elaine Goodale's husband—and Francis La Flesche. The Friends spent their mornings in formal policy sessions and passed the afternoons strolling the wooded grounds of the enormous hotel.

As far as I could tell, Catherine Weldon and the Blands never attended these retreats. In fact, the Friends of the Indian enjoyed portraying the NIDA as a bunch of out-of-touch crazies having their headquarters in Washington and

Pach Bros.

LYMAN ABBOTT AT EIGHTY
(1915)

13. The Christian reformer Lyman Abbott, who strongly advocated individual ownership of Indian homesteads and dissolution of the reservations, a policy opposed by Sitting Bull, Thomas Bland, and Catherine Weldon. Photo from the frontispiece to *Lyman Abbott: Christian Evolutionist, A Study in Religious Liberalism,* by Ira Brown.

representatives "so far as we know, no where else." The NIDA could boast only a few men of national repute, Lyman Abbott said, and these men were such extremists that one of them advocated erecting "a wall of adamant as high as the stars and permanent as heaven" around the Sioux Reservation. Certainly there existed "no student of the Indian question, West or East, in the field or in the Department, in Church or State, feminine or masculine," who did not accept the Dawes Act as the Indians' best hope.

Bland countered that his opposition to the Dawes Act was shared by any "*honest* man or woman . . . who has made a study of Indian management and of Indian character. . . ." Could Abbott find a single advocate of his policy among the scientists employed by the government's own Smithsonian Institution? No. But a goodly number of those scientists belonged to the NIDA. It was precisely to protect the Indians from Dr. Abbott and his brand of civilization that the NIDA wanted to see that wall of adamant erected.

So dangerous did Bland become in the government's eyes that when Sitting Bull traveled to Washington in October 1888 to express his defiance of the land bill, the NIDA was denied access to see him. Bland pushed his way into the Belvedere Hotel, but the government interpreter refused to translate for him. The Indians wanted "very much" to speak with him, Bland said, but the interpreter was under orders not to interpret for anyone but the government. That the president of the NIDA was denied access to Sitting Bull in the nation's capital makes clear Weldon's usefulness in traveling to Standing Rock the next summer and providing him with maps.

She enters the pages of the *Council Fire* late in its existence, after the editors came to share her vision of Sitting Bull as a radical chief trying to help his people retain their identity. In February 1889, the journal ran a list of members, including "Mrs. C. Weldon, of Hoboken, New Jersey, who has just paid $2 to renew her NIDA membership." Hoboken! So Weldon had lived in New Jersey before she moved to Brooklyn. Maybe she moved back to Hoboken later; I would need to check. For now, I moved on to a telegram from James McLaughlin to Thomas Bland announcing his intention, along with John Grass, Mad Bear, Gall, and Big Head, to "ratify the bill prepared by your association" to the effect that "the southern boundary of Standing Rock reservation will be set five miles north of the Moreau River." This proved that in April 1889, a few months before Weldon traveled to Standing Rock, the agent was still willing to cooperate with the NIDA, if only on a boundary dispute.

In the following issue, Bland refers again to "Mrs. C. Weldon of Hoboken, NJ, [who] sends $2 for THE COUNCIL FIRE, with good wishes, though confined to her room with illness. This friend has spent much time in years past among the Sioux, and is a warm friend of that people, and she appreciates our defense of their rights." Weldon, then, had already traveled among the Lakotas before her trip to Standing Rock to meet Sitting Bull. She developed her ideas about Indian rights *before* joining the NIDA. She joined the group because the Blands' ideas had finally caught up with her own—remarkable, given how far ahead of their time the Blands were. She already was a widow; she was using her first name, "Mrs. C. Weldon," rather than signing herself "Mrs. Richard Weldon," as a married woman of that era would have done. She was living in a "room," presumably in an apartment or boardinghouse, which makes her sound less wealthy than Bland tended to describe her. And she had been seriously ill, which correlates with a comment she made later to Red Cloud that Bland had invited her to Washington to meet him ("I am a member of the N.I.D.A. & he wished me to go and talk the Sioux question over with you and the other members"), but she was ill and couldn't go. A few months later, she traveled a much longer distance to Standing Rock to meet Sitting Bull, a trip Bland might have urged her to take, as he had urged her to travel to Washington to meet Red Cloud.

After that, Bland refers only obliquely to Weldon. In September 1889, after she already had been to Standing Rock, gotten thrown off the reservation, traveled to Cheyenne River, and returned to New York, Bland reported that during the recent turmoil on the reservation over the ratification of the land bill, an unnamed member of the NIDA informed Sitting Bull of the "doubtful meaning" of the controversial section 17 of the Act [which referred to the source of payment for Indian schools]. A letter from the NIDA "had been read to him and his band by a white friend in which he has the fullest confidence. We suspect that our letter failed to reach the other chiefs, and that the copies mailed to Grass and Gall were suppressed. We suppose, however, that Sitting Bull referred to this subject in general council. Grass and Gall stood firm for some days, but finally, and quite suddenly, they signed the agreement."

A few pages later, Bland lists the contributions of the association's newest members: Chief Sitting Bull, $2, Hoheci Kana, $2, Bear Ribs, Thunder Hawk, Walk in Your Duty, Wato-mao-yus-pa, Cega Agape, Matokawinge, each donating $2 to join. He fails to credit Weldon for signing up these men but reports elsewhere on his correspondence with "Mrs. C. Weldon, a cultured, wealthy, and philanthropic lady of New York" who has "spent much time, at her own expense, in efforts to educate the Sioux." Mrs. Weldon visited the Sioux this past summer "and wrote us many letters of interest," an admission that sparked me to wonder if Bland had bequeathed his papers to some archive and Weldon's letters lay among them. (No, on both counts.) He certainly didn't print them. Why didn't he, given that he habitually printed reports from other visitors to the Indians? Maybe Weldon's letters were so exaggerated in their passions or so radical in their theories that Bland feared they would hurt his cause. Maybe his catchphrase describing Weldon as "a friend" hides disdain for her flightiness. How else explain his refusal to quote even the briefest passage from her letters? Yet he tells his readers that Mrs. Weldon is "an active member of the N.I.D.A., and on this account and because of her true friendship for and influence with the Sioux, Government officials, and those personally interested in getting the Sioux to surrender their lands, tried in various ways to prevent her from visiting and conferring with the Indians." His sympathies seem to extend only as far as her treatment by McLaughlin parallels his own treatment by McGillicuddy. "She was even threatened with being arrested, if she attempted to visit her friends at Cheyenne River Agency," Bland raged on Weldon's behalf. "Is this a free country or a despotism?"

Unfortunately for our knowledge of Weldon, by the time she returned to Standing Rock in the spring of 1890, the *Council Fire* was near its end. With the passage of the Dawes Act and the cession bill, the Blands had lost heart in defending the Sioux from their liberal "friends." Weldon retired to the reservation and took as her goal painting Sitting Bull's portrait and writing his biography. The *Council Fire* ceased publishing in December 1890, a few weeks before Sitting Bull's death.

~~~

I folded the last issue of the *Council Fire* and slid it in its sheath. When I stood, brittle bits of history sifted from my lap. I couldn't go back to microfilm. Desperate to turn up some physical proof that Weldon existed, I asked the librarian to direct me to the branch of the Smithsonian that might know about her paintings. As far as I could tell from her letters to Sitting Bull, Weldon had painted four oil portraits of the chief. Two of those paintings seemed to have been stolen with the rest of her possessions when she fled the reservation. Vestal reported in the 1930s that Weldon's third portrait of Sitting Bull had recently been "sold at auction among the effects of Mrs. Van Solen. . . ." And the fourth portrait, which had been hanging in Sitting Bull's cabin when he was killed, what had become of that?

The answer turned out to be as near as the computer behind my chair. *That* portrait was listed in the Smithsonian's catalog as belonging to the State Historical Society of North Dakota; I could see it when I visited Bismarck. Even more exciting was the information that another Weldon portrait had come to the attention of the Smithsonian as part of a bicentennial project in which volunteers throughout America compiled an inventory of paintings executed before 1914. The Arkansas branch of the National Society of Colonial Dames had documented the existence of a portrait of Sitting Bull dated 1890 and signed "CS Weldon." Given the two stolen portraits and the portrait now owned by the Historical Society of North Dakota, three of Weldon's paintings seemed to be accounted for. This painting in Arkansas seemed to be the fourth—the painting Vestal mentions as belonging to Louise Van Solen and auctioned at her death. Whoever owned this portrait might also own a trove of Weldonalia.

Unfortunately, the computer printout mentioned that the owner didn't wish to be identified. The Smithsonian knew the owner's name but wouldn't release it.

No way? I asked the librarian. Not ever?

No way, she said. Not ever.

⟶

The next day I woke early and made my way to the Library of Congress, where I compiled a long list of Thomas Bland's publications, including that tantalizing monograph *A Brief History of the Late Military Invasion of the Home of the Sioux*, then handed in my call slips and took a numbered seat beneath the rotunda of a reading room so magnificent I wondered if I would be able to keep my gaze down. I had been dreaming of this room since hearing as a child of a magical place that held every book published. What a nation I lived in, building such a palace not for monarchs but books. The rotunda was ringed with poetic tributes to philosophy, art, history, commerce, science, and religion. A gold inscription around the top proclaimed that the Lord requires nothing of us but TO DO JUSTLY, TO LOVE MERCY, AND TO WALK HUMBLY WITH THY GOD.

The books began to come, and Bland's publications soon formed a tower beside my head. He was never called upon to demonstrate his bravery in a camp of hostile Indians like his hero Alfred Meacham, but in his own way, Bland was just as fearless. A farmer's son with little education, he kept inventing himself whenever he saw the need. America was still small enough and the individual citizen still confident enough that he could try to set the policy that would guide the nation for years.

The most extensive description of Bland's life appears in *Pioneers of Progress,* his 1906 memoir of the great people he knew—Abraham Lincoln, Ulysses Grant, Lucretia Mott, William Lloyd Garrison, Susan B. Anthony, Ralph Waldo Emerson, Julia Ward Howe, and, of course, Alfred Meacham. In the introduction, the Reverend H. W. Thomas recognizes that the reader might want to know a little about the author. Bland's parents were Quakers. They moved to Indiana and built a cabin just in time for the birth, in 1829, of "this now distinguished son." As a child, Thomas worked summers on the family farm. As soon as he reached fifteen, his father yanked him out of school. Young Thomas worked hard on the farm, but he found time to read the scholarly works he borrowed from his neighbors. It was a difficult schedule, but his mother sustained him by her encouraging words and love.

Then his mother died. His father sold the farm. Thomas drifted until he found another woman to guide him. At twenty-two, he married Mary Cora Davis, a native of Virginia with whom he would live happily for half a century. In the medical self-help book Bland published late in life, he acknowledged that he owed much of his success to his wife's "wise suggestions" and "kindly criticisms. . . . She has journeyed with me from the realm of youthful ignorance and false beliefs through the various stages of intellectual growth, and literary, scientific and philosophical development, to a place in the ranks of progress and reform."

At Cora's urging, Thomas studied medicine, returning to Indiana to open a practice. His interests weren't limited to the conventional treatment of the ill "but took the wider range of health reforms. He had been a student of phrenology from boyhood. He longed to reach and help the people in a larger way; and hence took the platform as a lecturer. . . ." During the Civil War, Thomas entered the army as a surgeon. In his absence, Cora started her own medical studies at "Dr. Jackson's Health Institute" in Dansville, New York. It might have made sense for the reunited couple to set up a practice; instead, they established a literary journal called *The Home Visitor*, ran it for a year, sold it, and founded a magazine called the *Northwestern*, then the *Ladies' Own Magazine*, with Cora as editor.

In 1870, Thomas published his first book, *Farming as a Profession*. Like books that advised disaffected middle-class kids in the 1960s to eschew materialistic lives in the cities and live closer to the land, *Farming as a Profession* appealed deeply to its readers. On the strength of its proceeds, the Blands moved to Chicago, then to New York City. Cora sold her magazine and went back to medical school. She and Thomas befriended Meacham and followed him to Washington, where Cora enjoyed a successful career as a physician and Thomas occupied himself "with his literary work and as Corresponding Secretary of the National Arbitration League, and, also, of the Indian Defence Association and as President of the Eclectic Medical Society of the District of Columbia." Bland wrote one book per year from 1879 through 1882, took a decade off to edit the *Council Fire*, then wrote a political novel called *Esau*, a medical self-help guide, and so many magazine articles they "would make more than fifty volumes the size of his books," the Reverend Thomas boasts.

As the clerks kept bringing books, I saw that Bland's writings were united by his vision of a nation in which the rising middle class would not set as its ambition amassing private wealth. While other reformers were trying to force the Indians to give up their devotion to the tribe in favor of private ownership, Bland was cautioning white Americans against becoming greedy individualists. People should remember they belonged to a community. It was to the tribe they owed their souls.

I wondered how many would-be capitalists were suckered into buying Bland's book *How to Grow Rich,* only to be informed that "any man can get rich if only he is mean enough." Bland himself needn't have worried that his royalties would corrupt him. He printed most of his books himself. The one work he meant to reach a large audience—*How to Get Well and How to Keep Well: A Family Physician and Guide to Health*—he priced low enough so everyone could afford it.

The guide is so commonsensical that most readers must have wondered why they bought it. The author prescribes no therapy more exotic than moderate meals, exercise outdoors (for girls as well as boys), avoidance of strong drink, tobacco, and overwork, music as a remedy for insanity, and laughter as a palliative for whatever ails a person. As to modern medicines like mercury and arsenic, antimony, opium, laudanum, and morphine, better to throw them in the sea than swallow them. For the majority of complaints, Bland recommends herbal teas and sweat baths.

But as soon as one tries to categorize Bland as a rational reformer, another side pops up. In his photo he looks like a cross between the thinner of the Smith Brothers and the abolitionist John Brown, with a piercing stare that indicates he has a plan for the world's betterment that involves more than cough drops. He pooh-poohs the Indian's belief that medicine men are endowed with supernatural powers, then describes his own faith in magnetic healing, especially in cases of "nervous prostration, paralysis, cerebro-spinal meningitis, nervous dyspepsia, etc."

After the success of *How to Get Well,* the Blands moved to Boston, where they spent three years "in professional, literary and reformatory work." Then they moved back to Chicago, where, in 1901, Thomas published *In the World Celestial,* the book that made him famous. Bland's belief in ghosts sprang from his belief in science. Apparently the electromagnetic vibrations of the spirit world had existed all along, but the angels had only recently learned from prominent dead scientists how to use the laws of chemical attraction to make their forms visible.

As the preface reveals, Bland considered his book to be "largely a record of actual experiences." Many Victorians came to spiritualism because they had lost a spouse or child. But Bland's beloved Cora still lived. Was he longing for death himself? The book is pervaded by a despair that seems odd in a man so vibrant.

Repeatedly we get hints of a middle-aged Bland who considers himself a failure and fears the years ahead.

The protagonist, Paul, is "an old bachelor" whose only love, Pearl, died when they were young. One day he dozes off and receives a visit from Pearl, who transports him to heaven, where they enjoy a kiss sweeter "than ever was enjoyed by mundane lovers since time began." Then she takes him on a tour of Paradise. And what does heaven look like? It has a high, gilt rotunda, a writing desk and easy chairs, and floor-to-ceiling bookshelves. The Library of Congress as Paradise! What writer wouldn't be thrilled to find out that he will spend eternity in a library furnished with the books he didn't get a chance to read on earth, not to mention his own books, which will remain in print forever? Pearl tells Paul that he mustn't think he was a failure on earth. As a writer and reformer, he has been "an instrument in the hands of a high order of spirits, who, through you, are enabled to send out their grand ideas and exercise their magnetic forces in the interest of human progress on many lines." Although Paul's labors have been so manifold as to seem diffuse and ineffectual, he is "an all-'round reformer, possessing a rare combination of mental and moral faculties that gives you great versatility. It is your mission to start reform movements and to enlist others in their interest. . . ." Nor should Paul be discouraged by the meagerness of his pay; he is laying up treasure in heaven.

With the nation entering a new century, Bland must have looked back and wondered if his life had made a difference. His campaigns on behalf of the Indians had been ridiculed, and few of his suggestions for agricultural reform had been adopted. America had become the coliseum of greedy capitalists he hoped it wouldn't become. Perhaps one afternoon he lapsed into sleep, only to gain the dreamy consolation that he had been fighting on the side of the angels after all. And he had a personal reason for believing in an afterlife. There was no lost Pearl to recover, but a love to keep loving. He loved Cora as a woman. He wanted to believe that even in heaven he might kiss her with a kiss sweeter than their kisses here on earth.

Bland's transformation from a radical reformer to a believer in ghosts must have disconcerted Weldon. When Sitting Bull and his followers became adherents of a religion that demanded they dance the Ghost Dance to communicate with their dead relatives, she tried to dissuade them (" . . . Your dead wives, sisters, brothers, fathers, mothers & grandmothers, your dead children will never come back to you & you will never see them again, unless *perhaps* when you die and go to the next world. Perhaps you will see them again! In this world *Never!*"). She probably assumed that her friend Thomas Bland would support her. Maybe he did, in 1889. But here he was twelve years later writing a book about the spirit world. She might have thought he had forsaken her. Unless, with so many of her own loved ones dead, Weldon now became his most ardent disciple.

I had been hoping to find Bland's monograph on the Ghost Dance, but one of the librarians told me it was lost. Check back later, he advised. Maybe it would turn up. For now, I sat beneath that magnificent rotunda reading its injunction to do justly, love mercy, and walk humbly with God. Maybe Weldon had received her inspiration to travel west sitting in this room. She had been reading about the Indians, and she simply looked up.

4

On the Cannonball

The Sioux who signed the cession bill expected better treatment in return for their land. Instead, the government cut rations. If the Indians were to become farmers—the reformer Lyman Abbott expected this transformation to take five years at most—they would no longer need handouts. But Lyman Abbott had never visited a reservation. He had no idea how dry the Dakota soil was, how second-rate the tools the government gave the Indians, how bitterly they hated farming. A drought hit. The crops failed. Measles struck, then whooping cough and influenza. In February 1890, President Harrison threw open the "extra" reservation land to white settlers, although none of the Sioux had received their allotments and the government hadn't bothered to mark the borders of the sections they could keep.

Weldon, in her apartment on Liberty Street, read reports in the *Council Fire* of her friends' deprivation. Not only did she send Sitting Bull advice, all that terrible winter she sent him money to keep his people alive. No matter how poor the spelling of his letters, Weldon understood how hungry his people were, how miserable, how ill.

Her apartment couldn't have been as overstuffed with furniture and knick-knacks as most Victorian dwellings. She traveled so often that she must have pared down what she owned. Even when she was living around New York, she moved every few months, renting flats on Box Street and Liberty Street in Brooklyn and rooms in Hoboken and Newark. When Christie was at school, she lived by herself. At most, there were only two of them. I imagine an artist's apartment, with an easel by the window, a kitchen table, a little stove.

Still, she ate well enough. She could afford to dress warmly. She probably received a stipend from her late husband's insurance. She had no job, but she had inherited silver, china, and jewelry from her mother, some of which, she makes a point to remind Sitting Bull, she pawned on his behalf.

But she could do only so much from Brooklyn. Sometime that winter, Catherine Weldon made a decision few other women would have made: she decided to go back and live among the Sioux. It's hard enough for most Americans to rouse themselves to travel to a land in crisis and help put things to right, then return to their comfortable lives with the satisfaction of knowing they have done something for the less fortunate. But to commit oneself to living out one's life in another land and engaging in the everyday hardships of its people is another kind of sacrifice. It's the difference between the relief worker who takes off a month to help the citizens of El Salvador or Rwanda avert a tragedy and, when the catastrophe has passed, returns to Manhattan, and the worker who devotes the remainder of her life to helping the people of a stricken nation endure their daily struggles.

What made Weldon's choice unique was that she had no reason to go back. There were no political battles left to fight. She had no job among the Sioux, no teacher's appointment, no missionary's post. Of course her decision was influenced by attitudes of paternalism—and maternalism—that saturated white society. But she also returned to Standing Rock because she missed her friends. She liked their way of life. She wanted their culture to survive, and if they were forced to switch to modern ways, she wanted to be the sympathetic white they trusted to guide them. She loved the Dakota Plains. She had nothing else to do and nowhere else to be.

And so, on April 5, 1890, Weldon sat down and wrote her letter to James McLaughlin. "You will doubtless be surprised to receive a letter from me after our not very amicable conversations regarding my intended journey to Cheyenne," she started. "And indeed it is with reluctance that I humble myself to address you, knowing that you cannot feel friendly disposed towards me. I do so however out of love for my Indian friends and because you are probably the only person who can furnish me with some necessary information and possible permission. Even enemies can act magnanimous towards each other, and I hope you will extend to me the courtesy of a gentleman to a lady, and answer my questions with a frank yes or no."

Weldon had the habit of portraying herself as a defenseless single woman in need of succor from a gentleman. She didn't see the contradiction between taking on a government bureaucracy and pleading with the man in charge of that bureaucracy to show her the deference due a lady. Or maybe she did.

In the language of a woman switching her gaze from her duties as a daughter, wife, and mother to a sensible older widow free to give up the burdens of society, she describes her desire to move west and live out her final days there. She had been intending for years to spend the remainder of her life in Dakota "among or near my Indian friends," she tells McLaughlin. Twice she has been there and returned disappointed. The last time she ventured west, *someone* spread rumors about her reasons for living among the Indians. The papers printed these libels, and she cannot imagine *who* would have been so unkind as to spread such lies. She is not vengeful, she says, but she cannot help but hope "that the instigator of these falsehoods will meet the reward he so richly merits. It is such a brave noble deed for a strong powerful man (created to protect woman) to trample upon, to annihilate woman."

Oh, excuse me, she writes coyly. So sorry for digressing. Her real motive is to figure out where and how she will live if she returns. She sees no choice but to take a claim on the land the Indians ceded the previous year—against her wishes and Sitting Bull's, "to build a house upon it, and have certain days set apart for Ind. women and girls to come to me for instruction in useful domestic accomplishments." She doesn't want to seem a hypocrite, building a home on land she cautioned her friends not to sell. But the Indians prefer she live near them. They have offered to build her a house in the reservation, but she doesn't think this prudent, since she would then be a white living illegally on the reservation and couldn't count herself the owner of whatever house they might put up. (No doubt she is thinking of Sitting Bull's resentment of Mary Collins's house. Weldon never mentions Collins, and Collins never mentions her, a telling silence, given that they were the only two white women living at Grand River during the fight about the land bill, the famine and drought that followed, and the messiah craze and Ghost Dance. Collins likely bore Weldon ill will, given that the missionary vigorously opposed the NIDA and spoke out to prevent Thomas Bland "from fencing [the Indians] in and shutting [them] away from the rest of our American brethren.")

The best idea, Weldon tells McLaughlin, would be if she were to look around and see what might become of the agreement to open reservation land. She has promised her friends that she will settle near them, and she never has broken a promise to any Indian, but she won't step foot on Standing Rock if McLaughlin is going to oppose her presence.

"I suppose it is needless to state that I have no intention to become either Sitting Bull's wife or a squaw, as the sagacious newspaper editors surmised." This brings her to the question of what she does intend to do. "I probably would not be able to dispose of first class paintings or plush lambrequins or be able to teach modern languages on the prairies," she muses in a jibe at the lack of culture in the Dakotas or the frivolity of her skills. Her real mission, she can't resist hinting to McLaughlin, is an exercise in what would later be called public relations. "I honor and respect S. Bull as if he was my own father and nothing can ever shake my faith in his good qualities and what I can do to make him famous I will certainly do and I will succeed, but I regret that at the present time he is so universally misjudged. . . ."

Weldon's not-so-secret plan, then, is to transmit to the wider world reports of the chief's good qualities to counteract the agent's campaign to defame him. She will write his biography, paint his portrait, and act as his secretary and translator. And she wants to transmit reports of the wider world to Sitting Bull. He had seen a few factories, ridden in the Wild West show, and smoked some cigarettes. But there was plenty left to teach him, and Weldon's letters convey the impression that she very much enjoyed the prospect of acquainting the most powerful representative of a noble, "savage" age with the wonders of white society.

Even in the voluminous archives of McLaughlin's correspondence in Washington and Bismarck, no copy of his reply to Weldon's letter has survived. But he did act the gentleman and allowed her to come back. Given that his answer couldn't have reached her before mid-April, she prepared for her journey with remarkable celerity. She packed everything she owned in two trunks and assorted cases. Victorian women were starting to simplify their wardrobes in recognition of the more active lives they led—many women had taken up bicycle riding, for example—and Weldon would have been at the vanguard of any such movement. But even an up-to-date Victorian woman wore ten to thirty pounds of underclothes and outer garments every time she stepped outside. Her underclothes alone must have filled one trunk; she couldn't have taken fewer than several pairs of drawers and chemises, a "light" corset of steel or bone, petticoats, and a bustle. And then, in the second trunk, flowing dresses, shawls, jackets, and skirts, a few shirtwaists, a riding outfit, shoes, boots, and hats, gloves, fans, and nightgowns. From a letter she wrote to Sitting Bull, we know she also packed bedding, silver, carpets, jewelry, art supplies, and books. She gave notice to her landlord, locked the door to her brownstone, passed the cigar store and its saluting Indian—I can see her saluting back—then called a cab and asked the driver to head his hack to the bridge across the river to Manhattan.

Long journeys by train were tedious. But the train Weldon boarded at Grand Central Depot in 1890 was vastly superior to the trains she would have taken even a few years earlier. For most of the nineteenth century, travelers needed to change trains every few miles. Stops were unpredictable. A trip seemed to last forever, and passengers couldn't stretch their legs by walking from car to car. There were no dining cars or sleepers. Travelers might spend a night in a poorly run hotel or eat a rushed meal in a filthy railway eatery. But mostly they endured a grueling ordeal of boredom and discomfort.

Only in the late 1880s did the notion of an express train enter the public's consciousness. No longer was it a miracle to get where you were going and start a new life. The modern idea of travel was to get where you were going, visit, and come back. Traveling from New York to Chicago in 1875 might take three days; the same trip a decade later took thirty-six hours, and by the 1890s, barely one day. Dirty, ill-equipped trains still carried immigrants to the farms they hoped to buy. The railroads couldn't function if no one was living on the Plains, so they sent misleading ads to immigrants, touting the fertility of the home-steads they could claim, then carted them to desolate places like Devils Lake for free. But the sort of train in which a paying passenger like Weldon traveled was far more luxurious than a similar train today, with a barbershop and bathing car, a ladies' maid to help the female passengers undress, an observation deck, a spotless Pullman where porters guarded the sleepers' privacy, a dining car, and a parlor car where Weldon could sip her tea.

All in all, her journey from Manhattan to Chicago, Chicago to Minneapolis, and Minneapolis to Bismarck took four days. It might have seemed faster than a similar trip today, given that she wouldn't be wishing she had flown. Perhaps she enjoyed the solitude. She needed the time alone to absorb the reality of what she had done. She had left behind few, if any, close friends in New York, but even the most reactionary New Yorker was more liberal toward the Indians—and the idea of a white woman living among the Indians—than most Dakotans. Even if she planned to send for Christie later, she must have had misgivings about leaving him alone for now, then uprooting him from all he knew and taking him to spend his adolescence on the most rugged reservation in the West. She was giving up every civilized convenience, not for a few weeks' camping trip, but for the rest of her life. She already had experienced the brutal Dakota heat. And she must have heard the Parkins and Van Solens talk about the rigors of a Dakota winter.

For all the hardships she faced, as she sat beside that window watching the landscape rush by, her mind probably raced with possibilities. How would she support herself and Christie while living in such a barren, uncultured outpost? She wouldn't be able to use her only skill, teaching painting and embroidery to the soldiers' wives and daughters. The whites who lived on and around the reservation had little use for art and even less use for her; they wouldn't allow their daughters to study crewel work or French with a woman of questionable repute who lived among the Sioux. There would be no market in Bismarck for the paintings that she might import from her artist friends in Europe or various galleries in Manhattan. Her own paintings of Indian life eventually might find a market in the East, but she would require years to complete enough portraits and landscapes to support herself and Christie.

In the meantime, maybe Louise Van Solen could persuade Major McLaughlin to allow her to teach at the day school at the Cannonball or, better still, at Grand River. If not, she could start her own school. There were trade schools for the boys. Why not schools in domestic science for the girls? There was no treaty or bill to sign. Sitting Bull had given in. Surely the Major wouldn't decline a willing outsider's help in easing the Indians' adjustment to their new lives. Even if he did, how could he possibly know if she, Catherine Weldon, helped the inhabitants of Sitting Bull's isolated camp keep their culture and crafts?

Oh, what schemes she had! She wasn't as sheltered and helpless as many people thought. Perhaps she couldn't ride as adeptly as a Sioux warrior, but she was no stranger to horseback. What she didn't know about ranching she could learn from the Parkins. The Lakota would be such magnificent ranchers if only the government weren't so determined to turn them into farmers! She could eke out a living somehow. If the Indians could survive on scanty rations, so could she. And so could Christie, if he must. The Indians would share what little they had, and she would give Christie all but what she absolutely needed to survive. It would do him good, to grow up knowing how to get by on so little. What was that book she had been hearing so much about, with all those photographs taken by one of those new portable little cameras, *How the Other Half Lives*? Well, if Christie wanted to see how poor Negroes and Jewish immigrants lived, he need only cross the East River and walk up the steps of any tenement. But to learn how the earliest and most noble inhabitants of his own grand country lived, only his mother was able to offer him that opportunity. Personally, she didn't care a fig what the ladies of Fort Yates or Bismarck or Columbia Heights might gossip about her. Why care, if she was never returning to their society? And if her scandalous behavior reflected poorly on her son, better than raising a son who believed that he could do nothing to help the downtrodden.

The country would grow up eventually. It must. Boys became men, and civilizations kept progressing. Not even America could remain a nation of children for eternity. And when those children grew up, they would applaud what they once had jeered. To think that not a single biographer had written an accurate portrayal of a man as great as Sitting Bull. She would read him stories of famous generals and give him a sense of what she was trying to do for him. Then she would listen as he told her the stories of *his* life. They would have many years to do this.

She looked around the coach, eager now to engage one of her companions in conversation, to enjoy that companion's surprise as she revealed her plans. *I am going west to live forever among my Indian friends.* But she was the only single woman in the coach. Those two older matrons toward the rear . . . she knew from experience such women could be the cruelest. Men were less willing to cut a woman with a direct rebuff, but a woman traveling on her own couldn't just strike up conversation. Were there no sympathetic souls on this entire train? That man in the severe black overcoat and the woman beside him, in that drabbest of skirts and jackets—with those few feathers in her hat, she looked like a mud hen— closing their eyes and bending their heads ostentatiously to bless the poor gray chicken legs the woman had produced from her shapeless canvas bag, no sense approaching them. If she never spoke to another missionary of any kind for the remainder of her days, it would be too soon. People who believed that God had ordered them to do a thing, well, there was no use trying to explain that other people had received other missions from other sources. And the remainder of her companions—soldiers, merchants, farmers . . . she knew the horrible things they would say. "Savages" this and "savages" that. *Eastern ladies like yourself have a tendency to romanticize the "poor Indian."*

She couldn't bear to hear a word of it. Everyone was an expert on how to treat a people they had never met in a land they had never visited. Why, there were whites who lived a mile from the reservation who had never set foot on Standing Rock.

She took her sketchbook from her bag and her colored pencils from their case. In soft greens and browns she sketched the gentle hills that had only just been plowed for the season's planting. Here and there she caught a glimpse of a rude lean-to for a pig. A farmhouse on a hill. It didn't matter that the train was moving, the landscape barely changed—hill, lean-to, horse, hill, lean-to, house. Such an enormous land, and the whites coveted every inch.

～

In Bismarck, Weldon would have stayed at the Sheridan Hotel to get a good night's sleep and buy some last supplies. She took her last indoor bath in a tub with hot running water, used her last indoor toilet, and said good-bye to middle-class comforts for what she assumed to be forever. There were several ways to travel the sixty miles south to Fort Yates and Standing Rock. You could book passage on the mail stage, which made the ten-hour journey along the eastern shore of the

Missouri. In Winona, you took the ferry west across the river (in winter, you walked across the ice). The fare from Bismarck to Winona was $5, baggage extra; the ferry cost a quarter. Or you could hire a team in Mandan—Bismarck's sister city on the western shore of the Missouri—and take the wagon road south. The team cost $10; spending a night at the Parkin Ranch cost another dollar.

Then there was the steamboat. From May through October boats plied the upper Missouri, making trips whenever the captain sold enough tickets. The stage tended to be faster for the upriver trip. But Weldon was traveling down

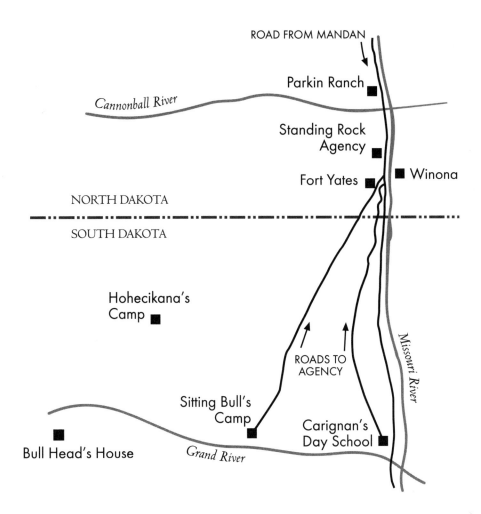

14. Map showing key sites on the Standing Rock Reservation, 1889–90.

the Missouri in the spring, when the river was at its deepest, so she probably went by boat.

She had written McLaughlin in early April; by May, she was living on the Parkin Ranch. The only writer who describes her sojourn on the Cannonball is David Humphreys Miller, the same author who tried to pass off the photo of Sallie Battles as Catherine Weldon. Most of Miller's article is a jumbled version of Vestal's earlier conjectures. Absurdly, he casts Weldon as a temptress in a romantic triangle that included McLaughlin as well as Sitting Bull, since, as Miller puts it, the agent could hardly "overlook her great physical attractiveness and there can be little doubt that he was disturbed by it far more than he cared to admit." Much of Miller's version of events is contradicted by Weldon's own letters and other sources. But his description of Weldon's stay at the Parkin Ranch might lead a reader to believe that he had spoken with informants who knew something of her time there.

"The Cannonball River bounded Standing Rock Reservation on the north," Miller writes. "Just beyond it lay Parkin Ranch, home of Mrs. Parkin and her sister, Mrs. Van Solen." This was the same Mrs. Van Solen who had advised Weldon on her earlier visit that an Indian could not leave the reservation without a pass. As Miller would have it, Parkin and Van Solen hated Weldon for "scandalizing their sex," and after McLaughlin kicked her off the reservation—on which visit isn't clear—they refused to take her in.

> Although these two women had been among Mrs. Weldon's more vociferous critics, she now appealed to them for shelter and advice. They refused outright to take her into their home, but permitted her to occupy an empty sod-roofed log shack a mile or so below the ranch house on the north bank of the Cannonball near its junction with the Missouri. Since McLaughlin's jurisdiction did not extend outside the reservation, there was little he could do to prevent the widow from taking up residence in this dreary region of drab sandbars, muddy water, and stunted oaks and box elders. It was hardly a fitting setting for Catherine Weldon's eastern elegance. But here she determinedly settled down, even adding a semblance of permanence and respectability by sending east for her sickly thirteen-year-old son, Christie, who joined her after traveling alone upriver on one of the antiquated side-paddle steamers that still plied the wide Missouri.

Whatever Christie thought about traveling to a remote reservation to join a mother he had rarely lived with, there is no evidence that he was sickly. He traveled to Bismarck on a train that was as safe as most trains of that day and only a few miles downriver on a steamboat, unless he took the stage. Weldon had expressed qualms about his safety to McLaughlin, but she couldn't have brought Christie earlier; school was still in session, and she didn't have a place to live. And she wasn't about to leave her only child back east while she retired to South Dakota. "It is a hazardous undertaking," she told the agent, "and my boy is not quite fourteen years old; consequently but of little protection. Yet I would like to live in Dakota and imagine that I can be happy no where else."

Even before I went to North Dakota and saw the Parkin homestead, Miller's description of Weldon's relationship to Louise Van Solen and Alma Parkin struck me as dubious. The sisters were part Indian. They were related to Sitting Bull. They wouldn't have viewed Weldon's attempts to help the Hunkpapas as scandalous. Both women had raised their own children on the ranch. How could they condemn another mother for doing so? If Christie's health really had been poor, they wouldn't have forced him to live in a dreary hut.

Maybe, when Weldon stayed with the Parkins, she rented a room at their hotel. More likely, she was a guest in the ranch house. You can stay with us, Alma might have offered. I can always use the company and help around the kitchen.

But Weldon wouldn't have found it comfortable to live in someone else's house. Oh no, she protested. I don't want to intrude on you and your husband.

Well, you and Christie might live in that abandoned soddy, Alma might have said. It's in terrible repair, but Henry could fix it up for you.

That would be wonderful! Yes, thank you, that's very generous of you, Alma. But don't trouble Henry on our account. It's only until I find a more suitable place.

Like the other heads of Sioux families scattered across the enormous reservation, Sitting Bull drove to the agency at Standing Rock every two weeks to collect his family's rations. According to Miller, on those days Sitting Bull trekked the extra twenty-five miles north to visit Weldon at the ranch. Given what we know from other sources—among them, McLaughlin's letters to his superiors—this part of Miller's story seems credible.

Driving a team of half-wild, loose-jointed cayuses hitched to the running gear of his wagon, the chief looked like an aloof old mummy sitting on planks laid across the bolsters, his hot-weather blanket and leggins of white sheeting soiled as old parchment after the seventy-odd mile trip from Grand River. Always riding with him on these occasions was one of his wives, for Mrs. Weldon thought to keep the tongues of soldiers' wives and ranch hands from wagging by insisting that Sitting Bull never come alone.

Although Sitting Bull couldn't avoid the dusty, bone-rattling trip to the agency to pick up his supplies, he wasn't required to travel the extra twenty-five or thirty miles on the rutted roads to the Parkin Ranch. He wouldn't have made such an effort to see a woman he didn't care about. After a winter of privation, Weldon's gifts and vibrant spirit might well have helped revive a defeated, tired "mummy." Her generosity caused Sitting Bull to admire her even more than he already did. Generosity was a trait he prized highly in himself. And he had great respect for Alma Parkin and Louise Van Solen and enjoyed the chance to see them.

The truth turns out to be that the Parkins and Van Solens, far from being Weldon's enemies, were among her closest friends. For all that she belonged to the NIDA, Weldon's name isn't recorded in the rolls of their meetings. She enjoyed no female traveling companion, as Elaine Goodale and Alice Fletcher did. Her only friends besides the Blands were mixed-blood Lakota women like Alma Parkin and Louise Van Solen.

The matriarch of Alma and Louise's family was a full-blooded Sioux whose Indian name was *Wambdiantapiwin*—it means Eagle Woman All Look At, but she took the less euphonious English name Matilda. Her father, Two Lance, was a chief of the Two Kettle band of Sioux, and her mother was a Hunkpapa named Rosy Light of Dawn, hence her relation to Sitting Bull. In 1825, as a five-year-old girl, she visited the trading post at what would eventually be Pierre, South Dakota, and met a Canadian trader named Honoré Picotte. He was an appealing man, tall and straight, with curly hair and a fine-featured face, so talkative and dramatic he stayed in her mind for years. At thirteen, Eagle Woman lost her father. Four years later, her mother caught "the great sickness"—smallpox—and died. An orphan at eighteen, Eagle Woman returned to the fort and married the handsome white trader she had met there as a child. He was twenty-four years her senior and the father of a son by his first wife, the sister of the famous Yankton chief Struck the Ree. (Picotte's first wife probably died in the same smallpox epidemic that killed Eagle Woman's mother.) Eagle Woman adopted her husband's son, Charley, and raised him so lovingly that most people assumed that he was her own child.

She put up with more than a stepson. Honoré Picotte was legally married to a Frenchwoman in St. Louis who raised their daughters and kept house for a husband who visited once a year. Eagle Woman knew about this white wife; in fact, she used her husband's journeys to St. Louis as a chance to maintain her ties with her own people, joining them on their hunting trips and visits to other camps. Her only complaint—and it was a large complaint—was that he took away their daughter, Louise, when she was three years old and sent her to live in with a white family in Council Bluff so she could learn to pass in white society. Later Picotte sent the girl to a convent school in Kansas. He visited her every few years, but Eagle Woman didn't get to see her daughter again until the girl was twenty.

In the meantime, Eagle Woman gave birth to a second daughter, Zoe Lulu, whom she was allowed to raise since shortly after Lulu's birth Picotte retired to St. Louis to live with his white wife. Before he left, he consigned Eagle Woman to the care of his young protégé, Charles Galpin. In one of those turns of fate that no one can predict, Galpin and Eagle Woman fell deeply in love and formed a marriage that needs no reinterpretation today. Galpin, a college-educated fur trader from New York, doted on Lulu and his own children with Eagle Woman—Samuel, Robert, Alma, Richard, and Annie. Louise Picotte had by now finished her education, and her father arranged for her to fill a teaching post in Nebraska Territory. There she married Charles DeGrey, a mixed-blood Sioux widower with three children, and they gave Eagle Woman her first grand-child, Eddy.

Eagle Woman had no patience for anyone of either race who was foolish or hateful. During the hostilities of 1868, she and Galpin accompanied Father De Smet on his journey to Sitting Bull's camp to try to make peace. Later the Galpins moved south to help Eagle Woman's people survive their transition to the reservation that later became Standing Rock. A lieutenant named William Harmon was assigned to the fort. He immediately fell in love with Lulu and proposed, although the wedding had to be postponed because her stepfather, Charles Galpin, died unexpectedly.

Finding herself a widow with two young daughters to support, Eagle Woman took over her husband's trading post and became the first businesswoman among the Sioux. Harmon resigned from the army to spare himself being sent to fight his mother-in-law's people; he opened a second trading post at Grand River and became her friendly rival instead. Harmon and Lulu gave Eagle Woman a second grandson, Leo Harmon. The following year, Eagle Woman's own son, Sammy, died of tuberculosis, but she set aside her grief to accompany a dele-gation of "hostile" chiefs to Washington, calming their fears on the train and ushering them around the capital before continuing to New York.

For all the times Eagle Woman helped the army, the government gave in to pressures from rival traders—led by Orvil Grant, General Grant's brother—and ordered her to close her trading post. She refused. A new agent sent his own order to close the store. Eagle Woman ignored that order too. The agent asked the captain of the fort to post a guard outside the store. The captain wouldn't do it. The agent demanded that the U.S. Marshal confiscate Eagle Woman's goods. The marshal said he wouldn't. Later, when Eagle Woman acted as a peacekeeper at the angry councils about selling the Black Hills, the agent became her greatest admirer.

Having earned her right to trade, Eagle Woman sent her youngest daughter, Annie, to school in St. Louis. In 1876 she convinced the agent at Standing Rock to cooperate on her pet project—a school for Sioux children, with Louise as head teacher. By May, Louise was leading a class of fifty mixed- and full-blood Sioux. Her half sister, Alma, was hired to assist her. Louise's husband died the next year, but she kept the school going.

Eagle Woman's household now included Louise, Alma, and Annie. Around this time, an artist for *Harper's Weekly* took a trip to Standing Rock while making sketches for the magazine. His description of Eagle Woman's house provides a glimpse of the hospitality Weldon enjoyed a decade later. Mrs. Galpin was a really fine character, the artist wrote. "She was the widow of an old French trader, and on more than one occasion had prevented attacks on the whites by her own people. She had several daughters who were educated and refined women. . . . We arrived after a four mile walk at one of the most curious homes it was ever my good luck to visit. The house, built of cottonwood logs and adobe, nestled in a draw. In part, it was a dugout, several rooms running well back into the bluff. The house was so much a part of the bluff that it looked small in the half light, but on entering, we were to our surprise taken through several good-sized rooms and passage-ways into the principal living room.

"We were received by the woman's oldest daughter, Mrs. D—[Louise De Grey], the graduate of an eastern college who had the well bred manners of a woman used to the refinements of civilization. Her mother, dressed in full Indian costume, greeted us pleasantly and called a woman servant to take our hats. . . ."

Louise Picotte DeGrey was charming enough that she attracted a second husband, George Van Solen, a sawmill engineer at Fort Yates. They married in 1879 and had a son who died young and one daughter, Lucille. Louise's half sister, Alma, married Henry Parkin, who had moved to Fort Yates in 1872. The homestead Henry Parkin established on the northern slope above the Cannonball was one of the earliest ranches between the Missouri and the Rockies. He built a store and a hotel. The ranch expanded from four hundred head of cattle to seven hundred. As a sideline, Parkin raised exotic mules, horses, and sheep. He ran a store in the town of Cannonball a few miles south and a meat market in Mandan and ended up one of the richest men in Dakota Territory.

Henry and Alma had no children, but Alma's sister, Annie, married a young clerk who came to Standing Rock with the McLaughlins. They had a son named Charles, who was orphaned at two when Annie and her husband died and who was then adopted by the Parkins. The boy was called Chaska, which, in Lakota, means "firstborn male child." Henry died in 1895, and Alma took over the ranch. (The only further mention I could find of Chaska Parkin was that he moved to Washington, D.C., and was so destitute that he sold the fillings from his teeth.) Alma inherited her mother's competence and compassion. "She never turned a soul away from her door," one account reports, "and if people were in need and couldn't come, she would go out to help them." Hardly a woman who would turn away a widow with a sickly son, especially if the widow was a friend of Sitting Bull.

Sitting Bull and Eagle Woman held each other in high regard. When the chief arrived in Bismarck after his surrender, he asked William Harmon to bring Lulu to the boat, in honor of her mother. In his first month at Standing Rock, Sitting Bull renewed his friendship with Eagle Woman. When he was shipped to Fort Randall as a prisoner, Eagle Woman was so concerned that she wrote a letter to her stepson, Charley Picotte, now a lawyer at Yankton, asking that he look out for Sitting Bull's welfare.

Toward the end of her life, Eagle Woman lived at Standing Rock with Louise, who had been abandoned by George Van Solen soon after they were married (he wandered off to live a hermit's life in the wilderness and died the same year as Alma's husband). Eagle Woman continued to do a little trading, but she devoted most of her time to caring for her aging friends among the Sioux, visiting Alma on the ranch, and traveling to Montana to see the Harmons. She died in 1888, a year before Weldon's first encounter with McLaughlin on the Cannonball and two years before Weldon returned to live with Christie at the ranch.

5

My Dakotas!

Weldon spent at least a few months living on the Cannonball before she moved to Grand River. She was waiting for Christie to finish school and join her. And she was hesitant to move to a location where she would be the only white, not because she was scared of the Indians, but because she was reluctant to set off further scandals. As she had written to McLaughlin, she wanted to see if she could, in good conscience, build a homestead on reservation land that had been opened to whites by the bill she opposed. And it must have been pleasant to spend the last weeks of spring on a ranch between two rivers among her women friends.

Eventually Christie did arrive and they moved to Grand River, early that summer of 1890. There, Vestal writes sardonically, "she continued her work for civilization, washing [Sitting Bull's] dishes, sweeping his floors, cooking for him, earning the name Woman-Walking-Ahead." Weldon was proud of that name. What's hard to imagine is why she risked worse—*dirty squaw, whore*—by moving in with Sitting Bull. She must have been frustrated, living so far away. She couldn't paint his portrait or gather facts for her biography. The trip was onerous for Sitting Bull, and few of his followers could travel so many miles. She assumed her reputation was safe because his wives were on the farm. She had a proper home on the Parkin Ranch and intended to build her own house before winter set in. Even in Victorian times, if a married man asked a widow to spend the summer on his estate, she could accept the invitation if his wife would be there. Two wives provided twice the supervision.

If this was Weldon's thinking, she misjudged McLaughlin's animosity, the boredom of the soldiers and their wives, and the entertainment value of her story. The white ladies denounced her infatuation with Sitting Bull as a disgrace to their sex and circulated rumors that she had become his third wife. She was carrying his child. She had given him a little gold bull, which he wore as a watch charm. His wives were so jealous they chased her around the camp with butcher knives.

Marriages between white men and Indian women weren't all that rare. A lonely white trader like Honoré Picotte might take an Indian "wife." But no respectable white lady would sleep with an Indian. Of course, the mere possibility fascinated everyone. Fanny Kelly seems aware in her autobiography of her readers' curiosity as to whether she was raped. For her sake, if not the Indians', she is careful to point out that the Indians didn't touch her. But she admits that a white woman *might* love a Sioux man. Meeting another captive, Kelly asks the girl, "Do you love your husband?" The girl gives her a bitter look. "Love a savage who bought me to be a drudge and slave? No, I hate him, and I hate his whole tribe!" The woman, Kelly learns, has borne a child by her captor, at which Kelly thanks God that no such indignity has been forced upon her.

Eighteen years later, when she appeared at the Blands' reception for Red Cloud, the question of whether the Indians had raped Kelly remained volatile enough that Thomas Bland felt called upon to answer it. "Learning that it is the almost universal custom of our soldiers to outrage Indian women who fall into their hands, it is difficult for the average white man to believe that Indians can and do rise above such temptations in most cases when our women are captured by them. But this is true, as Anna Meeker [another captive] and Fannie Kelly have both asserted in terms most positive."

In reality, Sitting Bull and Weldon rarely if ever touched, and Sitting Bull's wives didn't resent her presence. One of Vestal's informants, Robert Higheagle, reported that Sitting Bull's wives were women of quiet, patient dispositions. Many people came to their husband's lodge because "according to the old custom the chief was supposed to have an open lodge for anybody. I never heard of any of the Mrs. Weldon scandal stories. These are just invented stories." And one of Sitting Bull's descendants, Ina McNeil, told me that Weldon wouldn't have been allowed to live in Sitting Bull's camp if his wives had disapproved. "Grandpa Sitting Bull would have needed to get permission from his wives to accept her, to let her live there."

Given that Weldon and Sitting Bull were not sleeping together, Seen by the Nation and Four Robes had little cause to feel vengeful. The sisters had been Sitting Bull's wives for two decades. This new woman in their lodge was no younger than they. She *looked* younger—she had led an easier life—but she struck them as so outlandish they couldn't take her seriously as romantic competition.

Even if Weldon and Sitting Bull had been madly in love, they wouldn't have found it easy to carry on. Aside from barns and sheds, a chicken coop and a stable, the farm was composed of little more than two cabins—the larger one, in which Sitting Bull slept with Four Robes, their youngest child, and Crow Foot, and the smaller cabin, in which Seen by the Nation lived with her sons by her first marriage and the toddler she had borne Sitting Bull. Weldon was unconventional, but she repeatedly insisted to McLaughlin that she was a lady, and she was furious at gossip that she was sleeping with the chief. She would hardly have consented to make love to him in sight of his wives, various adolescents, and her son.

Seen by the Nation and Four Robes had less reason to stab Weldon than thank her. For two years she had been hectoring Congress to send more rations to feed them. She sold her silverware and jewelry to buy food to save their families. She even helped with chores. Whether she was being a well-mannered guest, making good on her promise to teach the Indian women the arts of domesticity, or making sure her food was cooked in what she considered a sanitary way, she certainly wasn't lounging around the camp mooning at Sitting Bull while his wives did her bidding. Even if the women needed to work harder to prepare the feasts her money enabled them to put on, they were glad to see their families eat, and they shared their husband's pride in acting as his people's benefactor.

Nor was living among the Sioux the misery that most whites assumed it must be. In photos, Sitting Bull's cabin looks surprisingly large. No pictures of the interior exist, but photos from Pine Ridge show airy, pleasant homes more inviting than the sharecroppers' shacks documented by Walker Evans forty years later. True, the chiefs at Pine Ridge were "progressives"; Red Cloud's cabin had been his reward for surrendering, and American Horse's cabin was trashed by the survivors of Wounded Knee to show their displeasure with his peacemaker's stance. But the quality of houses among Sioux chiefs on neighboring reservations couldn't have varied all that much. The chief of all Hunkpapas could boast wood floors in his cabin, while American Horse had dirt.

We know from the police who raided Sitting Bull's camp that the interior walls were covered with strips of canvas, giving the room a clean, bright appearance and keeping out the wind. The adults slept on low wood platforms. A cast-iron stove stood in the center of each cabin, and kerosene lamps dangled from the walls. No description has come down to us of Sitting Bull's furniture, but Red Cloud's house was equipped with a bookshelf and chairs, while American Horse owned a rocker and a clock. At Pine Ridge, the chiefs enlivened their

CROW FOOT,
(Sitting Bull's Son)
Crow Foot surrendered his father's gun to Major Brotherton at Fort Buford in 1881.
Sitting Bull claims the boy surrendered, not he.
D. F. BARRY,   BISMARCK.

15. Sitting Bull's son Crow Foot, who was killed in his midteens when tribal policemen attacked his father's camp at Grand River. Courtesy of the State Historical Society of North Dakota, Barry A7220.

16. Interior of American Horse's cabin at Pine Ridge. Note the cloth linings on the walls, similar to the linings used on the walls of Sitting Bull's cabin at Standing Rock. Courtesy of the Nebraska State Historical Society, W938-119-50B/RG2185: 119-101.

dwellings with pictures from magazines. American Horse nailed a photo of himself above his bed, while Red Cloud mounted a huge American flag and pictures of Jesus Christ and Mary. One of Weldon's portraits of the chief hung in a gilt frame in the smaller of his cabins. Most likely, that was the cabin she slept in, which would mean that she wasn't living with Sitting Bull, she was living with his wife.

Her decision to move to Grand River violated not only most whites' standards of propriety, but also of hygiene. It was one thing for McLaughlin to marry an Indian woman raised by nuns. But the imagined hardships of a white gentlewoman moving in with Indians, eating their horrid stews and sleeping in their dank cabins among all those greasy, sweating, lice-ridden bodies, repulsed ordinary whites. Weldon, however, was no ordinary Victorian gentlewoman. She had lived among Indians before. And the conditions she endured among the Sioux were more pleasant than the conditions most white pioneers faced.

When Rachel Calof, a Jewish mail-order bride from Russia, arrived at her in-laws' homestead near Devils Lake, North Dakota, in 1894, four years *after* Weldon's stay with Sitting Bull, she found nothing so civilized as a cabin. The shanty her husband showed her measured twelve by fourteen feet. The roof had blown off, and, until it could be fixed, Calof and her husband moved in with his parents. The holes in the walls were stuffed with paper "in hopes of keeping some of the flies out." The furnishings consisted of a table and two-legged bed hammered to the wall. There was no lamp, so, after an early dinner of boiled dough and cheese, everyone went to sleep. Nor was there an outhouse. "Each one simply picked a place in the prairie grass," she confided in Yiddish to her journal. Six people slept in that one shanty. "The boards of the bed, without mattress or spring, were covered with straw which pricked my skin at the least movement but did little to ease the hardness of the bare boards." Everyone snored, including her mother-in-law, with whom Calof shared a bed. Between them lay Calof's two-year-old nephew, who wasn't wearing a diaper. "Suddenly I began to feel quite warm. The little boy had emptied his bladder and quickly followed with a healthy bowel movement. I removed myself as far as possible from these immediate surroundings and gave myself up to utter despair."

With a river nearby and a store forty miles away, Weldon's "nightmare" would have been Calof's dream. Surviving on the Plains was arduous no matter what your race. The white settlement on the Cannonball was crawling with fleas and vermin; to discourage infestations, the settlers slopped their walls with lye. Mary Collins, who wasn't known for her sentimentality toward the Sioux, wrote a letter to the eastern ladies who sent donations to her mission. In answer to the question, "Are the Indians very dirty?" Collins wrote: "Yes. So are the Missionaries sometimes. The wind has been blowing at the rate of forty miles an hour for four days and the air and houses are full of fine dust and I have washed my hands about fifteen times today to keep them clean. When such days come I do not feel like using very strong adjectives in regard to the filth of the Indian and his home. Remember we live in a country of gumbo and alkaline waters and the Indian is without soap. . . ."

Collins couldn't resist adding that the Indian was not naturally "very cleanly," but other whites indicate that the Sioux were fastidious when they lived a nomadic life. Praying in a sweat lodge, then plunging in a river cleansed body as well as soul. Luther Standing Bear, who grew up on the Plains, then attended the Carlisle School and worked in Wanamaker's Department Store in Philadelphia, remembered his first glimpse of white Nebraskans in their dugouts. "These people were dirty. They had hair all over their faces, heads, arms and hands. This was the first time many of us had ever seen white people, and they were very repulsive to us." Confined to reservations, the Sioux found it hard to stay clean. Cabins couldn't be moved when the area around them grew foul with waste. Tuberculosis became a killer only after the Indians gave up their ventilated tipis for stuffy shacks. Forced to live on cereals, adding sugar to their diet, the Sioux grew ill with diabetes. Instead of heavy robes from buffalo hides and deerskins, they drew as rations undersized blankets of adulterated "wool." Instead of moccasins, they were given shoes with thin, stiff soles so carelessly nailed to the uppers that the soles became detached the first time the shoes were worn. Trousers were so poorly cut they split the first time a man sat down. As one missionary's wife discovered, an Indian cabin might show vestiges of traditional housekeeping—well-swept dirt floors, apparel hung from pegs, the pleasant smell of tobacco—along with the sort of mess associated with the newer way of life—dirty dishes on the floor, barefoot children in shabby clothes their mother had no means to mend.

Some Indians adapted. Others didn't. The same was true of whites. Two days of pioneer life brought Rachel Calof to desperation, but she vowed that she would "never surrender" to the conditions that threatened to overwhelm her. She refused to go to bed at dusk simply because she owned no lamp. "I went outside to see what materials nature might provide for my project, and soon found some partly dried mud which I molded into a narrow container. I shaped a wick out of a scrap of rag, smeared it with butter, placed it in the mud cup, and lit it and, lo and behold, there was light."

Elaine Goodale describes two Indian sisters who practiced housekeeping that was "a model of its kind—the one room and large, bare yard swept perfectly clean, their blankets regularly aired, their clothing washed, and all their belongings in order." On her camping trips, Goodale found Sioux tipis to be comfortable and the food to her taste (suppers consisted of roasted jerked beef, bacon, hot biscuits, potatoes, eggs, and coffee). She thought the homesteaders' soddies less attractive than the Indians' cabins, their occupants subsisting on little more than corn bread, gravy, mush, and milk. "At every stream or pond we bathed and washed our clothes—with soap, if we had it. . . . I found the Dakotas far more cleanly under primitive conditions than most of us habitual house-dwellers when camping out." She didn't like the dogs—they scratched their fleas and whined and stole her breakfast—but it was only when she stayed with a saloon keeper and his wife in a little Dakota town that she complained of a poor night's sleep; the house was alive with fleas and passing trains kept her up.

Even if conditions at Grand River weren't perfect, Weldon had everything she wanted there—her Indian friends, her son, inspiration for her art. A typical day began at dawn as she rose from her pallet and dressed in a shadowy corner of the room, drew water from the river, helped the women and girls cook breakfast for the men, then spent the morning tending chores—learning from the women how to bead a moccasin or dye porcupine quills to decorate a pouch, gathering sage and other herbs from the hills beyond the camp, picking wild berries, or teaching the Lakota women to mend a raveled sock, make soap, or bake a cake. She sat and sketched scenes of her friends at work, or took her easel to the fields and painted the prairie wildlife, or persuaded Sitting Bull to dress in full regalia and pose for hours beneath the sun as she painted and they talked.

Before she went to bed, Weldon might have sat up in the cabin's one chair beside a kerosene light and copied the phrases she learned that day: "*ma cuitan*—I am cold, chilly; *eya tka*—he or she said; *Owewakan*—a lie; *Eyi Jate*—forked tongue; *Leji nonpa*—double meaning; Bury—*Wicahapi* (grave) on the Earth." She translated the letters that Sitting Bull had received from around the world, in English, French, and German, and sent off the chief's replies. This was far from a useless task. The chief's own English was limited, and he could only write his name. Anything he said was open to mistranslation. On his first tour, in Philadelphia, he gave a speech about the need for Indian children to be educated in white ways; Luther Standing Bear, who was in the audience taking a break from his clerkship at Wanamaker's, said the translation came out as a gory rendition of what *really* happened when Sitting Bull's warriors wiped out Custer.

So Weldon wasn't acting out some grandiose fantasy of her own importance. She filled the much needed office of advising Sitting Bull on how to represent his people to the whites and providing him with information about white customs and inventions so he could decide if his people should adopt them. Weldon obviously enjoyed the sense of superiority that many nineteenth-century white liberals derived from offering rational explanations for phenomena that seemed like miracles to "savages." But understanding the secrets of white technology did make the Indians less susceptible to unscrupulous whites who used such marvels to cow them. A decade earlier, trying to convince the Sioux to surrender, General Miles had allowed several warriors to speak to one another by telephone. The warriors began to sweat and, "with trembling hands," laid down the instrument. A member of General Crook's staff hooked up a battery to a silver dollar in a pan of water and challenged the tribe's medicine men to lift the dollar while holding the battery. According to the officer, the thousand Sioux assembled to watch this spectacle conceived a deep reverence for him "as they had seen the most famous of their medicine men attempt to do this and fail, being almost thrown into convulsions in the attempt."

Weldon also took pleasure in reading to Sitting Bull from biographies of great white generals like Napoleon, Alexander, and Achilles. Weldon didn't know much Lakota, but she could have used signs and simple phrases to get across her point that Sitting Bull wasn't the only great chief who'd had his troubles.

Napoleon was a famous general, like you, she might have said. *His enemies put him on an island with lots of soldiers to guard him, but he and his most loyal followers managed to escape.*

Christie might have listened to those stories. Like many boys, he probably wanted his mother to himself. She should be telling stories to him, not sending him off to sleep on an itchy straw bed while she sat up talking in a language he didn't understand to some Indian she liked more than she liked him. What did Christie do while they lived on Grand River? Not once does Weldon mention him, except that one time, writing to McLaughlin to ask permission to come back. Even then, she only says how useless he will be. After Christie died, she lashed herself with guilt for ignoring him. Maybe her guilt was justified. The boy's father had died not long before. Christie must have been aghast at his new surroundings.

Unless he was thrilled, as most boys would be, to live among real Indians. This was Sitting Bull himself! Over there was the performing horse Sitting Bull had ridden in Bill Cody's Wild West Show. There were boys Christie's own age to take him hunting and fishing. There were woods and rivers to explore. Too many writers of the day make reference to Sitting Bull taking an interest in the boy and teaching him to ride a pony for their friendship to be a complete fabrication. The chief had a tradition of teasing little boys, playing with them, adopting them. He could show affection to his friend's son in ways he couldn't show her. And how could Christie not enjoy receiving attention from a famous Sioux chief?

Then again, the Plains were very dry that year. The crops shriveled. There was little to eat but what Christie's mother bought at the trading post by selling off her jewelry and using up their savings—savings Christie must have known they would need to get by for the rest of their lives. He loved his mother. And he didn't. He was confused about his feelings. Teenage boys often are. Sitting Bull scared him. Christie couldn't have picked up more than a few words of Lakota, and his life on the farm must have been a frustrating mime show, not least because one of Sitting Bull's stepsons was a deaf-mute.

But Crow Foot knew English. Crow Foot rarely played with other boys; even as a child he hovered around the grown-ups, learning his father's ways. But he would have seen it as his duty to help his father's friend's son.

Any mother who loses a child can find ways to blame herself, if not for causing his death, then for not spending enough time with him while he was alive. But Weldon had real reasons for her guilt. She *was* infatuated with Sitting Bull, in the sense that she couldn't pay much attention to anyone else. She was drawn to him as the noblest representative of a vanished way of life. Christie couldn't compete with that.

Given how many writers have insinuated that there was a sexual relationship between Sitting Bull and Weldon, and given how human it is to wonder about the bond between any two people from such different backgrounds, it's hard not to speculate as to the emotional connection between them. Independent women often are attracted to powerful older men. Muscular and well built, Sitting Bull had strong, dramatic features, sensuous hair, and always those eyes, those dark, intense eyes. He was sick the first time they met, in 1889. But by the following summer he was rested. A woman who spends her evenings reading to a man by the glow of a kerosene lamp might end up sharing more with her listener than an appreciation of Napoleon's genius. How could anyone live with a charismatic man who often walked around shirtless and slept with two wives in open view and not think about sex, even to dismiss the possibility? In his photographs, Sitting Bull is never shown smiling, but in life he smiled often. He must have smiled at Weldon. She made him laugh when she told him of Achilles fighting over the captured slave girl Briseis or described the rides at Coney Island or the conventions of Brooklyn society. And Sitting Bull couldn't help but revel in a new, receptive audience. As Othello said of Desdemona, "She loved me for the dangers I had pass'd, / And I loved her that she did pity them."

And they didn't only talk. Sitting Bull posed for her portraits, an intimate act even if the subject is fully clothed, artist and model intensely engaged in that most erotic of exchanges, being seen, looking. The very nature of life in such a confined space meant they must have sometimes glimpsed each other less than fully dressed. The cabins had no closets. Weldon kept her belongings in her trunks, but a few of her dresses and skirts must have hung on pegs. The doors had no locks. True, the Indians observed a complex code of decency. Elaine Goodale remarked that even on the nights she spent in crowded tipis "entirely surrounded by men, women, children, and dogs," she never felt self-conscious. "The etiquette of the tipi is strict," she wrote. "Each person has his bed, which is also his seat by day. . . . The privacy of each is inviolable, and no Dakota would think of transgressing, even by a look, that invisible barrier. If men were present, they stayed outside in the evening until the women had retired, afterward entering noiselessly, each to his own place. Again, in the early morning, they considerately disappeared while we made our toilets for the day. Like the native women, I did not undress completely—merely took off my shoes, loosened my garments, and let down my hair."

But Goodale's very insistence on her lack of self-consciousness shows how conscious she must have been that sex *might* have been an issue. The Sioux were famously modest. But their code of etiquette existed precisely because life in a small community requires such a code. Listening to Goodale describe the way

Sioux women bathed—they went into the water fully clothed, then, when they came out, slipped on a dry frock over the wet one and tugged off the garment underneath—I thought it might have been more erotic to see someone wriggling out of a wet dress than bathing nude. The men were always decently covered, Goodale says, but they were "more scantily clad" than the women, "occasionally in no more than is considered proper on a modern bathing beach. . . ." And the system couldn't have been perfect. There must have been times when the men entered the tipi too soon or came upon a woman squatting in the woods. McLaughlin once encountered Sitting Bull emerging from his sweat lodge in a loincloth. If Weldon rose at daybreak, she also might have seen him coming out from his morning sweat.

In the Hollywood version of their romance, all this reined-in passion would have exploded the afternoon that Weldon tried to win an argument about what women could or could not do. As Weldon describes the incident, the men were roping ponies and Weldon announced that she intended to rope and ride one, too. For her own good, the chief "forcibly detained" her. Perhaps at that moment, as she struggled in his arms, both of them knew that despite the differences between them, his deerskin and her petticoats, they were flesh and blood beneath.

What Sitting Bull felt about Weldon is impossible to know. He left no diary. Sioux men didn't often confide their emotions to a woman, especially a white woman who had the power to publish his words for other whites to read. "S. Bulls heart, secret, not open like to a friend, but secret, like to an Enemy," Weldon scribbled in her journal. "I am like an open book to him & have been all these years, & not one thought of my mind has been secret to him." Maybe he found her too odd to take seriously. This wasn't how Lakota women behaved—roping horses, bringing the chief knowledge of his enemies, painting his portrait. But it must also have been a heady experience to have a woman of the tribe that had conquered his people living in his lodge and washing his dishes. He must have been curious how white women lived, what their bodies were shaped like beneath those bustles and cinched-waist corsets. If nothing else, Weldon's son was evidence that white women did with their husbands in bed what Lakota women did with their husbands.

Not that Sitting Bull thought all white women chaste. In Bismarck, as he traveled home from his first visit to New York, a reporter boarded the train and asked Sitting Bull what he thought of his trip. Sitting Bull wiggled his hips and did an imitation of some dancing girls. Funny, yes. But not what he wanted his daughters to become. After his stint with the Wild West show, he told Mary Collins: "The farther my people keep away from the whites, the better I shall be satisfied. The white people are wicked and I don't want my women to become as the white women I have seen have lived."

The women of his own tribe were renowned for their chastity. When Sitting Bull was a young man, some Hunkpapa women decided that one of their Crow captives was a whore because she kept giving the come-on to their men. They tore off her clothes and prepared to set her on fire. Sitting Bull couldn't stand her cries of pain, so he sent an arrow through her heart. Whether the story is truth or myth, it's revealing to note that despite Sitting Bull's generosity toward other captives, the best he could do for this promiscuous woman was to shoot her.

Nevertheless, Sitting Bull seemed able to differentiate between white prostitutes and ladies. (The difference, he once remarked, must be that white men thought more highly of their prostitutes because they dressed them better than they dressed their wives.) He liked to whisper in the ears of the ladies who came to see him, and he gallantly gave women his autograph for free (what other gift could he give?). He was fond of Annie Oakley, with whom he became friends while they toured with the Wild West show. He called her "Little Sure Shot" and said that she was like a daughter, which he also said about Weldon. Maybe this was his way of reassuring himself—and whites—that his attentions weren't sexual. Sitting Bull knew that Catherine Weldon admired him. She believed what he believed. He wasn't threatened by her assertiveness. A Lakota chief had no reason to feel threatened by a woman.

And so he proposed. He wanted to do the right thing. Here was a woman who had traveled thousands of miles and given away her valuables for his sake. She moved into his cabin and performed the wifely chores a Lakota woman performed for a man she loved. And she needed his protection—from rumors that they were living in sin, from the dangers any woman faced on the Plains. She was a widow with a son, and Sitting Bull often had taken in widows and their sons. He gained great satisfaction from caring for the weak. He hated to be in debt. He might not have been attracted to her physically, but it's possible that he was, and was more able than she to put in words the feelings that had grown between them.

Whatever he assumed, Weldon grew outraged. How could he think that she would marry him!

Well, he argued, what about Chaska—not Alma Parkin's boy, but a Lakota warrior they both knew who had married a white woman.

And Weldon's reply: "You had no business to tell me of Chaska. Is that the Reward for so many years of faithful friendship which I have proved to you?"

This indignant rebuttal, in Weldon's penciled scrawl, was found in Sitting Bull's cabin with those snippets of Lakota she was trying to translate. Maybe this was what she *wished* she had said, the rejoinder she would deliver the next time Sitting Bull brought up marriage. At the least, the note seems proof that Sitting Bull did propose. It also hints at his mood. *Well,* he might have said, *why shouldn't we get married? This other Indian I know married a white woman.* A man consumed by passion would have been, well, more passionate. Even a warrior like Sitting Bull would have used the word *love.*

And Weldon's reply seems proof that the proposal did offend her. The obvious reading—and for all I know the true one—is that she considered herself superior to Sitting Bull and was insulted by a proposal that lowered her to his level. Fine to live with an Indian and keep him grateful for her charity; if he approached her as a lover she would be forced to reveal that Indians repulsed her. So what if Chaska *had* married a white woman? His wife might be a tramp. But there also is a way in which Weldon's acceptance of the proposal might have made her more suspect. When Charles Eastman proposed to Elaine Goodale, she admitted that the idea of marrying an Indian man caught her by surprise. She and Eastman had just been involved in caring for the survivors of the battle at Wounded Knee. "The gift of myself to a Sioux just at this crisis in their affairs will seem to some readers unnatural," she wrote in her autobiography. "Others will find it entirely human and understandable. In reality, it followed almost inevitably upon my passionate preoccupation with the welfare of those whom I already looked upon as my adopted people." Not that Elaine Goodale didn't love her fiancé. But she seems to have seen him less as an individual than a representative of a group. It made sense for her to marry an Indian because she had taken the Indians as her cause. Weldon can't be accused of marrying Sitting Bull simply because he was an Indian, and a famous one at that.

By Vestal's reading, Weldon was so repressed that she didn't even recognize the sexual longing behind her acts. "Poor lady," Vestal writes. "His words pierced to her Victorian bosom's core." Sex might well have been a part of it. If Weldon thought that Sitting Bull proposed merely to protect her, she wouldn't have sounded so indignant. He proposed that she become—in fact and deed—his third wife. Maybe she loved him. Certainly they were fond of each other. But more than an open heart is needed to transcend barriers as high as those between their cultures. Sitting Bull was a polygamist, and Weldon hated polygamy, as her diatribes against the Mormons show. If she loved Sitting Bull—especially if she loved him—she couldn't have wanted to share him with two other women. She and Sitting Bull could never enjoy the intimacy, of minds as well as bodies, she required of a man. He would never let her glimpse the most human parts of himself; Lakota men didn't reveal their innermost feelings to their women.

To Weldon, Sitting Bull's proposal reduced her from an adviser to a wife, a comrade to a bedmate, a single woman whose services were a gift to a wife whose services were expected. She had hoped that he would see her as an equal. "I think myself just as great as Sitting Bull," are the last words in her journal, "& my *Hankake* have been much greater." We can't be sure what she meant by *Hankake*. It might mean sisters-in-law or relatives. Maybe she was bragging about the status of her dead husband's family, although that would seem unlikely given all the drivers, carpenters, and joiners who made up the Weldon clan. But the meaning of the first part of the entry is clear. If she had said that to Sitting Bull, he would have laughed. But Weldon believed it. She mouthed clichés to McLaughlin about a gentleman protecting the defenseless sex, but that was only something she said to manipulate a conventional man. Sitting Bull had given her the name Woman Walking Ahead. How, then, could he see her as a wife, who must always walk behind?

~～⌐

So their friendship was strained even before the Ghost Dance reached Standing Rock. As early as the spring of 1889, rumors began sifting from the West that a messiah had come to earth to save the Indians. Representatives of many tribes surreptitiously left their reservations and traveled to a site in western Nevada near the Walker Valley. There they found a Paiute woodcutter and farmhand named Jack Wilson—his Indian name was Wovoka—a charismatically attractive holy man in his early thirties who claimed that he had gone into a trance and experienced a vision during the sun's eclipse on January 1, 1889. As Wovoka told these Indian emissaries from other tribes (and, a few years later, the white ethnologist James Mooney), he was transported to another world. There he saw God, "with all the people who had died long ago engaged in their old-time sport and occupations, all happy and forever young. It was a pleasant land and full of game. After showing him all, God told him he must go back and tell his people they must be good and love one another, have no quarreling, and live in peace with the whites; that they must work, and not lie or steal; that they must put away all the old practices that savored of war; that if they faithfully obeyed his instructions they would at last be reunited with their friends in this other world, where there would be no more death or sickness or old age."

As God bade him do, Wovoka shared with the Indians who came to see him this vision of a peaceful, honest, hardworking life, as well as the dance the Indians must perform to secure this happy fate. But two emissaries from the Sioux, Kicking Bear and his brother-in-law Short Bull, gave the prophet's teachings a more militant twist. According to Kicking Bear, a time would come the following spring when a wave of mud would flood the country, burying all the whites. Indians who believed in the new religion and wore feathers in their hair would be lifted above the mud. After the whites were smothered or transformed into fish, the Indians would drift down and begin their new lives. Lush, green grass would grow, herds of buffalo would return, and, with them, the dead Indians. In this new paradise only Indians would live. Why would the messiah allow whites to live there? The first time he came to earth, the whites tortured him and killed him. To speed this second coming, the Indians must dance and show their faith. This would anger the whites, but if the Indians wore special Ghost Shirts—these were fringed and painted blue, with eagles and other birds, stars, moons, and suns—the soldiers' bullets would be deflected.

Reports of the new religion reached Washington, and the Indian Office asked its agents what was going on. The Lakotas at Standing Rock remained peaceful, McLaughlin wrote. But he managed to plant the idea that any future "trouble and uneasiness" could be prevented by "removing" Sitting Bull. For his part, Sitting Bull thought Washington had the power to head off trouble by sending more food. Scorching winds that summer burned the Indians' crops, yet rations remained low and the tribes received no money for the land they had ceded. To whom should they turn but Sitting Bull? Even Mary Collins saw the chief's ability to bring—or, at least, predict—rain as supernatural. The people were much concerned about the drought, she wrote in her memoirs. One day, they went to the fort to draw rations, and Sitting Bull announced that it would rain. "He took a buffalo skin, waved it around in the air, made some signs, placed it upon the ground and—IT RAINED. Not immediately of course, but in a day or two. I had some practice myself in discovering signs of rain but on this occasion I was not prepared from the looks of the weather to agree with the prophet Sitting Bull. He saw, tho, by some means unknown to the rest of us that it *was* liable to rain. This is only one incident which shows *why* people had such faith in him."

At first, Sitting Bull didn't demonstrate much interest in the messiah. But his people were in misery. Indians at other reservations were sending word that the dances were enabling them to see their dead relatives. Curious, Sitting Bull sent several young men to Cheyenne River to ask Kicking Bear to come back and describe what he had seen in Nevada. On October 9, Kicking Bear and six of his apostles arrived at Grand River. He delivered a sermon that converted nearly everyone. "My brothers, I bring you the promise of a day in which there will be no white man to lay his hand on the bridle of an Indian's horse; when the red men of the prairie will rule the world. . . . I bring word from your fathers the ghosts, that they are now marching to join you, led by the Messiah who came once to live on earth with the white man, but was cast out and killed by them."

Sitting Bull's nephew and adopted son, One Bull, had grown increasingly loyal

17. Wovoka (seated), a Paiute shaman who became the prophet of the Ghost Dance, in a portrait taken in January 1892 by the ethnologist James Mooney, near the prophet's home on the Walker River Reservation in western Nevada. Standing beside Wovoka is the prophet's uncle, Charley Sheep. Courtesy of the National Anthropological Archives, Smithsonian Institution, 1659-A.

My Dakotas! ✎ 115

to the Indian police and took the news to McLaughlin. Enraged at the audacity of an outsider who dared to stir up trouble on his reservation, the agent sent a few Indian police to evict Kicking Bear. But the officers were so overwhelmed by Kicking Bear's powers that they could do no more than politely request that he leave. McLaughlin sent a less susceptible lieutenant to do the job, and Kicking Bear left, but Sitting Bull was insulted by this disrespect to his guest.

Sitting Bull may or may not have believed Kicking Bear's prediction. His belief was beside the point. He was doing what he always did—acting on his people's behalf. If a messiah did show up, he didn't want his Lakotas to be left out. As their chief, Sitting Bull felt bound to invite Kicking Bear to tell them what to do. That was how Sitting Bull approached any new practice. If it worked, he adopted it; if not, he didn't bother. If the messiah was supposed to show up that spring, why not wait and see? The Ghost Dance was giving his people something to think about besides how hungry they were. The whites themselves preached that Jesus Christ would return and bring the dead. Sitting Bull had plenty of dead relatives and friends he ached to see. Although he never reported receiving his own vision of the dead, Sitting Bull moved from his cabin to a tipi and began to advise the dancers about the ritual. He painted special signs on their faces—crescents, crosses, moons. By mid-October, hundreds of dancers had pitched their tipis around his camp. In the center of their circle they erected a sacred tree (this, too, may have been a Lakota innovation, a remnant of the Sun Dance, as Wovoka made no mention of a sacred tree). Although most Lakota dances were done by a single sex, male and female Ghost Dancers took hands with one another and sidestepped to the left, dancing in a ring until some of the participants fell into a trance and were granted visions of their dead relatives. The only photo of the Ghost Dance at Sitting Bull's camp—it was snapped by a reporter with a small portable Kodak camera concealed beneath his coat from five hundred yards away—shows Sitting Bull's tipi forty yards from the dancers' circle and a man who might be Sitting Bull standing between the tipi and the dancers, perhaps supervising the ritual or only looking on.

That fall, white settlers in the Dakotas began to hear reports of an Indian messiah coming to kill the whites and went crazy with fear. In 1890, the whites living in North Dakota outnumbered all the tribes seventeen to one. Only scattered homesteads bordered the reservations; Mandan and Bismarck lay sixty miles away. No more than a handful of whites actually lived at Standing Rock—clerking at the store, chopping wood, or hauling hay—and those whites had the soldiers at the fort to protect them. Still, the whites figured that the Indians could kill a lot of settlers before the army put them down. Everyone "knew" that the Sioux had stockpiled weapons and ammunition looted from Custer's troops—the same weapons Sitting Bull had warned them not to take—and what better time to unearth those guns than now? Even if the Ghost Shirts weren't really bulletproof, the warriors' belief in their power might fortify their nerve.

Weldon probably read about the settlers' panic in the papers that reached her at Grand River. She heard reports from back east and guessed that McLaughlin would use the settlers' fear as an excuse to get rid of Sitting Bull. Like the agent, she was more insulted than frightened by the messiah craze. How could a brilliant man like Sitting Bull give credence to such nonsense? Most whites denounced the Ghost Dance as a barbaric return to savage dances like the Sun Dance, which the government had prohibited. Weldon wouldn't have been upset if her friends had insisted on returning to their Native ways. But she saw the Ghost Dance as an example of the same Christian fanaticism she scorned in ignorant whites. And, as she later told the dancers, she didn't believe in Christ's first coming, let alone his second. An Indian savior wasn't on his way,

18.   The only known photograph of the Ghost Dance at Sitting Bull's camp on the Grand River at Standing Rock. The photo was taken secretly by a Chicago reporter named Sam T. Clover, who approached the camp in the company of Jack Carignan, a teacher at a nearby school. Unlike its form in other tribes, the Lakota version of the Ghost Dance took place around a central tree. Sitting Bull may be one of the Indians standing halfway between the tipi and the dance circle. Courtesy of George W. Scott, Minnesota Historical Society, E95-37r10.

and Weldon couldn't see that Sitting Bull would accomplish anything more by supporting this new religion than throwing away his life.

What she didn't understand was that for all its Christian undertones, the Ghost Dance was a revival of authentic Native practices and hopes, even as it incorporated certain non-Native tenets. The Ghost Dance of 1890 was an out-growth of a similar movement started in California in 1870 by a prophet named Wodziwob and witnessed by Wovoka's father. That dance, like its successor, combined old and new beliefs.

Mary Crow Dog, whose husband, Leonard, was a leader of the American Indian Movement (AIM) in the 1970s, said that Leonard always thought that the dancers in 1890 misunderstood Wovoka's message. The Ghost Dancers "should not have expected to bring the dead back to life, but to bring back their ancient beliefs by practicing Indian religion. For Leonard, dancing in a circle holding hands was bringing back the sacred hoop—to feel, holding on to the hand of your brother or sister, the rebirth of Indian unity, feel it with your flesh, through your skin. He also thought that reviving the Ghost Dance would be making a link to our past, to the grandfathers and grandmothers of long ago." In 1973, when AIM took over the settlement at Wounded Knee, Leonard Crow Dog staged a revival of the Ghost Dance. A religion that maintained its force eighty years after its followers were crushed can hardly be dismissed as a white-inspired delusion, as Weldon seemed to think.

The sequence of Weldon's actions during these troubled times is difficult to untangle from the few letters in Vestal's book. But a long-neglected account of the Ghost Dance written by a reporter named Willis Fletcher Johnson fills in many of the missing details. That account, published in 1891, has the hard-to-miss title *THE RED RECORD OF THE SIOUX: LIFE OF SITTING BULL AND HISTORY OF THE INDIAN WAR OF 1890-'91: A GRAPHIC ACCOUNT OF THE LIFE OF THE GREAT MEDICINE MAN AND CHIEF SITTING BULL; HIS TRAGIC DEATH: STORY OF THE SIOUX NATION; THEIR MANNERS AND CUSTOMS, GHOST DANCES AND MESSIAH CRAZE; ALSO, A VERY COMPLETE HISTORY OF THE SANGUINARY INDIAN WAR OF 1890-'91.* Johnson was a reporter for the *New York Tribune*, but in his spare time he wrote books on civil-service reform, the Johnstown Flood, Livingston and Stanley in Africa, and a two-volume history of American foreign relations that earned him a professorship at New York University. As he notes in the preface to his book about Sitting Bull, he rushed to get this volume into print while the recent war was still fresh in the public's mind ("It is the present purpose to record this history before the blood of the last grim chapter shall have grown dry"). But he tried to be objective. "The views of both friends and foes of the Indian are given a fair hearing, nothing extenuated, nothing set down in malice. In years to come, when some metempsychosis shall have translated passion into philosophy, a more discerning judgment may record in other terms these same events. For this day and this generation we can only tell the story as it comes to us in the echoes of war, in the prayer for relief, in the cry of despair."

Catherine Weldon's voice added to those cries. "MRS. WELDON'S REMARKABLE MISSION TO THE CAMP OF SITTING BULL," one chapter is called, "HER DESIRE TO CONFRONT THE PROPHET OF THE MESSIAH—FORCED TO FLEE FOR SAFETY—HER VIEWS OF THE SITUATION—HER LIFE IN DAKOTA." The chapter covers the same period as Weldon's letters to Sitting Bull but offers much more information. Johnson mentions those letters but doesn't quote them (by the time Johnson wrote his book, the letters were in the possession of James McLaughlin, whose widow passed them to Vestal; they now reside among Vestal's papers at the University of Oklahoma). Nor are Weldon's comments taken from documents published elsewhere, as is true of many of the other "interviews" in Johnson's book. He doesn't describe her appearance, as he does with other sources, so he probably never met her. But she seems to have written Johnson letters from the Cannonball and Kansas City—Johnson refers to her as "Caroline," a name she didn't assume until after she left the reservation. And with one exception, Weldon's voice in those letters sounds authentic. Johnson seems an admirer. He wouldn't have had a motive for making her look foolish.

"Of all white people who ever had any dealings with him," Johnson starts, "the one who best knew Sitting Bull, and had most influence with him, was Mrs. Caroline Weldon, formerly of New York City. On account of some disappointments in her early life, she went to the Northwest and devoted herself for many years to work among the Indians and to study of Indian character and history. She spent much time at Sitting Bull's camp, and indeed considered it her home. And she did much to bring about a better understanding between the Indians and the whites, and exposed and corrected many of the abuses practiced by the Indian agents."

Those "early disappointments" seem to include more than her husband's death. Weldon had been unhappy *before* her husband died. She wandered Long Island painting Indians. Then, after Richard's death, she left Christie in New York and began traveling the "Northwest," which then meant the Dakotas. She traveled for "many years," so Richard might have died as long as a decade before she met Sitting Bull. Her travels weren't inspired by religion, as Mary Collins's were, or a desire to educate the Indian so he could enter white society, as was true of Elaine Goodale. She didn't want to change the Indians as much as understand them, then use that understanding to mediate between Indians and whites.

Johnson briefly describes Weldon's return to Standing Rock in the spring of 1890. Then he skips to the messiah craze and Weldon's attempt to avert the war. Late in the summer that she lived at Grand River, she tried to stop the dances. Surprised at her resistance, the Indians came to regard her as a spy. Only Sitting Bull and his wives remained her friends, she told Johnson. She went to Fort Yates to try to convince McLaughlin that the Indians meant no harm, but her mission was "unavailing" and she returned to Grand River. While she was there, an Indian rode into camp to tell Sitting Bull that McLaughlin had forbidden the Hunkpapas to go to a "certain place" to hunt, which might have meant the agent considered the hunt a ruse to cover a clandestine trip to the lower reservations. If they persisted, McLaughlin threatened, he would confiscate their ponies and guns. The men muttered so angrily that Sitting Bull spent half the night trying to calm them. "He says he does not want war, and will do all he can to prevent it," Weldon wrote to Johnson. "He does not want to fight against the whites. Sitting Bull hastened to the Major to find out if the report was true, and to remonstrate with him. Sitting Bull, who loves his people, resents injustice done to them, and yet he wants peace with the white people. He said he would be glad if the soldiers would kill him so his heart would find rest. I told them what would be the result of a war, and that it would hasten their destruction."

Exasperated, depressed, and ill—she doesn't say with what—Weldon returned to the Parkin Ranch (she describes her departure from Grand River in a letter she wrote to Johnson on September 15, so she must have left before that). Tensions grew, and Weldon wrote a second letter to Johnson—that letter is dated November 4 but describes the events of mid-October. She had been expecting Sitting Bull to travel to the Cannonball to see her, she told Johnson, but he sent word that he wasn't coming because he needed to remain with his guest Kicking Bear, who had come to tell his people about the messiah. Weldon was furious that Sitting Bull would rather stay home and entertain a "fraud" who was "making all the Indians crazy with his teachings" than come north and visit her. She decided to go to Grand River to denounce Kicking Bear in person, take her friends' "blindness" from their eyes, and "confound the medicine men and prophets." She prepared a sermon that would accomplish these aims; maybe Alma and Louise helped her translate her ideas (the English version of the speech was found in Sitting Bull's cabin after his death, with Lakota phrases in parentheses).

Before traveling to Grand River, Weldon tried out the speech on the more progressive Indians who lived south of the Cannonball. Elsewhere in Johnson's book, these Indians are described as "thrifty, industrious, peaceable people who have taken up claims, built huts and houses, own cattle, ponies, and wagons, and are in good circumstances. They are Christianized Indians, having no faith in aboriginal superstitions and disliking this new Messiah craze for they say it interferes with the progress of the people." The younger people listened with "apparent belief," Weldon claimed, but she met unexpected opposition from the elders.

If the Christianized Indians at Cannonball resisted what she said, Weldon had to know that she would be poorly received at Grand River. But when she was healthy again and rested, she determined to make one last try. She intended to debate Kicking Bear, overpower him with logic, and end Sitting Bull's delusions that the messiah was on his way. This was no small decision. Traveling south from the Parkin Ranch around October 9, she must have had in mind Alfred Meacham's return to the Modoc camp in the Lava Beds to talk sense to Captain Jack. A white who tried to make peace with Indians being hounded for no good reason risked getting his—or her—face blown off.

The best indication of the complexities of the crisis comes from a lengthy letter McLaughlin wrote to the Commissioner of Indian Affairs on October 17. The agent gives his own self-serving perspective on the Ghost Dance. But he was the one who called the shots—literally—so his perspective is worth having.

"I trust that I may not be considered an alarmist," McLaughlin began, " . . . but I do feel it my duty to report the present 'Craze' and nature of the excitement existing among the 'Sitting Bull' faction of Indians over the expected 'Indian Millennium. . . . '

"It would seem impossible that any person, no matter how ignorant, could be brought to believe such absurd nonsense, but as a matter of fact a great many Indians of this Agency actually believe it, and since this new doctrine has been engrafted from the more Southern Sioux Agencies the infection has been wonderful, and so pernicious that it now includes some of the Indians who were formerly numbered with the progressive and more intelligent and many of our very best Indians appear 'dazed' and undecided. . . .

"'Sitting Bull' is high priest and leading Apostle of this latest Indian absurdity; in a word he is the Chief Mischief Maker at this Agency, and if he were not here this craze so general among the Sioux would never have gotten a foothold at this Agency. . . .

"He ('Sitting Bull') is bitterly opposed to having any surveys made on the reservation and is continually agitating and fostering opposition to such surveys among his followers who are the more worthless, ignorant, obstinate and non-progressive of the Sioux. . . . He has been growing bolder and more aggressive throughout the past year and it is undoubtedly only a question of time (a few months at the most) until it will be necessary to remove him from among his people, and I believe that if we can even ride out the present craze without removing him from the reservation it will be necessary to deal with him in a summary manner as soon as the Survey of this reservation commences. . . ."

On McLaughlin rants, detailing the particulars of Sitting Bull's "badness." The agent had sent such diatribes before. What's important about this letter is his apparently genuine belief that Weldon's presence made Sitting Bull's rebellious nature worse. "He has been a disturbing element here since his return from confinement as a military prisoner in the spring of 1883 but has been growing gradually worse the past year which is partly to be accounted for by the presence of a lady from Brooklyn, N.Y. named Mrs. C. Weldon who came here in June 1889, announcing herself as a member of Dr. Bland's Society, the Indian Defense Association, and opposed to the Indians ratifying the Act of March 2, 1889, demanding of me permission to pass through the Sioux reservation to Cheyenne River Agency and to take Sitting Bull with her. The Sioux Commission being then engaged negotiating with the Indians at the Southern Sioux Agencies, I, as a matter of course, refused to permit her either to pass through the reservation or allow Sitting Bull to accompany her and compelled her to cross the Missouri River at this point and travel over the public roads outside of the Indian reservation, in consequence of which she was very hostile toward me and wrote several letters to different parties in condemnations of my course and action. While here she bestowed numerous presents upon Sitting Bull, considerable being money, which had a demoralizing effect upon him, inflating him with his importance.

"After her departure she kept up a correspondence with Sitting Bull until early last spring when she again returned and located on the north bank of the Cannon Ball River just outside of this reservation and about 25 miles north of the Agency. Sitting Bull has been a frequent visitor to her house and he has grown more insolent and worthless with every visit he has made there; her lavish expenditure of money and other gifts upon him enabling him to give frequent feasts and hold councils and thus perpetuating the old time customs among the Indians and engrafting with their superstitious nature this additional absurdity of the 'New Messiah' and 'Return of the Ghosts' and in this coming, Sitting Bull whose former influence and power being so undermined and tenure so uncertain, asserts himself as 'High Priest' here and like a drowning man grasping at a straw is working upon the credulity of the superstitious and ignorant Indians and reaping a rich harvest of popularity, which with Mrs. Weldon's affection and numerous gifts he is doubtless self-satisfied. . . ."

McLaughlin knew by now that Weldon disapproved of the Ghost Dance—she had told him so in person—but he believed that her attentions provided Sitting Bull with the means to pursue it. Without her support—and she was able to visit Sitting Bull only because McLaughlin had been magnanimous enough to allow her to come back—the agent could have kept "his" Indians safe from the ideology infecting the reservations of his less vigilant colleagues. "Desiring to exhaust all reasonable means before resorting to extremes," he told his superiors, "I have sent a message to Sitting Bull by his nephew One Bull that I want to see him at the Agency and I feel quite confident that I shall succeed in allaying the present excitement and put a stop to this absurd 'craze' for the present at least, but I would respectfully recommend the removal from the reservation and confinement in some Military prison some distance from the Sioux Country of Sitting Bull and the parties named in my letter of June 18th last. . . ."

McLaughlin knew the Indians weren't going to attack, and he was the last person to want the army swarming onto the reservation and overruling his powers. But he couldn't resist the opportunity to rant about that troublemaker Sitting Bull and how he ought to be arrested and removed.

What about dead? Is that what the agent wished? I don't think he did. The two men excoriated each other in private (Sitting Bull told his friends the agent reminded him of his divorced wife Snow on Her, who foolishly tried to occupy a place that wasn't hers). But face-to-face, they were weirdly polite. As Sitting Bull's keeper, McLaughlin was famous. His frustrations were real. But so might have been his perverse need for the chief to keep living.

In the meantime, Weldon left Christie at the ranch and caught a ride to Grand River. Rather than head directly to Sitting Bull's house, she stopped a little way off, at the Ghost Dancers' improvised camp. She tried to reach her friend Hohecikana so he could "call the chiefs and men together, as I had something important to tell them." That is, she wanted to deliver the speech that had gone over so poorly at Cannonball and she needed a respected warrior to put her listeners in the mood. But Hohecikana was off hunting, perhaps to avoid Kicking Bear, or maybe to avoid Weldon. In his absence, she called for another friend, Circling Bear. And Circling Bear confounded Weldon by professing loyalty to the prophet. Although he "never forgot his dignity," Weldon was so incensed by her friend's "stubborn" adherence to the cult that she "grew warm and used harsh language."

Her anxiety escalated when she learned that Kicking Bear wasn't an Indian of another tribe, as she first thought, but "Sitting Bull's wife's sister's son, whose mother is dead." Weldon's plan to debate Kicking Bear failed because he wouldn't deign to face her. (She seems to have thought that Kicking Bear was scared of her powers of logic. More likely, he didn't consider a white female out-sider worth his time.) Sitting Bull and his wives protected her from the Hunkpapas' suspicions and threats, she told Johnson, "but when she asked to be allowed to confront Mat-o-wan-a-ti-ta-ka, the prophet of the Messiah [Kicking Bear], they refused." She decided to address the dancers instead. It was a courageous and foolhardy thing to do. Lakota women never lectured groups of men. Sitting Bull's great-great-granddaughter, Ina McNeil, told me that if Weldon gave a speech to the men in Sitting Bull's camp, "her speech had to have been arranged, because the council wouldn't have allowed it otherwise. If she brought information from the outside, she could speak, but she couldn't influence their decisions." Sitting Bull and his family would have been "courteous and accommodating" to a friend such as Weldon, but McNeil said the chief wouldn't necessarily have followed her advice. "He took advice only from one council of men. He didn't listen to outsiders. Catherine Weldon, even though she was a good friend, he might have listened to her, but he had a council to take his advice from."

Weldon must have known that Sioux men weren't accustomed to taking advice from women, but she gave the speech anyway. "My Dakotas!" she began, and one imagines how indignant her listeners must have been just hearing that pronoun. Not even Sitting Bull would have been presumptuous enough to start a speech: "My white people!" It wasn't only that Indians were in no position to speak possessively of whites. They didn't think in terms of appropriating other cultures. In the old days, they might take vengeance on an enemy tribe. But they didn't look upon the members of that tribe as dependents. No Indian would claim that someone else's gods were false. Yet here was a white woman scolding their bravest warriors as a mother scolds small boys.

"When I visited you last I was ill in body and mind and I could not speak to you then as I will now," she started. "Everyone tells me that the Uncpapas love me dearly. I believe it, and thank you all. Because I love you. I have come to speak to you, once more. I do not want any uncpapas deceived and you are deceived, and those who deceive you are leading you astray, leading you into trouble, out of which you cannot come out again. . . ." None of their hopes are true, she tells them—this from a woman who never danced the Ghost Dance, never had a vision. The dead aren't coming back. The Indians ought to be con-cerned for the living and save their money and clothes for them. None of the horrible prophecies Kicking Bear had made against nonbelievers will come true. She won't be turned into a fish, she scoffs. "It is false. I, your friend tell you so. I love you more dearly than my life & to prove it I will meet Mato Wanahtaka & tell him that he is either insane, crazy, or that he deceives you. They say that who does not believe in him, he strikes dead with the power given him by God. It is false."

It is false. It is false. The more she kept saying it, the more restless they must have grown. If Kicking Bear had any powers over the living, Weldon said, "it is the power that each of you can have if he will have it. What makes the telegraph wires speak? It is the same power of the lightning. The power that is in the air which is in each man, only he knows it not. It is in Each mans [*sic*] brain, in Each man's blood if he will only knew [*sic*] how to use it." Weldon dismisses anything she can't understand scientifically. Kicking Bear's power is nothing *wakan*, nothing holy. "It is quite natural. Let me prove it to you." She brings forth a magnet: the Great White Magician debunking an Indian charlatan, reducing their religion to a bit of metal whose powers the whites understand better than they do. "Look at this Magnet. A piece of steel so bent that it can attract— Do not fear, it is not holy, can do you no harm." She shows the Indians a battery and tells them that the whites now use electrical currents to cure rheumatism and other diseases and, lately, to kill murderers. (The first electrocution had just taken place in New York, and the papers were full of drawings of how the electric chair worked.) This is nothing supernatural, she tells them. Kicking Bear is using this same magnetic attraction—mesmerism, hypnosis— to make people his slaves. He has a strong will, and the Lakota are "weak fools to believe him. There are plenty of white men who have the knowledge of making people sleep for a while . . . & come to life again. It is the same power which is in Each one of you, if you only knew how to use it—It is the power of a strong mind, over a weak mind."

Now, about the coming of the Son of God, she goes on. Some medicine man among the Shoshones preached a sermon about an Indian messiah, and other Indians believed him. But the Indians shouldn't allow themselves to be blinded and deluded. Their dead wives, sisters, brothers, fathers, mothers, and grandparents, their dead children will never come back, she says, "you will never see them again, unless *perhaps* when you die and go to the next world. *Perhaps* you will see them again! In this world *Never!* Many Indians already have gone to the Northwest & to the Southwest to see & meet their dead. Their brain is sick with dreams & they are cheated into believing that which is not true. I who love you dearly, who have made greater sacrifices for you than any of you think of, tell you this because I do not want any Dakotas cheated by evil people who doubtless have their motive for leading you into trouble." Her fear for their safety is understandable. What she doesn't see is that Sitting Bull and his followers no longer want to live if they must relinquish their beliefs as Indians. She can't grant them the right to choose a path she doesn't deem logical.

At the time, Weldon hadn't yet met Kicking Bear in person, and she sets forth the possibility that he might be an innocent dupe of white troublemakers. She can't bring herself to believe that one Dakota would purposely deceive another. She has no proof, she says, but she is fairly certain that the Mormons are to blame, or perhaps a German immigrant who lives among the Mormons.

The possibility that her Dakotas might be pawns in a Mormon scheme to wreak violence on "gentile" whites left Weldon little peace. In a note found among Sitting Bull's effects after he was dead, Weldon asks, "Have the Dakotas heard of the White people of the West who have many wives? Do you not think that they might want to use the Dakotas as tools for their own purposes? & when the Dakotas have helped them and done their duty, they will then throuw [sic] them away again & perhaps fight them." She wasn't alone in her suspicions; the Mormons were uniformly reviled by mainstream Christian whites for their "blasphemy" and polygamy. The Commissioner of Indian Affairs, Thomas Morgan, attributed the Mormons' "deviant" social behaviors and "primitive" religious beliefs to a "racial reversion" that put them on the same level as the Indians. In light of this theory of mental atavism, Morgan wrote, "some of the excrescences of modern civilization, such as Mormonism, are seen to be relicts of the old savagism not yet eradicated from the human brain."

Everyone had a hypothesis as to the identity of the false Christ—the *New York Herald* identified the charlatan as one Isidore "Nosey" Cohen, "a Hebrew well-acquainted with the tongues and habits of the Dakotas"—but the Mormons remained the most likely suspects. Major General Nelson Miles, the commander of the troops charged with putting down the Sioux, told reporters in November, a month after Weldon's speech at Grand River, that he believed the Mormons to be "the prime movers in all this."

Though tinged by fear and bigotry, accusations that the Mormons had instigated the Ghost Dance among the Indians weren't so far-fetched. The Mormons' founder, Joseph Smith, was himself obsessed with Indians; they figure prominently in his theology as remnants of the Lost Tribes of Israel, a "Lamanite people" whose redemption was required for the messiah's establishment of his kingdom on earth. Not only did Mormon settlers treat the Indians more peaceably than other whites, they proselytized more vigorously among them, since the Indians' conversion seemed beneficial not only to the Indians themselves, but to Mormons. Given the proximity of Mormon settlements to Wovoka's home, the uncanny similarities between the two religions didn't strike most whites as coincidental. Both religions had begun with prophesies by contemporary American men. Both emphasized the second coming of a messiah, leading to the apocalyptic transformation of the land. Even more uncanny: in

1843, Joseph Smith had predicted that in his eighty-fifth year, the messiah would return in human form. Since Smith had been born on December 23, 1805, Mormons began to wonder if the Indians' messiah wasn't the same as theirs. Although Mormon leaders discouraged the belief that the Millennium was at hand, many lay Mormons kept an excited watch on events on the reservation. Some Mormons speculated as to whether Wovoka might be a celestial being called a Nephite, who, in Mormon legend, would minister to the remnants of the Indian tribes in the latter days of the current world.

With the Mormons themselves wondering if their salvation might be linked to the rise of an Indian messiah, it's not hard to see why General Miles and Catherine Weldon held the same idea. Everything pointed to the connection. Although Kicking Bear claimed to have received the design of the Ghost Shirt during his own trip to heaven, many white observers noted the similarity between those "bulletproof" shirts and the endowment robes and sacred undergarments worn by observant Mormons. That Mormons would give the Indians shirts to protect them from soldiers' guns fit with the general perception that Mormons took every opportunity to incite Indians to attack white "gentiles," a perception partly substantiated by the Mountain Meadows Massacre of 1857, in which a party of Indians led by Mormons attacked a wagon train of 140 Arkansas emigrants traveling through Utah on their way to California. After a four-day battle, the Mormons tricked the emigrants into surrendering, then killed all but seventeen of the youngest members. Thirty-three years later, memories of that massacre were still fresh enough that General Miles cited it as evidence that the Mormons were behind the Ghost Dance.

Modern historians now believe the Indians themselves invented the Ghost Dance and the Mormon presence throughout the West merely served to fuel the Indians' insistence that a new order of things was near. Although Wovoka's own daughter, son-in-law, and grandson became Mormons later (the grandson died a hero's death as a pilot in World War II and was buried with Mormon rites), Wovoka himself seems to have received his visions from his own god and lived by Indian customs until his death in 1931. Even then, his last words seemed to be a prophet's: "I will never die."

If the experts needed a century to discount all the circumstantial evidence that the Mormons were to blame for the Indians' new religion, Catherine Weldon can hardly be faulted for warning the Hunkpapas that they might be the Mormons' dupes. What's troubling is that even after she swept aside the Indians' faith as a Mormon-induced delusion, she tried to convince them to follow a religion she didn't believe herself. The true Son of God, she said, "was crucified & went to Heaven nearly 2 thousand years ago. . . . He will not come again until the End of the World (perhaps?). If the true Son of God was upon this Earth I would go from one end to the other to meet him & worship him. Not because I am a pious woman, but because I have not been true to him, not worshipped him, not obeyed him. To be forgiven by him & to look upon his face I would go all over the world. But he is in Heaven & only there will all good people meet him. There is no Son of God in shape of man upon this world *now* to help either white people or Indians. The true Son of God told all the people to avoid war & blood-shed to be mild & gentle & loving to one another & to forgive wrongs. That God would avenge all wrongs & to him should man leave it. Anyone who preaches of wars, of destruction & death could not be Christ. . . . He never destroyed those who did not believe in him. He gave life *to all and death to none.* It is my firm belief that this deceiver, this German (with the Mormons) perhaps is using the belief of the Christians and corrupting it to deceive the Indians who are either themselves deceived or are paid for deceiving the rest. I am willing to meet this false prophet at any time, to face him, & I am not afraid of his power."

Weldon's letters to Johnson indicate that after she finished delivering this sermon to the dancers, she started toward Sitting Bull's farm. Crow Foot ran ahead of the wagon to announce her arrival to his father; presumably Sitting Bull was staying at his homestead, entertaining Kicking Bear. Weldon expected that Sitting Bull would be displeased with news of her speech, "but when the wagon stopped he shook hands with me and told me how glad he was to see me; but in spite of his smile he looked sad and troubled, and seemed to have aged considerably since I saw him a month before."

The scene that follows is described in no other source but Johnson's book. Jumbled and confusing, the passage nevertheless gives insights into the atmosphere at Grand River and how enmeshed in the turmoil Weldon was. At times, the scene reads like great historical drama; at other times, the characters demonstrate the sort of histrionics one associates with six-year-olds.

When she followed Sitting Bull into his cabin, she tells Johnson, "the dishes were set for dinner. My plate was, with several others, on the table, and on the floor was a white cloth with eight plates for Matowanatitaka [Kicking Bear] and his followers. His followers came to eat, but Matowanatitaka and one of his disciples stayed away, and I did not see him that day. I never got a good look at his face. He always had a blanket drawn over his head, and when he looked at me it generally was from behind a couple of chairs or some other piece of furniture. Instead of coming around and asking for an explanation he avoided me and seemed afraid. The next day the Major sent some policemen to arrest Matowanatitaka and Sitting Bull. The majority of the police stayed four miles above Sitting Bull's residence, and the chief [of the tribal police force] and Catka [Lieutenant Chatka] were brave enough to come to the house to deliver their message. Of course, Matowanatitaka and Sitting Bull declined to accommodate the Indian policemen. Matowanatitaka lay flat on his back kicking his feet in the air in the most ridiculous manner, while Sitting Bull was delivering a speech to the policemen and Indians. I expected a fight every minute, for every man carried a gun and looked desperate, and the room was filled with them. Catka recognized me, as he met me a year before. He bent down and whispered to Matowanatitaka. Sitting Bull had already left the room and Matowanatitaka followed, and then one by one every one left; Sitting Bull's wife and myself were the only occupants in the room with the exception of the chief [of the policemen]. Catka and I chatted pleasantly about different things, he admiring Sitting Bull's full-length portrait which I had given to him. After a while the chief men came in and shook hands with the policemen, all but Sitting Bull and Matowanatitaka."

Weldon may have found Kicking Bear ridiculous, kicking his feet like a little boy, but she also was terrified. Kicking Bear probably was in the throes of a religious seizure, and his powers in such a state were unassailable. All the men were armed, and Weldon expected a fight to break out. Kicking Bear and Short Bull certainly had no reason to feel warmly toward a white woman who strenuously opposed the religion they believed would provide spiritual and material salvation to their people.

In a portrait taken by a white photographer not long after the Ghost Dance, Kicking Bear appears heavy browed, with angry eyes, a prizefighter's misshapen nose, and a full-lipped mouth drawn up on one side in the epitome of a sneer; Short Bull had thin lips, narrow eyes, and a deep scar tunneling from his hairline to his chin. Even after Sitting Bull was dead and all hope of an Indian messiah had proved futile, these two men were still plotting an insurrection. They weren't about to let some white woman from New York tell them what to do.

If Kicking Bear was an object of ridicule to Catherine Weldon, he was a holy man and leader among his own people. An Oglala and Brule by birth, he became a Miniconjou band chief after marrying Woodpecker Woman, the niece of Chief Big Foot. A somber warrior from the old days, when he had ridden beside Crazy Horse, Kicking Bear was known even before the Ghost Dance for his mystical leanings and uncompromising hatred of the whites.

In the summer of 1889, Kicking Bear's life was forever changed by a letter from his uncle, an Oglala named Spoonhunter who lived among the Arapahos. The letter urged Kicking Bear to come to Wyoming and attend a new ceremony that promised good things for the Indians. Without a pass, on horseback,

Kicking Bear traveled to Wyoming, saw the dance and heard tidings of Wovoka, then carried back this news to his band at Cheyenne River.

As enthusiasm spread among the Sioux, the chiefs at each reservation selected representatives to travel west and interview Wovoka. Kicking Bear was chosen, along with Short Bull, a Brule named Mash the Kettle, and four men from Pine Ridge. After a rendezvous at Wounded Knee Creek, the delegation rode across the plains and mountains to Nevada.

There, at Wovoka's homestead, the wandering Sioux converged with men from other tribes. The Plains Indians could communicate in sign language, but the desert and mountain tribes didn't share that skill. Wovoka himself spoke only Paiute, yet in such a way that other tribes seemed able to understand. Apparently Kicking Bear wasn't much taken with Wovoka's insistence that the Indians live at peace with the whites and send their children to white-run schools, but he was deeply impressed with Wovoka himself and the prophet's vision of a world in which Indians might again live honest, brave, clean lives.

Together all eight Sioux delegates rode back to Pine Ridge, where Red Cloud and a council of Oglalas grew so curious about the new religion that they ordered the delegates to return immediately to Nevada for still more information; the riders weren't even given the opportunity to see their families again before heading back west. Kicking Bear's son, Frank, who was seven at the time, later told David Humphreys Miller that his mother missed her husband terribly and feared the whites would kill him for spreading Wovoka's words. To his family, Kicking Bear's long absences seemed like periods of mourning. And as it turned out, Kicking Bear wasn't to return to his wife and children for many months.

It's not hard to see Kicking Bear and his companions as three Native wise men riding west instead of east to seek tidings of a new messiah. They must have given off an aura of importance; one time, they reached a railroad and were invited by a bunch of cowboys to board the train and ride, horses and all, thereby shortening their journey by several days.

After this second visit to Wovoka, the three men paid visits to the Umatilla Reservation in Oregon, the Arapahos in Wyoming, and Red Cloud's people at Pine Ridge. As Kicking Bear traveled from reservation to reservation and camp to camp, he melded Wovoka's vision with his own, glossing over the prophet's message about living peaceably with the whites and emphasizing instead a return to tribal ways, the resurrection of all the dead Indians and extinct herds of buffalo, and a lack of fear of whites afforded by the bulletproof Ghost Shirts.

Traveling without a pass, Kicking Bear repeatedly flirted with arrest. But Sitting Bull was more circumspect. After McLaughlin turned down his request to travel to Cheyenne River and speak with Kicking Bear, the chief declined to

19.   Short Bull (left) and Kicking Bear, apostles of the Ghost Dance religion among the Sioux. Courtesy of the National Archives, II-SC.85791.

go AWOL. Instead he sent word to Kicking Bear to come and see him. Having invited Kicking Bear to visit, Sitting Bull wasn't about to send him home simply because McLaughlin ordered the prophet's departure. At the least, Kicking Bear was a guest and deserved Sitting Bull's hospitality. But Weldon's repeated insistence that Kicking Bear leave the camp was harder to ignore. She still meant enough to Sitting Bull that he made a show of following her wishes: the day after the altercation between Kicking Bear and Lieutenant Chatka in Sitting Bull's house, Weldon was informed that Kicking Bear had left the camp. His weapons were gone, she told Johnson, and her friends assured her that he had returned home. Still, Weldon didn't believe them, "and subsequently I proved to be in the right. He had taken up his quarters somewhere else, for later on he was my traveling companion with Sitting Bull on my return to Yates. Circling Bear [Weldon's former friend, who now supported Kicking Bear] poisoned Sitting Bull's ears. He told him that the attempt to arrest [him] was my doings; that I was Sitting Bull's enemy; and that I was planning the destruction of both. He also called Sitting Bull's attention to a look which passed between me and Catka [sic]. Evidence was against me, for I had said that I would pursue Matowanatitaka, and Sitting Bull told me he knew that I was his enemy, and wanted him to be in prison. I simply laughed when he told me. There I had been working for his interest and the interest of the Indians for years; was ready to share all the dangers, and he was foolish enough to believe me his enemy."

That night, Weldon stayed in the smaller of the cabins on Sitting Bull's farm. A little way away, the Indians resumed their dances, which "sounded awful in the stillness of the night, and they kept it up until I could stand it no longer, so I arose and went through the crowd. It was dark, and there was the width of a street between me and Sitting Bull's house. I told Sitting Bull I would go away at daylight if he did not stop it, and he did. The next morning I asked him to have no more dances, as the troops would come and there would be a battle. He said it was not his doings, but the [other] chiefs', and he would be glad if the soldiers would kill him, for he wanted to die. 'If you want to die, kill yourself, and do not bring other people into trouble,' I said. He had the post removed to the foot of the hill, where it would not annoy me, but he acted as high priest, for I watched him. He expected the soldiers and battle every hour. You can imagine how pleasant it was for me."

Weldon doesn't describe her turmoil to Johnson, but it is easy to guess how she felt. The first time she came to Standing Rock, she came to help the Indians fight a battle in which they were clearly right, even if she was one of few whites who thought so. She returned to spend her retirement among them, teaching the women and girls to sew. What she found herself doing instead was mediating a confrontation in which she believed the Indians were partly right—the Constitution guaranteed them the liberty to practice their religion—and partly wrong—the religion was misguided, no messiah would ever come, and the army was going to use this ritual as an alibi to kill them. She wanted to be their protector, but they were scorning her advice. She tried her best, but they wouldn't listen to anything she said. She took their refusal personally, as an insult, although they wouldn't have listened to anyone. Alfred Meacham hadn't been able to make peace between the Indians and whites in a similar crisis. Thomas Bland wasn't even trying. If Weldon had been a man, she might have stood a better chance of convincing the men on either side that the Ghost Dance wasn't worth a war. As it was, her only option was to stay and try to protect "her" Hunkpapas from a massacre, or be killed along with them.

For a while, she tried to play both sides. In the chief's empty cabin—presumably Sitting Bull was at the dancers' camp—she secretly began to write letters to McLaughlin on the only paper she could find—small pages torn from a decade-old memorandum book. "Please have pity on the Uncpapas & Sitting Bull, who has been under the evil influence of Mato Wanah Taka [Kicking Bear]," she begged the agent. "Have pity on him & do not send the police or Soldiers & I will induce him to come to you of his own accord." And then, on a new sheet: "S. Bull will surely accompany me to the agency: but please do not detain him his brain has suffered; but his heart is good. He will be all right now that Mata Wanah Taka has gone." And finally, on the last sheet: "My heart is almost breaking when I see the work of years undone by that vile imposter. I will stay here of my own accord for several days & see what my influence can do."

In fact, her influence was able to do nothing. Sitting Bull remained cordial but beneath his polite distance was hurt. Compare Weldon's behavior to that of Mary Collins. Although Collins denounced the messiah as vociferously as did Weldon, Collins left Grand River only when the government ordered all whites to come into the fort. The Indians took this as a sign that the army intended to attack. As Collins tells it, the Indians heard she had gone to the garrison, and they said, "If Wenonah too has gone to the garrison then even she has deserted us and there will be war." Collins asked permission to return and assure them of her loyalty, "for I was not afraid of them. Colonel McLaughlin and Colonel Drum, who were in charge of the garrison, plainly saw the situation and asked me if I cared to go out and I told them that I did. Consequently they allowed me to go and as I rode over the prairie over each little butte I could see an Indian looking at us. As they discovered it was 'Wenonah' they spoke my name and dropped out of sight; we were not molested once. They were all delighted to think that I had returned to them."

If we can filter out Collins's need to prove the Sioux loved her, her testimony shows that the Indians were drawing hard-and-fast lines between their enemies and friends. Collins's flight to the fort meant she knew a war would come and preferred to spend it in safety with other whites rather than fighting beside them. In this light, the Hunkpapas saw Weldon's opposition to their dance and her threats to leave their camp as signs that she was privy to the army's plans to attack and was abandoning them because she didn't really care about "her" Dakotas as much as she claimed to.

Mary Collins ridiculed the dancers until the end. In November, she returned to Grand River and bullied her way into Sitting Bull's tent. "You know that the dead won't come back! The messiah won't come and kill the whites. The soldiers will come and kill you and your men and their families!" The chief only shrugged, and Collins went back outside. When a man named Louis collapsed in a trance, she marched up to him and said: "Louis, get up, you are not unconscious, you are not ill; get up and help me send these people home." According to Collins, Louis got to his feet and looked around and came out of his delusion. "All the people saw him obey me and of course lost their faith in the dance." Despite such interference, Sitting Bull and his followers did not turn on Collins the way they turned on Weldon. By returning to their camp, Collins demonstrated her willingness to risk her life with theirs.

Weldon, for her part, felt betrayed by Sitting Bull as Mary Collins didn't. He was already Collins's failure. She had never been able to convert him. She delighted in teaching him etiquette but delighted even more in his refusal to learn. (In a letter to the *New York Tribune*, Collins gleefully relates that Sitting Bull is now "thoroughly and hopelessly bad.") Collins saw Sitting Bull as a real—if comical—Indian, while Weldon fell into a more modern trap: she idealized him until he seemed incapable of error, then felt doubly deceived when he made what she deemed a mistake. How could someone she respected believe in bulletproof shirts and visions of paradise induced by shuffling for hours in a circle and then grasping Kicking Bear's thumbs? After all she sacrificed for Sitting Bull, he acted as if she were selling him to McLaughlin for a few silver coins. She was trying to *save* him. That was the real tragedy, that she left the friend she loved so he could pursue the course of action they both knew would kill him.

Even if she didn't remain at Grand River as long as Mary Collins, Weldon stayed longer than most whites. In a note to the agent, Weldon says that "Miss Carrigan" (a misspelling . . . she is referring to the sister of a schoolteacher named John Carignan) came to take her to the fort, "but I thought best to stay. S. Bull said after she had gone that I ought to have gone with her. He was willing." Weldon didn't leave from fear. She left because Sitting Bull and his people rejected her truths. No matter how much she loved "her" Dakotas, no matter what she had sacrificed on their behalf, no matter if they loved *her,* the gap between her way of seeing the world and their way seemed insurmountable.

I think she also was frightened that she would die and leave Christie an orphan. When Carignan's sister and One Bull offered to take Weldon to the fort (McLaughlin might have wanted her to come in for her own protection or to keep her from bollixing up his plans), Sitting Bull asked her not to go right then, since McLaughlin had taken five Sioux messengers as prisoners and he wanted her advice on how to get them back. (Perhaps he also feared that Weldon might be taken hostage and pumped for information or harmed.) Weldon was touched that Sitting Bull wanted her to stay. She agreed not to leave but sent money in a purse with Carignan's sister. "Not that I distrusted the Indians," she explained to Johnson, "for not a pin was ever taken from me, but I feared the battle, and if I was killed no one would get the benefit of it," meaning Christie would be left destitute. She wasn't being melodramatic. No women were killed at Grand River, but many women and children died soon after at Wounded Knee. If the army opened fire on Sitting Bull's camp, everyone there would die, and McLaughlin and the government would figure that Catherine Weldon had gotten what she deserved.

A few days later, Gall stopped at Grand River to take Weldon to the fort. Although Gall had been one of Sitting Bull's earliest friends, he wasn't the sort of savior most people would be glad to see. Even in middle age he weighed more than 250 pounds. (He was so corpulent that he had trouble riding horseback, and McLaughlin rewarded him for helping keep the peace during the Ghost Dance by making Gall a gift of a wagon. Legend has it that the old warrior eventually died from gulping down more than the prescribed dose of a patent medicine called Anti-Fat.) He had been one of the most murderous warriors at the Little Bighorn, where he avenged his family's deaths by hatcheting more white soldiers than anyone could count. Another time, soldiers pinned him to the ground with a bayonet through his lungs. When they came back to get his corpse, it wasn't there: Gall had staggered off through the snow (after a rest, he recovered).

When he first surrendered, Gall tried to do what McLaughlin wanted him to do. To please the agent, Gall divorced one of his wives. But he later fell in love with a younger woman. He begged the agent to let him marry the girl, but McLaughlin refused. You already have a wife, the agent said. Besides, she's married to someone else, and you promised to abide by the white man's laws. I know I did, Gall wailed, but I never guessed I would fall in love again at my age! Weldon suspected him of treachery, but Gall might have understood what Sitting Bull felt for her. He tried to persuade Weldon to go with him to the fort, "but Sitting Bull was not on good terms with him, and I feared Sitting Bull would think I might betray some secrets of the council, for I had always been present, so I stayed until Sitting Bull took me himself. He said:

"'Do as your heart dictates. If you want to go with Gall, go; but if your heart says stay, remain, and I will take you to Yates myself, and perhaps to Cannon Ball.'"

Weldon stayed. Sitting Bull and his family always treated her well, she told Johnson, even after she denounced Kicking Bear and many of her former friends grew bitter, accusing her of telling McLaughlin of the plans they had discussed in secret councils and causing him to throw Sitting Bull's messengers in jail. She suspected McLaughlin of spreading stories among the Sioux that she now was on his side. After all, she told Johnson, she had confided to the agent that her heart was breaking to see all her work undone by the "vile imposter" Kicking Bear. It made sense that McLaughlin would try to deprive the chief of her protection and the support of the NIDA by deepening the rift between them.

If so, the agent's plan worked. Weldon's friend Circling Bear had become such an enemy that Weldon threw back at him the painted robe he had once given her as a gift. Circling Bear refused to take the robe, and it remained in her possession until it was stolen a few weeks later along with her trunks. In those last days at Grand River, Weldon exchanged "many unpleasant words" with her former friends because she opposed their dances, which, she said, "destroyed their reason for days. They said I did not understand it, but that whatever disease they had was thrown off during these paroxysms." So many dramatic events had gone on, she could write a "whole book." Instead she dashed off to Johnson a garbled account of her final trip from Grand River to Fort Yates in Sitting Bull's wagon.

On October 22, she said, Sitting Bull drove her to the fort, the two of them bumping along in silence behind the plodding gray circus horse, dejected and aggrieved. (Was Kicking Bear with them? It's difficult to imagine such a trio traveling so far together, but Weldon indicates that Kicking Bear accompanied them at least part of the way to Yates.) When they neared the fort, Sitting Bull climbed down and walked ahead of the horse. That way, if the soldiers meant to shoot him, they wouldn't hit Weldon by accident. "He dressed as if for burial, wearing the black cloth about his head, which means he is ready to die at any moment," she told Johnson. "He expected to be seized, and was determined to defend himself and sell his life dearly. His followers were at the Grand River; he was brave to go alone. On the contrary, the officers treated him well and shook hands with him. I had the chance to go to Cannon Ball in a Government team. He thought I would remain there from Thursday until Monday."

They still hoped that their separation would be temporary. Weldon would remain at the ranch a few days or weeks and come back to Grand River when things were calmer. At worst, she would spend the winter with the Parkins. The Hunkpapas, she told Johnson, seemed now to feel sorry for what they had said and done. "They seemed to realize they had lost one of their best friends forever. Now I have gone, I fear that the last link between the white people and Sitting Bull is severed. The Utes, as well as other tribes, are ready to fight, and I cannot blame them. When one has seen how they are continually cheated, allowances can be made. I read an article about myself in a Washington paper which was sent me. All papers print the most dangerous lies, and I blame Major McLaughlin for allowing it. If he had not started these stories, they would not have been published, although he positively knows they are untrue, for I had sent several notes to him from the Grand River, and when I informed him of the unpleasantness between me and the Sioux on account of my opposition to their songs and dances, he knew I was trying to prevent war, and that my life had been in danger on that account, and yet he allowed these untruths to be told, and stated also the latter to the Secretary of the Interior. If you read romances, do not believe them. I would like to see these articles, for they interest me, and I know they are his doings."

Weldon considered returning with Christie to New York. Instead she remained a few weeks longer at the ranch. She kept writing letters—to Thomas Bland in Washington, to McLaughlin at the agency, to Sitting Bull at Grand River—trying to fend off the disaster she saw coming. But if Sitting Bull could have intercepted Weldon's letters to McLaughlin, he wouldn't have seen her efforts in a grateful light. On October 24, she assured the agent that all had been quiet at Grand River when she left two days earlier. Any unrest could be attributed to outside agitators rather than Sitting Bull, whom she portrayed as the pawn of Kicking Bear, the false Christ, and the Mormons. She exaggerates her triumph over the forces of unreason but not the warriors' animosity. "By attacking and defeating 'Mako Wanahtka,' I have turned my former Uncpapa friends into enemies, & Some feel very bitter towards me. Even Sitting Bull's faith in me is shaken, & he imagines that I seek his destruction, in spite of all the proofs of friendship which I have given him for many years. In fact His brain is so confused that he does not know friend from foe."

Unlike other visitors, who described the Indians as more scared of the whites than the whites had any reason to be scared of the Indians, Weldon tells McLaughlin that she has "every reason to believe the 5 tribes are ready to fight."

Although she previously admitted she isn't much of a Christian, she writes as any missionary would: "It is heart-rending to see how zealous they are in their faith of this false Christ, & reject the true Christ about whom I spoke to all the Indians explaining our faith. They believe that some terrible fate will over-take me for my sacrilegious [*sic*] utterances against their Christ. Poor mis-guided beings, so earnestly desiring to seek God, groping blindly for the true light & not finding it. If I had known what obstinate minds I had to contend with, I would not have undertaken this mission to enlighten & instruct them. It was money, health & Heart thrown away."

Of course, in writing such a message Weldon damned herself as the mis-guided party. No one had asked her to undertake this mission to "enlighten & instruct" the heathen. It's hard not to wish for a less condescending heroine who swallows her resistance and follows Sitting Bull and his warriors to their deaths. Or consider this scenario: Weldon is sleeping in the smaller of Sitting Bull's cabins when the tribal police show up to take Sitting Bull to jail. She upbraids the traitors—*Fools! You would arrest your own chief?*—until they slink back to the agency without the man they came for. Or she wraps her arms around Sitting Bull so no soldier dares to shoot.

In reality, few whites would have choked down their foreboding and stayed. *Was* the Christ coming? The buffalo? The dead? Were those flimsy shirts bullet-proof? What stronger message could she send? Any woman with the inde-pendence to defy her own race and stand up to the government would hardly be the type to ignore her own heart. And if she had stayed and saved him? We never would have known what fate she'd staved off. She would have been skew-ered in the press as a busybody who interfered with the army's attempt to arrest the leader of the Ghost Dance. Even the Hunkpapas might have bridled at the notion that they needed a white woman to protect their chief.

As it was, Sitting Bull dropped Weldon at the agency and took the oppor-tunity to gather his supplies—October 25 was ration day. One Bull informed him that McLaughlin wanted to see him about the Ghost Dance. But Sitting Bull suspected a trap. He picked up his groceries and started home. Vestal's ver-sion of the journey has Sitting Bull driving past the fort singing one of the songs he had learned from the eagle: "My Father has appointed me over this nation. I am fulfilling my duties until I grieve. In protecting my people I have had a hard time!" The soldiers heard him chanting. The son of a bitch, they said. Where does he get off chanting his war songs? We'll get him yet! But Little Soldier, who lived in Sitting Bull's camp, told Vestal that the chant was actually a love song, expressing Sitting Bull's sorrow at having driven away a friend.

Across the country, the newspapers chattered with reports of the "Indian uprising." Because of a delay in transmitting news, or the agent's ignorance of Weldon's whereabouts, or his plot to continue portraying Sitting Bull and Weldon as troublemakers, the articles in the press bore little relation to what was actually going on at Grand River. On October 28, the front page of the *New York Tribune* quoted McLaughlin as saying that Mrs. Weldon was to blame for the Ghost Dance. Although she had already left Grand River, the Bismarck paper told its readers that Mrs. Weldon, "a white woman from the east, who has more money than brains, is living with Sitting Bull at present and the Indians report her to be converted to their doctrine. She furnishes the grub pile—as with all their faith they cannot dance without something to eat."

To some extent, Weldon was responsible. If not for the money and encouragement she had earlier supplied, Sitting Bull might not have survived the previous winter and found the energy to lead the dances now. Not knowing the tenets of the NIDA, most readers would have found it ironic, if not infuriating, that a member of an Indian-rights group caused the chief's return to his earlier superstitions. Those groups affiliated with churches, as the NIDA was not, were exasperated with the dancers. A few kept faith: the *Herald* reported that the ladies of the New York Indian Association "adopted a resolution expressing confidence in the success of all Christian effort for the improvement of the condition of the Indians, despite reports from the frontier." But many groups remained silent in embarrassment. This was what the Indian haters had said all along: you couldn't give the vote to a bunch of heathen. (Never mind that the Baptist Pastors' Conference for Bible Study, "composed of believers in the pre-millennial coming of Christ," was even then holding a meeting in Brooklyn, its members having come not as "dreamers or stargazers, but to promote a revival of the forgotten truth in the words: Behold HE cometh in the clouds, and all eyes shall see Him.")

From a century's perspective, the government's response to the Ghost Dance strikes us as overblown. Why would anyone feel threatened if a few Indians, far from any town, set up a pole and put on canvas shirts painted with stars and moons, held hands, and danced in circles until they dreamed they saw their dead relatives? But the threat of an Indian uprising seemed real to many whites at the time. The same tribes now dancing had wiped out Custer's troops only fourteen years earlier. The average easterner's idea of how many Indians lived "out there" was hazy. One day, the *New York Tribune* reported that thirty thousand Sioux were ready to rise. A few issues later, the editors admitted that only seven thousand warriors were involved. This figure was still too high by a factor of ten, but how could most New Yorkers verify the numbers? The details of a battle between Indians and white soldiers in South Dakota probably seemed less real to a New England reader than the impending Ivy League play-off between Princeton and Yale (that contest ended in its own violence when the stands collapsed beneath the weight of overexcited fans).

And the agents at other reservations weren't nearly as competent as James McLaughlin in keeping their reservations calm. The removal of Valentine McGillicuddy from Pine Ridge had left the agency open to a succession of younger men who were no less tyrannical but more foolish. Daniel Royer— "Young Man Afraid of His Indians," the Oglalas called him—complained to Washington that the dancers were harassing nonbelievers. "It is useless to write more on this subject," he whined, then wrote a great deal more, sending a slew of frantic telegrams begging protection from the dancers, two hundred of whom had shown up to fight when he tried to arrest one of their number.

Given that the agents were hysterical, it is no wonder the settlers were. "We the under-signed settlers of eastern Mead County, South Dakota, and United States of America," began one plea to the government, "do here by ask in humble prayer for military protection during the trouble on the opening Reservation against the Sioux Indians . . . and further demand that we have protection of our lives and our childrens, and our homes and, our property." The citizens of Mandan threatened to kill off every Indian in the county unless the army did something to protect their city—sixty miles from Standing Rock.

Of all the newspapers reporting on the messiah craze, the *Herald* offered the Indians the most sympathy. ("My friends in the East send me the 'Herald'" Weldon wrote to Sitting Bull later from Kansas City. While most of the papers made "unpleasant statements" about the chief, called him "many bad names," and put forth spurious rumors about Weldon herself, the *Herald,* she said, "always speaks well of the Indians & you & me—instructs the public why the Indians want to fight because they are starving & because the Gov't does not fulfill the treaties.") With the demise of the *Council Fire,* Thomas Bland became a contributor to the *Herald.* On November 17, he informed his readers that the trouble on the reservations arose because the Indians didn't receive the rations promised them by Congress and settlers were taking over land for which the Sioux hadn't been paid. A few days earlier, he said, he had received a letter from "Mrs. C. Weldon, at Cannon Ball, North Dakota, a wealthy Scandinavian lady who is a voluntary missionary among the Indians. She had just returned from a visit to Old Sitting Bull. She had been endeavoring to persuade the old chief to use his influence with his people to abate their religious craze. She was not successful. Sitting Bull gave her small comfort. After her last interview with him, he shook his head and said, 'I don't know; the government is acting very bad. I want to die anyhow.'" Bland quoted Weldon's explanation that the Sioux "are much exasperated because the promise made them by the Sioux Commission to pay them for their 7000 ponies taken by the government in the hostilities of 1876 has not been carried out," an explanation that sounds odd only at this remove, since the Indians did hold a grudge for the confiscation of their ponies. (Bland's number, however, seems off by an extra zero, as the actual number of ponies confiscated from the Sioux in 1876 was closer to 700.) Apart from economics, the ponies represented the way of life Wovoka promised would return.

On November 18, a tiny article on page five of the *Herald* divulged "What Mrs. Weldon Found." According to the writer, "A very interesting letter from Mrs. C. Weldon, the wealthy voluntary missionary who has spent the past six months among the Sioux Indians, was received today by Dr. Bland, president of the National Indian Defence Association." Weldon reported that the government expected six Indians to subsist for two weeks on half a bag of flour, one pound of pork, a half pound of coffee, two and a half pounds of sugar, and "a bit of scrawny beef." The agent gave even fewer supplies to the Hunkpapas because they were Sitting Bull's band. Weldon explained the reasons for the Indians' unrest, but she didn't try to convince the *Herald*'s readers that the dangers were fictitious. Before she left Sitting Bull's camp, she heard "threatening language used toward her by the half crazed braves on account of her endeavors to put a stop to the ghost dances, although old Sitting Bull prevented any further demonstrations against her." Mrs. Weldon, who "put in several months arduous labor . . . endeavoring to induce them to abandon their fanatical religious ideas, has given up the case as hopeless and left the country." As of November 10, she was fleeing with her son for the safety of Kansas City.

Why Kansas City? A nephew recently had married and returned with his bride from their honeymoon in Europe. Weldon might have felt obliged to pay a call. More to the point, she figured she could stay in Kansas City until the messiah craze faded and she could return to Grand River. David Humphreys Miller claims that Christie stepped on a rusty nail while on "one of his many rambling solitary excursions along the riverbank," solitary because his mother was away at Grand River or otherwise preoccupied with trying to convince her Lakota friends to stop dancing, and the nail pierced the leather sole of Christie's right shoe, puncturing his foot. The Parkins and Van Solens guessed the wound was serious, but Weldon only "reluctantly gave up her last toehold in the Indian country and took Christie out to the Cannonball landing to catch a downriver steamer for Pierre where she might get medical attention for the boy."

Weldon's letters imply a different sequence of events. The puncture in Christie's foot didn't strike her as serious until they were already headed down the river. The decision to stop in Pierre happened midstream. This would make sense, given that she took the time to write Sitting Bull two messages from the Cannonball, and a third letter, which she sent by an unnamed Yankton Sioux when the steamboat stopped at Yates. All three letters, presumably, explained her reasons for deserting him and urged him to stop the dancing (the letters don't survive). The boat resumed its journey, and only then, on the way to Pierre, did the seriousness of Christie's wound become grimly apparent.

6

Sitting Bull's Heart

On November 17, a week after Weldon left the Cannonball for Kansas City, McLaughlin and his interpreter, Louis Primeau, drove in a buggy to Grand River to see what was going on. They found a hundred dancers circling around a pole, crooning, shrieking, and swooning, while an equal number watched. One woman fainted and was carried into Sitting Bull's tent. The chief put his ear to her mouth and reported her description of the promised land and the dead relatives she had seen there. McLaughlin and Primeau temporarily gave up the idea of interrupting and spent the night three miles upstream at the home of Bull Head, a lieutenant in the Indian police and Sitting Bull's fiercest opponent among his people. In his memoirs, McLaughlin reports returning to Sitting Bull's camp at dawn, in time to see the chief emerge from a sweat bath. Sitting Bull looked "very thin and more subdued than I had ever seen him." He wrapped himself in a blanket and stood shivering in the bright, chilly air as McLaughlin tried to persuade him the Ghost Dance was nonsense. I am your friend, McLaughlin assured him. I am speaking in your best interest. The messiah isn't coming for your people and you know it.

There's only one way to settle the question, the chief said. You go with me to the agencies to the west. Let me seek for the men who saw the Messiah. When we find them, I will demand that they show him to us, and if they cannot do so, I will return and tell my people it is a lie.

That's a waste of time, McLaughlin said. When you come to the agency to get your rations tomorrow, you can stay overnight and let me talk to you some more.

Maybe, Sitting Bull answered. I will consult my advisers, and if they think I should come to the agency, I will come.

By now, the dancers were awake, sneering at the agent, so McLaughlin took Sitting Bull's promise as the best he was going to get, and he and Primeau left. Sitting Bull's advisers didn't think much at all of their chief leaving their protection. Two days earlier, the army had invaded Pine Ridge and Rosebud, and the Hunkpapas at Grand River knew this. McLaughlin wanted Sitting Bull in jail, and his advisers weren't about to let him walk into a trap. So Sitting Bull sent another Indian, Kicks the Kettle, to tell McLaughlin that he couldn't come to the agency because one of his children was sick. Twenty other men from Sitting Bull's settlement sent their wives for their rations. McLaughlin issued an order that no family could draw supplies unless the male head of the household came to get them. The order reinforced the dancers' fears that he was trying to lure their leaders to the agency so he could jail them.

McLaughlin did intend to detain "the old mischief maker" until the messiah craze waned. But if he had wanted the chief dead he would have been more consistent in whipping up the public's frenzy. On November 21, the *Herald* relayed McLaughlin's report that he had been to Grand River and found Sitting Bull's influence had weakened greatly. "Now he has no more than a hundred or so followers. He received Major McLaughlin cordially, but the young bucks scowled at the agent as though he were not welcome. He had a long talk with Sitting Bull and is satisfied that the old chief's faith in the coming of the Messiah is in the decline. General Ruger's presence here last week had the effect of reducing Sitting Bull's followers by nearly one half, so that now he has not enough to make a campaign if he wanted to."

This was the same time that Weldon was sending warnings to Thomas Bland that the threat of war was real. McLaughlin could have sent similar warnings to the army. If the government had allowed the Indians to dance unmolested until spring, no one would have suffered more than disappointment. But the Indians' anger at the army for meddling in their religion, their fear that the soldiers would move in and kill their families, indicate that McLaughlin was soft pedaling the threat of war. It's a little far-fetched, but the Sioux might have risen up and tried to fight. Even without the ceded land, the reservations were so vast they would have been difficult to police. Homesteaders already had staked claims between the upper and lower agencies. Even the liberal *Herald* conceded that "the savages from either direction could make short work of the settlers should a massing of forces be desirable by the Indians." A society of warriors in despair, starved and maltreated, surrounded by armed troops determined to keep them from practicing their religion, might have risen up in its own desperate defense and struck out at scattered settlers, killing as many as they could before succumbing to their own suicidal defeat.

When the dancers at Rosebud and Pine Ridge found their camps surrounded by soldiers, they slipped off and joined forces on an elevated plateau between the two agencies. The dance site, protected by cliffs and bluffs, was dubbed the Stronghold by the press. As many as thirty-five hundred Indians gathered in this camp, an enormous number, if you think how much turmoil was caused a century later by a few dozen followers of cultist David Koresh in a similar standoff in Waco. The Lakotas at the Stronghold were led by Kicking Bear, who now assumed the role of fighting chief as well as holy man. Some chiefs, like Red Cloud, were quietly supportive of the dancers but wary of provoking an invasion (Red Cloud gave tacit approval to his son, Jack, to lead the dances in his place), while other chiefs, like Big Foot, Kicking Bear's uncle from Cheyenne River, refused to renounce his allegiance to the religion even though such a stance was clearly dangerous. While the Indians at the Stronghold kept dancing, the army tried to figure out how to get them down without too much bloodshed. The standoff at the Stronghold was one of the first modern news stories, and papers from around the country sent their best war correspondents and photographers to keep the public up-to-date.

At Standing Rock, McLaughlin retained control. The last thing he wanted was for troops to march in and stampede the Hunkpapas into fleeing to the Stronghold. He was even reluctant to send in his Indian police for fear of setting off a battle. Better to wait until the first blizzard struck, McLaughlin said. That would cool the dancers' ardor. They would abandon their tipis and hurry back to their farms.

But Sitting Bull had predicted a mild winter, and he turned out to be right. Warm weather persisted through the middle of December, unheard of in South Dakota. The Indians at Standing Rock kept dancing, the Indians at Pine Ridge and Rosebud kept dancing, and the army, commanded from Chicago by Sitting Bull's old adversary, General Nelson Miles, didn't think much of McLaughlin's plans to leave his charges to themselves.

Sitting Bull didn't fear only the white soldiers. Earlier that year he had gone to search for some ponies that he had left to graze in a meadow. At the top of a hill, he heard a lark call his name. Sitting Bull paid attention to birds. As a young man, he had been napping beneath a tree when he sensed a grizzly looming above him. He nearly gave in to the impulse to stand and run, but a yellowhammer sang out: *Lie still! Lie still!* Sitting Bull took the advice, and the bear finished sniffing him and lumbered off. In gratitude, Sitting Bull composed a song in honor of the birds: *Pretty bird, you saw me and took pity on me. You wish me to survive among the people. O Bird People, from this day always you shall be my relatives!* Now, on this hill, a meadowlark sang a new song: *Sioux will kill you! Sioux will kill you!*

But Sitting Bull didn't stop the dances. The temperatures remained above normal; it was the warmest winter in sixteen years. McLaughlin's knowledge of what was happening at Grand River came from spies like John Carignan, who, on September 1, had opened a school about a mile from Sitting Bull's camp. By October, attendance at Carignan's school had fallen from forty to fifteen, since most of the Indians kept their children home to join the dance. Carignan visited Sitting Bull's camp every chance he got. His presence caused no reaction, except one time, when he got so close to the dancers' circle that he was considered part of the ceremony and was asked to remove his hat.

On November 27, Carignan reported to McLaughlin that he had been out to Sitting Bull's camp twice since the previous Tuesday and had found everything quiet. "The Indians seem to be very peaceably inclined, and I do not apprehend any trouble," Carignan said. None of the Indians planned to join the dancers at the Stronghold. They weren't likely to do anything dangerous or foolish unless they felt threatened. "The Indians have been told that the Soldiers are coming down here, and are badly frightened if they were assured different there would be no danger of any of them leaving. I have done all I could in telling them that the reports they have heard are all lies, and that no one would try to prevent them dancing. I am positive that no trouble need be apprehended from Sitting Bull and his followers, unless they are forced to defend themselves and think it would be advisable to keep all strangers, other than employees, who have business amongst the Indians away from here, as Sitting Bull has lost all confidence in the whites since Mrs. Weldon left him."

If Carignan's assessment is right, Weldon's departure made the atmosphere at Grand River even more volatile than it had been while she was living there. When she left, Sitting Bull grew so distrustful that he wouldn't listen to any whites and so disheartened that he cared even less than before if he lived, a mood that contributed to his death. With Weldon gone, Sitting Bull had no white people he could trust. Bill Cody had just returned from a European tour. He read about the crisis and asked permission of General Miles to visit Sitting Bull. He would go out to Grand River with a bag of jelly beans and a few other gifts and bring in the chief single-handed, Cody crowed to the press. The success of such a plan would gain publicity for his show, although Cody also seemed to think that his strategy would allow the chief to be treated more gently than if the army manhandled him. Miles issued an order that Cody be allowed to secure Sitting Bull and deliver him to the nearest officer. McLaughlin was outraged. Not only was the army telling him how to run his agency, the fools were sending a circus performer to do the job. Colonel Drum, the officer in charge of Fort Yates, felt equally humiliated. He and McLaughlin launched a plan to get Cody so drunk at the officers' club that he couldn't carry out his orders. In the meantime, McLaughlin would telegraph his superiors to get Miles's order rescinded.

The plan was as screwy as something that a character on *F Troop* might cook up, and at first, it didn't work. Cody was such a hard drinker, the officers at the fort could barely match him. Drinking in rotation, they were able to delay Cody's journey to Grand River only by a day. On the twenty-ninth, showing few signs of what must have been a colossal hangover, Cody and a companion started for Sitting Bull's camp. McLaughlin sent his interpreter to catch up and inform Cody that Sitting Bull had left Grand River and was headed toward the agency along a different road. Cody fell for the lie and turned back. Just in time, McLaughlin received his telegram from the secretary of the interior, who had persuaded the president to overrule Miles. Disappointed, Cody left the reservation without seeing Sitting Bull.

Even then, Sitting Bull might have ended the dance. But Kicking Bear and the other leaders of the resistance at the Stronghold invited him to join them. Sitting Bull dictated a letter to a young man named Andrew Fox, whom Sitting Bull's daughter, Walks Looking, had married four or five years earlier. The couple had a baby; then Walks Looking died, leaving Fox to raise the child. Sitting Bull liked and respected his son-in-law, in part because the young man had been away to school. But Fox's written English was poorer than his father-in-law gave him credit for. If Weldon had still been living at Grand River and able to translate the chief's thoughts about freedom of religion into coherent English and edit out the threat of insubordination, this is the message McLaughlin might have read:

I wish no one to come to me with a knife or gun while I am praying. Like all the Indians, I am only trying to find the best road through life. You think I am foolish to pray to the God I pray to, and for this you don't like me. My friend, I am that way too; I don't like or respect a fool. You think that if I were not here, the Indians would become civilized. You tell the reporters I am a fool, and all the Indians are fools, and the newspapers back east publish what you say. But when you were here in my camp the other day, you spoke otherwise, offering me good words about my religion. And now you take back all those good words. Well, I must tell you that I am very eager to travel to Pine Ridge to find out more about my religion, and I hope that you will allow me to do so. . . .

As it was, this is the note McLaughlin received:

I wish no one to come to in my pray with they gund or knife: so all the Indians Pray to go for life & try to find out good road and do nothing wrong. in they life . . . you thing I am foll . . . because I am foll to pray to God. So you don't like me: My Friend. I dont like my self. when some one is foll . . . you dont like me because I am foll; & if I did not Here. then the Indians will be civilization: but because I am Here. & all the Indians foll, & I know this is all you put down on newspapers back East. So I seeing the paper but I thing it is all right: & when you was Here. in my camp. you was give me good word about. my Pray. & to day you take all back from me: & also I will let you know some thing. I got go to [Pine Ridge] Agency & to know This Pray. So I let you know that & the Police man. told me you going to take all our Poneys, gund, too; so I want you let me know that. I want answer back soo. Sitting Bull.

The letter, McLaughlin said, was "so incoherent as to be difficult to understand," a statement that might be disingenuous, given that McLaughlin had been deciphering such notes from his charges for decades, but the letter's apparent incoherence gave McLaughlin the excuse to consider it "full of defiance and implied threats." An eloquent, measured presentation of Sitting Bull's plea might not have prevented the agent from arresting him. But a comparison of the two versions of the letter shows how ignorant even a brilliant man can seem if he doesn't have a fluent, sympathetic translator. If Weldon had remained, she might have presented Sitting Bull's case to eastern liberals in such a way that they understood.

With the threat that Sitting Bull might join the rebels at the Stronghold, McLaughlin knew that he had every right to order in the troops and capture the chief. But relinquishing the job to the army gnawed at McLaughlin's pride. He was especially concerned about those Indians he considered well meaning but deluded. Without their leader, they would realize the absurdity of the dances and appreciate the magnanimity of a government whose "tolerance was only to save bloodshed and loss of life." There had to be a way to arrest Sitting Bull peaceably. Maybe when he came to the agency to draw his rations, the tribal police could grab him.

Unfortunately, Sitting Bull's note indicated that he planned to leave the reservation before the next supply day. McLaughlin sent a letter prohibiting Sitting Bull from going anywhere, then considered what to do. Reports from spies like Carignan indicated that Sitting Bull intended to travel to the Stronghold even if he was denied permission to go (later statements from Andrew Fox and One Bull contradict this claim). Not that it mattered. Colonel Drum was willing to let McLaughlin use his Indian police to arrest the chief, but that was as much leeway as he could grant, given that Sitting Bull's appearance at the Stronghold would enrage General Miles and cause Drum to lose his post.

So McLaughlin ordered his police to bring the chief in. He thought Sitting Bull would come quietly if his own people escorted him. Some members of the police force had been Sitting Bull's followers. John Loneman, who had hunted in Sitting Bull's band, regretted the order but saw it as necessary "to suppress this ghost dance which was becoming a menace to the Tribe." Loneman was "simply expressing [his] viewpoint as one who had reformed, from all heathenish, hostile and barbarous ways," he said. Other officers were Yanktonais and Blackfeet who didn't venerate Sitting Bull as his own Hunkpapas did. It's easy to disparage the policemen as stooges who toadied to the whites even at the cost of betraying their own leader, but many of them sincerely believed that the old ways were gone and that reactionaries like Sitting Bull were holding back their people.

At the very least, the tribal policemen knew they faced a fearsome order, marching into Sitting Bull's camp. The night before the arrest, Sergeant Shave Head told his relatives they must not be ashamed to see him reeling around as if he were drunk since he had good reason to act that way. "I am a dead man; I am as good as dead. I am here in spirit, but my body is lying on the prairie. We have been ordered to arrest Sitting Bull."

Sitting Bull's spy system was as effective as McLaughlin's. His warriors established a guard around his house. They weren't going to let a bunch of Lakotas from other tribes carry off their chief. They sat up smoking and telling stories about the old days. Crow Foot, who was fourteen, listened to the older men talk about their exploits. At dawn, after feeding everyone breakfast, Sitting Bull sent his guards home to tend their stock. He fed his own horses, then spent the day quietly, letting Kicking Bear lead the dances. Late that night, the dancers staggered home to sleep. Sitting Bull told them not to worry, he wasn't scared to be alone. Then he went inside and lay down with Four Robes.

That night, December 14, thirty-nine Indian policemen met at the home of Sitting Bull's enemy Bull Head. A mixed-blood interpreter and farmer named Charles DeRockbraine, whom the Indians called Chaska (most likely the same Chaska whose marriage to a white Sitting Bull had thrown up to Weldon when she refused his proposal), translated McLaughlin's orders to the police, ending with the postscript that they must not let Sitting Bull escape "under any circumstances." As Loneman put it, "We all felt sad to think that our Chief with his followers had disobeyed orders—due to outside influences, and that drastic measure had to be resorted to in order to bring them to discipline. Personally, I expected a big trouble ahead for during the time this ghost dance was indulged in, several times have the leaders made threats, that if the policemen tried to interfere with the matter, they would get the worst of it for the ghost-dancers were well-equipped with 'ogle wakan'—medicine shirts, which were supposed to be bullet-proof. . . ."

Like Sitting Bull's men, the police passed the night recounting their achievements in long-ago wars. The plan was to arrest Sitting Bull as he slept. The Indian policemen set off from Bull Head's cabin. They stopped at the home of the chief's brother-in-law, Gray Eagle, who volunteered to join them because he wanted Sitting Bull to stop this "heathenish" dance and because he had borne his brother-in-law ill will ever since they lived in Canada, where Gray Eagle had been caught stealing horses, and Sitting Bull, to keep from handing him over to the whites, punished Gray Eagle himself. With Gray Eagle and his friends, the Indian police rode through the icy night, owls hooting, coyotes howling, their horses slipping and clattering on the slick stones as they crossed the river.

Sitting Bull was sleeping naked with Four Robes and their toddler in the larger of his cabins. Also sleeping in the cabin were Crow Foot, two elderly guests who had been too tired to go home after the dances, and One Bull's hugely pregnant wife, Red Whirlwind. Sitting Bull's older wife, Seen by the Nation, their toddler, and her sons—one of them the deaf-mute—were sleeping in the smaller cabin across the road. The police kicked open the door to the larger cabin, and Shave Head grabbed Sitting Bull from the bed. Brother, we have come for you, he said.

Sitting Bull didn't resist. Fine, he said, I'll come.

More policemen crowded into the cabin, and everyone except Sitting Bull's wife and children slipped out. Sitting Bull's wife began to wail and scold the policemen, who were trying to carry Sitting Bull out the door. This is a great way to do things, Sitting Bull told them, not to give me a chance to put on my clothes in wintertime.

All right, all right, they relented. Get dressed.

Four Robes ran to the other cabin and brought back the clothes Sitting Bull wished to wear. But the policemen wouldn't let him dress himself. They were young and scared. They heard people gathering in the yard and wanted to get Sitting Bull out of the camp before trouble started. One policeman picked up a moccasin and tried to get Sitting Bull to put it on, but the shoe belonged to a woman and wouldn't fit. The officers tried to jam Sitting Bull into his leggings while he hopped around the room on one foot. He made a joke: You need not help me—I can dress myself. You need not "honor" me like this.

But the police kept mauling and insulting him, and he sat on the bed and refused to go. Several policemen yanked him up and tried to carry him, half clothed, in a ridiculous sitting position, out the door. The chief of all the Lakotas wasn't about to let his men see him in such a helpless state. He spread his arms and legs. The policemen struggled to budge him through the doorway. By now they were panicky. Several officers hung back. Others circled Sitting Bull, punching him between the shoulders with their revolvers, holding his arms and waist, trying to move him through a crowd of angry followers who had come running from their tents. The plan was to bring in the chief on his old circus horse, but the men were too nervous to get it saddled. The women were taunting them, and the men were shouting that if they killed the older Metal Breasts, the younger ones would run. Two troops of cavalry were on their way, and the police could have barricaded themselves in Sitting Bull's cabin and waited for reinforcements, but they wanted to get out of there.

Sitting Bull didn't want to be arrested, but he wasn't about to provoke a battle that would end in a massacre of his own people *by* his own people. He insisted that he would go with the policemen if they treated him with dignity, but they kept pummeling him and insulting him, and his people kept pleading with him not to go. Gray Eagle advised Sitting Bull to obey the police, but this angered the chief, that his own brother-in-law should throw in with the enemy, and he said that he had changed his mind. Well, Gray Eagle told Sitting Bull, I won't be responsible for what happens to you. Then Gray Eagle went to convince one of his sisters to leave with him. Whichever wife this was, she said she would obey her brother, then ignored him and stayed.

Several sources recount that Crow Foot came to the cabin door and shouted to his father in Lakota: You always called yourself a brave chief, but now you are allowing yourself to be taken by the Metal Breasts! This stopped Sitting Bull where he was. Bull Head, Shave Head, and Red Tomahawk tried to push him forward, toward the now saddled horse, and the crowd erupted, jeering. One of Sitting Bull's warriors, Catch the Bear, ordered the Metal Breasts to let go of his chief, then started jamming his rifle in their bellies, telling them to clear off. Maybe this was what Sitting Bull had been waiting for. He no longer cared if he got killed, the whole sad spectacle depressed him so much. When he saw Catch the Bear roughhousing the policemen, he called out: I am not going. Do with me what you like. I am not going. Come on! Come on! Take action! Let's go!

At that, Catch the Bear shot Bull Head. And Bull Head, as he went down, shot Sitting Bull. Red Tomahawk shot the chief at the same time, and Sitting Bull died. A terrible gunfight broke out, at close range. There's a legend—it might even be true—that the old gray circus horse, hearing all the shooting, imagined that he was back in the Wild West show and sat down and raised his hoof. That scared some of the policemen, who thought the spirit of Sitting Bull had entered the horse.

Red Tomahawk took command of the police and ordered his men to drag their wounded comrades into the cabin. The other officers sought cover around the barn. Inside the cabin, one of the policemen saw something rustling behind the strips of canvas on the wall. Loneman raised the curtain and there stood Crow Foot, terrified. My uncles! he cried out. Do not kill me! I do not wish to die.

The officers turned to Bull Head. But Bull Head was in agony from his wounds, and he blamed Crow Foot for taunting his father into resistance. Do what you like with him, Bull Head said. He is one of them who caused this trouble.

In an early account of the confrontation, Loneman claimed not to remember who fired the shot that killed Crow Foot. But he was more truthful in later interviews, admitting that he smashed the boy across the forehead with his rifle butt, "which sent him reeling across the room and out the door." Loneman and two other policemen, "tears streaming down their cheeks," pumped bullets into the boy.

After Crow Foot's murder, the cavalry rode up the bluffs above the camp and began firing artillery at everyone. Loneman ran out of the cabin, waving a strip of canvas from the walls to make them stop. The frightened Hunkpapas ran off, and Captain Fechet, who commanded the troops, found in the front yard two dead horses—though not the circus pony—and the corpses of Sitting Bull and seven followers, including Hohecikana, who had advised Sitting Bull to go peaceably and wasn't even carrying a knife when he was killed, and Hohecikana's teenage son, Chase Wounded. In the cabin lay four dead policemen and three wounded officers, two of whom died later. As the soldiers in the yard looked on, a relative of one of the dead policemen picked up a yoke and smashed Sitting Bull's face. The soldiers stopped the mutilation, but not before Sitting Bull's jaw ended up facing the wrong way.

⁓

At first, most of white America seemed glad that Sitting Bull was dead. President Harrison said he had long regarded Sitting Bull "as the great disturbing element of his tribe," and now that he was out of the way, a settlement of the difficulties could be reached without further bloodshed. But a backlash rose against the army. Reporters, private citizens, even army officials who had known Sitting Bull in Canada or at Fort Randall wrote articles to counter the image of a bloodthirsty obstructionist intent on killing whites. The same papers that had been waxing hysterical about the "Indian uprising" now called for an investigation into the premeditated assassination of a great statesman and his unarmed son. Even Americans who thought of Sitting Bull as Custer's ferocious and unrepentant killer saw him as a larger-than-life symbol of the nation's wild past and asked Congress

20. Sitting Bull's daughters and wives in front of the cabin where he was killed. Left to right: Many Horses, Four Robes, Seen by the Nation, and Standing Holy. Courtesy of the State Historical Society of North Dakota, Barry D0060-1.

to investigate the manner of his killing. A testimonial by the Reverend W. H. H. Murray, a friend of Thomas Bland, called Sitting Bull the George Washington of the Sioux nation. "Too intelligent to be hood winked and too honest to be corrupted by the influences that have been at work among the unlettered wards of our government, he stood firmly for the rights of his people.... He was a standing protest against the barbarity so often practiced upon his people under cover of protecting and civilizing the Indian.... And so he was slaughtered triumphantly, by his own fireside in his old age . . . by members of his own tribe wearing the uniform of our own government. . . ."

The chief's burial was as controversial as his murder. The same Bismarck paper that had delighted in castigating the chief as a wily troublemaker and Weldon as his lascivious groupie now took their side. "WHERE'S BULL'S BODY?" the editors demanded. "It is Said the Box in Which he Was Buried Was 'Very Light.'— And There's a Belief That Sitting Bull's Body is Still 'Out of Ground.'—The Last

Seen of the Remains They were in the Hospital Dissecting Room.—Perhaps the Government's Museum is to be Graced With the Chieftain's Skeleton.—From All Over the Country He Had Received Requests For His Autograph.—Mrs. Weldon Was Repeatedly Ordered From the Reservation, But Declared Her Love For the Old Warrior, With Whom She Wanted to Live.—Sitting Bull Actually Shed Tears When He and Mrs. Weldon's Son Were Separated."

The editors, if not sympathetic to Weldon, tried to understand her. "She was a remarkably fine looking woman 30 years of age and had a pretty little son 10 years old with long, curly dark hair. Indians say the couple lived together as man and wife, though there was no ceremony performed. Whenever Sitting Bull wanted a fresh partner he selected the prettiest of his flock, and his children are scattered throughout the Sioux nation by the score. He thought as much of Mrs. Weldon's young son as he did of the woman herself, and took great delight in putting the youngster on one of his ponies and riding with him on his own charger in triumph to the agency on ration days."

Although most of the report seems to be a deliberate distortion of the truth about Weldon's relation to Sitting Bull (they did live together in the sense that she was staying in his camp, and Sitting Bull did have many children, by blood and adoption, scattered through the camp, but he certainly didn't treat his people's daughters as his harem), the story of Sitting Bull riding to Standing Rock with Christie on his horse might have been based on the observations of Indians and whites who lived at the agency and saw them gallop in together.

The same sort of mixture of truth and distortion seems to constitute the remainder of the article. Mrs. Weldon, the reporter claims, had taken her departure from Standing Rock two months earlier. As Sitting Bull was parted from her little boy, "[t]ears actually trickled down the weather-beaten cheeks of the old warrior. . . . It was the first time he ever exhibited emotion. The boy had claimed a warm spot in his cruel heart. . . . Mrs. Weldon is a well-educated and refined woman. Her actions were a mystery. She is an able writer and fluent conversationalist, and a streak of mild insanity or crankism is the only reason assigned for her strange conduct."

Not only did the editors think Weldon mildly insane, they assumed that she had returned to New York. From there, they said, she wrote letters to Sitting Bull "foretelling the terrible tragedy enacted the other day. She warned him to be on the alert, telling him that the military and jealous Indians who sided with the government were seeking a pretext to put him out of the way forever. Letters from time to time were received to this effect, beseeching him to flee for his life. He paid but little attention until almost the last moment, when he began to realize the danger and was preparing to escape to the Bad Lands."

21. Oil portrait of Sitting Bull painted by Catherine Weldon in 1890 (the painting measures thirty inches high by twenty-three inches wide). It was hanging in one of Sitting Bull's cabins when he was killed; note the tear in the canvas where the portrait was slashed by a tribal policeman still angry at Sitting Bull. Courtesy of the State Historical Society of North Dakota, SHSND 12319.

Who knows where the paper got the story about Sitting Bull's body being sold, but the editors weren't about to let such a juicy rumor go unpublished. Bland heard the charge, possibly through Weldon, and demanded the punishment of anyone who had desecrated the corpse. Bad enough if the mutilation were the result of natural anger, he maintained; the only reasonable theory was that the chief had ended up in the dissection room because "the parties in charge" intended "to make his bones a subject of speculation, and perhaps his skin also."

McLaughlin was furious. The public ought to be grateful to the police for getting rid of the Indians who had been threatening the safety of the homesteaders and their own people's progress. McLaughlin's friends—and he had many—wrote effusive letters in his defense. He survived the ruckus, won a promotion, and went on to become the era's most important inspector of Indian affairs. For years he petitioned Congress to grant pensions to the survivors of the dead policemen. The notion that an Indian might risk his life for a white and never receive compensation so angered him that years later, on a trip to the Lava Beds, he went out of his way to meet Mrs. Toby Riddle, also known as Wi-ne-ma, and thanked her for saving Alfred Meacham's life, noting with satisfaction that she was the only Indian woman receiving a pension from the government—$25 a month—for her bravery and service.

Sitting Bull's family lost everything. After the battle at Grand River most of them fled the reservation. A few were taken prisoner and held at the fort for a short time before they were released. Thirty or forty dispirited Hunkpapas joined the ill-fated camp of Big Foot and fled south from Cheyenne River toward Pine Ridge. When Big Foot caught pneumonia, the refugees surrendered to a column of the Seventh Cavalry—Custer's old troop—and agreed to camp peacefully beside a creek called Wounded Knee, just north of the Pine Ridge Agency, and await the army's plans. The remainder of Sitting Bull's people accepted McLaughlin's promise there would be no retribution and straggled back to Grand River. According to One Bull, "Everything, trunks, boxes, and provisions in Sitting Bull's house were taken, his cattle—all that he had—all disappeared. Some of the horses were also missing. We were overwhelmed with grief. Sitting Bull's children, [Hohecikana's] children, all of them moved away to Red Cloud Agency." Only One Bull remained at Grand River, to take his uncle's place as chief.

Any gifts Weldon gave Sitting Bull were dispersed. According to the *Herald's* account of the melee at Grand River, when Bull Head seized Sitting Bull in bed, the chief "grabbed the revolver, the one given him by Mrs. Weldon, the Brooklyn woman who figured so prominently in Bull's affairs, but Red

Tomahawk wrenched it from him." If Weldon did give the chief a gun, it vanished in the pandemonium. Her letters would have vanished, too, if McLaughlin hadn't saved them.

The only other reminder of her stay at Grand River was the portrait of Sitting Bull that was hanging on a wall in the smaller of his cabins when the cavalry arrived. Matthew Forney Steele, a lieutenant at the time, said that he led his men into the smaller cabin and found Sitting Bull's wives and children sitting and crying on a low bed covered by a straw mattress. When the women refused to get up, Steele became suspicious and ordered his soldiers to pull them off. Hiding under the ticking were Sitting Bull's deaf-mute stepson and a second son of Hohecikana. The boys feared that they would be killed like their brothers, but the soldiers merely took away a broken jackknife they found on one boy. Steele ordered the soldiers and policemen not to loot the cabins, but, like Sitting Bull's warning to his people not to loot the dead soldiers at the Little Bighorn, this order was ignored. Steele was standing in the cabin when "one of the policemen, whose brother, another policeman, lay dead on the ground inside, killed by Sitting Bull's band, came into the cabin crying, and saw this portrait on the wall. Quickly he snatched it down and with his Winchester broke the frame in pieces and broke through the canvas." The rifle left a rent as pointed as a lance plunging through the chief's back, headdress, and arm, stopping just short of his heart.

Steele snatched away the portrait and carried it to the fort. He told McLaughlin he would like to keep it, "if the dead chief's squaws could be induced to let me do so." A day or two later, McLaughlin told Steele that the chief's widows had agreed he might have the painting for two dollars, which money Steele paid.

7

"I Am Informed That She Is an Adventuress"

*A*s I pieced together Weldon's story, I came to see the portrait that was hanging in Sitting Bull's cabin when he died as an emblem of their friendship, that friendship's bitter end, and Weldon's neglect thereafter. I wanted to go to Bismarck and see the painting for myself. I wanted to find the site of Sitting Bull's camp and stand on the spot where the chief and Weldon lived. Did any Indians remember her? If they did, did they consider her a kook, a traitor, or a friend?

But I couldn't just show up on the reservation. Besides, it was winter. I wasn't about to trudge around Standing Rock in a South Dakota blizzard. I put off my search and turned my thoughts from Weldon, only to find her footsteps close to home. At my department's weekly tea, a student asked the name of that woman I'd been looking for who was friends with Sitting Bull.

"Catherine Weldon," I told him. "Why?"

Well, a teacher had assigned his class Derek Walcott's epic poem, *Omeros,* and Weldon was in it.

She couldn't be, I said. How would Derek Walcott even know who Weldon was?

As it happened, *Omeros* was on the shelf above my head. The student took it down.

November. Sober month. The leaves' fling was over.
Willows harped on the Charles, their branches would blacken.
Drizzles gusted on bridges, lights came on earlier,

twigs clawed against the clouds, the hedges turned into bracken,
the sky raced like a shaggy wolf with a rabbit pinned
in its jaws, its fur flying with the first snow,

then gnawed at the twilight with its incisors skinned;
the light bled, flour flew past the grey window.
I saw Catherine Weldon running in the shawled wind.

Was this my Catherine Weldon? What was she doing in Boston, running along the Charles River? I felt elated and cheated. A Nobel laureate deemed Weldon a fitting subject for an epic. He could have picked Sitting Bull. But Walcott is the grandson of two white men and two black women, a native of the West Indies who teaches at Harvard. He felt closer to a woman caught between the worlds of privilege and want, Indian and white, than he did to Sitting Bull, who lived wholly as an Indian. Across gender, race, and age, Walcott felt drawn to Weldon, as I did. The convergence was uncanny. In the mid-1980s, both of us were sitting at desks in Boston writing plays each of us called *Ghost Dance*, with Weldon as the lead. Walcott's play was never published. Like me, he must have needed two tries.

Walcott based his poem on Vestal's version of Weldon's story, but he embroidered his own details. He has Weldon meet Sitting Bull while working as a hand "in Colonel Cody's circus," which she never did. He makes her a native of New England, fleeing her father's farm, although, as far as anyone knew, the only cities she ever lived in were Brooklyn, Hoboken, and Kansas City. The autumn of the Ghost Dance was mysteriously warm. Yet Walcott has her hair turning gray from snow as she carries logs on the Parkin Ranch. She sees the "tiny turret" of the fort above the trees, although in reality, Fort Yates lay twenty-five miles south. By the time Sitting Bull was killed and the remnants of his tribe cut down at Wounded Knee, Weldon was in Kansas City. But in Walcott's poem, she hears cannon from the fort, mounts a horse, and rides "downhill / away from the Parkin farm to the Indian camp," which she enters to find a starving dog, a deserted papoose, and white-eyed Omeros, the blind seer of the poem. "I walked like a Helen among their dead warriors," she says, as if, in her grief, she assumes guilt for the war; she ran off with Sitting Bull, as Helen ran off with Paris, and the whites killed him to get her back.

Whether Weldon feels responsible for the massacre or only helpless before its force ("This was history. I had no power to change it"), she retreats stricken to the ranch, where she sits rocking in the darkened parlor, refusing to move or eat.

> . . . Her shawl slipped from one shoulder
> but she left it there, in peace, since this was peace now,
>
> the winter of the Ghost Dance. "I'm one year older,"
> she said to the feathery window. "I loved snow
> once, but now I dread its white siege outside my door."

Walcott's vision of Weldon's later years isn't completely bleak. The dream in which he sees her running through the snow saves him from despair and sets him working on an epic that unfreezes Weldon from the wasteland of unremembered lives. Without denying that she suffered, he allows her the relief of knowing that sadness comes and goes. "Life is fragile," she proclaims. "It trembles like the aspens. /All its shadows are seasonal, including pain." This philosophy is clearer in Walcott's play, in which Weldon assures the audience that just because History wins, God hasn't necessarily lost.

> I feel a great victory in being on the losing side,
> in not having a heart as empty as that plain.
> I lived a rich and bountiful life out there,
> for all its losses. My ghosts are happy ones.

Walcott's poetry is achingly gorgeous. I felt churlish to complain that he got the details wrong. Yet if Weldon was now the heroine of a poem by a Nobel laureate, finding the truth about her life seemed more important than ever. Did the real Catherine Weldon feel a victory in being on the losing side? Were her ghosts happy ones?

All that dreary winter I kept rereading the stanzas in Walcott's epic that pertain to Catherine Weldon, stanzas that have baffled scholars since the poem appeared in 1990. One afternoon, on a hunch, I called the Museum of the American Indian in New York. Oh yes, the librarian said, she had heard of Catherine Weldon. The only printed material she had ever run across, besides the letters in Vestal's book, consisted of that article by David Humphreys Miller. But she wondered if I knew that a descendant of Sitting Bull lived on Long Island.

My first shock was that a descendant of Sitting Bull lived anywhere. I assumed that the murders of Sitting Bull and Crow Foot put an end to their line. As it turned out, Sitting Bull left as many descendants as might be expected from a man who married five women and adopted not only his own fatherless relatives, but nearly every orphan he ran across. Many of his descendants now hold positions of authority within the Lakota community. That one of these descendants should be living a few miles from the borough in which Catherine Weldon lived, not far from my own cousin's house in Levittown, that white middle-class suburb whose name is synonymous with white middle-class suburbia, struck me as an American story worth telling.

"Of course, she might not want to speak with you," the librarian warned. "But she is the family repository of the oral tradition about Weldon."

"She's heard of her?"

"Oh yes. She's heard the family stories about her. But she disparages the notion that Catherine Weldon was ever Sitting Bull's mistress." Sitting Bull's great-great-granddaughter, Ina McNeil, was so disgusted by the title of Miller's article, "Sitting Bull's White Squaw," she might not want to speak to another author, the librarian said. She promised that she would check to see if she was permitted to give out McNeil's address. A few days later I received it, with a letter advising me to write to McNeil "emphasizing how important you think it is to have a Native viewpoint on Weldon's visits to Sitting Bull, then follow up with [a call]. I have no idea how receptive she'll be."

I wrote the letter but heard nothing. A few weeks later, I called. The voice on the other end sounded reticent and distracted. She had been traveling, McNeil said. She didn't know much about Weldon. Maybe we could conduct the interview by phone?

I was tempted to say yes, get the information, and hang up. But I wanted to meet Sitting Bull's descendant. "I'll be in town next week," I said, "may I visit you then?"

"Next week? I won't be here." She sounded relieved.

"Maybe I can call you the next time I'm in New York?"

"You can try. You can call."

And so, a few months later, when I was planning another trip, I called Ina McNeil again. Yes, she said wearily, she remembered who I was. She was still extremely busy. There were trips to Manhattan for some project of Native history. She had her husband's dinner to prepare and a daughter in a town nearby to visit. I mustn't think she was putting me off. I should call when I arrived, and maybe I could come over.

I didn't hold much hope, but when I landed at LaGuardia, I tried Ina's number. She wasn't home, so I decided that I would spend the next few hours searching for Weldon's residence on Box Street, where she lived in the early days of her widowhood.

To drive through northern Brooklyn is to drive through the America white supremacists fear. The people on the streets that day seemed to represent every race in the world. The check-cashing emporia proclaimed their services in every alphabet. No one looked well-off. But on that sunny afternoon in June, no one seemed particularly destitute. Weldon had lived on Box Street more than a century earlier. That the street should still be there, with so much of the Brooklyn she knew buried beneath expressways, was miracle enough. But the very house she lived in?

I bumped up and over the potholed Pulaski Bridge, then coasted into Greenpoint. The main drag, McGuiness, was vibrant with shops, but the side streets were deserted. A century earlier, the neighborhood had been made up of working-class residences clustered among the factories strung along the East River and Newtown Creek. German and Scandinavian immigrants found jobs in those factories and the famous Brooklyn shipping yards. Darker-skinned immigrants live in Greenpoint now, but the rest of the description holds.

The sidewalks along Box Street looked forlorn, with blank-faced brick factories, steel-enclosed lots, and tilting tire towers. But just before the street vanished beneath the bridge, I saw four plain but neat houses, each three stories tall with shiny vinyl siding—brown, green, gray, and blue—and a tiny concrete yard with neatly clustered trash cans. Four black metal windows with drawn venetian blinds fronted each floor, not a breath of life in any. I climbed the canopied stoop of number 68, the house with green vinyl. The entryway showed six Hispanic surnames and a painting of a bullfight. The only possible renovation since Weldon's era was the siding. Yet every time she is mentioned—by reporters, her friends in Washington, or her enemies at Standing Rock—a tag describes her as "a wealthy philanthropist" or "a cultured lady from New York."

This tenement, then as now, housed working-class families. The other Weldons in this neighborhood were "joiners" and "drivers." Maybe Catherine lived on Box Street so her husband could be near the shipyards. Or she moved here as his widow so his relatives could help her care for Christie. This wasn't a neighborhood to which a person moved unless she had a reason—affordable rent, the proximity of relations. None of this fit with the repeated description of Weldon as wealthy. She learned to speak foreign languages and draw and paint as a child, so she must have been raised middle-class. Maybe she lost her inheritance by marrying beneath her. Standing by that tenement, I came to think that Catherine Weldon was called "wealthy" as a belittlement, an insult meant to characterize her, even by Thomas Bland, as a flighty society lady who had taken it in her head to help "the poor Indian."

I headed to the Historical Society to see if the Brooklyn papers from the 1890s carried articles about a local woman who became embroiled in the Ghost Dance. A few months earlier, a friend had succeeded in copying the will whose existence I had discovered on my previous trip to Brooklyn, in the basement of the Surrogate Court. I wanted to find out if the Catherine Weldon who wrote that will was my Catherine Weldon. The *Brooklyn Daily Eagle* must have run an obit. I could figure out the answer from what it said.

Around and around I drove, past the trendy shops and brownstones, the young businesspeople swinging laptops from their hands. Every metered spot was taken. I pulled into a garage—and pulled out again when I learned that parking there would cost more than twenty bucks. The 1990s, like the 1890s, were a decade of extremes in which the wealthier and better educated leapt ahead in life while other groups did not. Brooklyn in Weldon's day housed freethinking artists alongside Orthodox Jews who had just come over in steerage from Minsk and former slaves from Alabama. Whatever motivated her trip to the reservation wasn't the Indians' poverty. She could have found poverty a few blocks from her house. The Indians weren't the oppressed "other half," Jews and former slaves who had the motive to assimilate but needed a white Christian's hand. The Indians didn't want to assimilate. If they needed any help, it was to hang on to their culture.

I found a fifteen-minute spot and hurried down the street, only to be informed that the archives were closed for renovations. "You're kidding," I said. "I came all the way from Michigan."

The chubby-cheeked young black man behind the desk tsk-tsked, but he couldn't let me in. I stood in the vestibule, not knowing what to do. "Ma'am," he said, "have you tried the Brooklyn Public Library? They carry many of the same holdings as we do."

The library. Of course. I tried Ina McNeil again—she wasn't there—then jogged back to my car in time to shoo away the officer inspecting the "expired" sign on the meter.

～～⌒

The Brooklyn Public Library is an ornate fortress on a concrete island surrounded by a moat of horn-blaring traffic. The day I was there, nearly everyone inside was Hispanic or black. I placed an order for the *Eagle.* The young female clerk, chewing gum and bantering profanely with a friend, brought the rolls in minutes. The microfilm readers were old and temperamental, the mouths of the change machines taped shut with OUT OF ORDER signs, but that turned out to be true in the Manhattan branch as well. I found a working reader, sat down, and arranged my books and within a few minutes was laughing with the teenage boy on my left and the older woman on my right about how impossible it was to make out the newsprint floating across our scratched screens; we practically had to sit in one another's laps to get the right angle. I joined my fellow researchers in trading coins so we could use the copy machine. The sun began to set.

I found no mention of Catherine Weldon until December 20, 1889, a few days after Sitting Bull's death. On page six of that day's *Eagle*, Mrs. Lyman Abbott, president of the Brooklyn Woman's Indian Association, disavowed "any and all" sympathy for Sitting Bull and went as far as she could to disassociate herself from Weldon. The dispatches from Bismarck stated that among Sitting Bull's effects were letters from Mrs. Weldon, "a woman who, with her 10 year old son, had been living with Sitting Bull for some months, and who represented herself as the agent of an Indian society in Brooklyn." But Mrs. Abbott made it clear there was "but one Indian society in Brooklyn—the Brooklyn woman's Indian association," and Weldon was not a member.

In fact, Mrs. Abbott and her organization hadn't heard of Weldon until six weeks before, when someone wrote a letter to a Manhattan newspaper "sharply arraigning" the society for sending such a representative to the Indians and complaining that the present outbreak was largely due to the "coddling" of Sitting Bull by Mrs. Weldon, a prime example of the mischief done by women's associations "by introducing sentimental methods among the Indians." Rather than defend such methods, Mrs. Abbott's association "held a confab" with the aim of disowning Mrs. Weldon. None of the women knew her, "nor could they learn that she had ever lived in Brooklyn or was known here."

That a club of wealthy Brooklyn ladies interested in the "Indian problem" knew nothing of Weldon proves that she wasn't active in Society. She had lived in Brooklyn long enough that she might have been acquainted with someone in the club, if only she cared to be. This was a tight-knit community. Most of the women belonged to several clubs. They spent afternoons holding teas and receptions for one another and passed their evenings with their spouses at dinner parties, shows, and dances. If Weldon did not join these diversions, it probably was by choice, since people like Mrs. Abbott tend to know the social climbers whose hands they keep kicking off the ladder.

Having found to their relief that they had never heard of Weldon, the association published its findings in whatever New York paper had printed the accusation. "This statement brought them a letter from a town in New Jersey where Mrs. Weldon had once lived, stating that she had come back there last year and sold her effects, saying that she was going to make her home in the West, and that she had at some time lived in Brooklyn." The reference to New Jersey reminded me of the notice in the *Council Fire* that listed Weldon's address as Hoboken and the clipping from the *Bismarck Tribune* that gave Newark as her home. This was why her name appeared so sporadically in the Brooklyn directory. She lived in Hoboken or Newark, with her husband or alone, then traveled around the West, sketching and painting Indians, then moved to Brooklyn in time to be listed in the 1886 directory as Richard Weldon's widow, then moved back to New Jersey. Maybe she maintained a room in Newark while she rented her flats in Brooklyn, selling her possessions only when she decided to move to Standing Rock. No matter the sequence of her moves, Weldon clearly wasn't the sort of person to settle for long in any one spot.

The evidence that she was at least a temporary resident of New Jersey gave Mrs. Abbott the liberty to dismiss Weldon's claim to be a member of any women's Indian society in Brooklyn as "certainly fraudulent." Moreover, Abbott says, "I am informed that she is an adventuress." An adventuress! Not an adventurer, someone bold enough to travel far and engage in some quest. But an adventuress—I had to look it up—"a woman who seeks position or livelihood by questionable means." Mrs. Abbott is hinting that Weldon attached herself to Sitting Bull as his adviser or mistress to garner publicity and steal the chief's inheritance, an accusation Mrs. Abbott must have based on the dispatch from North Dakota the *Eagle's* reporter showed her.

> The dispatch says that Mrs. Weldon is a handsome woman of about 30, who went to the Standing Rock agency about a year ago and created so much discontent among the Indians that she was repeatedly ordered off the reservation but did not go. Finally she declared that she loved Sitting Bull and went to live with him on Grand river [*sic*]. Sitting Bull was particularly fond of Mrs. Weldon's son and used to take great delight in teaching the boy to ride a pony. Mrs. Weldon left the agency about two weeks ago and these letters received by Sitting Bull since she left are said to have warned him that he would be assassinated by the whites or the jealous Indians and saying that the military authorities were anxious to put him out of the way.

The correspondent omits any mention of Sitting Bull's two wives, his children, or his poverty, making him seem like an English lord with a stable full of horses. It sounds as if the other Sioux were jealous that Sitting Bull got to live with a handsome white woman and they didn't and that the whites killed him as retribution for an interracial love affair rather than for holding a religious ceremony of which they didn't approve.

The final few paragraphs of the article make it clear that even liberal eastern whites like Mrs. Abbott rarely if ever met an Indian, let alone discussed his wishes.

> Mrs. Abbott explained that the work of the Indian association was primarily among the whites at the East, and secondarily among the Indians. The promoters of the association feel that the Indian policy will not be wisely directed until there is a general public sentiment demanding wisdom and righteousness in the treatment of the Indian just as there is a demand for good business management and effectiveness in any other department of public business.

The problem wasn't that the Indians had lost their land and been confined to reservations. The problem was that the government didn't demand enough of them. Mrs. Abbott's husband, the famous Lyman Abbott, had earlier lectured the club on the evils of giving rations to the Indians without requiring them to work. Such enforced idleness and coddling would ruin even civilized whites, Abbott said. The charge sounded familiar. I had heard the same sort of talk not many weeks before on a visit to Montana: Make Indians go out and work and they won't have time to sit around drinking and bitching about all the bad things white people did to them. That the Indians' rations aren't welfare—Congress decided not to pay the Indians for the land purchased by treaty since they would only misspend the funds; the money was kept in Washington and the interest doled out in the form of supplies—escaped the knowledge of most white Americans a century ago, as it still does today. The Sioux had seen enough of white society to know that they didn't want to do the sort of work white people did, and this infuriated reformers like the Abbotts. The buffalo were gone. The Indians could no longer live as hunters. What else could they do but farm?

Weldon's distance from Indian-rights organizations other than the NIDA came because she didn't share their ideas. She was one of the only liberal white women who didn't. The organization to which Mrs. Abbott belonged, the Women's National Indian Association, had been established in the 1880s with the mission of gathering signatures of eastern whites opposed to the invasion of Indian lands; to achieve the greatest effect when presenting these petitions to Congress, the ladies tied their scrolls with red, white, and blue ribbons, which provided many men with cause to dismiss their work. Later, when the Indians were confined on reservations, the women's clubs switched to fighting for the passage of the Dawes Act. They joined the larger and more powerful Indian Rights Association and took the IRA's male leaders as their guides. Most branches of the women's auxiliary did little more than send a few boxes of used clothing to reservations once or twice a year. The more ambitious clubs—and the Brooklyn club was nothing if not ambitious—hosted lectures, raised money, and staged tableaux of Indian life, illustrating the ladies' favorite scenes from *Hiawatha.*

The Abbotts, who lived on posh Columbia Heights around the corner from the artsy neighborhood in which Catherine Weldon lived, represented everything about the Indian-rights movement, not to mention Brooklyn society, that Weldon chose not to embrace. The few radical notions Lyman Abbott had entertained in his youth were extinguished by his marriage to his cousin, Abby Francis Hamlin. As a young man, Abbott had written in favor of women's suffrage, but the article was never published, and he came to accept his wife's belief that women didn't want the vote. (Mrs. Abbott also served as president of the New York State Association Opposed to the Extension of Suffrage to Women.) He didn't support emancipation until after the Civil War began. Afterward he worked halfheartedly for the education of the Negro, then gave up and turned to editing the *Illustrated Christian Weekly,* a position he resigned to join Henry Ward Beecher as editor of the more successful *Christian Union.* In 1875, Beecher went on trial for a scandalous affair with the wife of a rival editor. Beecher won his suit, but his innocence remained in doubt and the *Christian Union* nearly folded. Abbott assumed its management and revived the magazine.

His views were strangely contradictory. Here was a man who published the most radical Indian-rights novel of its day, Helen Hunt Jackson's *Ramona* (her first book, *Century of Dishonor,* stirred up nearly as much sympathy for the Indians as *Uncle Tom's Cabin* created for black slaves), yet Abbott considered the Indians "barbarians," and, as he often said, barbarism had no rights that civilization was bound to respect. "A people do not occupy a country simply because they roam over it. . . . The Indians can scarcely be said to have occupied this country more than the bisons and the buffalo they hunted." Even Abbott's biographer, Ira Brown, was forced to conclude that the "story of Lyman Abbott and Indian reform is a good illustration of the limitations of his mind. Never a profound student of any problem, his ideas were often superficial and his judgments hasty. His knowledge of Indian affairs was entirely secondhand. . . ."

Still, Abbott and his wife were among the best people of their day. After Beecher died, Abbott was appointed pastor of the hugely influential Plymouth Congregational Church. Plymouth had drawn audiences in the thousands to hear Beecher's sermons against slavery. Abbott, with his subdued, otherworldly demeanor, didn't attract parishioners on the basis of his charm. Like many male

Indian-rights activists, he was fantastically whiskered and bald. (The Indians thought it funny that so many white men lost their hair. The only bald man among Sitting Bull's friends was John Grass. He and his brother-in-law were at a fancy dinner in Washington, and the brother-in-law chided John Grass for being ashamed of his bald scalp. *Why, John, these important white chiefs polish their scalps until they shine. Why don't you cut off your hair on the sides and polish your bald head like those congressmen?*)

Only half as many people showed up for Abbott's services as had come to hear Beecher's, but the parishioners who came wanted to do more than listen. Abbott and his wife transformed Plymouth Church from a citadel of gentility into a center of Christian service. The women's groups established free kindergartens; classes in cooking, dressmaking, millinery, typing, calisthenics, and current events; clubs for working girls; gymnasiums for boys; libraries; scientific circles; and a relief and savings association. Abbott resigned as pastor of Plymouth Congregational in 1899 but continued as a reformer. He tried to persuade Christians that the theory of evolution was compatible with their beliefs and was an early advocate of conservation laws, foreseeing a day when land would belong to the community (he didn't seem to realize that the Indians already had achieved communal ownership and the Dawes Act would destroy it). Abbott was so progressive that he remained a favored speaker on the college circuit until his death in 1922.

Sitting in the Brooklyn Public Library, surrounded by the descendants of the slaves Abbott believed should be given no more than an industrial education ("It is more noble to plow a field and furnish a crop which will feed hungry men, than to wield a pen and write a book that nobody reads," he wrote in a tribute to Booker T. Washington, a frequent contributor to his magazine), I shook my head at the injustice that Lyman Abbott should have died happy in the belief that his opinions were correct, while Catherine Weldon was ridiculed in her own day and only proven right long after she was dead.

I put aside Abbott's biography and turned back to the microfilm, scrolling forward fifty years to see if I could verify that the Catherine Weldon whose will I carried in my briefcase was the same Catherine Weldon who befriended Sitting Bull. The Weldon who wrote the will in my briefcase died on February 10, 1939, a resident of 103 Dean Street in Brooklyn. She left a minuscule estate to be divided among one son, three grandsons, and three granddaughters. Nothing in the will led me to think this was my Catherine Weldon. Nothing led me to doubt it. There was no signature to compare to Weldon's; my friend had run out of quarters before he could photocopy the final page of the will. The deceased left no surviving husband. I was beginning to doubt this could be my

Catherine Weldon, whose only child died soon after she left Grand River. To have given birth to the son mentioned in this will, she would have needed to remarry. But if she had remarried, her name would no longer have been Weldon.

Then, on page three, the statement appeared that a grandson and grand-daughter were the only children of Christopher Weldon, a deceased son of the decedent. A dead son named Christopher! Weldon's son Christie had been a boy when he died. He couldn't have left heirs. But if his mother had remarried and borne another child, she might have named him Christopher in memory of her first son. His name wouldn't have been Weldon, but the coincidence gave me chills. What if she adopted a son? What if Catherine Weldon decided that she could serve humanity best not by killing herself or joining a convent, as she threatened she might do, but by adopting an orphaned boy? Carried away by the idea of her own righteous sacrifice, as she often was, she adopted a second child in Kansas City and these other children later. The next paragraph of the will testified that "the above-named decedent left . . . no adopted child or children, no issue of any deceased adopted child or children other than those above named." The reference to adopted heirs might have been boilerplate language. Or it applied especially to Weldon.

I turned to the obits in the *Eagle* for February 12, 1939: "Weldon, Catherine, Feb. 10, beloved mother of Joseph, also survived by ten grandchildren. Funeral Monday February 13 from 103 Dean Street, Brooklyn, requiem mass at St. Paul's RC Church 10 A.M. to be celebrated by her grandson the Rev. Daniel Nelson. Internment Holy Cross Cemetery." The deceased had been a Catholic, which corresponded to my suspicions: Weldon wrote from Kansas City of visiting a priest. On some later trip to Brooklyn, I would try to find her grave and hope the headstone gave some hint that this was my Catherine. Meanwhile I had just enough time to call Ina McNeil before the library closed.

"Hello?" she said. "Yes?" She sounded unutterably tired. Driving back from Manhattan, she had gotten stuck in traffic. A chronic illness was flaring up. This evening would not be a good time for me to come. Maybe next morning?

Yes, I said, I'll be there. Then I purposely forgot to give her my cousin's number so she couldn't call me later and back out.

The next morning, I steered my rental car through the drizzle toward Hempstead, where Ina McNeil lives on a pleasant but nondescript street with small houses, small lawns, small driveways, and small trees. I took a breath and knocked. Ina came to the door, a short, congenial woman in stretch slacks and a black-and-white print shirt, her face round and brown as an acorn, her dark, shiny hair held back by a band. She led me through a living room with white walls and white carpeting, plastic slipcovers on the furniture, and a huge coffee-table book called *The Native Americans.* Other than the book, the only clue that the woman facing me was a full-blooded Lakota Indian was the arrangement of tiles in her kitchen—a star burst that might have been a Native American design, unless it wasn't.

She caught me looking around. "I was hoping to see your dolls," I said; the librarian had told me that Ina was an artist who crafted Native American dolls for museums.

"New York dust isn't regular dust," she explained. "It's more like soot. If I leave the dolls out, it ruins them."

I asked if making dolls was the work she kept mentioning, the work that left her so exhausted.

"My work is everything we were taught at home," she said. "My work is everything I learned from my great-grandparents, and my grandparents, and everyone around me. The doll I played with as a child, my grandmother Cecilia made it for me to play with; it wasn't purchased. Being Lakota was a wonderful thing to me, a beautiful philosophy." Ina serves as a consultant for the Museum of the American Indian—the new branch of the Smithsonian under construction in the capital—and she helped to plan the Powwow Now exhibit at the Museum of Natural History. She was developing a CD-ROM about the history and art of the Plains Indians. One day, she said, someone in her family would write Sitting Bull's biography, to give the world a richer and more accurate view than white historians had provided.

I opened my case and pulled out the new biography of Sitting Bull by Robert Utley, with its striking portrait of Sitting Bull on the cover and, inside, a photo of Ina's great-grandfather, One Bull, as a gaspingly handsome young man. Had she read the book? I asked.

Yes, yes, she had been meaning to read it. But she always found it so hard to read what was written about her people. The white historians got so much wrong that she ended up upset.

I cringed. She meant that I would get everything wrong as well. I switched the subject to Stanley Vestal. What about his books? Were they inaccurate, too?

Vestal was a friend of the family, Ina said. He had been invited by Sitting Bull's relatives to come live with them and interview them, and he still was remembered with some fondness and respect. Ina's Grandma Cecilia, the daughter of One Bull, spoke highly of Vestal, but "he never really understood our culture." She ran her fingernail across the lid of the sour-cherry preserves I had brought as a gift from Michigan. "Vestal's account of Sitting Bull's life was like scratching the surface."

Vestal's chief informant was Ina's great-grandfather, One Bull. "Grandpa One Bull was four or five years old when Sitting Bull decided to take him as a son. He raised him with all the rights inherent thereof." White people have a hard time understanding Lakota family relationships, Ina said, how close everyone is, how a person's uncles and aunts are like fathers and mothers. First cousins are as close as brothers and sisters, which is why the Lakota don't marry their cousins. "Family relationships are so much closer than in European families. Even a fifth cousin is too close to marry. So, Grandpa One Bull, in our culture, he was Sitting Bull's son. This was announced by public statement. He became the chief after Sitting Bull's death."

One Bull, like his brother White Bull, was the son of Sitting Bull's sister, Pretty Feather Woman. One Bull fought with Sitting Bull at the Little Big Horn, fled with him to Canada, then settled near him at Grand River. Unlike other warriors who fought with Sitting Bull in the old days but turned against him at the end, One Bull resigned his commission in the tribal police rather than arrest his adopted father. If anyone knew the facts of Sitting Bull's life, it was One Bull. Other Indians might have fabricated stories to please agents and reporters. But One Bull was an old man with little to lose when Vestal interviewed him. "My friend," he said, "I do not care to hear the lies that white men have made about Sitting Bull. I will tell you the truth!"

By her family's calculations, One Bull was 106 when he died. Ina McNeil was born at Standing Rock in 1940. "There's a photograph that shows him walking with a cane in one hand and my hand in the other," she said. "I remember that, walking with him." What Ina knows of Sitting Bull and Weldon came down to her through One Bull, and, later, through her father.

The phone rang, and I could barely sit still while Ina finished talking about some matter related to the CD-ROM project. Yes? I said. Your father told you about Catherine Weldon?

She balanced her elbows on the round, glass table and intertwined her hands. "Catherine Weldon was a very close friend of my great-great-grandfather Sitting Bull. Let me start it by saying that no one, especially a woman, comes to live in the house of a Lakota chief unless she's invited as a family member, as a daughter or a sister or a wife. Maybe short-term, as a guest, but not to live permanently or even for an extended stay." But Weldon had a different road to travel from Sitting Bull. "She was a very close friend, an advocate, she was befriending him, warning him of all these dangers and things," but her role in the chief's household was limited. There was only so much Weldon could understand about the Lakota culture. When any white person lives among the Lakota, "it's as if she is looking in a window. A soundproof window."

The help Weldon could give Sitting Bull was limited, Ina said, and he might not have needed as much help as Weldon guessed he did. "My great-great-grandfather was not a man who had no insight into what was going to happen to him. He knew his own people would kill him. At the same time, the Great Spirit guided him and gave him direction. . . . He told our family to take that which was good, the whites had some good to offer. But he would not take advice from a woman." Not that the Sioux didn't hold women in esteem, she added quickly. "Women were the life givers. Women were greatly honored. If I were given in marriage but wasn't treated well, my family would take me away, and I'd take my lodge with me. The home belonged to the woman." Like most white people, Weldon had great difficulties understanding Lakota behavior. "Out of respect and kindness, let's say she was a friend, but there was much she couldn't understand."

Instead of defending Weldon, I asked if there was any truth to Vestal's claim that Sitting Bull proposed marriage to Weldon. Had anyone in Ina's family mentioned their "affair"?

Ina shifted on her kitchen seat. No, she said. In her childhood she never heard Weldon spoken of at all. As an adult, she read about Weldon's supposed love affair with Sitting Bull. A composer in Canada was working on an opera about this great love romance, so Ina asked her father about Weldon—was what the whites said and wrote true? "Papa looked at me, and it was clear he didn't want to talk about it. I broached the subject again later that day, and Papa was very indignant. 'How dare you speak to me about that!' he said. 'There was never *any* relationship between them, never a romantic relationship. He never invited her to be his wife. She was a friend. That was all she was. She never understood what Grandpa could or couldn't do.'"

I pointed out the lines from Weldon's diary that made Vestal think the chief had proposed ("You had no business to tell me of Chaska. Is that the Reward for so many years of faithful friendship which I have proved to you?"), and Vestal's footnote to those lines ("The reference to Chaska was Weldon's reply to Sitting Bull when he asked her to marry him, and reminded her that Chaska [another Sioux] had married a white woman").

Ina wrinkled her broad forehead. "That's it?"

I nodded. Then I offered my own theory: that Sitting Bull and Weldon were friends, but Sitting Bull felt called upon to offer Weldon his protection. She was a widow with a young son living in his camp, suffering slander from her people. She had no way to earn a living. She had given him many gifts. How could he repay her? Maybe he was offering to adopt her. Weldon's Lakota was poor. Sitting Bull barely spoke English. How much room for misunderstanding gapes between women and men who speak the same language!

Ina agreed that plenty of room for misunderstanding might exist between a white woman living on a reservation and the Indians she lived among. "It wouldn't be acceptable even today for a single white woman with a child. The men would think she was looking for a man. She would have to be careful even today." But she considered it unfair to both Sitting Bull and Weldon to reduce their relationship to a romance. "She cared about his welfare. What she did was a display of true friendship. She wasn't just a woman he wanted to make a wife."

What about the Ghost Dance? I asked. Weldon turned out to be right, didn't she? No Indian messiah arrived to save the tribe. The government, as she predicted, used the dance as an excuse to kill Sitting Bull. Was she really so misguided for trying to convince her friend not to throw away his life?

Ina's answer was indirect, but she seemed to be saying that Weldon couldn't understand why Sitting Bull would hold his own life less dear than his people's desire to keep dancing. Whether he did or didn't believe in the coming of the messiah, he never would have stopped his followers from practicing their religion. "He couldn't act like a tyrant," Ina said. "By the fact that he was a chief, he had to live an exemplary life. The tribe's spiritual teachings had to be incorporated into his life, had to be part of his moral character." In other words, Sitting Bull's personal beliefs didn't matter. If his people wanted him to lead the Ghost Dance, he must risk his life to lead it. He was ready to die so his people could see how important it was to maintain their religion. He knew that his descendants would need his example if they were to resist the pressure that they stop living as Indians. In Lakota culture, Ina said, "when one does anything, he must always keep in mind he is affecting seven generations to come, so he has to be very careful. He was thinking of my future, not just decisions related to Mrs. Weldon. He couldn't do things considering his life alone."

At least Ina believed that her great-great-grandfather and Catherine Weldon *were* friends. Maybe Weldon wasn't revered as a hero. ("There are no traces of her on the reservation," Ina said. "No one speaks of her. We know of her but don't speak of her. Nothing.") But the whites were the ones who saw Weldon as an object of derision, a sentimental easterner who fell in love with Sitting Bull's image but recoiled from the realities of living in his lodge. The Indians took her seriously. Her image as a crank was created by Stanley Vestal, and, before that, by white reporters, and, earliest of all, by James McLaughlin, who hated her almost as much as he hated Sitting Bull.

I asked Ina if the agent's hatred for her relative didn't seem a bit overdone. Sitting Bull and McLaughlin reminded me of a couple who enjoy fighting so much they can't bear to divorce.

She clapped and laughed. "McLaughlin hated Sitting Bull! He just hated him! And he hated any white who helped him. Catherine Weldon became a friend of a person who had annihilated the U.S. Army." The defeat of Custer's troops was terribly upsetting to non-Indians, Ina said. Not only had Sitting Bull's warriors wiped out so many soldiers, Sitting Bull was the symbol of those Indians who refused, even after their surrender, to allow themselves to be wiped out as Indians. Even today, she said, many whites can't accept that Indians haven't disappeared. "I once took a sociology course at Nassau Community College. The instructor kept speaking of Native Americans in the past tense. Finally I took him aside and I told him, 'Excuse me, but I am a full-blooded Sioux Indian, and I am taking your class.'"

Ina's son, Ron, was the president of the tribal college at Standing Rock. He held a doctorate in jurisprudence, she said, he could have done anything he wanted to do, but he chose to run the college—his mother said this with a shrug of frustration, but she also seemed proud. She had given the college a gift of Sitting Bull's double headdress "to inspire the young Lakota men and women at the school to get an education and rise to the standard Sitting Bull held." By Ina's stipulation, the headdress can never be sold. She is the only person allowed to take it from its case to repair it.

I asked if there was any sort of museum devoted to Sitting Bull. Maybe on Grand River?

No, she said, the cabin there was long gone. The whites wanted to leave no traces of Sitting Bull. But yes, of course I could go to Grand River and walk around. I could see the cottonwood trees that Sitting Bull so loved. Ina returns to Standing Rock often. Her father's oldest sister still lives there. This relative was getting on in years, she was having some trouble cutting out the diamonds for the intricate eight-pointed star quilt she was sewing, so Ina brought her a rotary cutter as a gift. Ina lives on Long Island because her husband's job demands this. But she returns to Standing Rock every summer to attend the Sun Dance her relatives hold near Sitting Bull's old camp. "Tree day is on July eighteenth this year. You really ought to try to go."

A Sun Dance? I knew enough about Lakota culture to understand that the Sun Dance is the tribe's most sacred ritual. A Sun Dance isn't a public spectacle like a powwow, but a four-day religious ceremony of intense prayer and sacrifice, culminating in a rite in which the male dancers pierce their chests with skewers attached to a pole and dance backward until the skewers rip free. Banned from the mid-1800s until Jimmy Carter's time, Sun Dances were held in secrecy until recently. Even now, they are only held in a few isolated sites. To be invited to a Sun Dance led by Sitting Bull's descendants on the land where he was born, the land where Catherine Weldon preached against the Ghost Dance, where

Sitting Bull died, where his son and friends are buried, made me so excited I could barely take notes.

Then fear rose in my throat. I would need to travel to the reservation and camp among Indians who might resent my presence at their Sun Dance as deeply as the warriors resented Catherine Weldon's presence at their Ghost Dance. With the time it would take to do research in the archives in Bismarck and Pierre, I would need to be away from my son for ten days. I hated camping out. What equipment would I need? I had intended to spend the entire coming year reading about Lakota culture and learning to speak the language. If I accepted Ina's invitation to attend the Sun Dance that July, I would have only six weeks to get ready. On the other hand, if I waited, the invitation might never be repeated.

"Here's my son's number at the college," Ina said. "You can call him there and ask permission." She mentioned a relative named Isaac. I would need Isaac's permission, too. If Isaac said I could attend, I would need to pack long-sleeved, modest dresses. I couldn't wear makeup or jewelry. Ina pointed at the sleeveless black minidress I was wearing that day for an appointment in New York. She covered her mouth and laughed. "Just don't dress like that!"

Part 2

8

Prairie Knights

~ℐnlike Catherine Weldon, I didn't need the government's permission to visit Standing Rock. I had only to ask Ina McNeil's son. Ina would be arriving a few days late for the Sun Dance. If Ron knew that I was coming, he could show me around and introduce me. I wrote a letter and explained my research. When Ron didn't write back, I called. I heard a kind, hearty voice; amused at my request, he raised no objections to my coming, although he wouldn't be able to greet me since he also would be delayed. And I would need to get permission from his uncle, Isaac Dog Eagle (actually, Isaac is his cousin, but in Lakota terms of kinship Isaac Dog Eagle is many people's uncle). I couldn't attend the ceremony unless Isaac said I could.

I promised I would ask Isaac. In the meantime, what could I do to get ready?

Well, Ron said, camping day would be July twenty-fifth. The twenty-sixth was tree day. On the twenty-seventh the dancing started. It would continue through the twenty-eighth, then on through that night before ending on the twenty-ninth, when the dancers pierced their chests. "I guess I have to tell you that a woman can't attend a Sun Dance if she's having her period," he said. The medicine of a bleeding woman was so powerful it might interfere with whatever medicine the dancers' own sacrificial bleeding was meant to bring about.

I made a noncommittal noise, wondering what I would do if I traveled all that way, only to find out my period had chosen those days to come, while Ron went on telling me more rules for a woman's behavior. I would need to bring dresses that covered my arms and legs. As Ina had said, I couldn't wear makeup or jewelry or anything made of metal. The dancing would take place in a circular arbor whose eastern gate couldn't be crossed. I must be careful not to waste water, out of respect for the dancers, who wouldn't be drinking water while they danced. It gets very hot, Ron said. The sound of someone opening a can of Coke might drive a dancer crazy. "Another thing, we try not to use too many lights after dark, and we keep conversation to a minimum. You can't talk to the dancers—they'll be sleeping in a cordoned-off area to the west of the arbor."

I would respect the dancers' privacy, I told Ron. I wouldn't do anything I shouldn't do. But was there anything I *could* do? To help set up, I meant.

Ron supposed that I might help the women cook. Isaac's wife would introduce me to the other women, and I could hang around with them.

So, I should bring food for five days? Should I bring a tent and all my gear?

Ron laughed. "That would be a good idea. The nearest hotel is forty miles away." He advised me to rent a four-wheel-drive vehicle. If it rained, the roads would turn to gumbo and I wouldn't be able to reach the camp. He started to give directions. I would need to fly to Bismarck, take the highway south from Mandan . . . turn off here, turn off there. . . . By the end of the directions I was supposed to be driving down a gravel road, watching for a pole with a red bandanna tied around it, at which I was to turn south and drive another seven miles. I jotted the directions frantically, worried that if I got lost, no one would set me right.

"There's another thing you should know," Ron said abruptly. "Indians believe in self-torture. The way we see it is, we come into the world with nothing but our bodies. Putting some money in a collection plate doesn't seem much of a sacrifice to us. If you're really going to give something to the Creator to show how serious you are about your prayers, you give your pain and suffering."

Sure, I said, as if ritual self-torture were an everyday event in the university town I live in. I asked if I could stop at Ron's college. Of course, he said, stop by. He wouldn't be there, but the woman at the desk could show me around.

Encouraged by Ron's warmth, I phoned the tribal court where his uncle presides as judge. Isaac Dog Eagle was out of the building, the receptionist said. The next time I called, he was in court. At last I got through to a man who sounded gruffer than his nephew, though still cordial. He didn't object to my writing a book about Weldon. He knew only a little about her, but he was willing to tell me what he knew. I should come to the Sun Dance. "Just leave your negligee home!" He laughed.

Oh, I said, I will. I knew he would be busy leading the dance, but maybe we could talk after it was done?

"I would like that very much," Isaac told me. "After the ceremony, we must sit down and have a talk."

I should have felt ecstatic. But I couldn't shake the premonition that something might go wrong. I give little credence to premonitions. In college, I studied physics. I married a biologist. I don't believe in horoscopes, miracle cures for cancer, aliens, or ghosts. But before my trip to Standing Rock, I was queasy with foreboding. I had an inkling of how isolated the reservation was. I might get lost or have a flat. What if no one found me? What if someone did? Many Indians would object to a white academic coming out and studying them. I wasn't an anthropologist, and even if I were, the idea of any white writing an account of the most sacred ceremony of a culture to which she didn't belong was so problematic that I could never overcome it.

In the weeks before the Sun Dance, I dreamed three vivid dreams. In the first, I was speeding down a road in a foreign sports car when a black truck came hurtling toward me. My steering wheel wouldn't turn. The truck kept weaving toward me until I startled awake and screamed. I began to fear obsessively that I would be killed by a drunk driver. I'd had a milder version of this fear before moving to Ann Arbor, where, I had been warned, the students start drinking Thursday afternoon and stay drunk until Monday. Students in Ann Arbor do drink to excess, but the town is so small that they usually don't need to drive where they're going. If the Indians at Standing Rock drank the way my students drank, they wouldn't have the luxury of taking a cab or bus.

I wasn't making up that Indians on reservations drink more than most other people. I had read Michael Dorris's book, *The Broken Cord*, and knew the causes to be complex—a genetic susceptibility to alcohol, a cultural predisposition, the effects of poverty, depression, and unemployment. But understanding the causes didn't allay my fears. Studies conducted at Standing Rock in 1980 found that of the eight thousand Indians who lived there, roughly half the adults and adolescents over the age of twelve regularly drank alcohol, including one-third who drank heavily. Seventy percent of those who drank couldn't stop once they started. Indians who drink mostly hurt themselves. The Indian Health Service estimates that Native Americans are three and a half times more likely than other Americans to die from cirrhosis of the liver, four times more likely to die from accidents, and three times more likely to die from suicide and murder. But any white who visits a reservation exposes herself to becoming one of those statistics, from the drunk drivers at least.

I vowed I wouldn't drive the reservation roads after dark. I couldn't believe that Indians celebrating their most serious ritual of the year would drink while they were doing it. Ina McNeil wasn't the sort of woman to abide rowdiness.

And why would her son warn me not to wear provocative clothes to a drunken orgy? Everyone at the Sun Dance would ignore me. That was the real danger.

As if to illustrate this fear, I dreamed a second dream. I entered the dancers' camp and came upon Sitting Bull sitting crossed-legged on the ground, bare chested, with the heavy belly and sagging breasts of a well-fed older man. "I wasn't really killed," he said, smiling. "That was a ruse to fool the agent. I hid out for a few years, and everyone forgot me. Now I can come out and live in peace with my people and celebrate the Sun Dance." I was happy and relieved—until I looked down and saw what he was doing. He had something in his lap. A head. A severed head. He was scalping the head of a bald, brown-skinned man.

But no. It wasn't a head. It was a crusty loaf of pumpernickel! I hadn't seen that kind of bread since my childhood in the Catskills. He was carving off the crust so it peeled back in one layer. It came to me, the way things come to you in dreams, that Sitting Bull was putting on, for my benefit, a cross-cultural display of his scalping technique. "I have many things to show you," he said. "After the Sun Dance, we'll have to sit and talk."

In real life, Sitting Bull spoke barely any English. Much of the ceremony I had been invited to witness would be conducted in Lakota. Not that I could expect to learn a meaningful amount of Lakota in six weeks. But it couldn't hurt to know as many words as I could. Driving around Ann Arbor, I listened to a tape called "Lakota for Beginners," glancing at the vocabulary lists on the seat beside me. I belong to a generation raised to believe all languages are equal, as are the cultures that produced them. But the only thing I learned from listening to that tape was that studying a language with little knowledge of the land and culture that produced it is as difficult as learning to play a flute without ever having heard one.

The first lesson included the Lakota words for *cactus, coyote, forest, fire, windy, sharp,* something called "swelling medicine," and the names of places like Porcupine, Wolf Creek, and Wounded Knee. Several lessons consisted of nothing but the grammatical forms appropriate in conversations among various family members ("female cousin on father's side addressing a female . . ."). There was a lesson on the senses—no one had ever taught me that my senses were important. The Sioux have beautiful names for months—*ducks come together moon, tree leaves potent moon, wild turnip moon, black chokecherry moon, red plums moon, tree leaves turn yellow moon.* Where I grew up, the calendar was dictated by Memorial Day, when the tourist season started, and Labor Day, when it ended.

I practiced making sounds only Indians could make, although they reminded me of the guttural rasp required to speak Hebrew. My pronunciation wasn't bad. I retained more words than I had predicted. But I wasn't much encouraged by the nature of those words. On and on went the lists of animals I might run into—wolf, bear, grizzly, porcupine, fox, prairie dog, hawk, ferret, lizard, mouse, snake, rat—and the foods I might be expected to eat—buffalo cherry, chokecherry, sand berry, service berry, dried meat, fat parts, soft fat parts, fresh meat, pemmican, pounded beef, juicy fat parts. I don't much like insects, but I was traveling to a place where it was useful to know how to say bedbug, bumblebee, ant, louse, maggot, wood tick, spider, and wasp. By the time I reached the last lesson—*Tohan Wiwanyang Wacipi hwo?* "When will they have the Sun Dance?," the answer being, *Bloketu cokanyan kin Wacipi yelo,* "They will have the Sun Dance in midsummer"—I knew that my fantasies about showing up at Standing Rock, amazing Ron McNeil with my proficiency in Lakota, and being accepted by the tribe were as crazy as most white people's fantasies about Indians. Weldon had a facility for languages, but the notes she left behind prove that her Lakota wasn't fluent. The people accepted her because she joined her fate with theirs. She brought her son. She helped with chores.

Preparing for my trip, I read the memoirs of Elaine Goodale, who, in 1886, went to teach at Pine Ridge. In the summer between sessions she didn't return east, as the other teachers did, but planned a little jaunt across the thirty thousand square miles of the Great Sioux Reservation. She bought a pony, ordered a miniature tipi, and joined a family of Oglalas on their way to visit relatives near the Rosebud Agency. When they reached their destination, Goodale thumbed a ride with another group of Indians. The agent was so shocked that a white girl of twenty-three would be traveling alone with Indians that he ordered two members of his Indian police to go with her. No, thank you, Goodale said. But the agent insisted, so she slept in her little tipi while the Sioux family slept in their big tipi and the two Indian policemen slept beneath the stars, although one evening, when it rained, the women woke Goodale and asked if they could sleep with her so the policemen could stay dry in the other tipi with the men.

Finding the experience "delightful," Goodale arranged to spend the next summer with another family on a hunting trip to the Sand Hills. The Indians weren't thrilled. They would be gone a long time. A white woman couldn't possibly enjoy the way they lived. But Goodale paid for their supplies, and they gave in. At least she spoke Lakota. She ate the food they ate. She slept in their tipi and responded to their giveaways of onions and wild cherries with gifts of coffee and sugar. She shared the women's work, gathering wood, fetching water, pounding and drying cherries, picking mint and balm, making and mending moccasins, putting up the tipi, taking down the tipi, watering and harnessing the ponies (the only work she didn't do was to dress the meat or tan the hides since she was so clumsy at both). Sometimes she was bored. It rained a lot. The Indians told the same stories over and over—maybe they liked those particular stories or they didn't know as many stories as folklorists today would lead us to believe. Goodale had brought along no book except the Bible. She craved fresh fruit and something sweet. But the men watched their language in her presence. Everyone was modest. She had been warned that the men wouldn't take food from a woman who was undergoing her "mysterious monthly ordeal," and Goodale feared this taboo might lead to embarrassing questions, but she was spared any such inquiry. Her white acquaintances urged her to travel armed, but she felt safe among the Indians and was certain that a revolver "would only have served to advertise my lack of trust in my companions—and in the fact that I did trust them completely lay my sole and sufficient guarantee of safety."

Packing for my own trip to Grand River in July 1997, I tried to travel light: toilet paper, soap, a compass and a knife (for slicing bread and cheese rather than for protection), insecticide and sunscreen, a first-aid kit, a sleeping bag, a tent, a single-burner stove, notebooks, pencils, a tape recorder and a camera I doubted I would get to use, my two most modest dresses, a sweatshirt and scarves—in my mind's eye I saw Indian women wearing shawls, and these flimsy paisley scarves were the best I could come up with. I learned that renting a truck for ten days would cost $500. But the thought of getting stuck on some remote, muddy road loosened my purse. Hadn't I been driving a little car in my nightmare when that truck came barreling toward me? I reserved an Explorer, strapped my tent to my backpack, kissed my son good-bye, then drove to the airport, trying not to look back to see if he was crying.

～⌒

My trip from Detroit to Bismarck, even with a layover in Minneapolis, took less than half a day. At the rental counter in Bismarck, the clerk asked where I would be staying.

"The reservation," I said. "I'll be camping out all week, and I won't be near a phone."

"You're going to Standing Rock?" She was pert and well scrubbed. She had never been to the reservation, she said. She plucked a brochure from a rack— *Prairie Knights Casino & Lodge. The Finest Gaming, Lodging & Dining.* "You'll want one of these. The casino is the only place to stay on Standing Rock. You get a coupon for a free breakfast and a discount on staying at the lodge."

"I'm not here to gamble. I was invited to a Sun Dance."

"A Sun Dance!" she chirped. "How nice!"

"Nice" didn't seem the right word to describe a Sun Dance. Never mind. I took my gear and staggered out the door. The land stretched for miles, flat in all directions. No other visitors were to be seen. The airport employees stared, unabashed, as I tried to make my way across the stifling tarmac lot without fainting from the heat.

On the outskirts of town I passed gas stations decorated with red neon flying horses and enormous yellow clamshells. The Capitol reminded me of the photos in a 1950s civics class—the stark lines, the glossy aura of promise, the building rising stark as a stack of keypunch cards against the azure sky. There was a pleasant modesty about the town. Even the governor's mansion looked like a tract house.

I found the Days Inn. The clerk sported five earrings in one ear, a pierced eyebrow, and a tongue stud. Watching that pierced white girl fill out the proper forms made the piercings I would see at the Sun Dance seem less exotic and threatening.

Settled in my room, I leafed through the phone book, which, thin as it was, covered not only Bismarck but surrounding towns like Yates. A listing for a man named James McLaughlin, Jr., caught my eye.

Hello? he said. Yes, I had reached the right person. The agent James McLaughlin was the great-grandfather of the James McLaughlin I was speaking to. Yes, he would be happy to meet me and talk about his relative. How about the Prairie Knights Casino, two evenings from now, when he got off work and drove up there?

I hung up, elated. I had a descendant of Sitting Bull and one for James McLaughlin. Now all I needed was a descendant of Catherine Weldon.

There were no Weldons in the book. No Van Solens. But there, a Harold Parkin. On the phone, Mr. Parkin was a courtly, slow-spoken man who told me that he wasn't related to the Parkins who owned the famous ranch, but he knew about those Parkins because his wife's grandparents had built a homestead three or four miles from the Parkin cemetery and his wife's parents lived in Solen, which wasn't far from Cannonball. He had gone grouse hunting in that area every year for fifty years. He passed the graveyard every time, and since he accidentally shared the same name as the people beneath those stones, he became curious and did some reading. The two Parkin brothers, Walter and Henry, came to Dakota Territory from somewhere near Pittsburgh before Custer was killed. One brother became the first postmaster of Solen and married Sitting Bull's granddaughter. The other Parkin was the rancher. "I don't really know what happened to their descendants." Harold sighed. "They lost the ranch in the dust bowl years and moved into Mandan. No one around here knows anything about them now." If I looked along the road in Parkin Township, I could find the foundation of the Parkin store, he said. If I kept on along the farm-to-market route west of Fort Rice, I would find the family cemetery.

I thanked Harold Parkin and hung up. After an icy shower I went for a drive around Bismarck, then crawled into bed and dreamed my third dream. A man in a white coat entered a waiting room and said to a crying woman who might or might not have been me, "I'm sorry about your son." I went cold and woke abruptly. *I'm sorry about your son.* I couldn't get back to sleep and at eight the next morning was waiting outside the North Dakota Historical Society, which wouldn't open for another hour.

❧

I suspected that Weldon's portrait of Sitting Bull would be difficult to find, but the museum knew exactly where it was. A large, affable, bearded curator named Mark Halvorson went to a back room to get it. Then he stood it on a table, a full-length portrait of Sitting Bull, signed in red and black paint "C. S. Weldon 1890." Before I knew what I was doing, I reached out and touched the scar where the tribal policeman slashed it the day Sitting Bull was killed.

"It would make a great tobacco ad, don't you think?" Halvorson laughed. "Or the painting on a can of Calumet baking powder."

This seemed sacrilegious, but he was right. The painting measures thirty by twenty-three inches, on a Masonite board in a simple wood frame. Sitting Bull stands sideways in his double eagle-feather headdress, a fringed shirt and fringed pants, moccasins, a beaded sash and pouch. He holds a Winchester and looks blankly in the distance, his face featureless and wooden.

"It's a very European portrait," Halvorson went on. "It's got a typical sylvan backdrop. He could have been a burgher or poltroon in New York State, with a brace of grouse at his feet. And the forest in the background—the trees are all wrong. Birches don't grow in North Dakota." Weldon, he said, had painted the portrait based on a photograph taken in Montreal in 1885 by a man named William Notman.

She hadn't painted it from life? What about all that romantic heat I had imagined sizzling between them as Sitting Bull posed for her in his headdress on a steaming summer day? But the curator showed me a copy of Notman's photo, and the similarities were inescapable. I had noticed them myself—the photo was the illustration for a widely reproduced poster for Cody's Wild West Show ("Foes in '76, Friends in '85")—but I had dismissed the resemblance, thinking Sitting Bull would look pretty much the same in any portrait in which he posed in full regalia. Now, seeing the photo and the portrait side by side, I couldn't

22. Publicity photograph of Sitting Bull and Buffalo Bill Cody taken in Montreal in 1885. Courtesy of William Notman.

credit the coincidence. The only major difference was that Weldon had replaced Cody with a birch. And Sitting Bull's face was less wrinkled and expressive in her portrait than in the photo. He looked like a cartoon. Or a cigar-store statue.

It came to me that Weldon must have painted this portrait of Sitting Bull in Brooklyn, between her first trip to Standing Rock and her return the next spring. She passed the winter of 1889–90 painting her hero from a photo and dreaming of spring, when she could paint him from life. She had the portrait framed in Brooklyn; several descriptions indicate that when this portrait hung in Sitting Bull's cabin at Grand River, it was encased in an elaborate gilt frame, and she couldn't have found that sort of frame on the reservation. She brought this portrait from Brooklyn as a gift for Sitting Bull. But the other three portraits? Had she painted those from life?

I asked the curator what he thought of Weldon as an artist.

Oh, she was a very talented amateur, Halvorson said. She grew up in a time and place when middle-class young women learned to do needlepoint and play a musical instrument and paint. That was fortunate for us, he said. If she had been raised as a scullery maid, she wouldn't have acquired such talents.

I was disappointed not only by the artistic qualities of the painting but how accessible it was. The Historical Society had used the portrait to illustrate a 1984 exhibit called "The Last Years of Sitting Bull," and I was able to buy a copy at the gift shop. What startled me was that the Historical Society held the deed to another Weldon portrait. In 1984, the curators received a letter from a Mrs. J. R. Harmon, whose husband administered the estate of Lucille Van Solen, Louise's daughter. Mrs. Harmon had seen the poster for the exhibit and remembered a deed she had found among her husband's papers. "My husband died twenty years ago and I have no idea why the deed was in our file," she told the society.

Halvorson handed me the deed. It was dated "this Seventeenth day of February, A.D. 1912." So Weldon had been living in Brooklyn in 1912, under the name of Caroline. Maybe historians had failed to trace her whereabouts after she left Grand River because she had changed her name, not wanting to be associated with that *other* Weldon, Catherine, the one who lived with Sitting Bull.

"For and in consideration of the affectionate regard which I have for the grantee hereinafter named," Weldon wrote, "and in Consideration of One Dollar to me in hand paid, I, CAROLINE WELDON, of the Borough of Brooklyn, City and State of New York, hereby grant, convey and transfer unto Mary Louisa Van Solen, and her daughter Lucille Van Solen, the picture, Sitting Bull, painted by me, and now in possession of said Mary Louisa Van Solen, To have and To Hold the same upon the conditions as follows: To the said Mary

Louisa Van Solen, for and during the term of her natural life, and upon her death, to her daughter, the said Lucille Van Solen, with the instructions, that upon the death of the survivor of them, the same be left and given by such survivor to the North Dakota Historical Society forever. . . ." And then, in a neat hand, Caroline Weldon's signature, in the presence of a lawyer named Michael C. Gross, who attested that "before me personally came and appeared CAROLINE WELDON, to me known and known to me to be the same person described in and who executed the foregoing Deed of Conveyance. . . ."

In 1912, Louise Van Solen was seventy-three years old; she died in 1920. Her daughter Lucille died in 1929, at forty-eight. According to a sheaf of notes taken by Robert Hollow, a former curator of the Historical Society, the second Weldon portrait did briefly reside with the museum, on loan from the Van Solens in 1914. After Lucille's death, the painting vanished. "Whether the painting was later returned or whether it somehow mysteriously disappeared from our collection I have not been able to ascertain," Hollow replied to Mrs. Harmon. "A complete inventory of the collection was done between 1925 and 1930, and the Weldon portrait is not mentioned in this document. We have a list of items acquired from the Van Solen estate in 1929, but again the Weldon portrait is not mentioned. Stanley Vestal in his 1934 book *New Sources of Indian History* indicates that he believes the portrait to have been sold. I was completely surprised to discover that we appear to have a legitimate legal claim to it if it ever turns up!" Elsewhere, Hollow notes that when Lucille Van Solen's effects were auctioned, the Historical Society bought "buffalo robes and Indian relics" worth $100, but there was no record of the painting. His worst fear was that it perished in the capitol fire of 1929.

From his files, I could tell that Hollow had become as fascinated with Weldon as I was. Less comforting were letters from other writers following Weldon's trail. A man named John Baker wrote the superintendent of the Historical Society in 1977 to say that he was researching a biography of Weldon, who, he seemed to think, "was a redhead and an Easterner who favored flamboyant styles. She also had a hot temper and apparently was more spirited than political. No doubt her intervention caused Sitting Bull more harm than good." Baker's description seems based on nothing but the stereotype that women of temperamental natures always have red hair.

"I like the lady," he went on. "I believe that 'Woman Walking Ahead' deserves an honorable mention in History and would like to attempt to write about her. . . . Catherine was always mistily Romanticising 'the Indian' yet she'd never known people who had been on the receiving end of a War Party. She envisioned the Indian as a Clean spirit moving majestically across the land. It must have shocked her to see him dirty and smelling. No doubt her endless chatter fell on deaf ears and uncomprehending eyes of old Indians who wondered if she would ever shut up." Baker's affection and disdain seemed curiously entangled. On the one hand, he portrayed her as a chattering romantic; on the other, he expressed the sentiment that "Catherine would have missed Social evenings, walks in the Park, hot baths and picnics under the trees. She is a Mystery Woman, My 'Lady from Brooklyn,' and I hope you can help me pierce the mystery." His letter allowed me to see an aspect of Weldon's story I hadn't seen before: she bewildered most men because she was an attractive widow who didn't care about remarriage. Even at this remove, she caused men like John Baker to feel superior and spurned.

Other biographers seemed more serious. In 1987, a writer named Kenneth Brooks of Vashon, Washington, discovered the existence of the same Weldon painting I had seen listed at the Smithsonian. He got as far as asking the museum to forward a letter to the Colonial Dame who had directed the inventory of American paintings in Little Rock, but the Dame didn't write back. In a letter to the Historical Society, Brooks speculated that, given the slashed painting in the Historical Society's possession and the two paintings that Weldon claimed were stolen with her trunks after she left the reservation, the portrait in the Smithsonian's files might be the one deeded to the Van Solens. Maybe the current owners were averse to being associated with the once notorious Mrs. Weldon. Or they might not want to make known the existence of a painting not legally theirs. "[T]here were Harmon, Van Solen and Parkin heirs to the Zoe Lucille Van Solen estate, in 1929, not just in North Dakota, but in New York, Vermont and Minneapolis," Brooks informed the Historical Society. "With just a *little* unaccounted handling, the Van Solen portrait could easily have slipped away to one of those." Brooks noted that he had placed notices in several periodicals, requesting information about the painting, but no one had replied. He was $300 in the hole. Would the society perhaps care to defray his costs?

Brooks must have given up before he incurred the kinds of expenses I was incurring. I felt like an explorer who finds skeletons by the trail and is torn between the fear that she will end up beside them and relief that they didn't succeed in reaching the North Pole first. In the case of Bob Hollow, who died in middle age, I felt sad that he hadn't lived to complete his work and grateful that he had left clues for his successors. From an article he had clipped from the *Emmons County Record* of February 19, 1914, I learned that Louise Van Solen had indeed lent her portrait of Sitting Bull to the Historical Society for display. The reporter gave some background on the artist, who lived for some time

Fort Yates, *Geo. W. Scott,* Dakota.

23. Alma Parkin and her son Chaska, circa 1890. Courtesy of the State Historical Society of North Dakota, Scott 0192-37.

in a small house on the eastern side of the Cannonball, at the south side of its shore—a house that would have placed her *on* the reservation—where she painted the second portrait. "Mrs. Weldon was of Swiss birth," the reporter noted, a fact that I had never seen mentioned anywhere before.

Weldon, the reporter wrote, "had a high artistic temperment [*sic*] and with her admiration for the hero of another race she found it easy to portray in oil the respect and reverence she felt. The artist did not have any relation in this country and fearing that the portrait would fall into the hands of strangers who would not appreciate it she sent it to Mrs. Van Solen so that it would be out in this country where the friends of her hero lived." So Weldon deeded the portrait to the Van Solens because she had no relatives out west and never returned to live there. (Did she ever go back to Switzerland? Was that why no one knew what had happened to her after she left the reservation?) If nothing else, the article proved that the portrayal of Louise Van Solen as a bigoted, mean-spirited prude who hated Catherine Weldon was a figment of David Humphreys Miller's imagination.

Since I was trying to track down which of the Van Solen heirs might have taken Weldon's painting, I copied everything I could find about the family. Alma Parkin died in the late 1890s or early 1900s. She left the ranch to Louise, who made ends meet by continuing to teach at the Cannonball day school. After Louise died, her daughter Lucille attempted to keep the ranch going but eventually lost it and died of a broken heart. Henry Parkin's brother, Walter, was appointed Indian Trader at Fort Yates in 1889; he must have been in charge of the store when Weldon lived at Standing Rock. In 1893, he chaperoned a group of Sioux to the Chicago World's Fair, where they saw "Sitting Bull's death cabin," complete with Weldon's slashed portrait of the chief. Walter Parkin died in 1914. His widow and three of their children died soon after, leaving one daughter in Bismarck. The only other relatives of the Parkins and Van Solens were descendants of Lulu Harmon, who might have been related to the Harmon who wrote the letter to the Historical Society.

None of these people seemed real to me until I found their photos. The pictures are the sort every family would love to own, conveying as they do a sense of character and place. Few of the photos are dated, but there are hints from the subjects' ages, the locations of the studios, and the captions, neatly penned in Lucille Van Solen's hand. In my favorite portrait, Louise Van Solen sits at the bottom of the photo, bespectacled and jowly as Queen Victoria, in a flat, broad-brimmed hat. "Miss Agnes Fridette" poses above Louise in identical spectacles and hat. A younger woman, the wife of the schoolteacher, John Carignan, stands above Fridette in a slightly less ostentatious hat. And above Carignan rises Lucille

24. Louise Van Solen and her daughter Lucille, 1890. Courtesy of the State Historical Society of North Dakota, Scott 0192-30.

25. From top to bottom: Lucille Van Solen, Mrs. Jack M. Carignan, Agnes Fridette, and Louise Van Solen. Courtesy of the State Historical Society of North Dakota, Fiske 1680.

26. Military band playing at the Parkin Ranch for Chaska Parkin's seventh birthday party, August 15, 1889. Courtesy of the State Historical Society of North Dakota, Fiske 7632.

Van Solen, with a wide, unsmiling face and the largest hat of all. They appear to be the very backbone of midwestern womanhood, the flat, broad-brimmed hats so many disks in a spine, all this fortitude built on the back of Eagle Woman, whom we can imagine at the bottom, beneath Louise.

The next photo that caught my eye is labeled "Military band from Fort Yates at the Cannon Ball Ranch Aug. 15, 1889 on Celebration of (C. L.) Chaske Parkin's Birthday—7 years old," which means that it was taken six weeks after Weldon argued with McLaughlin and was driven to the ferry by Sitting Bull and one year before Christie came to stay on the ranch. A military band plays music while observers stand beneath an arbor. Six children fill out the shot: an older girl, her back to the camera; a younger girl on the ground, turning to glance at the photographer—according to the caption, this child is Lucille; an indifferent boy in knickers playing in the dirt; and two younger boys, one of whom must be Chaska. Far from being a dreary outpost, the ranch could offer Christie other boys his age to play with, picket fences, shade, a party that any child would be happy to attend. There was even a pond to swim in. One photo shows Louise Van Solen and Alma Parkin sitting in the Cannonball River fully clothed: "The Last Frogs in the Pond," the caption reads, in Lucille Van Solen's hand.

Lucille was the photographers' darling. Here she is at nine, a clear-faced, thoughtful child leaning against her mother in a studio at the fort in 1890, and there, a year later, an impish girl of ten tugging on the sashes of an oversized bonnet, and there, all grown up, in the bead-and-bone regalia of a full-blooded Sioux, hair parted and braided, moccasins on her feet—she looks the prettiest in that picture, her broad-cheeked face at ease, although she looks happiest while riding her ponies at the ranch, in a long, simple skirt, a blouse, and a tall straw hat.

After all the photos of Lucille, I flipped to the bottom and saw a picture that made my heart thump. It was Weldon. I was sure of it.

The setting was the ranch; I recognized the fence. Three women are trying to fit in a wagon built for two. "Lucile Van Solen and Alma J Parkins," the caption reads. But who was the third woman, perched awkwardly above the older woman's lap? It's hard to tell her age. Early thirties? Late forties? Older? If this indeed is Weldon, the actress I would cast to play her in a movie would be Sally

27.   Alma Parkin (left, back to camera) and Louise Van Solen, bathing in the Cannonball River. Photo captioned "The Last Frogs in the Pond" in Lucille Van Solen's hand. Courtesy of the State Historical Society of North Dakota, 0192-16.

Field or Patty Duke, someone who had kept the pudgy face of youth into middle age. The woman in the photo is wide cheeked, with an overly large nose, smiling a smile that might be called free spirited, unless it's the half-collapsed smile of a woman in need of dentures, or the smile of a mental defective. The photo is cropped in such a way that the top of her head is missing, but she wears a frilly bonnet tied beneath her chin. Her gloves seem to be made of black mesh; she folds her hands demurely on her knees, beside a whip that rises from a holder beside the buckboard. The most striking feature of the photo is the woman's shawl. The satiny material is trimmed with a yoke of lace around the shoulders and long frills of lace around the sleeves. It flows luxuriously in folds that nearly reach her feet, covering her heavy skirt. This is a shawl that surely would have earned its owner the label "overdressed."

The older woman, on whose lap the mystery woman appears to sit, regards her with disapproval. But the younger woman, who holds the reins, smiles in bemusement and admiration. This younger woman wears a heavy, ungainly cloth coat and a visored cap. In 1890, when Weldon visited the ranch, Alma Parkin would have been thirty-four years old, which seems to be this woman's age. But I couldn't figure out who the older woman might be. Lucille Van Solen was born in 1881, so she would have been nine that year. If the caption is correct, then the *younger* woman has to be Lucille, the older woman must be Alma, and the date of the photo must be much later than 1890, which means that the unlabeled woman couldn't possibly be Weldon.

I started flipping back through the pile of photos, comparing faces and names, trying to guess who was who. I got more and more confused. None of it made sense. Could the photo be mislabeled? It wasn't captioned in the same hand as the others. "Lucile" and "Parkins" were misspelled. I didn't trust the information. Maybe the younger woman was Alma Parkin and the older woman was *Louise* Van Solen, not her daughter Lucille. Louise would have been about fifty the year Weldon lived on the ranch. It made more sense for the sisters to be riding on the ranch than for Lucille and her aunt to be there.

Unfortunately, this theory had to be questioned when I was informed by the photo archivist that Frank Fiske, who took the picture of the three women in the carriage, didn't begin his work around Standing Rock and Fort Yates until 1900, ten years after Weldon's last known visit to the Parkin Ranch. Could she possibly have returned? If Fiske took the picture in 1900 or 1910, the caption might be right; the younger woman might well be Lucille and the older woman Alma. Then again, at least a few of the photos in the Fiske collection are dated *before* 1890; witness the photo of Chaska Parkin's party in 1889. Perhaps, in some cases, Fiske merely preserved other people's photos rather than snapping them himself.

28. Lucille Van Solen beside a pony on the Parkin Ranch. Courtesy of the State Historical Society of North Dakota, Fiske 2654.

I couldn't prove that the third woman was Catherine Weldon, so why was I so sure? Because she was overdressed? Because she was smiling the slightly demented smile I imagined Weldon would be smiling, squeezing in where there was no room for her, making a spectacle of herself? Because it was impossible to read and dream about a person for a decade without knowing her when you saw her? Maybe I was only doing what David Humphreys Miller had done—wishing an unidentified woman to be who and what I wanted her to be. But without evidence to the contrary, I was determined to keep believing that I had found a photo of Catherine Weldon.

Bob Hollow wouldn't have approved. For each item that reputedly belonged to Sitting Bull, Hollow arduously searched for documentation. (If all the relics purporting to be Sitting Bull's were genuine, Hollow once joked, there would be enough relics in circulation to rearm and reclothe the entire Sioux nation.) For several items, Hollow relied on testimony from McLaughlin, who might have been responsible for Sitting Bull's death but was a painstakingly honest man. The authenticity of Weldon's portrait of Sitting Bull was vouched for in a letter by Matthew Forney Steele, who described to his mother his participation in the attack on Sitting Bull's camp:

I have two relics of the day, which I wouldn't part with for a good deal. One is Sitting Bull's beadwork tobacco-bag and the other is a most excellently painted portrait of that old devil, painted and presented to him by his great admirer Mrs. Weldon of Brooklyn. I keep the latter rather quiet for fear that old crank may try to get it away from me. She can't have it, tho by a law suit. It represents old Bull standing in the woods with full war costume on holding a Winchester rifle ready to take aim. It is a most artistic picture. Every feather & bead and every little detail is perfect, the likeness is life-like. It, however, has a great rent in it. This hurts it as a work of art, but rather enhances it as a relic. This picture hung in old Bull's house and was the pride of his vanity. It was set in a deep gold frame. The way I came by it was this: after the thing was all over, I saw one of the policemen with it in his hand. He had smashed the frame to pieces and tore this rent in the canvas with the butt of his carbine. He was just about to finish the picture when I spied him and

29.   Lucille Van Solen, left, in heavy coat and cap, with her aunt Alma Parkin, partially obscured, and an unidentified third woman, in shawl, in a carriage on the Parkin Ranch. Courtesy of the State Historical Society of North Dakota, Fiske 3798.

asked him to let me have it. The way I got the tobacco pouch was thus: After we drove the hostiles away, Red-Tomahawk (the policeman who shot old Bull at the same instant Bull Head shot him) came out of the house bearing a white flat on a pole. He came up the hill to meet us. My troop (F) was in the advanced part of the skirmish line & I was with the left of it. Red Tomahawk came up to me. He had this pouch in one hand & gave it to me, telling me that he took it away from Sitting Bull.

Maybe Steele atoned for appropriating Sitting Bull's belongings by donating them to the Historical Society. And he did say nice things about Weldon's talents. But I found it hard to forgive him for calling her a crank. Before I found this letter, I had supposed Steele saved the painting out of respect for Sitting Bull. But even with the chief bleeding in the yard, Steele was calculating the painting's worth as a relic. The policeman who slashed the portrait acted out of hate. Steele was thinking in terms of lawsuits before the chief was cold.

Intrigued by Hollow's notes, I took a tour of the museum. Most of the items made Sitting Bull seem more human. Here was a child's dress with intricate quill embroidery that One Bull had identified as belonging to Sitting Bull's daughter, Stands Holy, or to Crow Foot. I saw an embroidered bag that hung from the chief's saddle when he galloped off to war and a tobacco pouch that belonged to Hohecikana. Other objects made Sitting Bull seem *less* human—the telegram in which the War Department granted him permission to travel in the charge of Bill Cody; the 1890 census, in which McLaughlin listed every Indian on the reservation, including No. 1169, Indian Name: *Tatankaiyotake*; English Name: Sitting Bull; Sex: M; Relation: father; Age: 58; and the order for his arrest, in which the agent stated his belief that Sitting Bull could be brought in by the Indian Police "without much risk," although McLaughlin affixed a PS that Lieutenant Bull Head "must not let him escape under any circumstances."

What made Sitting Bull most real of all were the gifts he gave and got: a buffalo robe he painted for the trader who taught him to write his name, a pipe he gave to the proprietor of the hotel where he was entertained in Bismarck, a buffalo-horn spoon carved with SITTING BULL, given to Lulu Harmon in return for having served as Sitting Bull's interpreter, and an autographed pipe he gave the Harmons when he and five warriors unexpectedly stopped at their ranch in Montana, on their way to make peace with their old enemies, the Crows. I saw a drum presented to Sitting Bull by Bill Cody and a monstrosity of an inkwell, hodgepodged from stones collected at various historic spots around the West, with a thermometer cemented in the middle, given to Sitting Bull while he was traveling with Cody's show. To many Native people, a gift only carries force if it is passed along to others. Hoarded, it becomes wealth and brings its owner bad luck. On display in a museum, a gift can still be seen—not passed along in space, but passed along in time. Weldon sent her portrait to North Dakota so Sitting Bull could be seen by those who knew him. It didn't belong in Little Rock in some aristocrat's safe. The curators at the Historical Society in North Dakota were angry that the Smithsonian, a government institution, refused to divulge the "owner" of a portrait to which they had the deed. I promised the museum's curators that I would eventually go to Little Rock, learn who owned the portrait, and try to bring it back.

Meanwhile I settled in for two days. One of the librarians brought me a book that provided a census of the earliest residents of the Cannonball; it listed a "Mrs. C. Weldon" as living in Cannonball in 1888, a full year earlier than her first recorded visit, verifying her account that in 1889 she was visiting mixed-race friends from an earlier trip.

"And look at this," the librarian whispered. The article she showed me— "Was Mrs. Weldon Sitting Bull's White Squaw?"—was the one published by Handleman. Most of his story was cribbed from Miller. But Handleman portrayed his Weldon as a hero. Her counsel, had Sitting Bull heeded it, would have allowed him to live to a riper age than fifty-six. Unremembered in her native Brooklyn, Handleman wrote, Weldon is nonetheless "an honored and forever living tradition among the memorable chieftain's tribe of the Sioux—the Hunkpapas." In a time when few white people showed the principle to speak out against the mistreatment of the Indian, Weldon became a "genuine friend of a vanquished people." This woman from a comfortable eastern home "had all the personal integrity and dedicated courage of a pioneer woman who saw something wrong and went out hell-bent to correct it. Catherine Weldon might be compared to Esther McQuigg Morris, who was responsible for Wyoming becoming the first American commonwealth to adopt woman suffrage; to Bethenia Owens Adair, who had the guts to set up practice as the West's first woman doctor; or to that other champion of the Indian, Helen Hunt Jackson, whose stinging book, *Century of Dishonor*, had so influenced Catherine's thinking about aboriginal Americans."

Never mind that Jackson was aligned with the IRA, and, for all we know, Weldon never read her book. I was glad to see Weldon get credit for being more than a crank. She wasn't in love with Sitting Bull, Handleman wrote, "not in 'love' with him as we understand the word. Much more she loved his people and respected him as their heroic symbol. . . ." Nor was she a bad mother. Soon after Christie came West, "he was learning happily from Indian urchins how to carve arrows and fork ponies. . . . Young Christie began looking on the feared chief of the Hunkpapa Sioux as a second father. And Sitting Bull, who had once routed white warriors, liked batting balls with this appealing little white boy."

What disturbed me was that Handleman felt the need to demonize the other women in Weldon's story. Like Miller, Handleman characterizes Alma Parkin and Louise Van Solen as Weldon's abusive adversaries. "Those two pious souls would not offer a harassed woman and her frail little boy shelter under their roof. But they grudgingly let her have the use of a vacant empty soddy a mile or so from their house. . . ." In a spin-off from Vestal's conjectures, Handleman surmises that McLaughlin's wife "began a feud against Catherine Weldon for her fine clothes and distinguished manners. Mary McLaughlin already felt humiliated enough for being a half-breed girl born in a wigwam. In addition she had a grievous grudge against Sitting Bull" because he had supposedly refused to go to England with Bill Cody's circus and so denied her the chance to meet the queen. Such an achievement would have forced "the snobbish wives" of the officers "to invite her to their teas and stork showers. . . . Mary had many mouthfuls to spill after Catherine went off to live at Sitting Bull's encampment on Grand River to start the picture."

For all this foolishness, one of Handleman's hypotheses struck me as true. Had Weldon been a lesser person, she might have "turned up a pretty penny lecturing on her life among the Sioux or doing illustrations for lurid dime novels portraying all Indians as born homicidal maniacs. Many a false white 'Friend' of the red men perpetuated just such outrages." She was as destitute as Fanny Kelly, but Weldon refused to play the role of a writer who "specialized" in Indians.

Unlike Weldon, James McLaughlin wrote voluminously about the Sioux—in his autobiography, *My Friend the Indian*, and in thirty thousand pages of correspondence, most of it on film at the Historical Society. (So neat and appealing are McLaughlin's handwritten letters, they are easier to read than the typewritten correspondence of more up-to-date agents.) McLaughlin also was blessed with a sympathetic biographer, a monk named Louis Pfaller, who took the agent at his word that his fifty-two years of association with the Indian had transformed him into *The Man with an Indian Heart*. Pfaller recognizes that modern civil-rights groups might look upon McLaughlin's career "as one of the greatest swindles in that he used his persuasive skills to lure the Indians into giving up their native ways and trying to make them into 'white men.'" But he defends the agent as believing that the old Indian style of life could not survive and he must do everything he could to help the Indians adjust to a new way.

James McLaughlin was born in Ontario in 1842, the seventh of ten children. He attended school through eighth grade, served as a blacksmith's apprentice, then worked odd jobs outside St. Paul, where he met and fell in love with Marie. They had two daughters who died as babies and a son, Harry, who lived. With blacksmithing too light to support a family, McLaughlin traveled around the West peddling tools and watches. When a second child was born, he applied for a job at the new agency at Devils Lake, a mistranslation of the Lakota name for Spirit Lake but an accurate description of the way white homesteaders like Rachel Calof felt about the place, with its salty lake and marshes, the vicious winters and scorching summer heat. McLaughlin supported his family by working as the official agency blacksmith and unofficial overseer of everything else. He built a school and staffed it with nuns from Montreal. He set up a sawmill and taught the Indians to build log houses, tables, chairs, and beds. The commander of the agency asked Washington to raise McLaughlin's monthly salary from $60 to $75, but this still didn't go far, considering that Marie had given birth to three more children.

When the agent in charge of Devils Lake died, McLaughlin wrote to the bishop of Northern Minnesota, asking for the post. "I have the advantage of being born & raised a Catholic. . . . Accordingly, if ever agent, I will do my best to abolish poligamy [sic] and eradicate from my agency all kinds of Superstitions there existing, viz., *medicine dances or feasts, Sundances, &c. . . .*" The bishop supported McLaughlin. But the commissioner gave in to pressures to appoint a "greenhorn Hoosier politician" the Indians couldn't bear. McLaughlin maneuvered to have his boss fired. The agent maneuvered to have McLaughlin fired. McLaughlin won.

Most agents were political hacks who stole from their charges. But McLaughlin saw it as his duty to "try to prove by our acts that there are some honest Agents." At one point, he got so angry at Congress for reducing the agents' salaries that he applied for a job as trader. But his services were requested at the wild new agency at Standing Rock, and he agreed to take the post. After ten years at Devils Lake, he and Marie and their five children took the steamboat to Fort Yates.

The fort, named for one of Custer's dead officers, was an orderly arrangement of barracks, warehouses, and stables and a huge parade-ground with a flagpole at the center, gas lights on poles, and spindly trees. The steamboat landing lay at the foot of a steep embankment beneath the fort. As McLaughlin stepped ashore, he found Sitting Bull and the last two hundred of his followers camped above the river. They had been there for a month and hoped to remain. Instead they were forced onto the *Sherman* and taken to Fort Randall.

In the chief's absence, McLaughlin did his best to convince the six thousand Indians under his supervision that they must become farmers. "I occupy the same relation toward you that a father does toward his children, and as the first thing that is necessary on the part of children is obedience, so I look to you to willingly obey me and listen to the commands of the government without demur. . . . I appeal to you, great chiefs, to bury the hatchet forever and learn what happiness you may have with your children by tilling the soil. May yon hills be covered with corn and vines, and may the smoke of your cabins arise amidst peace and plenty. Each individual must do his part. If the whole Sioux nation joins hands they can be as comfortable and as wealthy as the whites. . . ."

We don't want to farm, they said. Why won't you let us continue hunting buffalo?

McLaughlin told them that the few buffalo left would soon be extinct and they should prepare now by farming. To gain their favor, or speed that extinction, or divert them from his decree that the Sun Dance be abolished, he allowed the Indians to go off on a buffalo hunt. In fact, he went with them. The Sioux slaughtered five thousand buffalo—McLaughlin killed one himself—and two thousand more on a second hunt that fall.

The Indians couldn't keep hunting buffalo. But the Sioux—and the tribal lands they held in common—were better suited to raising cows than farming. The Indians, with their love of horses, could have become the ultimate cowboys, running communal herds of beef and living in the old way. Even McLaughlin saw the merits in such a scheme. His objection was that it might succeed too well. A pastoral life on the Plains would be "but a small remove from the hunting life of the wild Indian and it will perpetuate that nomadic spirit and love of roaming without any of the comforts of a fixed abode, which an agricultural life (for an Indian) alone affords." Farming, McLaughlin claimed, would bring the Indian under "powerful civilizing influences, 1st by identifying himself as an individual, 2nd a personal responsibility, 3rd a separation from Band affiliations and, lastly, a cultivated field, with house, barn and domestic cares which a permanent home can alone give."

Year by year, McLaughlin cajoled "his" Indians into following the path he laid out. During his tenure, nearly all the Indians at Standing Rock moved from tipis into cabins. He visited each of the 1,180 families on the reservation, even the families that lived farthest from the agency. When he started, a hundred of Standing Rock's 763 children were enrolled in the reservation's two schools; by the time he left, six hundred children were attending nine schools. He convinced the army to prohibit soldiers from visiting the Indian camps in search of women. To let the Indians continue their tradition of policing themselves, he created the tribal police and a Court of Indian Offenses.

But the "achievement" in which he took the most pride was eradicating the Indians' dances. "When I first assumed charge of this Agency," he wrote, "the 'Sun Dance,' 'War Dance,' 'Scalp Dance,' 'Kiss Dance,' 'Buffalo Dance,' 'Horse Dance,' and 'Grass Dance' were all in vogue and the 'tom-tom' orchestra could always be heard in some of the camps, no regard being paid to Sunday. . . . I at once commenced breaking up these pagan practices and gradually prohibited one after another, leaving only the 'Grass Dance,' which I granted them the privilege of continuing, on Saturdays only, after eliminating all the more objectionable features connected with it," namely, the giving away of property, which the agent couldn't abide. He wasn't a hypocrite. He advocated assimilation for the Sioux, and he married one himself. He was born poor and worked and saved his way up, and he wanted the Indians to do the same. His real failing was his arrogance. You can see it from the cover of Pfaller's book. The agent's hair and whiskers have gone gray, giving him an air of benevolence he didn't have in his youth. But there's still that insufferable smugness.

McLaughlin wasn't predisposed to dislike Sitting Bull. Had the chief cooperated, Pfaller says, "McLaughlin would have praised him to the skies, as he did the other members of the Sitting Bull band, such as Gall, Crow King and Crawler. . . ." Nor was he inventing charges when he called Sitting Bull "wily." What he meant was that Sitting Bull pursued his program of keeping his people from assimilating even when he made a show of obedience. In 1886, Sitting Bull petitioned to be allowed to visit the Crow Indians in Montana, ostensibly to close the wounds of animosity between the tribes. He had been behaving peacefully, and McLaughlin let him go. Imagine how betrayed the agent felt when Sitting Bull used his trip to convince the Crows that they were foolish to agree to break up their reservation into farms. Weldon's attempt to take Sitting Bull to the lower agencies to defeat a similar scheme fit the chief's own aims. Her support for Sitting Bull's shenanigans enraged McLaughlin. Bad enough that Sitting Bull should resist his own power being broken. McLaughlin hardly needed his plans for the Indians' welfare to be thwarted by a scatterbrained female artist from New York.

Even after Sitting Bull and Weldon gave up their resistance to his policies and retired to Grand River, McLaughlin refused to credit her motives. Among McLaughlin's letters I found a request from Weldon, at the Cannonball, asking permission to teach at the day school at Grand River or open her own school and teach domestic science to the women. On July 11, 1890, McLaughlin wrote back:

"Madam—

"Replying to your letter of the 5th, I have to say that there is no vacancy now existing in our Grand River Schools, and I do not deem it necessary to establish an Industrial School in that neighborhood at the present time.

"The Fort Totten and Pierre Indian Training Schools together with the recent addition to agency Boarding schools afford ample facilities for all Indian Children of this reservation."

The assertion that he saw no need for a white appointee to teach domestic economy was insincere. Official government policy prescribed the assignment of white women to reservations as "field matrons," whose duty was to indoctrinate Indian daughters and wives into a proper, civilized division of labor between the sexes and provide them with models for middle-class white domesticity. Although Victorian women were considered by most men—and often by themselves—as unfit to engage in strenuous thought or work, these same women were deemed ideal in carrying the values of democracy and domesticity to savage men. Not long after Weldon's request, McLaughlin created the post of Matron of Domestic Economy for a Mrs. Lucy Arnold, who spent her time visiting Indian women at Standing Rock to teach them how to sew, decorate their homes, care for the sick, plant flowers, and raise pigs to eat instead of dogs. McLaughlin apparently judged Weldon an unsuitable role model for Lakota women. He didn't want her around Sitting Bull in any capacity, not even to teach the Hunkpapa girls to sew.

Not satisfied, Weldon wrote the Commissioner of Indian Affairs, Thomas Morgan, making it clear that the demand for her services was the Indians' own. This remarkable letter, which Weldon wrote from the Cannonball on August 7, 1890, let me see her handwriting for the first time; it was calmer and more orderly than I had predicted, the only affectation an excessively long cross to each *T*.

"Allow me to call your attention to a request of the Dakota Chief Sitting Bull and his people," Weldon wrote.

"They deem it necessary that a school be established on the Grand River, especially to instruct women and girls to live and clothe themselves, like white people. They have asked me to live among them, and I have expressed my willingness, provided I can get permission to do so. I hoped that I could secure a position as teacher in a day-school, and then intended to have sewing-classes after school-hours, two or three times a week. I am familiar with the mode of teaching in the Indian Schools as I have taught the children at Mrs. Van Solen's school, during her illness.

"Most Indians have a taste for Art, and all artistic work, done either by the brush or needle; and I think that they could easily be instructed in such work, and then be more capable of supporting themselves. There is no reason why they should not be able to do this, as well as the white people; they are by nature

30. Louise Van Solen with her students outside her day school between Fort Yates and the Cannonball River. Catherine Weldon substituted for Van Solen when the latter was ill. Courtesy of the State Historical Society of North Dakota, Fiske 5239.

fully qualified, and thoroughly appreciate what is beautiful and good; but what the women and girls need most at the present time is the knowledge of making and repairing their clothing; and other useful household duties. Sitting Bull is anxious to have his people improve and become civilized, notwithstanding what may have been published and spoken of him. He feels friendly to the white people; and he loves all the Dakotas, as he does the members of his own family; and all his thoughts and wishes are for their welfare. He sees the success of the white people and he knows that the Indians must follow in their footsteps or perish; and he wishes his people to become civilized as soon as possible; He has begged me repeatedly to come and live among them.

"I love the Indians, and I would like to help them even if I must make sacrifices. Sitting Bull requested me to write to Agent McLaughlin and apply to him for an appointment as teacher. I have done so; Maj. McLaughlin answered that there was no vacancy now existing in the Grand River Schools & that he did not think it necessary to establish an Industrial School there at the present time. The Indians were disappointed and begged me to write to Dr. Bland, Sitting Bull dictating the letter, and Dr. Bland advised me to write to you. I think that the Indians would be willing to put up a log-house for me, as they had logs cut for that purpose last year. If the Gov't would allow me rations for myself and my son, aged fourteen, and fuel, I would try to furnish the rest; although I can ill afford to do so.

"Hoping that you will kindly consider this subject, I am Very Respectfully, Mrs. C. Weldon, Cannon Ball, North Dakota."

If Weldon took Van Solen's place as a substitute teacher at her school, they must have been friends, with Van Solen holding Weldon in high enough esteem that she let her teach the class. Her desire to teach seems genuine, not to mention that teaching was the only way she could support Christie and herself while living among the Sioux. Most interesting of all is her claim that the Indians have an affinity for beauty and might support themselves by selling their handicrafts. Although a similar trade had already been established in the American Southwest, proposing that the warriors who killed Custer might sell beautiful objects to the whites who, until recently, had tried to destroy them reveals extraordinary foresight. Her avowal that she was helping the Sioux from love might ring sentimental to our ears. But this was a widow without an income offering to live among the Indians, eat the rations they ate, teach them to cook and sew.

That she let everyone know she was martyring herself doesn't make her generosity less real. In the language of the day, she is assuring the commissioner that she isn't one of those inebriated illiterates who often applied to teach at reservation schools. It wasn't, as John Baker claimed in his letter to the Historical Society, that Weldon was disillusioned to find Sitting Bull "dirty and smelling." She had spent months living close enough to know exactly how he smelled. She chose to settle at the most remote camp of the one Indian who was trying to preserve the old ways. That wasn't an accident. She didn't love the race blindly. Some Indians she liked; one senses a special affection for Hohecikana. And some Indians she didn't like—Kicking Bear, for one. It is hard to come up with another white person who did what Weldon did for love of specific Indians rather than a love of Christ. What propelled her to help Sitting Bull was an aesthetic response. She perceived the Indians' lives as beautiful and was repulsed by the prospect of seeing that beauty ruined.

On July 23, 1890, Weldon sent Bland a letter dictated by Sitting Bull at the Parkin Ranch, asking Bland to use his influence with the commissioner to pressure McLaughlin to accede to Weldon's wish to open a school among his people. Bland wrote the letter, although his penmanship is so atrocious and his grammar so slipshod I found it hard to believe that he took her case seriously. He couldn't have written letters as careless as this on a regular basis or he would have been laughed out of Washington. Some of the roughness of the language mimics Sitting Bull's. ("He says, 'The agent McGloughlin, says this is not necessary, hurt me. Indians find that we need a school here, and we want Mrs. Weldon for teacher. She is our friend and if the President would let her come and teach our children it would make our hearts glad.'") But much of the confusing language is Bland's. ("Such a woman as Mrs. W. who has the confidence of the Indians, and who desires to teach not for money, but for their good for I learn that she does not look for pay for her services, can do more toward lifting them toward civilization and self-support than hireling teachers of the [unreadable].") The commissioner probably couldn't be bothered to decipher Bland's scrawl. He regarded Bland as a crackpot even before he got the letter. And he didn't want to overrule an agent. In any event, Morgan declined to intervene.

Bland wrote again. "Sitting Bull desires me to ask you if any order has gave to Agt. McGloflin which contains a threat of any sort, directed at Indians who decline to have their lands surveyed and set off to them, &c. He desires also to know if rations will be continued to those who take up claims and if so, how long." The commissioner passed the letter to McLaughlin, who answered that no such threats had been issued. The letter had little effect other than worsening relations between Weldon and the agent.

Even the simplest request created tension. Weldon wrote to McLaughlin in August to ask permission for herself, Alma, and Louise to take an Indian woman named "Kate" on an outing to Mandan. (This letter confirmed my suspicion that Alma and Louise were more likely to be going on a journey than Alma and Lucille; maybe the photo of the three women in the wagon was made the day they all drove up to Mandan on a shopping trip, although Kate would have had to stand the entire way.) McLaughlin wrote back to say that he offered no objection, but the letter is so terse and artificially polite it sounds more like a rejection.

Weldon's presence on the ranch must have created strains between the agent and the Parkins, but the Parkins and Van Solens had been the agent's friends for a long time before Weldon showed up. In 1886, at Louise's request, McLaughlin wrote to a marble works in St. Paul to order a set of gravestones for her son, Eddy, who had died the previous year. The descendants of Eagle Woman would have taken as their mission to act as mediators between Indians and whites rather than as advocates of either view. Whatever friction Weldon caused, the friendship lasted. When McLaughlin was promoted to inspector in the Indian Bureau in 1895, five years after Weldon left the reservation and Sitting

Bull was killed, the Parkins held a reception in his honor. As the *Bismarck Tribune* described it, the approach to the main building was lit with Chinese lanterns "so ingeniously arranged as to form the letters M.L., whilst a large limelight shed its halo over a radius of several hundred feet." Mrs. Parkin and Mrs. Van Solen served a midnight supper, with tables groaning under the weight of the "luscious viands" they'd prepared. At evening's end, the sisters presented the Major with a gold-headed cane they hoped would symbolize the strengthening of their friendship.

The promotion was double-edged. The McLaughlins didn't want to move to Washington, but they had five children to educate. They had sent all five children to the local mission schools, but those schools stopped at junior high. Harry and Imelda went on to Catholic boarding schools in Minnesota, an impossible burden on an agent's salary. James McLaughlin was a shrewd man—he invested in land around Devils Lake and Bismarck and built a ranch not far from Yates—but his financial worries ended only with his promotion. Imelda was married by then, and the boys were raising cattle at the ranch (a photo shows four handsome young men with identical handlebar mustaches and dark hair parted in wings to expose their large ears). Mrs. McLaughlin preferred to stay home near her children rather than live alone in Washington while her husband traveled on business.

Like Sitting Bull, the McLaughlins knew what it was to lose a child. Imelda died four years after her father's promotion. Their third son, John, was given to hard drinking and squandering his money. His father wrote a letter advising him to mend his ways, but a few months later, John fell from a horse and died. Harry, the eldest child, died in 1913. Charley and Sibley, the surviving sons, remained on the reservation. Charley was popular enough to win the post of Sioux county sheriff, but he sold some of his father's property, giving up land like an Indian who didn't understand its worth, or so his father thought. Some property McLaughlin had bought in South Dakota turned out to be worth a lot of money to the railroad, which named the town in his honor. Mrs. McLaughlin and Sibley moved there, and the three McLaughlin children were reburied in the family plot. The Major increased his fame by publishing his autobiography. He worked as an inspector until his death at eighty-one and was buried in the town that bore his name. The guard of honor was composed of eleven tribal policemen who had survived the fight at Sitting Bull's camp.

When I left the Historical Society late that afternoon, having browsed my way through thirty-seven rolls of McLaughlin's correspondence, the temperature was still ninety-six degrees. I drove to the river and ate dinner on the dock beside the paddleboat depot, watching some sleek creature—a beaver? a muskrat?—swim along the bank. Then I boarded the *Lewis & Clark* for a scenic cruise along the Missouri.

The explorers for whom the paddleboat is named spent the winter of 1804–5 among the Mandan Indians not far from where I had eaten dinner. Seventy years later, the Northern Pacific Railroad reached Bismarck from the east. Advances in technology finally allowed steamboats to navigate the shallow Missouri this far north. The Grant Marsh Bridge, which carries the highway across the river, is named for the pilot who brought the news of Custer's defeat from the Little Bighorn and the first boatload of survivors. Marsh traveled the nine hundred miles from the Little Big Horn to Bismarck in a record fifty-four hours. Then he went back for more wounded. In 1883, he piloted the boat that brought Sitting Bull from Fort Randall back to Standing Rock. This wasn't a coincidence. Few men gained the expertise to keep a boat afloat on this treacherous river.

The history of steamboating on the upper Missouri is known more for all the boats that got stuck on sandbars and the boilers that exploded than the successes of pilots like **Marsh**. "A channel today might be a sandbar tomorrow morning," chimed the recorded narration on the *Lewis & Clark*. "The average depth of the Missouri is seven feet. The current is four miles per hour—too strong for many swimmers. The cottonwoods along the shore are two centuries old." Which meant that these same trees had been standing here when Lewis and Clark camped among the Mandan, and when Sitting Bull was a boy.

The other passengers on the paddleboat were celebrating a family reunion. The man in charge of the group spoke louder than the guide. "Up ahead on the left you'll see really fancy houses," he announced. Trees had been cleared, and enormous houses were going up, most with docks and boats. The recent floods had created moats, and the houses sat atop their islands like castles. We spent half an hour traveling down the river, then an hour going back, fighting against the current. Two kids on Jet Skis chased across our wake, playing chicken with each other. They seemed so young and irresponsible, I wanted to ask a woman with a cell phone to call the cops.

She slipped the phone inside her purse. "Who owns those houses, anyway?" she asked.

"Doctors, mostly," the man said. "Lawyers, too, I guess. And Indian chiefs."

Everyone laughed. "North Dakota is a happy place," the recorded guide assured us. "The state dance is the square dance. The state drink is milk. The state bird is the meadowlark"—the bird that warned Sitting Bull that his own people would kill him. I looked back to watch the boys. I heard their Jet Skis but couldn't see them. A train blew its whistle and crossed the bridge, silhouetted against a bruised and brooding sky.

~~~

By the end of three days in Bismarck, I felt the self-conscious isolation that comes to anyone who isn't a light-complected blond Christian in a city where most people are. My last morning at the Days Inn, I took my coffee to a table and was joined by two couples who held hands and said grace over their cornflakes. Looking up, one of the men asked if I was saved. Well, I said, I'm Jewish; I don't think in those terms. Jewish? the man repeated. He had never met a Jew and didn't know what to say. Finally he broke the silence by asking what brought me to Bismarck. I mumbled some reply about writing a book about a woman who had lived among the Sioux.

Indians! the man said. He knew about Indians. His mission was to minister to the Indians in Canadian prisons. He used to remodel homes. Then he had a vision of what God intended him to do. "I used to rebuild houses, now I rebuild lives!" His companions nodded and crunched their cereal. They had traveled from Saskatchewan to a religious conference in Tennessee, and now they were headed back. "Indians!" the man repeated. "You probably haven't had as much contact with Indians as me. It's easy to, you know, entertain romantic notions about them. But not if you've known as many Indians as I do. Ten percent of Canada's population is Indians, and ten percent of those ten percent are in jail. All they do is sit around and bitch and moan about having their land taken away, what's been done to them by the government. They're living in the past! All that stuff happened a hundred years ago. It's time to move on. It's time they started to live in the modern world. When I preach in the prison chapel, they don't like to hear what I'm telling them. They yell out and interrupt, and I tell them right from the pulpit to shut up and listen to what I'm telling them. After I'm done, I'll give them a chance to speak." The man's wife looked anxious, as if I might start a fight. "I know my view is not a very popular one," the man admitted, "but you can't convince me that it's wrong."

I checked out and drove to the grocery store in Mandan. The air-conditioning was heavenly, but I had to consider what provisions would last for five days in this heat. I bought a cantaloupe, smoked cheese, breakfast foods, and pasta I could cook on my little one-burner stove. I bought fresh carrots in a bag, lima beans, and peas. And cans of diet Coke; I would hide these in the truck and open them only if the dancers couldn't hear. I filled two big jugs with water—for drinking, not washing. We were camping beside a river; how dirty could I get?

I was standing at the register when I noticed that the woman in front of me was black. She was the first African American I had seen since landing at the airport. She was joking with the cashier, but I wondered how it felt to live in a city where she could go days without seeing anyone else who looked anything like her. I had to laugh at how ridiculous I was. When I was the only white person in a black neighborhood in Brooklyn, I felt out of place. But when I was the only Jew in a Christian town and saw a black person, I felt as if we ought to give each other the secret high sign and make plans to meet for drinks.

I loaded the groceries in the Explorer and started south from Mandan. I chose the longer route, winding through the forested hills along the western bank of the Missouri. I passed Fort Lincoln, where Custer held his last command, and the remains of Fort Rice, against which, in 1865, Sitting Bull led three hundred warriors in an attack that gained him his first notoriety among the whites.

I reached the Cannonball in an hour, and right away I knew that Miller was wrong. No boy Christie's age could be unhappy in such a place. Maybe the Parkin Ranch was dreary in winter, but in summer it was lush, the small river widening into the larger, the bluffs shaded with trees whose leaves glittered in the sun, the land rolling in soft, inviting hills on either side. Even Fanny Kelly, who had been marched here by her captors, wrote that the valley of the Cannonball was "a magnificent sight—a sight that made my soul expand with lofty thought and its frail tenement sink into nothingness." Animals darted everywhere, Kelly wrote. Birds of striking plumage skimmed above the river. The scene was "the most lovely, most sublime" she had ever beheld.

I had brought along an old WPA guide to North Dakota published in the 1930s. I love those old guides. Written by out-of-work novelists, they offer insights into what the country was like midway between Victorian times and our own. The Cannonball, the book explained, "is so named because of the odd spheroidal formations found in its waters and in the steep banks of its valley. These concretions, believed to have been formed by the action of moisture within the Fox Hills sandstone, have been carried away in such large numbers by collectors that today only the small 'cannonballs' are found along the stream." Christie Weldon might have been one of the earliest white collectors of those cannonballs. Maybe that was what he was hunting the day he stepped on a rusty nail and got the wound that caused his death.

I drove west above the river. All this land must once have belonged to the Parkin Ranch. I could believe that Lucille Van Solen died of a broken heart at the prospect of losing it. A portly older man in suspenders and a feed cap climbed from a truck on the opposite side of a gate. He shaded his eyes and watched me walk toward him, then listened as I asked if he knew anything about the people who used to live there.

No, he said. He didn't know much at all about the place. His name was Merle Allen. Monty, his son, had bought the ranch a year and a half earlier. Monty was planning to raise buffalo. He and his wife were off on a tour of other buffalo ranches to see how it was done. Merle was just minding the ranch. He was attentive and polite, but he had chores to get done.

I drove across the Cannonball, thinking how ironic it was that the whites had killed the buffalo and forced the Indians to farm, and then, when most Indians had given up farming because the land was too dry, the whites bought up all the land, imported the world's few remaining buffalo, and reintroduced them on their native range, this time behind fences on land white people owned.

I entered the reservation. "Take good care of the land, your family, your life," said the welcome sign to Standing Rock. (In my mirror I could see that as you exited, the sign warned you not to drive drunk.) My guidebook described a tour in which a visitor could follow a gravel road to see the HOLY HILL OF THE MANDANS. "The Mandan legend tells that an ark came to rest on this hill near the Cannonball River, and after the waters subsided the First Man and First Woman stepped out on the hill. Mandan, Arikara, and Sioux all revere the place, and the older natives are reticent about approaching the hilltop." Four granite boulders stand on the hill. "Carved into the face of the largest, a red stone, are many symbols: buffalo tracks, bear paws, thunderbird tracks, serpents, and turtles. . . . Through legend and story the existence of the writing rocks had been indicated for many years, but, because of Indian reticence regarding sacred objects, their exact location was not definitely established until early in 1937." The carvings aren't mentioned in modern guides. I was tempted to try to find them. But I didn't want to be insensitive, intruding on a site that the Indians tried to keep private.

I turned off the main road at the tiny town of Cannonball, "a good place to observe the Sioux in his native surroundings," the guidebook advised. "During the winter months he lives in a tiny log hut, clay-chinked and sod-roofed, heated with a crude open hearth or a modern heating stove, depending on his affluence. In the summer he takes to the cooler tents or brush wickiups. Sioux beadwork and other articles of handicraft can be purchased in the stores at reasonable prices. Many of the Sioux here are well educated and will talk freely with strangers on current issues, but they are decidedly reserved concerning information and legends of their people. This is, of course, typical of the entire agency; the Indian will pretend ignorance of the identity or whereabouts of any Indian about whom a white man may inquire, unless the white man is known to him."

As I drove around the streets, I saw people looking out at me. Some of the houses were dilapidated; others looked neat. A few skinny kids in shorts were playing in the yards. The only adult I saw was riding a mower around a church. The town was flat, with few streets; a stranger couldn't remain unseen for five minutes. Every road ended in a gate that said "KEEP OUT" or "NO HUNTING." The fields were gold and green, with daisies and rolls of hay. Cannonball was a pretty place, but there seemed little to do but hunt, gossip, and fish. As far as I could tell, there were no movie theaters, stores, or sources of employment.

Driving into Yates, I passed the only restaurant I had seen since leaving Mandan, a fast-food stand called Taco John's. I parked along the river. Dragonflies as big as fists batted my ears like boxing gloves. I walked toward a pedestal with a misshapen rock on top. The stone was the size of a pubescent girl with her arms around her knees. "STANDING ROCK, INYAN WOSLATA," the marker read. "A famous stone which many years ago came into possession of the Sioux. According to Dakota legend, it is a body of a young Indian woman with her child on her back who were left in camp when she refused to accompany the tribe as they moved south. When others were sent back to find her, she was found to have turned to stone. The stone is held in reverence by the Sioux and is placed here overlooking the waters and the empire once held by the mighty Sioux nation." In the version in my guide, the woman refused to move out of jealousy of her husband's second wife. Whatever her motive, the legend seemed a warning against following one's own individual will instead of the tribe's. Hardened in the solitude of ego, the mother brought the same lonely fate on her child.

A few yards away stood an obelisk of colored stones cemented in a column with a round, red stone on top. Was this a cannonball from the river? There was no explanation. But a little way down the path, another plaque noted that the Lewis and Clark expedition had proceeded to a site three miles north of the present town. The leaders saw thirty Arikaras and stopped to eat and trade. "Those people were kind and appeared to be much plsd at the attention [we] paid them." Clark, who kept the journal, liked the Sioux far less than he liked the Arikaras. A band of Sioux in South Dakota had grown belligerent and tried to prevent the expedition from continuing. "These are the vilest miscreants of the savage race," Clark wrote, "and must ever remain the pirates of the Missouri, until such measures are pursued, by our government, as will make them feel a dependence on its will for their supply of merchandise."

If there was merchandise for sale in Standing Rock—other than tacos—I didn't come across it. Down the bank, in the river, two boys were floating on a log, laughing and trying to shake each other into the green-brown waves. Weldon's son might have gone swimming in this river. Or Sitting Bull and his sons. I could just make out the clearing on the other side where the old "Devil's colony" of Winona used to be. As the guidebook discreetly put it, "Across the river from Fort Yates, in the heyday of the military post, there sprang up a little town called WINONA, a natural corollary of the restrictions of military life on an Indian reservation. By ferryboat in summer and over the ice by bobsled in winter went the soldier, trader, bullwhacker, Indian, and cowboy, to taste the 'night life' offered in the gaming houses with their expansive bars and amiable hostesses. In Territorial days no less than nine saloons were operating, and an excellent race track was the scene of many financial exchanges."

The woman who ran Winona was a onetime schoolteacher named Clara Bell Rose. Finding teachers' pay too low, she opened a saloon, then added a hotel, a dance house, and a gambling hall. Her photo shows a moderately attractive woman without a hint of facial hair, but Clara Bell Rose somehow became known as Mustache Maude. The women of Fort Yates ostracized her, "but the men found her well educated, an astute business woman, a good poker player, and an excellent cook." Not only did she own Winona's brothels, she owned the only decent library for miles around. A rancher named Ott Black was bewitched enough that he married her and made her Mustache Maude Black. She cut her hair, began smoking Bull Durham tobacco, took over the branding and horse breaking on Black's ranch, and prospered until she died.

In addition to its brothels and saloons, Winona was known for its literary society and a dramatic club run by a man named Jolly Stiles. Weldon could have lived there. Winona might have been a comfortable home for an artist. But she wanted to live among the Indians. And she was too proper to enjoy engaging Mustache Maude in conversation. Most of the women in Winona were whores, and Weldon wouldn't have approved of selling liquor to the Indians.

As long as McLaughlin prohibited soldiers from visiting Indian women, Winona prospered. The schoolteacher, Jack Carignan, opened a store there. Even the Major bought land in Winona. But in 1895 the government decided to abandon the fort, and with the soldiers went the reason for the town. Two years later, Winona became infamous as the site of a mass murder—Thomas Spicer and his family were killed by five Indians. At least, the Indians were blamed for the murder, and three of them were lynched. By the time the writer of my guidebook visited Winona in the 1930s, nothing was left but a few cellars.

I went to find the tribal court; I couldn't imagine anywhere in Fort Yates I couldn't walk to. The dragonflies slapped my ears. The heat weighted my jeans with sweat. I wondered how many of my groceries were ruined. Where did people here shop for food? The only public building I had seen besides Taco John's was the high school.

Two round, middle-aged women in sunglasses sat by the back door to the tribal hospital. They studied me without expression as I asked where I could find the courthouse; I hoped to have a few words with Isaac Dog Eagle before he got busy with the dance.

"Over there." One woman pointed to an alley.

"Thank you," I said, too shy to try saying *pilamaya* in Lakota. The women shifted on the bench as if they wanted to ask me something. Maybe they thought my husband was in jail. But neither said a word. "Thanks," I said again, then walked off to find the court.

Two totaled cruisers and three accordion-pleated heaps lay crumpled in the lot. At the entrance, a sign warned: "If you enter this court with an odor of alcohol upon you, or if you are under the influence of alcohol, you will be lodged in jail until you are sober." Another sign stated that no cases would be heard that day, as no judge was available to hear them. I asked the receptionist if Judge Dog Eagle was in, and she said no, he was off preparing for the Sun Dance. Well, I said, could she point me toward the college? Her directions made me realize that I had passed it twice without knowing.

The building was low and drab, like a bowling alley beside a service road in New Jersey. The Word of God Ministries had put up a blue-and-white revival tent next door. The cars in the lot were junkers. Weeds sprouted in the court-yard. Someone had scrawled "SCOOL SUCKS" in red paint. Students milled about in jeans, T-shirts, and caps. Except for the boys' long, braided hair, they looked like any students. The inside seemed only a little less dispiriting: the decor ran to posters of Sitting Bull, soda machines, chairs with the stuffing coming out. But I felt what I rarely feel at other schools—the excitement of people coming together to build something that needs building.

The dropout rates among Indian students at colleges off the reservation used to be 70 percent. Tribal colleges seemed a way to prepare Indians to enter schools outside and give students an education that would help the tribe (among other things, the program at Standing Rock gives students practice building houses for people who desperately need them). Standing Rock Community College started in 1973 with three teachers serving ninety students. It received national accreditation in 1984. The name was changed to Sitting Bull College in 1996. The faculty and staff now number forty, with two hundred students. On a reservation whose unemployment rate fluctuates between 25 percent in the summer and 75 percent in the winter, more than 95 percent of the graduates are employed or pursuing further study.

One of Ron McNeil's assistants, a young woman named Carol Garza, showed me around the campus. "If it weren't for this place, I would have gone to school off reservation and never come back," she said flatly. She had gone to business school in Denver, and she had done okay, but she'd had to come back to Standing Rock for other reasons. She had loans to pay off. Enrolling at Sitting Bull made sense, since her mother could look after her child while Carol went to school and worked at the housing authority. She led me through an auditorium with a buffalo head nailed to the wall and a poster detailing the parts of the buffalo in English and Lakota. Then we entered a lab filled with computers. "I admit it," she said, "at first I thought this college would be lightweight." But she loved the staff. They took an interest in her. Not like the faculty in Denver. She was broke, she wasn't doing well in her classes, and members of the faculty helped her get a loan. Now she was studying computer science. Maybe she would go to school off the reservation for a four-year degree. Maybe the college would get a similar program here.

We walked across the courtyard to the library, which smelled of wet carpet from the recent floods. There were books and magazines, although not as many as would be found at a good suburban high school. In a narrow glass case I saw Sitting Bull's double eagle-feather headdress, the one Ina McNeil had donated. A crown of white feathers rose from the headband, each one tipped in black, with a red ribbon trailing from each. Two rows of red-fringed feathers cascaded gracefully to the ground. The headdress was longer and more impressive than I imagined it would be. Magnificent, really. But a little shabby. It was a century and a half old.

Garza led me back to the main building. When a lot of Indian kids go away to college, she said, it's the first time they've left the reservation. They go to a big city, maybe they have to work an extra job, maybe there's prejudice, cultural differences. This way, they can get used to going to school and build some confidence before they go away to finish their degrees. What Sitting Bull is fighting is a perception that it can't be a top-rate school because it's run by Indians. Garza, who is young, vibrant, and outgoing, was chosen to be Miss Sitting Bull. She made a tour of schools to recruit students, but some administrators wouldn't let her speak because they perceived the college as being only for Indians.

We walked through a carpeted room in which a smiling woman stood and introduced herself as Cynthia Antelope. She runs the small-business advisory center, giving tribal members advice on how to set up companies—a day-care center, a construction company, a firm that hauls away reservation garbage. Like Antelope, most of the faculty are Lakota. Many come from Yates, but Garza told me that some come from "far away—as far away as Bismarck!" One teacher originally lived in Grand Forks, but now he lives in Yates. It occurred to me that Indians are less inclined to accept whites who come to visit or observe them than whites who come to stay.

I was halfway to my truck when Garza handed me a catalog. It fell open to a picture of Ron McNeil. There is no other way to say this: Ron McNeil is a very handsome man. He has long, thick, dark hair, eyes that seem confiding or mischievous, depending on your interpretation, graceful Asian features, and a smile so blinding it could be a weapon. He has a law degree. He runs a college. He is Sitting Bull's descendant. If he ever ran for public office, he could win a lot of votes.

Oddly, I saw no signs to Sitting Bull's grave. In a town of two hundred, I assumed that if I kept driving, I would stumble on the site, but it took me another hour. I passed Taco John's three times, some dusty playing fields with goalposts, a deserted dugout, an empty track. The foreboding brick building behind the baseball diamond made me wonder if this flat expanse might have been the fort's parade-ground. I turned right at a sign nailed to a tilting post: BURIAL SITE OF SITTING BULL. Beyond the lot stood an inviting copse of trees and a dike overlooking the Oahe Reservoir, but the burial site was bare, with no facilities except a rusty metal awning. The monument to Sitting Bull consisted of a concrete block with a boulder on top and a plaque against the boulder.

Few grave sites have been as controversial as this one. The details of what's been done to Sitting Bull's remains would fill its own book. After he was killed, his corpse was brought to the fort and turned over to the post surgeon, who was under orders not to mutilate it, though he did remove Sitting Bull's blood-stained leggings. A private named John Waggoner was ordered to build the coffin. Sitting Bull's contorted, frozen body was still wrapped in his blanket, frozen stiff with blood. "He filled the box chock-a-block," Waggoner wrote. "They had to sit on the lid to close it." A burial detail of prisoners from the fort dug a grave at the northwest corner of the post cemetery. Sitting Bull had never converted to Christianity, and so he couldn't be buried in the Catholic graveyard. Besides, the angry families of the Indian police wouldn't have allowed it. Some witnesses claimed that quicklime and muriatic acid were poured in the coffin, but McLaughlin, who watched the burial, vehemently denied this.

Nevertheless, there were those rumors about the coffin being empty and McLaughlin selling the chief's body to a businessman in Bismarck, with the object of making Sitting Bull's bones and skin "objects of speculation." Bland wrote a letter to the Commissioner of Indian Affairs, which Morgan transmitted to McLaughlin for investigation "relative to reports that the body of Sitting Bull was removed from the coffin before burial and taken to a dissecting room, &c." Perhaps a letter from Weldon instigated Bland's concern; it doesn't seem that Bland ever wrote to Morgan on Sitting Bull's behalf unless Weldon prompted him. McLaughlin, who had done nothing to the body except clip a lock of hair, was able to refute the charges. But in 1905, the historian Frank Fiske dug up the grave and stole a thighbone (his accomplice stole a rib). He showed off the bone as a conversation piece for years.

Three years later, with the fort now long gone, the War Department tried to have the chief's body removed, along with the bodies of the soldiers buried in the graveyard. The department's representative dug up some remains, but the historical societies of North and South Dakota protested the removal of such an important figure and the bones were reburied in a smaller box inside the coffin. In 1931, stray horses knocked over Sitting Bull's headstone and cracked it. E. D. Mossman, the Superintendent of Indian Affairs at Yates, sent the broken marker to the museum in Bismarck with a letter that they could have it if they provided something to take its place. The new marker, Mossman said, should be more substantial than the first, but with exactly the same lettering ("Sitting Bull, Died Dec. 15, 1890, Chief of the Hunkpapa Sioux"). Mossman said that he would object to anything more "pretentious . . . anything that will laud the life and deeds of Sitting Bull. I object to any more fame being attached to the name of Sitting Bull, than has already been given him. . . ."

Mossman recognized that his protests made him seem "quite an objector." But, he said, when it came to Sitting Bull, he *was* an objector. Sitting Bull was "one of the premier demagogues of all time. He kept his ear to the ground and whenever objection to the established order were made, whenever there was disaffection, disloyalty, or any other discontent of any kind to be voiced he made that cause his own and proceeded with all of the wily qualities of his nature to make as much trouble for every one concerned as possible. He lies now in full sight of the school the church and the agency, which is a representative of the Government, which he fout [*sic*]. I recommend that he lie where he is until time shall be no more and we shall all be called before the Great White Throne to receive our just deserts, Sitting bull [*sic*] along with the rest of us."

The Historical Society reluctantly complied with Mossman's wishes. At the installation of the new headstone, Mossman had Sitting Bull exhumed, finding in the coffin the smaller box of bones buried by the War Department in 1908. Only a femur was missing—this might have been the bone the historian made off with. The remains were reburied and a slab poured above the grave.

But Sitting Bull's descendants kept agitating for his removal. As a boy, Clarence Gray Eagle had watched from a clump of brush as his father—the brother of Sitting Bull's wives—helped the police attack the cabins at Grand River. Now he led the campaign to move the chief's body from the fort that

Sitting Bull so hated. In 1953, when water from the Oahe Reservoir threatened to flood the grave, Gray Eagle and his followers dug up the site with a backhoe and carried off some bones, which they encased in a steel vault in a twenty-ton block of concrete and reburied in Mobridge, South Dakota, on a bluff overlooking the place where the Grand River used to flow into the Missouri before the reservoir was built. *That* burial site is commemorated with a seven-ton bust of Sitting Bull sculpted by Korczak Ziolkowski—the same Ziolkowski who started sculpting the gargantuan relief of Crazy Horse near Mount Rushmore.

Many Sioux believe that Sitting Bull now rests in South Dakota. Most white historians don't think so. The grave at Yates was reexhumed in 1962, when the Army Corps of Engineers was building a dike. Investigators found a small box of bones within a larger coffin, fitting the description of the remains reburied in 1908.

Wherever Sitting Bull is buried, I was curious to find out what was written on his monument. Let's put it this way: Superintendent Mossman wouldn't have been pleased. I traced the graffiti on the stone—"Cory White Bull '78," "Little Warrior." Had the vandals written their names from ignorance or a wish to be connected to their chief? Other visitors had left wild sage, an empty Coke can, hair from a horse's tail. In my religion, the way to show respect for the dead is to leave a pebble on the headstone. I found a flat red rock and left it on the stone beside the sage.

～◦

By four o'clock I was heading up the drive to Prairie Knights Casino. A row of colored flags snapped against their poles. A bus from Grand Forks disgorged senior citizens in pastel pantsuits, plaid shirts, and knit slacks. They walked past the sculpture of a chief in buckskin riding among four contorted bronze ponies. "This Facility is owned by the Standing Rock Nation," a sign announced.

An hour early for my interview with James McLaughlin's great-grandson, I drifted among the slot machines and blackjack tables. I had never been in a casino, but this one seemed much more modest than the pictures I had seen of casinos in Las Vegas or Atlantic City. I kept checking the lobby. By now, McLaughlin was late. I asked the clerk if anyone by that name had stopped by. She was young, with olive eyes, smooth, dark hair, and a brilliant smile. "Sheriff Jim? His niece works at the casino. I could go and ask her if he's coming."

No, I said, that's fine. I sat beneath a mural of an Indian woman with Edenic bunnies, elk, and buffalo looking up as if they wanted her to play. A tall, skinny man in his forties came in. "Hi, Jimmy," the clerk sang out. He sat nervously on the couch beside me. Fair, with a sparse mustache, he was the kind of quiet man who hides his height by slouching. He wore a Dakota Nation T-shirt and black aviator-shaped bifocals. He folded one leg and crossed it so his boot rested on his knee, then put that foot on the floor and folded his other leg so the other boot rested on the other knee. He was carrying a book whose title I couldn't read. He put it on the couch and answered what I asked, although he tended to mumble and break off his sentences.

Jimmy McLaughlin had been born forty-eight years earlier, the grandson of Charley McLaughlin, the agent's second-eldest son, the son who had been elected Sioux County sheriff and whom his father had reprimanded for mortgaging his property. Only Charles and Sibley lived beyond their father. They sold the family ranch. Sibley died in 1924. Charley died three years later, at fifty-five. "Mr. Kenny Bam owns the Circle M now," Jimmy told me wistfully. "It's not far away. In Shields. The house is still there."

Except for three years in Denver, Jimmy had lived his entire life at Standing Rock. "I know everybody here. After I came back from Denver, I promised myself I'd never live in a city **again**." He loved it here, he said. He loved to hunt and fish. He was an enrolled **member** of the Lakota Nation, although he could get along in both societies, Indian and white. In his lifetime he had been a policeman for the Bureau of Indian Affairs, a sheriff, and, most lately, a child-services worker for the tribe. He was divorced, with two grown boys who lived with their mother. Jimmy lived with his sister.

I asked what it had been liked growing up at Standing Rock as the great-grandson of the man who caused Sitting Bull's death. (Even whites have it in for McLaughlin's descendants. Stanley Vestal was asked to judge the Miss Indian America contest in 1955, and he hesitated about giving the award to Rita Ann McLaughlin, the agent's part-Sioux granddaughter. Only after some soul-searching did Vestal decide that the girl deserved the prize.)

Well, Jimmy said, some people said his great-grandfather was no good because he ordered the police to arrest Sitting Bull. A few kids in high school gave Jimmy a hard time. But they didn't take it out against him personally. They only said negative things about his great-grandfather. As for his own opinion, Jimmy thought James McLaughlin was as fair as he could be, given the circumstances. He did the job he was ordered to do. Jimmy admired him. He wished he could have met him, not so much because James McLaughlin was a historical figure as because Jimmy hadn't known any of his grandfathers.

Some historians consider James McLaughlin the best Indian agent who ever lived. Others vilify him. How did Jimmy interpret his namesake's place in history?

"That Ghost Dance," he said. "A lot of people were afraid of it. He wasn't afraid, though. He was married to an Indian. He knew it was nothing to be afraid of. He was just following orders. The non-Indians were afraid. The government had to act. If he'd wanted to get rid of Sitting Bull, he could have had the troops go in. He had Indian children himself. He used his own people so there wouldn't be any violence."

Why had his great-grandfather hated Sitting Bull so much? Did he really think the chief was a coward and a wily cheat?

"McLaughlin was just mad at himself because Sitting Bull was the only one he couldn't get to plow the fields. He had to take his anger out because he couldn't convert Sitting Bull or convince him to give up the Ghost Dance or give up what little bit of freedom he had along Grand River." Jimmy could understand that an Indian leader would see himself as defending his people's rights and yet pose a problem to the government, as well as to other Indians. Jimmy had been a police officer at the Wounded Knee uprising in 1973, when members of the American Indian Movement occupied the village where their ancestors had been cut down after Sitting Bull's death. The radicals, led by Russell Means, demanded a Senate investigation into the mistreatment of Indians across the country.

"I could see where Means was trying to stick up for the elderly," Jimmy told me. "But in the meantime, AIM trashed their homes and their church. He didn't end up helping them." Jimmy was on duty at Wounded Knee for twelve days, then he got sick and was sent home. As an Indian and a police officer, he had mixed feelings about the protest. "The government was afraid the protesters would trash the [Bureau of Indian Affairs] office and the hospital. It was built into us on the reservation—when you work for the government, there's a code you do the best you can, no matter how hard it is." Because of his experience, he could place himself in the shoes of a tribal policeman in his great-grandfather's time. "They got five dollars a month to take care of their families. They were proud to be chosen. It was a big deal in those days, a way to be outstanding. You got to carry a gun. Get your bullets free. Today, if you're a tribal policeman, you get to drive a car. You get your gun. Your holster. Your nightstick and your radio. You get a chance to be responsible."

Jimmy hadn't known of Weldon's existence until four months earlier, when the Bismarck public television station mentioned her on a show about the history of Standing Rock. "I'd never heard of her before. I'd never heard of her growing up."

What did he think of a white woman coming to the reservation to help the Indians?

Jimmy considered for a while. "If that was in her heart, if she felt strongly about helping someone out, a person like that can at least try. The worst they can do when you get there is say no. It had to take her a lot of guts to come out here from New York to no-man's-land. She must have been very brave. She had to oppose the government. She lost her boy. That had to have been hard, to lose her boy. She must have been a strong woman, to oppose a man like James McLaughlin. Sitting Bull and McLaughlin were strong-headed men. Great men. That lady must have been a strong lady."

As for his great-grandfather, "he was just doing his job" in opposing Sitting Bull and Weldon. "If he lived today and was, say, a computer manager, and his boss told him to fire someone, he'd fire them. He had a wife and four kids to support. The challenge was to do what the government wanted him to do."

I could understand what Jimmy meant, that his great-grandfather was sometimes caught between the government's idea of what was best for the Lakota and his own judgment. But I couldn't see James McLaughlin as a flunky. He was a stubborn man who lived by his principles. He believed in most of the policies he carried out.

"Who won?" I asked. "If Sitting Bull and your great-grandfather were sitting here today, in the lobby of this casino, which one would think he'd won?"

Jimmy shook his head. "Neither won. It was a standoff between the government and Native Americans. And neither won." Sitting Bull's efforts had resulted in the Lakota people keeping a larger part of their reservation than they otherwise might have kept. "So we won, in a way. Sitting Bull won. He got his people to be free. To a point. There's still Sun Dances. The government will never stop that. Sitting Bull would probably be proud of the casino. He told his children to go to school. But McLaughlin would be proud that they'd succeeded. He wanted the Sioux to plow a garden, plant a field. He wanted the Indians to better themselves."

Sitting Bull had won. McLaughlin would be proud. It wasn't the standard version of history told by either side, Indian or white. Well, I said, to an outsider, the reservation seemed to be undergoing some improvements. The casino. The tribal college. Was this a renaissance for the Sioux?

"That's a hard question." Jimmy took off his glasses and rubbed his eyes. "Things are changing. Yes. But sometimes I think the only thing that's come down to the reservation that's new is the gangs. The kids go off to the cities and bring that crap back. They're disrupting the court system and the schools, preying on their own people. But some other changes are good. It's good they're putting the Lakota language back into the schools. It's good the kids can understand it. Sometimes a kid needs to know his heritage. It's important to know your heritage."

And his own heritage? What did Jimmy consider himself to be?

"I'm an Indian. I'm a Native American. I can function in both worlds. But in my heart I'm Lakota. Some people might dislike breeds, but I'm proud of what I am."

I asked if there was any truth to the claim that his great-grandmother, Marie McLaughlin, was embarrassed about her status as a quarter-breed Sioux, that she hated Sitting Bull because he refused to go to England and caused her to miss her chance to be presented to the queen.

"I've never heard anything about that," Jimmy said. "I never heard she had any status problem. One of my favorite stories as a kid was about my grand-mother's grandma, how she had to run for her life from the massacre in Minnesota. They had to cross the river in boats in the middle of the night. She always talked about being an Indian. That was the story I asked for all the time."

Jimmy is proud that his sons are more Indian than he is. He showed me the book he'd brought, *Iyan Woslate Wo'oyake: A History of Standing Rock.* "Here, look at this." He pointed out a photo of a very dark-skinned man named Herbert Buffalo Boy. "I married his daughter. That's why my boys are so dark."

I had seen a photo of Charles and Sibley McLaughlin as children, riding ponies with Indian boys. They grew up playing with Indians, studying with Indians, flirting with Indians. Like their father, they married Indians. What their father hadn't considered was that his descendants might *become* Indians.

Jimmy shut the book, untangled his legs, and stood. Awkwardly we shook hands. He went to find his niece. I watched him walk off—social worker, cop, a man who functions in both societies but considers himself Lakota—and felt my own belief in integration stir. Wasn't that the best for everyone, if each of us felt comfortable in his or her own world but could function in many others'?

I had a coupon to stay at Prairie Knights at a discount and eat breakfast there for free. But I wanted to find the site for the Sun Dance and set up my tent before dark. I filled the Explorer's tank with gas at the Prairie Knights Quik Mart, and, at the last minute, remembered to fill the stove. I decided to call home to see how my son was doing. The lines chattered with static, as if a storm were coming on. I could barely hear my husband. What was that he said? Was everything all right? Well, mumble, mumble. Something I couldn't make out. Something about Noah falling and getting hurt. A cut? A broken bone? "Did you take him to the hospital?" I asked.

A few months before, Noah had fallen off the monkey bars at school—or rather, he was pushed. He asked to be taken home, but the nurse assured me that his arm was fine. My husband thought so, too, as did the young doctor at the clinic to which I took him. But I was certain that they were wrong. I put Noah to bed, only to hear him wake screaming in the night: "Mommy! Help! It hurts! Please stop the pain!" It doesn't sound very serious, a child with a broken bone. But at two in the morning, when your son is screaming in pain, nothing seems trivial. My husband took Noah to the hospital, and yes, the arm was broken. As soon as the bone was set, Noah fell asleep, and the next morning, bright and early, he begged to go to school.

And so, at Prairie Knights, when I heard my husband say that Noah had fallen and gotten hurt, I shouted above the static: "Take him to the hospital. Promise you'll get it x-rayed." I tried not to think of my son in pain without me. I would be out of reach for five days. Breaking a bone was minor—but so was stepping on a nail. Christie's wound had healed. When he started to complain of achy joints and headaches, his mother thought he was coming down with a cold. What had the doctor said to the woman in my dream? *I'm sorry about your son.* No, that wasn't real. My husband and I had our differences, but he was a responsible adult who loved our son as much as I did. He would take Noah for an x-ray. What if I flew home and nothing much was wrong? When would I ever get another invitation to a Sun Dance?

I climbed in the truck and drove. The Explorer was an oven; the smell of rancid food made me gag, so I drove with the windows down. I turned off the highway. My tires threw up a screen of dust so thick that I nearly missed the pole with the red bandanna tied around it. I turned through a gated fence and bumped down a road so winding and steep that even in the truck I was scared I would plummet off. The valley stretched for miles, green and gold beneath a sky that swirled with yellow clouds. A truck rattled up the road in the opposite direction, filled with dark-skinned boys too young to be driving. I let it pass. The driver waved. That seemed a good sign. Then I drove around a bend and saw a headless, rotting calf. That seemed a bad sign.

On and on I drove. I had heard that even after McLaughlin banned the Sun Dance, the ceremony continued to be held in hidden locations. That was easy to believe. Woodstock could have happened here and no one would have known. The seemingly endless drive made me understand how much Sitting Bull enjoyed Weldon's company. Why else would he have been willing to travel so far to see her? And her willingness to travel all this way to see him, to share his tribe's hardships and the beauty of their lives, must have proved she was their friend.

9

Grand River

I drove into camp an hour or two before dark. The dancers had built a circular arbor of forked poles with a trellis across the top. In a second ring, the width of a street around the first, stood three tipis, dozens of battered station wagons, old-fashioned metal trailers, new minivans, pickups, and shelters made of canvas, camouflage net, and boughs of cottonwood and willow. Most of the participants had come in groups, with tables, chairs, and coolers. At the edge of the field, closest to the latrines, squatted a few nylon tents. Clearly this was where I belonged, but the grass was high, and there wasn't shade. I drove around the circle to inspect the other side. I reached the end and turned back. Men came running toward my truck, waving and shouting. I had been at the Sun Dance fifteen minutes and already had broken Ron McNeil's first rule—I had crossed the eastern gate.

Shaken, I drove back to the latrines. Swarms of grasshoppers settled on every bag and pot I set down. But I was making good progress—snapping poles together, fastening Velcro straps—when two women and a man came to say hello. The darker of the women introduced herself with a Lakota name I couldn't pronounce. "You can call me Donna," she said. She might have been anywhere from her late twenties to her forties; I suddenly felt more sympathy for the men who had offered such wildly differing guesses for Catherine Weldon's age. Donna's companion's name was Wox; at least, that's how it sounded. She was softer, sweeter, and lighter skinned than Donna.

"You can call me Uncle Charlie," the older man said. He looked like everyone's Uncle Charlie, short and round, with a doughy face, less successful than your other uncles but the one you hoped would show up at reunions. He asked if I had come by myself.

Yes, I said, but I had been invited by Ina and Ron McNeil. Isaac Dog Eagle had given his permission. Were any of them here?

"Sure, that's Isaac's tipi there." Uncle Charlie pointed. "He's having a birthday party later—you can talk to him then."

"You're friends with my grandma Ina?" Donna's eyes lost their coldness.

"We're not friends, exactly, but I met her a few weeks ago and she told me I should come."

"She isn't here now," Donna said.

"I know." I wished she were. "But I'm looking forward to seeing her."

Donna stared at me suspiciously, as if to ask what sort of relationship I might have with her grandma Ina if we had met but weren't friends.

"That's quite a tent you've got," Charlie said. "We'll help you set it up."

I protested, but my visitors began fitting poles together, and I didn't want to interfere. I had the notion that because they were Indians they must be better at setting up tents than I was. I only hoped they wouldn't peek inside the truck and see my diet Coke. Already I could tell that my tent was worse than useless. I hadn't given a thought to shade. Unprotected in the sun, my supplies would sit here cooking. I looked enviously at the tipis—roomy and light, with flaps on either side to let the breezes flow through.

Donna and Charlie gave up. "Just be sure you stomp down the spear grass," Donna said. "It's really prickly, and it'll keep you awake all night, poking you in your back." She and Wox and Charlie trampled the spiny grass.

"And you'd better put those pegs in real good," Charlie warned. "Wind's picking up. Get a storm out here, these winds get so strong they'll blow you across the field." The year before, there had been such a bad windstorm several tents got blown across the Plains, with their occupants still in them. "And watch out for tent crawlers."

Tent crawlers?

"Young men who come at night and sneak into the tipi of an eligible young girl. They slit the side and go in, then sew the canvas back up."

"What's the sign to show you're married?" I asked.

"Just don't hang out your moccasins!" Charlie laughed and said to come over to their camp after I got set up. I wondered if he and Donna would be so kind after they learned I was a writer.

I didn't take time to trample the spear grass, but I shoved the plastic pegs as deep as they would go in the hard-baked ground. I couldn't put my food outside: coyotes might steal it. If I put the food inside, animals might shred the tent to get in. I would have left it in the truck, but a voice announced that all campers should move their cars above the field so as not to ruin the atmosphere around the circle. I put my canned food inside the tent and the rest around the back. At least there weren't bears.

By now I was exhausted. I wriggled inside the tent to rest, but a grasshopper got in with me and boinged noisily against the nylon. Multitudes of giant hoppers hurled themselves against the tent from outside; sleeping here would be like trying to sleep through a drum solo—if you were lying inside the drum. The grasshoppers flocked the tent's exterior, their upside-down shadows magnified by the setting sun. As I lay trying to ignore the spear grass skewering my back and the sweat pooling on my chest, I thought of how Sitting Bull held that Sun Dance before the battle at the Little Big Horn and saw soldiers falling into his camp upside down like grasshoppers. That his prediction came true isn't surprising. It's rare for a commander to predict his own defeat. What I thought as I lay beneath those upside-down shadows was that a poet's metaphors come from the world around him. Anyone might see grasshoppers. A poet uses what he sees.

I crawled from the steamy tent and walked to the edge of the bank above the river. The lip crumbled beneath my shoes. Far below, the river meandered through its shallows. Boys waded across a sandbar while flashes of heat lightning played above their heads. Thunder rumbled like a jet. Not many feet away, a woman my age was setting up a tent. The wind whipped her wavy, dark hair around her face and snapped the tent flap from her hands. I asked if she needed help. Thanks, she said, she did. She reminded me of my best friend from junior high, the friend who played the flute and liked to talk about things that mattered, then moved to California in tenth grade and disappeared. "I'm Tristan," she said, and really, she was the only person I have ever met who looked like a Tristan.

We sat on my poncho and shared my runny cheese. The carrots I had bought in Mandan had boiled in their plastic bags. The cans of soup had swelled, bulging in a way I knew was fatal. (The diet Coke cans bulged, too, but what could be unsafe about a can of hot chemicals?) Tristan was no more Indian than I was. She was from Silverfish, in the Black Hills. She worked with handicapped people and had that tranquilizing calm the best social workers have. The year before, she had taken a course in Native American spiritualism from a professor in Silverfish. He and his wife invited her to the Sun Dance. She was going through a bad time, and the experience saved her life. That was their camp, the big one. She would be spending time with them, cooking and doing chores. I should come over and she would introduce me.

We were sitting there like that, juice from a warm cantaloupe running down our chins, when an older man came over and squatted by my tent. He looked like George Plimpton or Spalding Gray, tall and bony, with whitish hair and an aristocratic face, eyes hidden by tinted glasses. His name was Ted, he told us. "No last names, right?" He had lived in New York. Then he moved to Boston. Now he lived in Santa Fe. I was a writer? That was great. Did I like John le Carré? Ted was a big fan of John le Carré. He was trying to write his own book. Not like le Carré's. It was the story of Ted's own life. He would send me the manuscript and I could help him revise it. This was his second Sun Dance, but he wasn't here with anyone.

The sky grew heavy. Sprinkles fell. Then a rainbow came out. Beneath its misty bow, a dozen shirtless boys stalked fish in the river. I must have thought I was in some Disney replica of an Indian village. How else can I explain what a stupid thing I did? I asked Tristan where I could find the site of the camp where Sitting Bull lived with Catherine Weldon.

"It's over there." She gestured vaguely. "We hiked there last year. Just keep following the trail." Then she excused herself to say hello to her friends.

For a while the walk seemed easy. I followed the road I had driven in on, past a fork where it divided, then took the western branch. The ground was parched and cracked. Grasshoppers flew up, catapulting against my chest. I remembered an article from the Yankton paper when the government was trying to persuade the Sioux to sell their land. Why, the reservation was so poor that not even a grasshopper could live upon it. The Indians should be glad to get fifty cents an acre. Although why the whites would want to buy such worthless land, or how the Sioux could support themselves on land that wouldn't provide sustenance for a grasshopper, the reporter never said.

A bird whistled. Ordinarily I can't tell one bird from the next. But Sitting Bull felt an affinity for birds: a yellowhammer saved him from a bear, and that meadowlark warned him that his own people would kill him. I had looked up the meadowlark's picture in an on-line encyclopedia, and here it was, whistling from a fence. No wonder the Indians attached such significance to every animal. What else was there to notice?

I passed a few derelict cars, an empty cabin, an abandoned farm. The trail petered out. The spear grass pierced my jeans and scratched my ankles until they bled. Night fell faster than I'd thought. I hadn't brought a flashlight. No one but Tristan would notice I was gone. Two hundred people were camped a mile away, but I had never felt more lonely. I thought of how scary it must have been for a family of whites to live here, not knowing if a band of Lakota warriors might gallop across that ridge at any time. Or a small Lakota band, not knowing if a troop of soldiers would thunder into camp. The enemy could find you sleeping or drawing water, your children playing in the river half a mile away. The Indians were known to pick up a crying baby and smash its head against a tree. When soldiers sacked a village, they took bets on who could hit the Indian toddlers running for their mothers' arms.

I had the sense to turn back, but I couldn't see where I was going. I followed the fence by feel; it cut through higher grass but kept me headed east. Mosquitoes feasted on my face. I am not prone to being bitten, but those mosquitoes were less choosy than any mosquitoes I had ever met. At last I saw smoke. Isaac's tipis glowed whitish in the dark. You didn't just wander off. Only the most rugged individual could make it on his own.

When I got back from my useless hike, I heard cries from the latrines. The women's outhouse lay cockeyed across the planks meant to keep it from falling in the pit. The men came running. "We'll save you, girls! Don't make any sudden movements!" I put my shoulder to the outhouse, but, as small as I am, I was in danger of slipping in. I stepped back and let the men do what they were good at. They righted the latrine. The women stumbled out and took the teasing with good humor. It was a story I would hear again and again that week, a story that would be repeated at dances in years to come. I wanted to be at those dances. Already the outside world seemed distant and unreal. This tiny band of strangers constituted my entire world.

Everyone gathered at Isaac's camp. A POW/MIA flag stood beside his tipi. Many of the men were vets; you could tell this from their caps and the stickers on their trucks. They were big-bellied men in jeans, tank tops, and tattoos. Gentle and soft-spoken, they had long braids and bad teeth; they carried their knives in sheaths and had names like Riley and Bazooka. The women wore long, colorful skirts with long-sleeve tops, sandals or heavy shoes. The young people led their elders to the metal chairs in a half circle by Isaac's tent, then sat on the ground and waited.

Isaac came out. He looked impish and fierce, a cross between the Keebler elf and a Sioux warrior, which is to say he looked like someone you would be glad to see if he were your uncle and someone you would not want to see galloping toward you with a lance. He stretched his arms and smiled. His birthday was actually later that month, he said, but with everyone gathered for the dance, it would be a good time for a celebration. Everyone come! There would be dinner, he said, and everyone would get a slice of cake.

Then he talked about the dance. I couldn't write down what he said. It was too dark. Besides, Ted had warned me that writing anything at a Sun Dance was forbidden. Ina had invited me knowing that I was a writer. I had told Isaac and Ron. Allowing me to come but forbidding me to take notes would ensure that I would get important details wrong. If I went back to my tent to record the day's events, I would need to use a flashlight; people would see my silhouette and know what I was doing. In the daytime, I wouldn't be able to write inside the tent without passing out from the heat. That night, as was true the entire week, I found myself repeating stories in my head so I wouldn't forget the details. It gave me some idea of what it must have been like to be the storyteller in a culture that had no written word, or Catherine Weldon, hiding in Sitting Bull's cabin, scribbling notes to James McLaughlin while the Indians danced outside.

Isaac, meanwhile, was talking about the Sun Dance and how quickly it had grown since he had started holding it fourteen years earlier. More and more people kept turning up, even though the dance wasn't advertised. This made Isaac glad. The next morning, he would meet with the men who intended to pierce their chests, to make sure they understood what a commitment they were undertaking. Many men vowed they would pierce, but they didn't perform the act with the right respect. "I'm going to tell these men I don't want to see them again a month from now in my court, as tribal judge."

He welcomed everyone who had come to support the dancers. Most of the dancers' prayers were for help in overcoming problems like alcoholism, cancer, and sugar diabetes. That was fine; Isaac just wished more of the prayers might be given for thanksgiving. But no matter why anyone was there, Isaac wanted everyone to sing along to show support. Sing along, he said. You'll learn the songs if you listen every day. The year before, the dancers' whistles had gone dry because not enough people were singing. Everyone ought to learn the language of the tribe. The elders couldn't use English for important rituals like the Sun Dance or they would be beating around the bush, trying to give the people some idea of what they meant. The audience clapped. Isaac stretched out his arms and said he wanted to introduce his helpers. He called forward his sons and daughters—they seemed embarrassed but proud—and his wife, who was one of those older women you can't describe later, except to say that she was handsome and retiring.

Then Isaac gave a loving introduction to Uncle Charlie, who, it turned out, had promised he would dance. I hadn't thought that an older man would take part in the Sun Dance, especially an overweight older man with diabetes. But Uncle Charlie had vowed to help Isaac run the ceremony. The two men would do things the way their grandfather had done them. They would sing the prayers their grandfather had sung and use the same kind of sacred tree. The next day, at noon, they would send scouts to find that tree. They would need virgins to cut it down. Virgins, Isaac joked, were always in short supply. More virgins were always welcome, but everyone should come and watch the tree being cut. Isaac himself had a wedding to perform back in town. The other elders would supervise the ceremony, and Isaac would hurry back and join them.

Other men stepped forward. The first man, a Korean War vet, explained that there were four kinds of prayer. There was silent prayer, and prayer a person spoke. There were singing prayers—the kind we would hear the next day. But the fourth kind of prayer most people didn't know. The fourth kind was crying. If a man was sincere when he was praying, he might cry. Men cry, the man repeated, and he himself was near tears.

Another dancer, Isaac's adopted son, had come all the way from Germany. His friends sent their love. (*"Hau! Hau!"* the crowd responded, and it was jarring to hear real Indians say "How!," Hollywood having rendered it impossible for a white person to hear real Indians talk without thinking they were actors.) The guests brought their own utensils. I went back to my tent and got mine, then filed past Isaac's children as they ladled out bowls of chokecherry soup, soup from wild plums, stew lumpy with potatoes and chunks of fatty beef. People helped themselves to Indian tea and fry bread. I sat on the ground with my knees together and my ankles to one side, as I had read Indian women were supposed to sit, although it was too dark for anyone to give me points for good deportment. At least I wouldn't go hungry. I don't eat beef or pork, but even a vegetarian could love the refreshing soups and hot, doughy fry bread. I was less afraid of not eating than I was of being eaten. Dragonflies buzz-bombed around my head, eating the mosquitoes, but there seemed plenty to go around. No wonder the Indians refused their agent's order to give up wearing blankets. What else would keep off the bugs? I doused myself with a repellent that didn't deter a single fly. Even the grasshoppers bit.

Isaac and his wife were receiving guests. His wife was delighted to receive the preserves I had brought as a gift from Michigan. Isaac took the plasticized packet of vacuum-packed lox and asked me what it was.

"Smoked salmon," I said.

"Smoked fish! I love smoked fish!" He slit open the cellophane and ate the slices then and there. "Welcome!" he said again. I reminded him about our talk. Yes, he said, later, after the dance was done.

Buoyed by my success, I brought pints of maple syrup to Donna, Wox, and Charlie. Donna's aunties were sitting in a circle, digesting the feast and murmuring in Lakota. They seemed pleased to get the gifts. Donna was cutting hide in the shapes of a buffalo and a man to adorn the sacred tree. Charlie invited me to sit. What was I doing here? he asked. Why had I come all the way from Michigan?

"I'm a writer," I said softly. I told them a little about Catherine Weldon and how she had worked for the Hunkpapas.

Donna's back stiffened. "You're a writer?"

Uncle Charlie didn't care. He asked me if I had ever worked as, what was it called, a ghostwriter. I should write a book about *his* life, he said. He had been trained as a mortician and tried to get a job at various funeral homes in Chicago. "But the mortician's business is very clannish. Whites like to go to their own funeral homes. Blacks go to black funeral homes. Jews go to Jewish funeral homes. Spanish people go to Spanish funeral homes. I would get a very hot potato, they would say on the phone there was a job, they didn't know I was an Indian—my last name isn't an Indian name. Then I'd show up and they would see me, and it would be a very cold potato." He gave up working as a mortician and studied to be an optician. "I'd grind those, you know." He pointed to my glasses. "I was the straw boss of the whole place."

For some reason, that didn't last. He studied law for a while and served as a tribal judge. He settled at the Rosebud Reservation, where he worked as the first Indian mortician in South Dakota. Then he went to jail—he didn't say why and I didn't ask. He served his two years, but the authorities took away his mortician's license. It was double jeopardy: you got punished once in jail and a second time when you got out and lost your way to earn a living. He supported himself by making crafts to sell to dealers, with help from "these two lovely ladies"—he nodded to Wox and Donna. Things were starting to go right. His family and friends had been praying for his life and health to improve. "So I'm here to pray, too."

Charlie looked around. The silence was the kind that lets you know your hosts wish that you would leave. Well, I said, thanks, I'll see you all tomorrow.

I went to use the outhouse. The line on the women's side was long, and we passed the time joking about the outhouse falling in. The kids dared one another to stand at the very edge of the bluff. The men rested their hands on their bellies and talked in low voices. No one asked me who I was. In the four days that followed, I visited the latrines more often than my bladder required. There was nothing else to do. The women shared the camaraderie of any rest-room line.

By the time I got back, two women and their kids had set up a trailer behind my tent. I tried to sleep, but another grasshopper sneaked inside and I had to trap him and send him out. Sounds carried across the field; I heard every snore and groan, every whisper, every belch. In a band as small as this it was impossible not to know who was courting whom, sneaking around at night, quarreling with his wife. You had to live an honest life or bet on being caught. I smelled something like marijuana. Other tribes took peyote. Did the Lakota smoke pot? No. I remembered. What I smelled was burning sage. I had read dozens of books about Lakota culture and I was still making false judgments. In Weldon's time, there were no reliable books about the Indians. She had even less to go on than I did.

Thunder jolted me from sleep. Rain pounded the flimsy tent. If the thunder that afternoon had sounded like a jet, it now sounded like a squadron of fighter planes crashing in the field beyond the camp. The ground shook. My brain shook. The lightning was so bright that even through the nylon I could see the sharp, searing bolts. I was sure my tent poles would draw lightning; my only consolation was that the trailers must be higher. I remembered Elaine Goodale describing a night in which a thunderstorm struck. The Indians had made sure everything was snug. The lodge poles were well braced. But everyone was afraid the tipi would collapse. The Indians sat up all night, talking. One of the men was telling a story about someone dying in a thunderstorm when a woman in a nearby tipi was struck by a lightning bolt and killed. The wind tugged my tent so hard I stretched in a human cross and tried to keep it down. Right at that moment, I would have been glad to have anyone beside me, adding his weight to mine.

Tree Day: Saturday, July 26

The next day dawned cool. People moved about their business so serenely they seemed to float. The women ladled scrambled eggs and chopped ham for the men, who had risen at first light to build shelters for the dancers. To the west of these huts they erected two latrines and two bent-sapling mounds covered with canvas tarps that looked like giant turtles. Mountains of wood and stones would be used to heat the sweat lodges in which the dancers would cleanse their souls and bodies every morning before they began to dance. A tank of drinking water had been hauled in and left behind the arbor; it seemed to me that hearing someone pop a Coke wouldn't be nearly as infuriating as hearing that spigot run.

Isaac had said the scouts would hunt the tree at noon, but I hadn't worn my watch, watches being jewelry, and I had no way of guessing time. The morning clouds burned off. The sun was so intense that even with my sunglasses I could barely keep my eyes open. Donna had warned me to take off my glasses whenever I approached the arbor since the lenses would reflect the sun and distract the dancers, but for now I kept them on, consoling myself that Sitting Bull thought smoked glasses to be one of the white man's best inventions, protecting an Indian's eyes from the blinding summer sun or shining winter snow. Maybe if Sitting Bull had been able to buy sunscreen, he would have worn that, too. In any case, I wasn't about to let Donna see me slathering on lotion. I crawled in my tent to put it on—the interior was hot enough to bake bread—then positioned my perishables in the sliver of shade behind the tent. I kept moving my supplies around the tent, following that bit of shade, and by the end of four days, I could tell time within the hour by where the shadows fell.

I sat and watched the women in the campsite next to mine. I coveted their shade and the third chair beneath their awning. Sitting on my poncho was hard on my arthritis and made me too conspicuous. I had never felt so *seen*. When I lit my stove to boil coffee, everyone stared. The stove was an elegant contraption—a burner and tripod attached to a cylinder filled with gas—but it seemed tiny and effete compared to the huge open pits the other campers kept blazing. Behind my tent, men doused logs with gasoline to barbecue the side of beef that would be the meal that night. I primed my stove and lit it. The Plains were tinder dry. Lightning might strike at any time. No wonder Native parents raised their children to be calm.

The children at the Sun Dance were the best behaved and most gently treated kids I had ever met. I missed my own son. But Noah would have been complaining how uncomfortable he was. Poor Christie Weldon. Life might have been pleasant at the ranch, but he couldn't have borne the discomforts at Grand River as patiently as an Indian child. Through five days of the hottest weather, the most ferocious bugs, the fewest diversions, and the longest, most repetitious religious services I have ever lived through, I didn't hear a single child complain. Not a parent raised a hand. The boys invented things to do—hunting grasshoppers, juggling sticks, exploring the river, and skimming stones. A troop of girls wandered, giggling, from camp to camp. At the giveaways and feeds, the children took their elders' arms and led them to their seats, then went through the buffet and brought them plates of food. I was almost relieved to hear a child calling in the night, "Ma, my throat is sore. Ma, I can't stop coughing." His mother murmured a few words of comfort and the boy went back to sleep, but at least I had been assured that Lakota kids were human.

"Why don't you come join us?" One of the women at the adjoining campsite pointed to the empty chair. "I'm Suzanne. This is Carol."

I hated to accept their shade under false pretenses, so I told them who I was. They didn't seem to mind. They had come to the dance to pray for their nineteen-year-old grandson, who had just had open-heart surgery. The voice in my dream had said, *I'm sorry about your son.* It hadn't said "grandson." I wanted to tell Suzanne that her grandson would get well, but I wasn't accustomed to reasoning based on dreams. I promised to add my prayers to theirs. Then, to make conversation, I told them about Catherine Weldon.

"She sounds like she was a fine lady," Suzanne said. Carol nodded. Then they switched the subject. They had grown up speaking Lakota, they said, but had almost forgotten how—it was prohibited at school—and now they were happy that the language was coming back. They only hoped they wouldn't get their periods because then they would have to leave. A woman in her moon time was too powerful, they said. She would draw strength from the men. The year before, two men had gotten very weak, and Isaac went around looking at all the women until he found one of the Germans and took her aside. The German woman left, and later they found out that she had been in her moon time. Isaac could just tell. Women in their moon time are powerful beings, Carol said. "That's why women rule!"

We talked about the weather and laughed about the outhouse tipping in the pit. I asked if they knew where I could find Sitting Bull's old camp. They had been coming here for years, but neither woman knew. "Just be careful of snakes," they warned.

I started down the road, hoping that if I went far enough, I would stumble on the camp. A little way beyond the parking lot, I came upon two women walking with a boy. Maybe they were making a pilgrimage to Sitting Bull's camp? No, they were trying to catch up with a sage-cutting expedition. They were sisters, they said. I'm Peggy; this is Pat. They had driven from Ohio with a Cherokee clan allied to the Lakota. Why didn't I come with them? The Indians used sage to drive away evil. There could never be too many people cutting sage at a Sun Dance.

Peggy and Pat were overweight, and the sun was so oppressive that we needed half an hour to catch up to the other women. We found them on a hill. Tristan was there, and a white girl named Michelle, who was the girlfriend of a young Indian man about to join the army. The leader of the expedition loaned me a knife and taught me to cut only the sage growing in single stalks rather than in bunches. This woman was the matriarch of the Cherokee clan. She had sinewy arms and legs, crooked teeth, and straight brown hair. She never raised her voice, but I don't recall her laughing. Her son, who seemed ten, stuffed the sage in trash bags and left these in a pile to be carted back later. Don't cut your fingers, the woman warned. Watch out for rattlers and poison ivy.

I enjoyed the work, at first. The meadow smelled sweet. I was doing something useful. Then I started sweating. My throat went dry. My back ached. My knife slipped and cut my leg. I had doused my skin with DEET, but the mosquitoes kept biting. I decided to take a break and find Sitting Bull's camp. I asked Tristan if she could give me more precise directions, and she pointed out a clump of cottonwoods to the west. Off I went again, wincing through the spear grass, the sun parching my skin and scalp. The grove was farther than it seemed. I glanced back and saw the harvesters coming down the hill and hurried back to join them.

Later that afternoon, the Cherokee women spread their sage and set to work, trimming stalks and plaiting them. I wanted to help but knew that I would only get in the way. An old woman with long, unkempt white hair and the sort of weathered Georgia O'Keeffe face I have always hoped I might age into was using a plastic swatter to kill flies. (In the old days, the Indians used buffalo tails as swatters; for their sakes, I hoped buffalo tails were more effective than plastic.) But there was only one swatter. I couldn't find anything to do to justify my time in their shade.

So I was thrilled to hear the drumming. A voice summoned us to pray for the scouts going to hunt the tree. Tristan told me that a woman couldn't approach the arbor unless she wore a shawl, so I trotted to my tent, delighted that I had brought those paisley scarves—only to find out how ridiculous I looked compared to the other women, all of whom wore *real* shawls of heavy patterned wool hanging to their knees. The other women looked like Indians; I looked like an artiste on a stroll through Greenwich Village. I wondered if Weldon wore that magnificent lacework shawl when she lived at Grand River or if she traded it for wool. Either way, she and the Lakota women had this trait in common—they loved to dress up. Come to think of it, Lakota men loved to dress up, too.

We gathered at the arbor. Isaac's daughter carried in the sacred pipe. She was a beautiful adolescent girl in a deerskin dress and long, red shawl, so innocent and dignified I could see her as the chief's daughter she would have been in years gone by, sought by the bravest men. The drummers drummed their songs. The scouts filed out the east gate, hunting for the tree.

Again the vexing question of what to do to pass the time. How often could I visit the latrines? Where could Catherine Weldon have been walking when she received that Lakota name? I opened a can of tuna while, at the other camps, the other women cooked real lunches for their men—meat sandwiches and stews washed down with Kool-Aid. Thankfully, I had accumulated enough trash to make a trip to the dumpster. On the way back, I stopped to see Donna. The temperature was in the high nineties, but she and Wox were cooking that night's dinner over a flaming pit, boiling fry bread in oil, and fashioning balls of *wasna*, an old-fashioned pemmican of buffalo fat, chopped meat, and cherries that

Donna took pride in knowing how to make. She told me that she would be throwing the giveaway feast that night to celebrate her *hunka* ceremony with her brother, Fred. She said the word *hunka* as if daring me to ask what it meant. But I knew that much. A *hunka* ceremony joins two people in a vow to give their lives for each other. The rite's fullest form usually involves two men, but the ritual can create or reinforce any family tie. "I would slit my throat to save my brother," Donna said. And I didn't have the slightest doubt she would.

I asked if I could help. No, she said, surprised. She and Wox had the cooking under control. But they needed someone later to help cut up the meat.

The speaker called us to go out and get the sacred tree. We followed the scouts through a field into a little grove where the mosquitoes were so hostile we must have invaded their homeland. The women gracefully flipped their shawls to cover their necks and arms while I used my flimsy scarf, which offered no protection. My hands began to swell. I got bitten on one eye. The tree had been roped off and tied with red flags. The custom was for warriors who had proven their bravery in battle to speak about their deeds. Two vets were called forward. As they spoke, I realized how much of Lakota culture still revolves around war. To prove your devotion to your people, you have to risk your life protecting them, or mortify your flesh for the common good in the Sun Dance, or gather food and share it. Like most Lakota men, Sitting Bull believed that the only way to gain honor was by contributing to his tribe. His father let him ride to war when he was only fourteen. If Sitting Bull had died, his parents would have grieved, but they would also have been proud. If whites had permitted Indians to continue living as they wished, they might be our most loyal citizens. Even after centuries of abuse, many Indians take pride in having fought in World War II, Korea, and Vietnam.

Both vets who spoke at the tree-cutting ceremony had taken part in the bloody charge on Hamburger Hill, but they chose not to describe that battle. They talked about friends who survived the war only to kill themselves later—directly, with guns, or indirectly, by drinking. Other vets were still fighting addictions to drugs and liquor. The men hoped we would remember those survivors in our prayers.

The third speaker wasn't technically a vet. He was asked to speak because he had won his fight against drinking and was helping others to win that fight. Sitting Bull's message, this man said, was that an Indian should not fight his own people. There were very good things in the Indian nation of which an Indian should be proud. The man told a legend about the sacred tree and how it would become the people's path south. If a person shared his belongings, if he was humble and didn't care for personal fame, then Grandmother would send him along the tree to the Milky Way, where he would live with all his relatives. But if a person was very selfish, if he had too big an ego, that person would try to take the path along the tree and fall off, condemned to stay on earth forever, hungry, cold, alone.

A medicine man blessed the tree. Each of the virgins took symbolic swings with an ax. Then the men took their turns. The tree began to fall. I was forty-one years old, but this was the first tree I had ever seen chopped down. I had never seen an animal killed for food. I had never seen a corpse.

"Careful!" someone cried. The men caught the tree, hacked off the bottom branches, and carried it back to camp. The women walked ahead, laying their shawls on the ground so no part of the tree would touch it. "This is our relative now," the medicine man announced. "Don't step over the trunk. That wouldn't be a respectful thing to do to a relative." They carried the tree through the arbor's east gate and set it gently on logs and shawls. The bottom of the trunk rested on the lip of a hole in the center of the circle. A medicine man painted sage on the tree's wounds, then tied banners around the top, and the effigies of the buffalo and human being that Donna and Wox had cut, and the ropes the dancers would use on the last day, when they pierced. The men hoisted the tree until the trunk slid inside the hole, and the earth was tamped around it. Then the drummers led the people in a memorial song that Sitting Bull had composed. To protect the dancers' feet, the rest of us were asked to trample the spear grass and pick up cacti, twigs, and dung. While the drummers drummed, we danced. Even I joined in, shuffling around the mystery circle, picking up as many cacti as I could.

I returned to Donna's camp, where huge joints of beef were roasting in aluminum pans. My job was to carve the meat in big chunks. The Sioux really love their meat, Donna said, and the pieces should be equal. She handed me a knife so lethal it could have severed a man's head. I set to work, hacking beef from bones and trying not to be repulsed by the gristle and fat Donna told me to leave on.

After the meat was cut, I had hours until the feast. I provisioned myself with water, a pocketknife, a stick, a compass, and some crackers and set off for the third time to find Sitting Bull's camp. Maybe I could also find a spot to take a dip in the river. (Grown-ups didn't go swimming, Donna said. It was a frivolous use of water, and the sounds of people splashing would drive the dancers mad.) I was caked with mud and sunscreen, sweat and DEET. My hair was dry and tangled, my scalp sunburned raw; I'd had to tie a scarf around my head and try to forget how badly it itched.

The longer I walked in the scorching sun, the more I came to respect the Victorian convention of wearing hats. I wasn't sorry not to wear a corset, but maybe the long-sleeved shirts and ankle-length skirts protected Weldon's flesh from bites.

I walked about a mile. The road ended. Pushing through the briars, I came upon two young men who glanced in my direction and shyly turned away. "Please," I said, "I'm looking for Sitting Bull's old camp. You know, the monument where he was killed?"

One of the men motioned toward the next grove of trees. "Just keep going west," he mumbled, looking at his feet. "Keep going along the trail until you can't go any farther." Then he and his friend waded deeper in the woods.

I kept walking down a trail that no longer seemed a trail, hallucinating about how refreshing it would feel to dunk my head in the river. I reached the grove and saw a cabin with an enclosure nearby. After he was killed, Sitting Bull's cabin was transported log by log to the World's Fair in Chicago, where it was rebuilt on the Midway. But there had been a smaller cabin and several sheds. I walked around the farm but couldn't find a monument—only the muddy river, flowing slowly between its banks. I slip-sided down the cliff, which dissolved beneath my feet in such a treacherous way I panicked. I made it to within a few yards from shore but kept sinking in the mud. I had to plunge my arm to the elbow to retrieve the shoe I'd lost. The mosquitoes and biting flies seemed even thicker here. My dress grew heavy with clotted mud. If Sitting Bull and Catherine Weldon had been waiting around the next bend, I couldn't have gone another step.

In the distance I heard drums. I didn't want to miss the *hunka* ceremony, so I crawled up the bank on all fours and started back to camp, hotter and dirtier than ever.

I have little memory of the ceremony that joined Donna and Fred as *hunkas*. It happened in the dark. Isaac escorted Donna's relatives around a ring, then waved an eagle-feather fan over the two *hunkas* as they repeated their vows. I helped serve the feast. The Indian women worked with the energy and pride that comes from devoting yourself to tasks that have become fashionable for others to denigrate. I had spent my life avoiding anyone who thought that I ought to spend my time cooking food and serving it, and even now, I went about it all wrong. A barrel-sized kettle of potatoes needed to be moved, and I volunteered, knowing that I could lift heavier weights than most women. "Put that down!" the women ordered. "That's too heavy for a woman to lift. That's what men are for!"

The woman with the Georgia O'Keeffe face turned out to be another white New Ager from Santa Fe. She walked around chatting to herself and slept in the jalopy she had driven from New Mexico. She wasn't shy about asking why the Sioux did this or that, how the Cherokee were different. The women told her that she wasn't supposed to interrupt the men or speak to them first, but she didn't take the hint. When the men weren't chopping wood or fixing what needed fixing, they sat in chairs beneath the camouflage net. The older men told war stories to the younger men, who were thinking of joining up or had already been through boot camp and were here on a few days' leave. I sided with the old woman for thinking she was entitled to sit with the men. But I was mortified that one of the only other whites would violate Lakota etiquette. I could imagine the seduction of being Catherine Weldon and thinking you were special because you were exempt from the rules that governed the Native women. But if your powers are derived from being an exception, eventually the rules can be used against you.

Other customs I grew to love. How could whites denounce the giveaway? Even if a giveaway leaves the giver poor, gifts travel in a circle. Eventually a person gets back most of what he gave. In the meantime, why not entertain your friends and kinsmen with a feast? What else was there to do? The tables at Donna's giveaway were piled with Tupperware and pillows. Peggy and Pat handed me a blanket. Oh no, I said, I can't, I'm only here to watch.

But you've come so far, they insisted. You have to take the blanket or Donna will be hurt.

I accepted the gift and thanked them. I loved the rich, soft colors. If I put the blanket beneath my sleeping bag, it would keep the grass from pricking through. But I was afraid that accepting a gift from someone who didn't like me would bring me bad luck. I shoved the blanket inside my tent, then crawled in myself. A voice summoned the women who would be dancing next day to come to the arbor and offer their tobacco, but I couldn't bear the thought of going back outside and facing the mosquitoes. I wet a towel and washed my legs, but the mud was sticky and wouldn't come off. I cursed and fell asleep and was woken by a storm even fiercer than the one the night before. I covered my head with Donna's blanket. The tent bucked like an angry horse. I heard the first few pegs tearing from the ground, then fell asleep praying the remaining pegs would hold, only to wake at dawn to the throbbing of a drum and the mournful call of whistles—*wheee-hooo, whee-whee-hooo.* The Sun Dance I had come a thousand miles to see finally had started, but I was so tired, stiff, and drained I couldn't crawl from my tent and watch.

First Day of Dancing: Sunday, July 27

By the time I got up, the first round of dancing had ended and the Cherokee women were clearing away the feed they had provided for the camp. The men sat around trading war stories while the women twisted offerings of tobacco into colored cloths to attach to the sacred tree. Tristan and Michelle washed dishes in plastic tubs. The German women in the neighboring camp went about their business, hauling water, cooking. I walked over to a solemn blonde toting a rubber jug. Why had she traveled so far? I asked. Why was she here?

Her body went rigid, as if she expected to be told to leave. "We are coming here to support one of the dancers," she said stiffly, then walked behind a tent.

The drummers started drumming. The women got their shawls. The children dragged lawn chairs to the arbor for their elders, then settled on the older people's laps or by their feet. The dancers filed in. There were seventeen male dancers, among them Uncle Charlie. Most of the men were fleshy and middle-aged. They wore long, bright red blankets tied around their waists, with gym shorts underneath. Their hairless chests bore scars from earlier piercings. But the youngest boy was so skinny, his unblemished chest so tight, I flinched as I imagined the skewers going in. His hair was shaved in a buzz cut, but the older men wore their hair long. One man had a beautiful Indian woman tattooed on his back; she peeked from behind his hair whenever he twirled or swayed.

The nine women behind the men were all middle-aged, in full-length deer-skin dresses or skirts of colored cloth with fringed shawls around their waists. All the dancers wore sage wreathed around their heads, wrists, and ankles. Whistles carved from the wing bones of eagles dangled from thongs around their necks.

In everything they did, the dancers were led by Isaac, his hair hanging thick about his shoulders, the blanket around his waist white instead of red. The dancers danced in lines facing the sacred pole. They lifted their feet and set them down, raised their arms to the sun. The men blew their whistles. Anyone who has taken an aerobics class can guess how exhausting it must be to jog in the blazing sun, raising your arms and whistling, hour after hour. To give the dancers strength, Isaac and his helpers brushed them with eagle-feather fans, then led them to the pole, where the dancers knelt and prayed. Each of the eight drummers was led to the pole and blessed. A boy walked around the circle swinging a can of smoldering sage, bringing it close to the spectators, who cupped the fragrant smoke in their palms and tossed it like water up and over their hair. Waving the boy away seemed more disruptive than doing what everyone else was doing, so I fanned myself, too.

I am reluctant to describe more. I couldn't take notes, and my memory is blurred because I wasn't allowed to wear my glasses. I was torn between the sacred nature of what I saw and my writer's wish to show a Sun Dance to my readers. The only known photos of the Ghost Dance were taken by white reporters. The portable Kodak camera had just been invented. At Pine Ridge, one young photographer entered the dancers' circle and revealed a small brown box. The Indians heard a click but didn't know what to make of it until one of the boys who had been away to school cried, *Etoape wachee!* He takes a picture! The men dashed the camera to bits. At Standing Rock, an adventurous Chicago reporter named Sam Clover prevailed on the teacher, John Carignan, to take him to Sitting Bull's camp. Carignan agreed, and Clover used a small hidden Kodak to snap that one illicit photo. Procuring photographs by chicanery isn't right. But that picture is the only record—for Indians and whites—of the way the Hunkpapas' dance was done.

Most whites gain their impressions of Indian life from photographs and movies. The Germans have been obsessed with Indians since the Wild West shows began touring Europe in the 1880s. The shows—especially Cody's—inspired the fantastic Western novels of the writer Karl May, who had never been to America. No German child could grow up without reading May's books. In the 1960s, East German filmmakers started a genre called the *Indianerfilme*, in which the cowboys were the bad guys and the Indians were the heroes. An estimated eighty-five thousand Germans belong to more than three hundred clubs devoted to studying and reenacting life in the American West. Critical of the life of overly civilized Europe, German "Indians" pay admission to parks where they can dress in full regalia, camp in tipis, and pretend they are living on the Plains. I couldn't help but be reminded of the Germans I know who are obsessed with all things Jewish, allying themselves with the victims of a genocide rather than its perpetrators. I was bothered that the Sioux could be so easily bought off—the Germans throw tremendous feasts. Never mind that my grandparents hadn't arrived in New York until twenty years after the last Indian war. I was white and an American. My presence at the dance had to be resented more than the presence of a few Germans who got off pretending to be Sioux.

Then again, even I didn't want some of the other white Americans to be there. "Did you know the CIA implanted a tiny computer chip in our wrists?" Ted asked me that afternoon. "The chip has your social security number in it. The government can track us from satellites." He saw my disbelief. "The rabbis are worried. It's like the numbers the Nazis tattooed on the wrists of inmates in the concentration camps."

To escape Ted, I went to the parking lot and hid in the wedge of shade behind my truck. Sitting there, I overheard a conversation between the leader of the Cherokee camp and the old white woman from Santa Fe. The white woman had taken it in her hands to discipline the Cherokee woman's son, whom she caught tormenting a grasshopper. The boy's mother didn't approve of her son's cruelty, but she told the woman that it wasn't the Indian way to shame a child. "It's our way to hope that a child who is given the proper love and examples will grow up the right way." She kept repeating this, but the older woman kept objecting.

Still, the Indians let her stay. A vision had brought her from New Mexico, and the Indians honor visions. When Catherine Weldon asked Sitting Bull to stop the Ghost Dance because she foresaw what would happen, he didn't demand that she leave. *Do as your heart dictates. If you want to go, go, but if your heart says stay, remain.* My own heart had told me to follow Weldon here. I believed I would learn something I needed to learn—about her, about myself. But I wondered if that knowledge was worth making my hosts uncomfortable.

In the long, scorching hours between rounds, I stood beneath the camouflage in the Cherokee pavilion and tried not to bother anyone. I washed dishes and helped to cook. Why hadn't Ina shown up? I couldn't interview the dancers. I had brought books to pass the time, but I hadn't seen anyone else reading.

I welcomed the round of drumming that started every dance. The women got their shawls. The older people found their lawn chairs. The men stood farther back, arms crossed. The medicine man came in and approached the buffalo-skull altar west of the sacred tree. Praying, he offered his pipe to each direction. The male dancers came in first, followed by the women. As the drummers sang and drummed, the dancers rose and fell on the balls of their feet, chests and chins thrust forward. The men whistled on their whistles, licking their cracked lips. They raised bundles of sage and feathers. They moved where Isaac led them—west, north, east, south. The youngest dancer had the most trouble—Isaac and his helpers fanned him with their fans—but I worried most for Charlie. He had a painful-looking sunburn and sweated so profusely I couldn't imagine him going on. Boys circled with smoking censers, and we fanned ourselves with sage. Each round ended with the medicine man taking the sacred pipe to the eastern gate and pretending to hand it off to another man—three feints in all, to test the receiver's sincerity—before the dancers filed out and retired to their huts to meditate on whatever visions they had been granted. If I had planned to study the Sun Dance as an anthropologist would study it, I would have given up. The only thing I learned was how much I didn't know.

I stopped at Donna's camp. Casually I asked if she had ever taken part in a Sun Dance.

"I need to get some tea," she told her relatives, then pulled me across the field. "I didn't want my aunties to hear me talking about the Sun Dance. They would kill me if they heard me tell you anything about the Sun Dance." She informed me that girls who hadn't yet begun to menstruate and older women past their moon time could take part in a Sun Dance, but not women like her. I apologized for my ignorance. I was trying to learn what I didn't know, I said.

This gave Donna the chance to tell me what she had been so eager to tell me all along. "People don't want to talk to you because you're a writer." Her people hated when white writers came to the reservation, she said. The writers asked the people questions, then they wrote lies. Or the people told them lies because they didn't like white people coming in to study them. The writers went away, published their books, made themselves famous and rich, and what did they give back? Nothing. They never gave anything back.

I looked around this camp of polite, gentle people who didn't want me with them. They wouldn't tell me to go home, but maybe I should take Donna's hint and leave. What good would come of telling Weldon's story? Other whites might travel to the reservation. But they probably would be less like Tristan than Ted. As Ina had warned, no matter whom I spoke to, I would remain an outsider. I would get everything wrong.

Still, I had been invited. I didn't want Donna to forget that. "Your grandma Ina," I said. "Do you know if she's planning to show up?"

Donna stared at me darkly. "She was here for weeks. Until the day before tree day. Her son Donald was Jet-Skiing with a friend off Long Island and disappeared. They found the Jet Ski, but not Donald. We drove her to Bismarck to fly home."

I was dumbfounded. "Her son? You mean Ron?"

"No. Her other son. Donald."

"Her son drowned? And you didn't tell me?"

Donna shook her head. "I didn't say he drowned. I said he disappeared. The medicine man says they'll find him in four days, alive, next to something red."

A man didn't disappear in the middle of the Atlantic Ocean, then reappear, unharmed, by something red or not. The voice in my dream had said, *I'm sorry about your son.* He had meant Ina's son, not mine. I had seen those two boys playing chicken on their Jet Skis and hadn't tried to stop them. Ina had lost her son. I wanted to drive to town and call her. But I didn't know what to say to comfort a parent who's lost a child.

I left Donna and started walking. "I've got to get out of here," I told Tristan. Would she go with me to Sitting Bull's camp? Sure, she said, she wouldn't mind getting away for a little while herself.

We climbed in my Explorer and drove along the path I had walked so many times. The camp was two miles farther than I thought. The path ended. We left the truck. Tristan showed me an enclosure with a plaque, a small bench, and a modest white obelisk. "In Memory of Sitting Bull and his friends who fell with them here. . . . Erected by their friends. Faith. Hope and Charity. But the greatest of these is Charity." I read the list of the dead and was stricken to my knees with pain for Ina McNeil, Catherine Weldon, Sitting Bull, Hohecikana, even James McLaughlin, anyone in the world who had lost a child.

Tristan wandered off to give me time alone. I scribbled down the words on the plaque, the most controversial of which had been partially scratched out.

SITTING BULL'S TRAGIC DEATH

December 15, 1890

Sitting Bull, best known American Indian, leader of the ["hostile groups"] for a generation, a powerful orator, a [clever] prophet who believed that white contact only degraded the Indian, an Uncpapa Siouan patriot, was killed here at dawn, Dec. 15, 1890. Slain with him were seven "ghost dancers," his followers, buried here Jan. 2, 1891, by Rev. Thomas L. Riggs with Indian helpers. The slain men's names are on the nearby marble monument, placed here in 1958, but provided for by Missionary Mary Collins and kinsmen of the dead men half a century ago. . . .

An unnecessary and tragic end of a notable [misguided] Indian leader, this marker briefly tells the sad story.

Erected 1958 by State [Historical] Society.

All of it had happened. This is where they lived. It came to me more strongly how brave Weldon was. Outside the cabin in which she stayed, the people danced and chanted. Inside, she wrote letters to McLaughlin on the only paper she could find, torn from an old datebook. She betrayed Sitting Bull by doing this. But she was pleading for his life. Her friends wouldn't credit what she knew. They saw her as an enemy. She was angry and hurt. But maybe some things are more important than being right. Maybe, if she had stayed, this marker wouldn't be here. Or her name would be carved on the monument with the other names.

It's easy to say that someone else should rise above history. One insult and I had left. Perhaps if Weldon had known how sad her life would be after she left Grand River, she would have stayed and been killed beside her friends. As it was, the only white woman mentioned on this marker was Mary Collins, who gave money to buy it, and the Reverend Thomas Riggs, who'd had no use for Sitting Bull but found the decency to come out and bury his dead followers.

No one else would do it. Two weeks after the battle, Sitting Bull's relatives were still afraid to return to Grand River because the survivors of the dead police might be lying in wait to kill them. Only Riggs and a friend were willing to accompany a few surviving Hunkpapa warriors on the two-day trip on horseback in the dead of a Dakota winter. They hacked a grave from the icy ground. Then Riggs picked up Crow Foot's frozen corpse and laid it in the hole. The Sioux brought Catch the Bear, the warrior who had fired the first shot, and, one by one, the others. The Indians were quiet while they worked. Afterward they relaxed. "They talked and smoked and joked as if a shaft of sunlight had engulfed them all," Riggs recalled later.

Crow Foot. Hohecikana. Chase Wounded. Catch the Bear. Black Bird. Chief Spotted Horn Bull. Chief Brave Thunder. All of them were buried here. Sitting Bull had died not knowing that his people, a century later, would be dancing the Sun Dance a few miles from where he lived. Or maybe he did know. Maybe he died because he knew it was more important to bequeath his people an idea than live a long life without one.

~~◦

When Tristan and I got back, another round of dancing had started. This time, anyone who wanted could join in. Parents escorted their children to the circle's east gate; the dancers held out sage and led the boys and girls to the tree. The children bent their heads while the dancers sang around them, brushing them with fans. Then the grown-ups prepared to enter. They took off their shoes and glasses, bowed their heads to the tree, and prayed. An old woman was wheeled in and helped to stand. Bent, she hobbled forward, then stood against the tree. Like my own dead grandmother, this woman's face had shriveled and left her nose as prominent as a mountain on a plain. I remembered my grandmother in synagogue on Yom Kippur, pounding her fist against her chest as she repented whatever sins she needed to repent. I realized that I was crying. I am not one to think all religions are the same. But in many ways they are.

I noticed a man standing next to Donna. Even without my glasses I guessed that he must be Ron McNeil. I tried to ignore how charismatic he was, as Catherine Weldon must have done with Sitting Bull. I waited until Donna had left, then went up to Ron and stammered out my hope that his brother was all right.

He looked as puzzled as if Donna had made up the whole story. "We're hoping this isn't all that serious," he said. "The young man and his friend have been known to stay away for several days. We're hoping it's a prank."

"I've been praying for him," I blurted out.

"Why, thank you," Ron said.

There was a night dance that night. In the dark I didn't feel white. I didn't feel so *seen*. The stars pulsed to the drums and whistles. I had read that Indians danced at night to scare away their enemies. If a spy sneaked up on a camp, he would see a band of warriors dancing with their shadows and count them twice as numerous. But the Indians also must have danced because dancing made them feel less alone beneath those vast, cold stars.

Monday, July 28: Second Day of Dancing

Monday dawned cloudy. The dancers faced east, raised their arms, and sang, and the sun rose above the clouds as if dragged up by their arms. I couldn't imagine how I could endure another day. Here I experienced life directly, unmediated by a microfilm reader, a word processor, a telephone, or a book. I spent my time moving food around my tent, lighting my stove, making trips to the latrine, salving my burns and cuts. But coping with survival can be dull.

There was more to my failure to appreciate the Sun Dance than being spoiled. The Indians saw self-sacrifice as a way to prove one's devotion to one's people and one's Creator. Pain wasn't a barrier to the life of the spirit so much as a path to that life. The dancers were jogging in the sun hour after hour without food or water as a way to induce their visions. Their families and friends were undergoing their own less drastic deprivations to lend support to the dancers' prayers. But I had been brought up to see pain as an obstacle to spiritual endeavors. Hunger and repetition interfered with my ability to think, which was how I reached the spirit. Judaism prohibits mutilation. Not even a corpse may be marred by autopsy or cremation. Only on Yom Kippur is deprivation seen as a way to reach God. I could pitch my tent and live beside my Lakota hosts for days, but I would never get anywhere near them in the spiritual landscape of a Sun Dance.

And Weldon? Was she bored at Grand River? I don't think she was. She was more like Tristan than like me, less a distant guest than a friend intimate enough to be allowed to help with chores. Weldon didn't approve of self-torture. But she never saw a Sun Dance, and the Ghost Dance didn't require physical mutilation. I doubt that she would have wanted Christie to dance and pierce. But she wouldn't have disapproved of the dances that honored nature or celebrated life.

At the second round of dancing, a teacher and his class wandered in from town. A few middle-aged white couples walked around the circle in T-shirts, shorts, and hiking boots. One of the drummers took the microphone and thanked his uncle Isaac for giving the dancers heart. Not that Isaac was his uncle by blood. But each of us is related, the drummer said, no matter what his race. *Tunkashila* doesn't see a person's color, the drummer repeated. He talked about how hard it was for Isaac and his helpers to offer their prayers over such a long time. None of us is here for presents or recognition, the drummer said. We're here because we must be. He was missing a few teeth and had an accent. "It's not supposed to be a fun t'ing," he said. "It's not just a weekend t'ing."

The man, it turned out, was a veteran of both Korea and Vietnam. In Vietnam he had been part of a platoon that destroyed a village with napalm. He went in with the other men and stumbled over a baby's corpse. When he tried to pick it up, the baby fell apart. He wrapped the pieces in his shirt and tried to find a villager to bury the child. But everyone had fled. He looked down at the baby's face, and its face looked Lakota. He carried it up the hill and dug a hole, put some plants in the hole to purify it, then he buried that child. To this day, he hoped that child had crossed the river. That's why he dedicated himself to helping all the young people. To honor that dead child.

After the man stopped crying, another healing ceremony started. A man carried his little girl to the circle. In a flowered hospital gown and bandages, she walked weakly to the tree. As the dancers prayed around her, I doubted that anyone would care if she were cured by *Tunkashila*, or Jesus Christ, or the head of pediatrics in Pierre.

A female dancer took the microphone to encourage her comrades to keep dancing, despite their thirst. Like everyone there, she said, she'd had a hard life. She had been an alcoholic. She had barely survived her drinking. But here she was, praying to be strong, praying not to drink.

Then one of the dancers offered his vision to the crowd. He spoke in Lakota, but the lead singer translated. On the first day, this dancer had been praying for his family's health and the health of all our families. He had been looking at the sun, and he saw a woman and a child covered by dark clouds. *This is not what we are here for!* he prayed, and the cloud disappeared. Our prayers are strong, he said. Today he had seen that same woman and her child, but no clouds were covering them. The coming year would be a healthy, good year for our children. But we must care for them. Our children are very precious, the dancer said. We must care for every one.

All the grown-ups who wished to be healed removed their shoes and entered the sacred circle. Tristan went in to pray, and the Germans, and Michelle. If every round had been like this one, with everyone taking part, I might have joined in. It's hard not to be drawn into whatever ritual your hosts are putting on, sing the songs they sing, dance to the persistent beat of their drum. No one would have stopped me. But at the last moment, I balked. This wasn't my path. Although what my path was, I couldn't have yet said.

That's when I received my own vision, even though I was the only person at the dance who didn't believe in visions, and I received it from a man who didn't intend for me to have it. A young *heyoka* came in. A *heyoka* is a warrior who does everything backward. It's one of the most difficult paths a man can take. This *heyoka* danced backward, counterclockwise. He had a sharp face, like Isaac's, and fierce, unblinking eyes. Half his face was red, the other half was blue, and a brilliant white stripe was painted down his nose. He wore red leggings and a blue fringed shirt and carried a savage knife. He made my heart stop. That's all I can say: he was the only human being who ever made my heart stop. The dancers were unsteady from their fasts, but he bumped them with his chest. He even jostled Tristan. As the drummers sang and prayed, the *heyoka* shrieked and laughed. When the dancers raised their arms toward the sun, the *heyoka* stood in the opposite direction and raised his arms away from the sun. He ran out of the circle and came back with a large bowl of water, which he wafted beneath the dancers' noses, flicking drops in their faces—not enough to refresh, only to torment. Then he raised the bowl and drank a long draught, smacking his lips and pouring the rest over his head, shivering and howling.

Around the circle he skipped, making kissy faces at the men, brandishing his knife. When he saw a woman pushing up a branch that had fallen from the trellis, he danced over and yanked it down. He was a clown who wasn't funny, a jester whose jokes were meant to confuse and instruct. But his teasing was directed at members of the tribe. He ignored me in a way that couldn't have been an accident. I wasn't even worth teasing. For a moment, I imagined that I had been born a century earlier as a Hunkpapa. Would I have been a model wife? A medicine woman? A *heyoka?*

That's when I saw that the only culture in which I'd ever fit was the one I lived in now. I was exactly what I was: a woman, a Jew, a feminist, the mother of a son, the writer of stories I felt called upon to tell, the teacher of students who wanted to tell their own stories and the stories of their tribes, whatever those tribes might be. I'm an American, I thought. I couldn't have lived in any other country at any other time and done what I loved doing.

And Catherine Weldon? Where did she fit in? She wasn't talented or trained enough to make her living as an artist, or was the wrong gender to be allowed to do so. She was a Victorian lady in some ways, but in most ways she wasn't. She certainly didn't fit in society life in Brooklyn. She couldn't be taken seriously as a painter, a teacher, or a reformer anywhere but here.

The *heyoka* swept past. My legs had gone so weak that I needed to leave the circle. I needed to leave the camp. I began walking along the path I had traveled earlier with Tristan. I sensed someone up ahead. It was Weldon, I knew. Like me, she had felt the need to get away for a little walk. I could hear her skirts rustling. She was wearing black, I saw. And—how odd it seemed—she was carrying a cup. A porcelain cup. Of tea. The liquid trembled near the rim, reflecting the evening sun, this light she loved better than anywhere on earth.

Still, the poor quality of the cup made her angry. It was inferior and expensive, like everything the Indians were forced to buy at the agency store. If only she hadn't sold her china in New York. True, it would have been ridiculous for Sitting Bull and his family to be eating from her family's Swiss china. But if the Indians no longer could carve utensils from buffalo bones and horn, they must use china plates and forks, and if someone had to buy china plates and forks for Sitting Bull's family, she, Catherine Weldon, ought to be that person.

Sitting Bull valued her gifts. He loved the little gold charm in the shape of a bull she had brought him from Brooklyn; he wore it on a horsehair braid around his wrist. He didn't use the table and chairs she had ordered from the trading post, but he was proud his cabin had them and proud his wives had learned to set the table properly, although Sitting Bull himself preferred to eat on the floor.

And there was of course the food. When the rations ran out, she, Catherine, sold her silver to feed the camp. Sitting Bull's wives threw a feast, and everyone ate well for one night, then no one ate anything until it was ration day again. Sitting Bull was pleased to see his people eat, although he wished he were the one to provide the food. He disliked owing so much to anyone. To a widow with a child.

Well, no harm if she allowed Sitting Bull to show his gratitude toward her son. Already the boy seemed happier. He was learning to love the outdoors. He and the other boys whittled little tops, then built corrals of sticks and played a game in which they shot their own tops in such a way as to bump their opponents' tops from the enclosure, or they fashioned bows and hunted, or they waded in the shallows, chasing fish in the muddy stream. Christie was putting back weight, thank goodness, having found that he enjoyed the chokecherry soup, the wild plums and fry bread Seen by the Nation served.

The rich, woody scent of the cooking fires drifted toward her. She should return to the camp and wash her plates or the other women would do it for her. She should help them cook *wasna* for tomorrow's feast. But she could not bear the prospect of going down to the river and exposing her hands to the biting flies. If she were to approach the river in this heat, she would not be able to stop herself from walking in, dust swirling from her skirt, the cape billowing around her shoulders as the cool, refreshing water rose above her head.

She walked toward the hill where she and the other women went to gather sage and, with every step, a scattering of grasshoppers flung themselves against her. One grasshopper shot up beneath her crinoline, and she fluttered the folds of cloth and danced to get it out; she was glad that no Indian men were near, or they would have swirled imaginary skirts and petticoats to mock her. She wore heavy leather boots, although no rain had fallen in months and there was no mud anywhere but near the river. Snakes hid in this grass, and the grass itself was sharp, the blades burrowing in her flesh like a porcupine's quills. The earth was so parched that she might have stepped in a fissure or a prairie-dog hole and broken a leg. There was no doctor within forty miles, and the surgeon at the fort was an army hack. She would as soon have had the leg amputated as let that foul man put his tobacco-stained hands beneath her skirt and ask how she liked living among the filthy savages. That was all they ever called them, *filthy savages, filthy savages.* The whites derived as much pleasure from linking those two words as from sneaking looks at coupling dogs.

With one hand she held her cup, and with the other hand she shook the insects from her skirt. Her shawl slipped. She clasped it against her throat, the silk rustling like the hot, dry wind through the spear grass. It was utterly ridiculous to be wearing a long, black silk shawl at Grand River in July, but Indian women wore shawls and so must she. The men walked around any which way, vain of their flesh, even the heaviest old men, especially the heaviest old men, the Big Bellies, the Silent Eaters. She once saw Sitting Bull coming out of his *Ini ti* in nothing but a cloth, and his smile told her that he was not sorry. But Sitting Bull was a man, and men were ever so. The women wore long dresses, and most were tidy and clean, and they changed modestly beneath their frocks. Even at her friend Alma's ranch, when no men were present, Alma and her sister Louise, both of whom had married and borne children, were modest as virgins. They would, without flinching, reach inside a laboring cow and pull out the bloody calf. But they never would do anything to jeopardize their reputations as modest Sioux women.

The one day they all went swimming at the ranch, with Christie, and Alma's son Chaske, and Louise's little girl Lucille, Catherine made certain that no men were nearby, then went into the bushes and changed into her swimming dress. It was old and out-of-date, with a moth hole in the leg. She would have been hooted off the beach at Coney Island. But here it was risqué, and Alma said it would be a very good thing if little Chaske did not see her like that. Alma marveled that Catherine would allow her own son to see her so exposed. As for Alma and Louise, they wore their dresses and underclothes right into the water, crouching in the shallows in their good white frocks, Louise still wearing that ridiculous hat that looked like a stovepipe and sweet Lucille giggling and calling out: Mrs. Weldon! Don't my mother and Aunt Alma look like frogs! Chaske said there were no more frogs in the Cannonball, he caught them all, but here they are, the last two frogs in our little river!

The shawl snagged a burr, and she snatched it back. Something fluttered near her hand; she started and spilled some tea. A pale grasshopper had trapped itself in her cup. Had the drought turned the insect white, or had it been born that way? She used to shudder every time a grasshopper brushed her leg, but now she was quite used to them and would have missed their company. The creature was panting out its life in her tea, and she was torn between wanting to see it keep struggling and wanting to rescue it. She tipped the cup, and the grasshopper flowed over the lip like a daredevil down Niagara. The earth sucked in the liquid, and Catherine knelt and laid her palm to the dirt, resisting the fantasy that moisture would spread from her thin white fingers to heal the cracked, brown fields. The government wanted the Sioux to farm, but even a woman such as she, who could barely grow parsley in a window box, knew the ground was too dry. She slapped her hand on the hollow earth, thinking of what magnificent ranchers her Dakotas would make, if only that infuriating agent would allow them to run their herds.

But no. She had given up that fight. She had given up all fights. If the Sioux must live in cabins and wear shoddy clothes and cook the rations they were given, someone must show the women how to keep a cabin clean, how to repair those clothes, how to sew on a button, how to cook a loin of pork or boil a cabbage or churn a vat of butter, although their stomachs absolutely could *not* tolerate milk, and someone must teach the men to set the outhouses far enough from the river so the water wouldn't grow foul and to ventilate the cabins so the air inside wouldn't grow stale and infect their lungs. She would have liked to build a school and teach the Hunkpapa women these things. But the agent didn't trust her enough to teach the girls to hem a handkerchief, or even how to use one.

The grasshopper crawled away. Catherine struggled to her feet, trying to ignore the stiffness in her hip. In the distance, she could just make out the shapes of men on horses. A few days earlier, she had read Sitting Bull an excerpt from a book of Greek mythology she had brought with her from Brooklyn. She translated the story into Lakota—she was nowhere near as fluent as she would have liked to be, but she was becoming more so each day. It was the story of the centaurs, and Sitting Bull said it was the first story the whites had ever told him that he liked. Lakota men are that way too, he said, half man and half horse.

That tall shape must be her friend Hohecikana. She would never get over thinking it humorous that they called him Little Hohe, a heavyset man nearly as tall as Sitting Bull. And those two smaller shapes must be Crow Foot and Chase Wounded. And the smallest forms, the twins. And there, farthest behind, the double shape of Christie and Sitting Bull. The sight filled her with such pleasure, she thought her heart might crack like the brittle cup she held. The joy was even greater because it was mixed with the knowledge that if she had been a farm wife who had settled on this land twenty years earlier, she would have been terrified to see these Indians, especially if she knew one of them to be the dread warrior Sitting Bull. Terrified of a man who teased her about the shape of her bustle, who cried when someone's infant couldn't stop coughing, who was teaching her son to ride.

He once deserved such fear. He had killed many whites, she knew. The whites were killing Indians, the Indians were fighting back. She and Sitting Bull had not discussed this, but she was certain that he never killed women and children. And he saved Little Hohe. If Sitting Bull had come upon her that way, as he came on Hohecikana, he would not have killed her either. She took a certain ugly pride in thinking how cruel Sitting Bull's warriors were to white soldiers and how kind they were to her. She suspected that Hohecikana felt this same satisfaction, that Sitting Bull was so cruel to other Assiniboines, even to Little Hohe's own family, yet so kind to Hohecikana himself. But Hohecikana was a man and would not put such feelings into words. Even if Sitting Bull had been vengeful in the old days, the killing times were over. Who was there left to kill? And no one wanted to kill him. He had no power left, no land. She could live with him at peace, here, at Grand River, and learn all he had to teach. She wanted no more scandals. She had been daughter, wife, mother, and now she need only be herself, *Toka heya mani win*, Woman Walking Ahead. After she passed her moon time she would not be set aside, as she would be in New York. Here, among the Sioux, she would be consulted and looked up to. In the old days, before the agent prohibited the Indians from dancing, a woman past her moon time was allowed to dance the Sun Dance and sacrifice her flesh. The dance still went on in secret, she was sure of this, although the Indians did not yet trust her enough to tell her where and when. But someday they would tell her. Someday she would see them dance.

By now I had reached the monument. The sun was going down. I sank beneath a tree and wept. *Take heart*, a voice said. *Take heart. I say this now. I am Sitting Bull.*

Tuesday, July 29: Piercing

Before I traveled west, I imagined piercing to be the culmination of the Sun Dance. Now it seemed anticlimactic. I'd had my vision, and it said I didn't belong here. Ina wasn't coming. I felt sick about her loss. I was filthy with mud and bug spray. The evening before, in a flash of desperation, I had rubbed my scalp with cooking oil; it itched less, but now I reeked. Changing fuel tanks to cook breakfast, I had spilled gasoline all over my dress and shoes. I wanted to get home, take a bath, and hold my son. Even before the first round of dancing, I had taken down my tent. I was dragging my supplies to the truck when I passed Peggy and Pat.

"You mustn't leave!" they said. "It's been so good to have you. We really enjoyed meeting you. We're staying with the rest of our group to clean up. You could stay and help. We'll have a giveaway tonight. Will you come back again next year?"

I nodded ambiguously and hugged them. It occurred to me that the last time Weldon left Grand River, she was thinking of her friends, not her enemies. She must have hugged Sitting Bull's wives and daughters. Crow Foot would have stood aloof, but she went over and shook his hand. She must have been sad not to have the chance to say good-bye to Hohecikana. He was away from camp, hunting. Maybe he was discreetly avoiding the dance. Whatever his reason, Weldon never mentions that they argued. In her letters to Sitting Bull, she asks him again and again to remember her to her friend and brother Hohecikana.

The first round of dancing was no different from the others. But the second round began with the helpers unfurling the dancers' ropes and staking them full length from the tree. When the dancers filed in, I saw that five of the men had painted red circles above their nipples. Uncle Charlie wasn't piercing, thank goodness. I liked to think that *Tunkashila* had accepted his prayers already and granted him a long and prosperous life.

A buffalo robe was spread west of the sacred tree. The helpers led the first dancer, a heavyset young man with long red-blond hair, to lie on the robe. They removed his sage headdress. Isaac and two helpers rubbed his chest with sage. Then Isaac peeled the wrapper from what appeared to be a scalpel. He pinched the man's chest, sliced the folded flesh and slid a stick through the slits, then tied it to the rope. Isaac pierced the other side, then helped the man stand up. Attached to the sacred pole, the man jogged in place while the next two dancers were pierced.

Then the youngest man came in. He was even thinner than before. How could Isaac find a finger's worth of flesh to pinch on that skinny boy? But he did. He finished working, and the boy jumped up and raised his arms in a victory salute. The holy men led the boy to the perimeter of the circle, then tapped his rope with their fans to make the skewers work out faster. When all five supplicants were pierced, the women raised the tremolo. The five men danced forward and huddled around the tree while the holy men fanned them. They danced backward, then forward, up and back four times. Then, at a signal, all five men ran backward and hurled themselves away from the tree so violently, the skewers tore from their chests. All but the first dancer, whose skin stretched but wouldn't rip. I had to turn away. When I turned back, his skin had torn. Blood trickled down his chest and the chests of the other dancers. Still, the piercing was less bloody than I had feared. I had been more disturbed watching my son's circumcision.

I said good-bye to Tristan, then climbed in my truck and left. This time, instead of driving along the river, I took the inland route through a landscape so dramatic, with its valleys and sandy buttes, I thought I had taken a wrong turn and strayed onto another planet. I turned on the radio and got music from a powwow. The only other station I could get was public radio from Mandan, and the Mahler they were playing fit the majesty of the land in a way that set me crying. I couldn't have said until that moment that any music was truly mine, but Mahler's Ninth was, right then.

My flight home wasn't scheduled until the following day. I could try to fly standby. But my promise to go straight home and make sure Noah was all right already seemed to fade. What I wanted to do was drive to Pierre, where Weldon went with Christie after she left Standing Rock. On the map the trip looked easy—140 miles due south. The sun wouldn't set for hours. I could make Pierre by three and spend an hour or two ransacking the archives. I would find a motel, finish my research the next morning, then drive to Bismarck and fly home.

I stopped at a diner I assumed would serve the white-people food I craved— a hot open-faced turkey sandwich, mashed potatoes, rolls, a salad, and a vanilla milk shake. I got out of the truck and stretched. I was wearing an ankle-length dress that I had bought in a trendy boutique in Boston, but I had been wearing it for days, with a sweatshirt and heavy shoes. I smelled of gasoline, smoke, sage, bug spray, sweat, and mud. The dust from the reservation had caked the Explorer brown. The interior was littered with diet Coke cans, cracker boxes, and crumpled napkins. I stuffed these in a bag from the grocery store in Mandan and went inside to order lunch.

"I'm sorry," the hostess said. "I'm afraid you can't come in." She was blonde and well scrubbed. I wouldn't have been surprised if she were a cheerleader at the high school.

"I can't come in? You aren't full."

"I'm sorry," she repeated in the sort of stern voice you might use to discourage a persistent beggar. "You can't bring in your own food and eat it here."

My own food? Oh, she meant the grocery bag. "This is just trash from my truck. I'll go throw it out and wash up. Could I sit in that booth there?"

She shook her head no. "You can't use the bathroom—it's only for paying customers."

But I was a paying customer. "I just want to wash up and make a phone call. Then I'll order lunch. I've been driving for miles. I'm tired."

"Oh, all right," she said, and led me to a booth near the kitchen. I ordered the turkey special and went to find the ladies' room. I took off my sunglasses and studied my reflection. My face was ten shades darker than it used to be. My sweatshirt was torn and stained. My hair hung lank and oily. The waitress must have thought that I was a dirty Lakota squaw who had straggled in from Standing Rock and didn't belong in town.

10

Pierre

After I ate my lunch—the warm, bland food tasted heavenly—I went outside to call home. A bare-chested boy was talking on the phone. He turned his muscled back, curled the metal cord around his arm, and knelt beside the booth. The sun was a heated anvil on my head. Twenty minutes went by. I was about to walk away when the boy freed his arm—the cord had branded its impression—and hung up. I grabbed the phone and dialed my husband's lab. He wasn't there, which was unusual. I called home, but no one answered. Maybe he was picking up Noah from school. I would call again from the road. If the news wasn't good, I could turn around and speed back to Bismarck. If not, I could reach Pierre by three.

I got back on the road and drove. It occurred to me that I hadn't known a thing about Sitting Bull or Catherine Weldon before coming to the Dakotas. This was land that made you think nothing was more important than feeling close to whatever powers could create such beauty. If a stranger claimed this land was his, you would be angry enough to kill him. The entire Sioux nation could be living between that river and that hill, and every white South Dakotan could be living behind that bluff, and neither group would know the other group was there. Before venturing west, I thought the Indians couldn't withstand the whites' invasion because there wasn't room for both. But the whites could have taken the best farmland, settled all the cities, and left the Indians to wander the Plains for game. In 1890, fewer than 350,000 whites lived in South Dakota. Even today, when the number of whites has doubled and

Indians constitute 7 percent of the population, the density is fewer than nine people per square mile.

I also understood why the Indians resisted carving their land into farms. Not only did owning land violate every Indian idea of what was right, accepting an allotment meant that a family needed to separate itself from other families. A mile on the Plains is longer than a mile back east. The Plains aren't flat but rolling. The land stretches forever, yet a person can't go far without disappearing behind a ridge. The river offers water, boundaries, friendship, shade. The Sioux couldn't understand why homesteaders would leave their friends, dig a soddy in the ground, and go about their business with no companionship or help. How vulnerable a family was, dependent on a single plot of land for food, medicine, and clothes. If the rain didn't fall that year, you had to stay and starve.

Drought was the greatest danger the summer Weldon lived here, but flooding was the catastrophe the spring before I came. Long stretches of road had washed away. I kept coming up to spots where a construction worker stopped me and explained that I had to wait while another vehicle negotiated the single muddy lane in the opposite direction. Then it was my turn. I clenched my fists and drove along a narrow, slippery dike, trying to keep my wheels from catching in a rut and causing the Explorer to slip down to the flooded fields.

In 1948, the Army Corps of Engineers began building the Oahe Dam six miles above Pierre to try to end the cycle of flooding, erosion, and drought that brought so much grief to settlers. The dam turned the shallow Missouri River into a deep blue lake longer than Lake Ontario and deeper than Lake Erie. Lake Oahe is pretty. But the flooded land I passed made me wonder if the dam had been successful even for the whites who built it. The Oahe certainly was a disaster for the Indians, inundating more than 160,000 acres of land at Standing Rock and Cheyenne River. The government didn't bother to consult a single tribe while planning the Oahe. Only in 1947 did the Indians at Standing Rock learn that construction of the dam would mean flooding fifty-six thousand acres of their reservation. One-third of all the families at Standing Rock would be forced to abandon their farms—the very farms the government had been browbeating them into running since Sitting Bull's time. Sixty percent of the most successful Sioux ranchers would be required to move their cows to higher ground. Ninety percent of the reservation's timber grew along the river, providing the only source of fuel and wood for most members of the tribe, as well as the best land for wildlife and the berries and fruit that formed a staple of their diet. The dam would strand the agency, including Sitting Bull's grave, as the town below was flooded.

The Sioux protested, but their legal resources in the 1940s were very limited.

When they understood that the government would take their land no matter what, the Sioux argued for a settlement of $26 million, money that would provide assistance to a tribe in which most people lived in shacks with no electricity or plumbing, three-quarters were unemployed, and the average family earned $1,100 a year. The government derided the request. In the end, the Sioux received less than half of what they asked.

In January 1960, 190 Indian families were forced to evacuate their homes and live in cold, unfinished trailers, although the actual flooding wouldn't take place for many months. The government agreed that the Indians would be given time to cut their trees before the reservoir rose. But the Army Corps of Engineers demanded that *they* be the ones to clear the land. The courts ruled against the Corps, but by then there was no time for the Indians to cut the trees. No Sioux were given jobs building the dam itself. Little wonder they didn't show much enthusiasm when President Kennedy arrived with Stewart Udall and George McGovern to dedicate the Oahe as a "striking illustration of how much a free society can make the most of its God-given resources."

Some of the $12 million the government gave the Sioux did help the reservation, but no other good came from losing all that land. Flooding had never been much of a problem at Standing Rock until the government started playing with the level of the river. The rapid rise and fall of the water caused the banks to erode. Cattle tumbled in. The reservoir was meant to irrigate the Plains, but Standing Rock is so full of shale that most of the land there isn't arable even with irrigation. No hydroelectric power was set aside for the reservation. The lake was ruined for pleasure boats by the forest beneath the surface. A few outsiders showed up to swim and fish, but even with the Prairie Knights Casino, Standing Rock never became a mecca for tourists. The whites who come to the Dakotas to fish or see the Badlands usually stay in Pierre, as I discovered when I straggled into town and couldn't find a room.

It had taken me eight hours to cover the 140 miles. Not long after I started driving, the wind began to gust, smacking the truck so hard I could barely stay on the road. The sky went black. The rain fell in blocks. I had driven in storms before, but never with such violent wind. Colossal red forks of lightning speared from sky to ground in every direction. I couldn't pull off the road; there was no shoulder to pull off on. Finally I saw the exit for Pierre. I hadn't bothered to make a reservation. Who would be staying in Pierre, South Dakota, in the middle of July? I saw a ribbon of motels, more than I had predicted for a town of thirteen thousand. But the signs all flashed NO VACANCY. In and out of the drenching rain; every room was booked. When I found a place after midnight, I wanted to call my husband and make sure our son was safe. I knew that

I was overreacting, but I was spooked to be in the city where Weldon's son had died. I dialed our house and waited. Static distorted the line so badly I could hardly hear the ring. I heard a click. The line went dead.

I barely slept that night. At seven the next morning I drove to the park where the steamboat landing used to be. The morning was so misty that I couldn't see the opposite bank. In the middle of the river some bureaucratic hocus-pocus changed the time zone by an hour. And somehow, in that mist, time began doing strange things. I imagined that I could see a steamboat stranded on a sandbar and could hear a boy's faint screams.

"Chief Sitting Bull, My friend," Weldon wrote from Kansas City. "My boy, my Christie, died on the Missouri River Steamer 'Chaska.' He stepped on a nail while we were at Mrs. Parkins; the foot got better; but on the boat he got cold in it & spasms & lockjaw set in & he died, suffering the most terrible pains. We could not land, the boat stuck on a sand-bar opposite Pierre, and when the boat could land, and the Doctors were sent for, it was too late. He did not like to die, but clung to life & to me; for day & night. I could not leave his side & held his hands until he died. I took his body on shore & left the boat at Pierre. Put him in a coffin & an extra box & took him with me to this place, Kansas City. Last Monday the 17th we buried him here. . . ."

A steamboat stranded on a sandbar on the Missouri wasn't rare. For a certain kind of passenger—one with lots of time and an appreciation for the lore and romance of the river—getting stranded posed no problem. There was an entire vocabulary of running aground, and part of the entertainment was watching how cleverly the pilot got you off. "Plant a dead man!" he might order, and the crew would row to shore, bury a log upright in the mud, tie a rope to the "dead man" and winch the other end around the capstan, dragging the enormous boat up and off the sand. If this failed, the boat could be hoisted on huge wooden spars that dangled off the deck and "grasshoppered" free. The last resort was "double-tripping"—putting half the freight on shore, which lightened the boat enough to pass the shallows, then going back for the rest.

The fall that Weldon took Christie south from Fort Yates, the state of navigation on the Missouri was at its worst. The owners of the shipping lines were being driven into bankruptcy by the railroads, and this meant putting off repairs. Because of that summer's drought the river was at its lowest. The surprise was that Weldon's boat made it so close to Pierre before running aground. On the night of November 12, she endured what no parent should have to go through: her son lay shrieking in her arms, lips pulled above his teeth and frozen in a grimace, muscles contorting in violent spasms, breaths coming in rasps, his larynx nearly paralyzed, sweat pouring from his skin. There was nothing she could do. She couldn't walk ahead. She couldn't walk back. She couldn't lift this massive boat or swim to shore for help. The Indians had predicted that some dreadful fate would overtake her for mocking their messiah. She must have thought that they were right.

As I watched, the mist lifted. The day grew hot; it was in the eighties by the time the Historical Society opened. I found a phone and called home. He's all right, my husband said. Noah just broke his hand. The doctor put it in a cast. Stay as long as you need to.

I slid down the wall and cried. It was only a broken bone. I would drive to Bismarck that afternoon, catch the next plane home, and see him.

For now, I had only a few hours in which to work. The archives in Pierre were smaller than those in Bismarck, but there was still a lot to do. I hoped the local papers would reveal something of Christie's death. A boy dying of tetanus couldn't have been an everyday occurrence even then.

Sure enough, the *Pierre Daily Free Press* of November 13, 1890, acknowledged the arrival of Weldon's boat. The real topic of interest that day was the contest for state capital, which Pierre had just won. But Dick Talbot, captain of the newly arrived *Abner O'Neal*, also brought news of "the Messiah racket," which, he said, was continuing "in a white heat" among the Indians. According to the reporter, the "gigantic frame" of Captain Talbot loomed up in the lobby of the Locke Hotel and mentioned that among his passengers were "a Mrs. C. Weldon and her little son. Their home is in Brooklyn, N.Y. They have been living at Standing Rock for some time and Mrs. Weldon says the papers have indulged a great deal of unjustifiable rot about her affection for old Sitting Bull—there being no ground for such talk. A few days ago her little boy ran a nail in his foot and on the way to Pierre lock-jaw set in and the boy suffered horribly. As soon as the boat touched the Pierre landing Dr. Robinson was sent for, who is doing all possible to relieve his sufferings—with the chances very much against the lad's recovery."

So Christie had still been alive when the boat finally docked. A doctor tried to treat him. As it turned out, scientists in Germany were developing the anti-toxin even as Christie Weldon lay writhing in Pierre. I had been skimming head-lines about Robert Koch's advances against tuberculosis since starting my research. Koch's associate, Emil Berhing, and a Japanese bacteriologist named Kitasato Shibasaburo had discovered that injecting the serum of an animal infected with tetanus into an uninfected animal produced an immunity against the disease. Weldon might have read of these discoveries not many days after she buried Christie.

As it was, in cases like Christie's, when the onset was so rapid, there was very little hope. The mortality rate from tetanus before the discovery of the antitoxin was 80 percent. The hospital in Pierre had been started the year before by five nuns who had arrived in the city with $50 and the intention of founding a school. D. W. Robinson, the same doctor who later treated Christie, assured the sisters that Pierre already had enough schools; what it needed was a hospital. The nuns used their money to buy one room of an abandoned hotel and furnish it with instruments. The best they could have done for Christie was keep him sedated in a darkened room and quiet his convulsions with alcoholic drinks.

No one can say that his mother didn't go to pieces. On November 20, the *Bismarck Tribune* reprinted a notice from the *Pierre Capital*. "A 12-year-old son of Mrs. C. Weldon, from Buffalo, N.Y., [*sic*] died on the steamer Abner O'Neal yesterday morning. He was the only child, and the unhappy mother, who is now stopping at the Grand Pacific Hotel, is nearly crazed with grief. Mrs. Weldon is a very intelligent and highly educated lady. She has been working the past summer among the Indians at Standing Rock agency as a disciple of the religious ideas of Dr. Bland and is on her way to Kansas City to spend the winter. The body was in charge of Undertaker Kelley yesterday and was being prepared for shipment to Kansas City where the interment will take place."

Aside from Undertaker Kelley, no one paid much attention to Weldon's grief. While she ordered Christie's coffin, the citizens went to the landing to inspect the first "real live steamboat" they had seen in days because of the low level of the river, the *Abner O'Neal*'s presence a "practical demonstration" that the Missouri was still navigable even in this present "universal stage of low water." Back and forth the steamboat went, ferrying cattle across the river as Captain Talbot held court at the hotel.

Big Dick Talbot was a celebrity along the river. A businessman from Bismarck, he and a druggist named Brandt had gone east on a secret trip earlier that year. The river towns were rooting for pilots like Talbot to keep pace with the railroads, so the *Bismarck Tribune* cheered the news that Talbot had purchased "the well known river steamer, the Abner O'Neil," for $10,000 and had the boat refitted so he could put it to work on the shallow upper Missouri. (The lighter a steamboat was, the more likely she could keep navigating the river during the winter months when the water was low and the railroads stole the steamboats' business.) Talbot rechristened the steamer *Chaske*, took on a heavy load of freight in Pittsburgh, and left for St. Louis. The steamer's arrival in Bismarck created quite a stir; the excitement would have been noted by Alma Parkin, who, by coincidence, was visiting the capital that day, although the *Tribune* gave her name as "Mrs. H. S. Partin."

A report in the *Bismarck Tribune* that summer clarified why Weldon referred to the boat by two names ("the Steamer 'Chaska' 'Abner O'Neil,'" she wrote to Sitting Bull); the government had a rule that no steamer could change its name, and so the *Abner O'Neal* "must cling to her old name." On August 14, the steamer advertised a trip to Standing Rock "with a party of excursionists," to return the seventeenth. The excursion, which seems worth reporting since it gives us insight into how other whites who took the trouble to visit Standing Rock viewed the Indians Weldon counted as her friends, "was a sort of impromptu affair,—the people at the other end of the route knowing very little about it,— but it was none the less enjoyable for upon the boats arrival, the people of Fort Yates and Standing Rock did everything possible in the way of providing teams and in other ways looking after the welfare of their guests. The steamer Aber [*sic*] O'Neal left the Bismarck landing about 2:30 Friday afternoon, the intention being to make Yates that night. The high wind prevented this, and it was only after considerable struggle that the boat reached Lincoln, where it tied up until the wind went down late in the afternoon, and then proceeded to a point a short distance below Riverside ranch, where it tied up for the night. Starting again at daybreak, after encountering high winds and sand bars it finally arrived at Standing Rock shortly after dinner Saturday."

On the return trip, the passenger list was increased by several women who had been visiting friends in Winona, a party of artists connected with Frank Leslie's publications, as well as "Mr. and Mrs. H. T. Parkins [sic] and children and Mrs. Van Solen, who had been down to Standing Rock to attend the funeral of George Faribault," the agency interpreter and a relative of the Louis Faribault who had walked Sitting Bull to the jail and warned him not to carry off Mrs. Weldon. The funeral now complete, the Parkins and Louise Van Solen were returning to their Cannonball home on the boat.

Although the *Abner O'Neal* didn't arrive at the agency in time for "the excursionists" to witness the killing of cattle issued to the Indians as rations, "the visit was none the less enjoyable for a visit among the teepes [*sic*], where the squaws were busy with the 'jerking' of the beef and later in the afternoon to *the* grand dance and dog feast, about three miles out from the agency, was well worth the time and trouble to the excursionists. Through the kindness of an interpreter, on the right side of whom the party made haste to get by the payment of half a dollar each—those who desired were escorted into the inner circle where the big chiefs, hideously—some of them artistically—painted from head to foot and arrayed with war bonnets, feathers, skins and ornaments of all kinds, danced to the tune of the tom toms around that most delicate of Indian delicacies—a pot of dog soup." One passenger brought along his Kodak and took many "views" of the dancers, some of which, the reporter speculates, "are doubtless fine—especially that one where one of the dancers is feeding another chief with a piece of cooked dog meat from the end of a long stick." The stay at Standing Rock was a success, with the reporter giving special thanks to Major McLaughlin, who, though "grieving over the death of his head farmer and right-hand man, Mr. Faribault, lost no opportunity to contribute to the comfort of the excursionists. . . ."

For all the frivolity, Talbot was desperate to recoup the $10,000 he had shelled out to buy his boat. The *Abner O'Neal* couldn't stay afloat carrying fifty passengers at a dollar a head when the boat was designed to haul tons of cargo on long journeys. The drought that year meant the river would become too shallow to navigate even earlier than usual. On October 25, the *Trib* reported that the river men were unable to predict how long the navigation season was liable to continue. "They say the Big Muddy gets more uncertain and mysterious as each year rolls by. The steamers Abner O'Neal, Bachelor and Rosebud are in waiting at the landing for cargos." Talbot must have scrounged enough passengers to make a final trip. He left Bismarck in mid-November and picked up Weldon and her son on his way past the fort. If he hadn't been so financially pressed, he might not have made a trip when the river was no longer safe.

When Weldon took Christie off the boat, she left everything on board except a small trunk of clothes. "I could not look after so much baggage, so I let that follow me as freight," she wrote Sitting Bull later. "All my silver, & you know how much I had; all my valuable books & paintings, including your two portraits are with it. My clothes, beds, carpets & artist materials in fact all I possess. Our letters & all valuable documents. I arrived here [Kansas City] on the 16th Nov. Now we have the 1st of Dec. & my goods are not here and noone knows anything of them. Captain Talbot of the Steamer 'Chaska' 'Abner O'Neil' promised to put my goods on shore at Sioux City & then send them by mail to Kansas City. I had paid for the freight until Sioux City; from there it was to come C.O.D. all the freight officers here have telegraphed to Sioux City, but no one knows anything at all about my goods. You can imagine how I feel. . . . If I had not always helped others as I have done, I would not feel so bad; but as long as I can remember, I have done all to help others, whites & Indians, & gave my time & my money, & now when I am childless & helpless people seem to take advantage of it. If the Captain would have acted right I would have my goods long ago. All my beautiful Indian trinkets are with them & Circling Bears painted robe. I have nothing of value with me at all."

The *Bismarck Tribune* reported on November 19 that the steamboats had gone into winter quarters and would be making no more trips that season. Maybe the trunks showed up in Kansas City the following spring. Or they were stolen, and the thief tossed everything except Weldon's silver in the river. I can't imagine Talbot keeping the trunks himself, unless he had grown so desperate to recoup his losses that he would steal from a grieving mother.

The archives in Pierre held another source that made the ordeal of getting there worthwhile—Willis Fletcher Johnson's book about the Ghost Dance. Weldon must have kept up a correspondence with Johnson while she lived in Kansas City, because she complains about how much she hates living there. But she ends her last letter looking back on the Dakotas. "No one in the world was as happy as I, and I wish that all might have shared that happiness. A city seems a prison to me. One must work hard to get along in the city, and I enjoyed the freedom of the wilderness. I enjoyed the trees, and the hills, and the clouds. The flowers and the birds make me happy. I love the solitude, with its songs and its scenery, and I was loath to leave it. But I had to go, as my life was in danger."

The description of her joy on the Plains sounds to me pure Weldon, as does her defense of the Indians' right to go to war. But the passage that follows is perplexing. "Those who were friends were now my enemies, and I left against the wishes of the Sioux. They wanted me to remain for the winter, as I knew too much. I had been at every council and was acquainted with all their plans. They needed an interpreter and a secretary, and they wanted me to so act for them. I feel that I have escaped with my life, and I laugh to think how I have outwitted that cunning Sitting Bull. After I left I was informed that Sitting Bull rode through Yates at night, singing his war songs, which were awful to listen to. If the Indians can gain anything, I say fight, for they are starving. As it turns out, they get only one-fifth of what the Government allows them. If I could only live, and had power enough to see the agents exposed and brought to justice, I should like it, for I know they are stealing goods intended for the Indians. I always urged them not to fight, for they would get the worst of it. I feared the leaders would suffer, and all their ponies and arms be taken, and that would be awful, but it would be what I have said all the time. I often wonder if they remember my words, and things are turning out different from what they anticipated."

The sentence in which Weldon describes herself as laughing to think that she has outwitted "that cunning Sitting Bull" seems to come from someone else. Maybe Johnson couldn't read her writing and invented what she said. The phrase is such a strong echo of McLaughlin's oft-printed disparagement of Sitting Bull that Johnson might have picked it up from him. Or Weldon wrote the phrase in a fit of anger.

I had become so engrossed in Johnson's book that I overstayed my intended departure time. I didn't want to miss my flight, but the long stretches of road that had been swamped the day before were flooded still deeper now. I drove carefully along the spots where the pavement was washed away, then sped to make up time. The highway carried one lane of traffic each way, but everyone drove fast. The distances were huge, but it was easy to see another car before it came. Unless a hill obscured it. Unless you were from the East and weren't accustomed to the tricks of perspective, and you saw a truck ahead and couldn't tell that it was stopped until you were nearly on top of it, so you had to slam your brakes and spin the wheel violently to avoid the truck and the construction worker leaning in its window with his little red STOP sign, your tires screaming as the worker watched your Explorer turn a figure eight and come to rest beside him.

"Hey," he said, surprised.

"Sorry," I whispered. "I couldn't tell that you were stopped." He nodded, then motioned the other driver to take his turn while I wondered if I had just avoided the accident I had been fearing so many weeks or the disaster was still to come.

I drove more slowly after that, trying to keep to seventy, but it was three in the afternoon and I didn't want to miss my plane. The highway sent up heat waves. I drove another hour, wondering how far it was to Bismarck, and when I glanced ahead, I saw two pickups rise above the hill and come barreling toward me. The driver in my lane kept weaving back and forth. Maybe he was drunk. Or he was trying to pass the other truck and couldn't get back in his own lane. Both trucks hurtled toward me. One truck was black, the other red; I can't remember which was which. My impulse was to swerve, but the embankment fell steeply twenty feet. If I cut my wheel at seventy, I would flip the truck and somersault. If I swerved into the other lane, I would hit that truck head-on.

I punched my horn. The driver in my lane swerved so wildly his truck lifted on two wheels. I decided to try flipping off the road, but I couldn't bring myself to do it. I closed my eyes. When I opened them, both pickups were behind me. I stopped and sat shaking. My legs had turned to sand. Fifteen minutes later, an ambulance and a police car screamed past me. Had my premonition saved my life? It wasn't as if I had been more alert than usual and avoided the crash through quick thinking. Maybe some Higher Power was trying to shake me from my lifelong adherence to rational belief. I wasn't used to sitting in the middle of a road trying to figure out the meaning of a dream. But that might have been its point.

⁓

When I got back to Michigan, I tried to find out what happened to Ina's son. I didn't want to disturb Ina at such a time, so I did a search on the Internet and turned up a string of stories from *Newsday,* the paper near their home.

Ina's son's last name turned out to be Jackson; he must have been Ron's half brother from another marriage. On Saturday, July 19, a week before tree day, Donald and a friend had gone out on a Jet Ski in the ocean off Long Island. Both men were twenty-eight. The Jet Ski belonged to Donald's brother-in-law, Jonathan Smith. Donald was a novice who had taken a few lessons; his brother-in-law asked him to drive the Jet Ski to the marina, get gas, and come back. Donald and his friend, Alex Montalvo, rode off together. They didn't return that day, but no one was concerned. Both men were known to spend a lot of time on the beaches and at clubs around New York. Montalvo was a singer and guitarist in a band called De Facto. Jackson was a student at Long Island University's Brooklyn campus; he planned to start a hospital internship in pharmacology. He loved to scuba dive and fish and knew the waters of that bay. His brother-in-law told reporters that Don often stayed out all night. But that was in a car. The water that afternoon was choppy, with three- to five-foot swells. Neither man was wearing a life preserver.

By Saturday night, Donald's sister, Jacqueline Smith, had grown worried enough to call the Southampton police. Early Sunday morning, the Coast Guard joined the search. Helicopters skimmed the water, and jeeps tracked the sand. The cops sent around a flyer stating that Jackson had last been seen wearing a white T-shirt and khaki shorts. They searched Shinnecock Bay, the Inlet, and the margins of the sea. Around 8:30 P.M. they found the Jet Ski not far from the Shinnecock Canal, high and dry, in good condition. An eyewitness told police that he had seen the scooter wash ashore around 5 P.M. Saturday. Not until Wednesday did the first body turn up. It was Alex Montalvo. A fisherman found the corpse floating in the Inlet. Donald's sister, Jacqueline, didn't give up hope. "Donald hasn't been found yet," she said. "We can't just stop hoping."

But that Sunday, when a fisherman did find Donald's corpse, Jacqueline told reporters she felt a "sick kind of relief." The body was badly decomposed, but the top and shorts were similar to the ones Donald had been wearing. He had been missing two weeks. "It's a disturbing mystery," his sister told the reporter. "How both of these very healthy men could drown . . . is beyond us all." The article didn't mention whether, as the medicine man had predicted, her brother was found beside anything red.

11

Kansas City

After she left Pierre, Weldon was torn between anguish about the Indians' fate and bereavement about her son. In a letter dated November 20, she writes from Kansas City to "Chief Sitting Bull." *My friend*, she addresses him, grief having shrunk their differences. "My boy, my Christie, died on the Missouri River Steamer 'Chaska,'" and one can hear her think, even in her torment, of the Lakota brave, Chaska, whose marriage to a white woman Sitting Bull threw up to her when she refused his proposal. Then every memory vanishes before the excruciating nightmare of her son's ordeal. "He stepped on a nail while we were at Mrs. Parkins; the foot got better; but on the boat he got cold in it & spasms & lockjaw set in & he died, suffering the most terrible pains. . . ."

Her letters are laden with woe over Christie's death, but her fears about the turmoil on the reservation pierce through her pain. Above all, she desires to convince Sitting Bull that her opposition to the Ghost Dance was the opposition of a friend. That she could write about such matters not three days after Christie's death—and twice the following week—might demonstrate that she did neglect her son in favor of the Indians. But the grief and guilt are wrenching. "Away from the Dakotas, my boy gone forever, what is there left for me? Unfortunately I cannot die, it seems to me that nothing will, or can kill me, and I would be so glad to go where the rest have gone. If I only knew where my boys spirit is. I never can dream of him since he has died, & before that I dreamt of him always." A more compassionate interpretation is that even through her pain, she remained concerned for her friends.

"The papers are full about the Indians," she wrote Sitting Bull, "and that they may make war upon the white people. I have nothing more to say and advise that what [sic] I always said. I always advised you & your people for their own good and the day will surely come when you all will know it. War can do no good, only hasten your destruction. Oh, my friend, and my Uncpapas, you are deceived by your prophets, and I fear some bad white men who are leading you into endless troubles. I said enough when I was among you, you ought to remember my words. If I spoke harsh to you sometimes, forgive me; a true friends warning is not always pleasant to hear. I meant it for the best."

Plenty of soldiers surround the Indians on all sides, she warns. Should the Indians make trouble, it will go badly for them. "Be reasonable," she says, "& take care!

"Remember my boy! He was the only son of your best friend; Mourn for him. Tell Hoheci-Kana, my brother, & all my friends. And if your prayers to the Great Spirit are heard, pray to him to give me a speedy death, that my heart may find peace."

And she signs the letter *Toka heya mani win*, Woman Walking Ahead.

Frenzied by regret, Weldon found herself among unsympathetic whites in a city where no one cared about the Indians. Three days after her first letter, she wrote a second. "Sitting Bull, Once my best friend, what now?" She wonders if he received her first letter—perhaps the agent intercepted it. She is enclosing a newspaper clipping that surprised her very much (the clipping hasn't come down to us). Then her sorrow pours forth. "Since my boy is dead it seems that I have turned to stone. I could not weep until today when I went to Church; then the ice around my heart seemed to give way & I feel more human. When he first died I was strongly tempted to kill myself; so that my heart might find peace; but then I thought of my niece & nephew & how such an act would disgrace them; and our religion teaches me that anyone who would do such a thing would not meet their friends again in heaven. My boy has been taken from me here, I would not want to be separated from him in the next world."

Weldon, it turns out, is a lapsed Catholic, and Christie's death has renewed her religiosity. She goes to church, something she never before mentioned doing, and speaks about meeting Christie in heaven. She is trying to strike a resonant chord in Sitting Bull. He, too, has lost children, and she is admitting that she now understands his desire to dance the Ghost Dance in the smallest hope of seeing them. She is writing as a parent who knows despair, cautioning Sitting Bull as much as she is cautioning herself that suicide would deny them the chance to see their dead children—and each other—in heaven. "I wish you would try to live an honest, noble life, & do what is right in the eyes of God,

& let your heart be true to those who deserve it, that when death comes to both of us we may not be eternally separated, but meet again in a better world."

Even if she is too religious to take her own life, she wishes death might come soon. "God took my boy from me, because I did not deserve to have him. I gave my heart & soul to you & to the Dakotas, & their welfare alone was my care; & my poor boy was motherless. Had I taken better care of him, he would be with me still & we could be happy; instead of that black despair has seized my heart, & it never can find peace again until I close my eyes in death. If God only will be merciful to me I hope it will be soon. I cannot see the green grass here, nor the sunshine without a heartache, for my boy in his grave cannot see them."

Although this last passage, in a convoluted way, places the blame for Christie's death on Sitting Bull and his Dakotas, she considers traveling back to Standing Rock to die beside her friends. Then she relinquishes that idea in favor of a less futile sacrifice. She will retire to a convent and devote the remainder of her life "to God alone, & to the memory of the dead who have gone before me," by which she seems to mean not only her son, but other loved ones she lost before him. She speaks to a priest about joining a convent. He counsels her to do nothing "under the influence of this passionate grief" since she might regret her rash actions. But day by day she feels "more determined to renounce the world. What right have I to enjoy what my boy cannot have, what he can not see? I always had a heart for all unhappy people & tried to help & comfort them; but now it seems I am dead to all on Earth & only everlasting sleep I want."

Yet even as she longs for death, she cannot keep from worrying about the Indians. She tells Sitting Bull that she has written to Washington "and stated how very small the Indians rations are. Your wife showed me what she received & I wrote everything to Washington, also that the Uncpapas do not get clothing. The major [McLaughlin] in his report to the Ind. Com. Morgan made many false statements about me & you. I send you the paper. He knew that he was lying about me while he wrote it. Will God ever punish him for his double dealing." She ends by sending her love once more to Hohecikana. "I know he will grieve for my loss," she writes, with the unspoken refrain *even if you do not.*

Weldon forced herself to wait a week before writing one last time. With the papers full of news about the standoff at the Stronghold and Cody's aborted attempt to capture the chief, she is afraid the letter will never reach him, but she is going to send it and trust to luck. She tries to impress upon Sitting Bull the extent of her own troubles. "You will understand me better than anyone else, for the death of your own daughter left a wound in your heart never to be healed." If Christie had died on the Cannonball, she would have been more content, since she could have buried him in the Dakotas and stayed near his grave, among her friends. Instead, she is alone among people who hate the Indians and despise her as an Indian lover who brought about the Ghost Dance, Sitting Bull's "rebellion," and the death of her own son. This is nonsense, and Sitting Bull knows it. "You know that I always warned you not to be deceived. . . . I wish that 'Mato Wanah'taka' would have come forward like a man when I was staying at your house so that I could have talked to him & convinced him of the truth of what I said. I fear that my poor Indians must suffer for opposing the Gov't & fear for you. All the Mandan, Bismark [sic], Chicago & St. Paul papers have been making statements about me which are quite false. Because I am your friend they denounce me, & even lay the blame for the Ghost Dance & the threatened outbreak at my door; & you know best that I opposed the dance, & always counciled against war, & opposition against the Gov't. I had not slept for months while in Dakota fearing this; for I knew the minds of your people; but I always hoped you would keep your people in check; you had assured me that for my sake you would not fight against the white people any more."

Cast out by the Indians for opposing the dance, disdained by the whites for causing it, Weldon can think of nowhere to retreat but back in time. If her nephew and niece had not returned to Kansas City from Europe, she says, she never would have come here. It was "the very worst thing" she could have done and will probably destroy her. If only she had returned to Brooklyn as she intended to do in September or October, her dear boy might still be alive. "When I think of it I become almost insane. There is no one here who sympathizes with the Indians; people take no interest in them. This is a very poor place & there is no business doing here. One could starve."

Not only is Kansas City a poor place, Weldon herself is poor, having suffered misfortune after misfortune since Christie's death. ("It is as if an Angel had left my side. And I feel like a poor Eagle shot in the wings not wounded enough to die & too helpless to fly.") She tells Sitting Bull about the captain of the steamer promising to put her goods ashore at Sioux City and ship them to her nephew. That was in mid-November, and now, two weeks later, the trunks still haven't arrived. She inventories her losses and complains that she has nothing of value left. The self-pitying tone can be excused by the reality that she was destitute, childless, and friendless among people who spurned her for siding with the Indians. Sitting Bull, she assumes, is sitting in his tipi maintaining his grudge and wondering what gives a rich white woman the right to ask his comfort. Yet she demands that he imagine how she feels.

"If I should lose my goods I would be poorer than any poor Indian"—not poor *as* any Indian, but *poorer than any poor Indian,* by which she means that a destitute white lady could hardly make do living in a tent, wearing patched rags and trying to survive on maggoty meat. "If I had not always helped others as I have done, I would not feel so bad; but as long as I can remember, I have done all to help others, whites & Indians, & gave my time & my money, & now when I am childless & helpless people seem to take advantage of it. . . . I wish you would write to me. Dr. Bland & his wife wrote to me when they learn [sic] of Christies death & their letter did more towards softening my heart than anything else could have done. It is such a comfort to hear from one's friends when our hearts are bad & hopeless from grief."

She also has received letters of condolence from "Mrs. V. Solen Parkins & Mr. Parkins & all my Eastern friends & Christies death has caused more grief among them than I ever imagined it would, for he was but a child." The phrasing is ambiguous. It almost supports the view that the Parkins and Van Solens were Weldon's foes and she is surprised that they grieve for Christie. But it is more likely that she is commenting on the disproportionate effect of a small person's death rather than the kinder-than-expected response by her enemies. People don't send notices of their children's deaths to enemies.

Sitting Bull's silence torments her. How can he allow their argument to come between them? In her closing lines she begs him not to class her with the other whites who betrayed him. "I never gave you cause to be displeased with me in any way. If I spoke against the dances & war it was because I am your true friend, have seen more of the world & knew what the result would be. A true friend will warn, & point out the dangers." She reminds him of the afternoon she wanted to ride that wild horse and he "forcibly detained" her for her own good. He saved her life, and, in speaking against the dances, she was doing the same for him. "Oh, my friend, may the Good God who used to watch over both of us, open your eyes to the truth."

Although Weldon didn't know it, Sitting Bull did receive her letters. And he did share her sorrow. On December 20, the *Bismarck Tribune* reported that "Mrs. Weldon was grief-stricken [at her son's death], as was Sitting Bull on hearing the news, and he sought solitude for several days." Why didn't he answer? His own troubles weighed him down so heavily he couldn't respond to hers. Soldiers might swoop down and massacre his followers at any time. He expected his own people to kill him. It wasn't that he had hardened his heart against her and was refusing to offer sympathy because he wished her more pain. Ina McNeil thinks her great-grandfather didn't respond to Weldon's letters because "it was more kindly to let her go. He had a different idea of kindness than a European. Why continue the friendship when he knew what would happen to him? It was better to end the friendship while he was still alive, that was so much kinder."

That's a variation of my own theory that Sitting Bull had given up not only on his friend, but on life itself. Weldon's prediction that the dances would bring soldiers had proved true. She ought to have deferred to his leadership and stayed to die with her friends, but she had apologized for that. ("How I do regret having left Dakota; I might have prevented much unpleasantness had I remained with you.") Sitting Bull was in such despair that he couldn't summon the energy to find a piece of paper and a pencil, an envelope, a stamp, an interpreter to translate his message into English, a courier to take the letter to the agency and mail it to Kansas City. He couldn't send his friend comfort he didn't feel. Her woes added to his own and weighed him to paralysis. Indians and whites agreed on one thing: if a man died a good death, he would see his loved ones in heaven. If their reunion came this spring or a thousand years hence, what did any of it matter?

Whatever his reasons, Sitting Bull never answered. I can see Weldon putting on her coat and leaving her nephew's apartment to avoid his disapproving stares. She went to the post office to check and see if her friend had written back. She bought the latest paper and read the reporters' accounts of the coming war, then walked the streets of Kansas City, arguing with what she read and holding her handkerchief to her nose to filter out the stomach-turning odors from the stockyards. After her years in Brooklyn, with its museums and cafés, and those idyllic months at Grand River, she found herself trapped in the dirtiest, rawest, least cultured cow town in America, at its most economically depressed, in the dreariest season. Specks of greasy smut floated in the air. A journalist named Emma Gage visited Kansas City in the early 1890s and noted in disgust that a lady could wear a white dress only once before the soot ruined it. Of all the town's dismal features, this one, at least, didn't add to Weldon's grief—she was already wearing black.

Of the 132,716 residents of Kansas City in 1890, ten thousand of them slaughtered livestock for a living. Trains bringing pigs and cows from Texas and Colorado clotted the sky with smoke. The cows were crammed in pens in the sprawling wasteland called the Bottoms. In the bloody killing-rooms of giant packing companies like Armour, a pig could be split, gutted, and skinned before it had time to squeal. Poor immigrants and blacks drifted to the Bottoms in search of work, camping in shanties among the plants. Homesteaders heading west got stranded at the river, unable to pay the fare to cross. Boys Christie's age and younger swabbed the killing-room floors, losing hands in the machinery and scalding their arms in boiling vats. The shantytowns were filthy, primitive, and lawless. A corpse could lie on the levee for days before anyone did anything about it.

The stench of human feces, cow manure, and burning hides filled the lowlands and rose to the mansions on Quality Hill. The revolting smell, like the sight of the slaughterhouses and the screeching of the trains, was a reminder of the source of wealth of those who lived there. Livestock accounted for 90 percent of the value of everything in Kansas City (the next-most lucrative business was the manufacture of clay sewer pipes for expanding western towns). The residents knew that they were looked down upon (a journalist from the East described the city as an "overgrown country town . . . consciously citified, like a country jake in his first store clothes"), but they couldn't understand why. They had a modern business district a dozen blocks square, with a new ten-story building put up by New York Life. City boosters could tout an opera house, a theater, art schools, a polo and yacht club, and a bunch of swank hotels. By 1890, the wealthiest families had figured out that one's social standing was inversely proportional to the distance one lived from the source of one's wealth, and many of them had moved to gingerbread mansions in newer neighborhoods to the south or northeast. Middle-class families followed. Kansas City was the third city in America to install a cable-car system, with thirty-five miles of track running up and down its hills.

But as can happen when you are trying to impress, the city went too far and ended up looking foolish. The cable-car companies laid lines to suburbs that were never built. The eastern press scorned the city as "an unattractive hodgepodge of unplanned sprawl lacking sufficient paving, sanitation, police and fire protection, zoning restrictions or parks to make it in any way urbane." The price of real estate soared. Then a recession struck. Businesses went bust, as did investors who had paid exorbitant rates for downtown lots. Buildings stood empty, apartments offered themselves "TO LET," and the city's homeless boys slept in the basement of the Board of Trade.

Unlike smaller western towns, Kansas City was full of single women, many of them abandoned by men who couldn't afford more than one ticket west. Other women migrated from rural towns to look for work in factories—stitching clothes, gluing boxes, making hats, dropping and wrapping candies—then lost their jobs to the recession. The most desperate sold themselves to traveling cattlemen for as little as a quarter. Seven thousand whores lived in Kansas City, one for every fifteen men. The nicest brothels were located not far from the boardinghouse where Weldon lived. She must have walked the streets among women selling themselves to cowboys. She had no means to earn a living. She had lost her art supplies and books. She wandered among the prostitutes in her somber mourning clothes, thinking what to do.

This was a city for pioneers who came in from the frontier and needed R and R. Drunks reeled from saloon to saloon on Battle Row. Cowboys strutted the streets—in drag. Whites accused blacks of stealing their jobs and beat them.

Sometimes the blacks fought back. The police beat anyone they felt like beating. With all the fights and epidemics, the venereal disease, the limbs and fingers left on the killing-room floors, the Kansas City Medical College was able to promise students ample opportunities of witnessing "every kind of disease and injury, all of the common and many of the rarer surgical operations."

But the city offered little to Weldon. She had no savings or skills that Kansas City could appreciate, and she wasn't about to support herself by slaughtering cows or gluing boxes. The nephew upon whose generosity she relied could barely support himself. Frederick Schleicher was Weldon's sister's son, a language teacher at the parochial school attached to St. Peter and St. Paul's Roman Catholic Church. In the 1887 directory, he is listed as living alone in rooms at 1510 Oak Street. The establishment of parochial schools was a recent development, and he couldn't have earned much money teaching at a struggling school on the frontier. The church was a stolid brick edifice with uninspiring stained-glass windows for stolid German parishioners (its site, at the southwest corner of McGee and 9th, like most of the other sites associated with Weldon's story, is now a parking lot). No Fritz or Frederick Schleicher is listed in the 1889 directory; he might have been in Europe on his honeymoon. When he returned, he took new rooms; in 1890, Schleicher is listed as living in room 406 of the boardinghouse at 1106 Baltimore Ave. The following year he is still there, with "Caroline Weldon, artist," listed at the same address. (In her last letter to Sitting Bull, she urges him to write back to her care of her nephew, so she was sharing quarters with her relatives rather than renting her own room.) By 1892, no Caroline Weldon is listed, and in the 1895 directory "Schleicher, Fred. W." is noted as having moved to San Antonio, Texas.

The rooming house at 1106 Baltimore Avenue was a narrow, unassuming structure about six stories tall; the buildings on either side still stand, the alley between them having been converted to a lot for Allright Parking. The brick wall on one side is still painted in faded letters "HOTEL BRAY, FIREPROOF, Rates Start at $1.50," so it hardly seems as if Weldon's accommodations were as luxurious as the other hotels on the street. Photos from the time show cavernous tiled lobbies, swirling marble stairs, rococo domes and balconies, cigar shops with grand circular displays, suites with skylights, divans, and marble fireplaces spanning entire walls. The old Muehlenbach still stands, a Marriott now, with tiled mosaic floors, daunting chandeliers, and frosted-glass windows. Weldon found her rooms with her niece and nephew incommodious, but I doubt she was impressed with the fancier hotels; she had seen nicer in Manhattan. Better to be living in a cabin on the Plains, where at least the air was pure. Her niece and nephew must have hated her complaining. Like the other residents of Kansas City, they were touchy about easterners who found their city squalid. They didn't need to listen to snobbish, self-righteous carping from a destitute aunt who had caused an Indian war.

The only Indians in Kansas City were vagrants and drunks—at least, that's how the whites saw them. The last open conflict in that vicinity had been a dozen years earlier, and the residents of Kansas City had no patience with Indians elsewhere who hadn't gotten the message that they had lost. The *Kansas City Star* didn't run stories about Weldon, but she must have lived in dread that the editors would notice the stories running in other papers and seek her out. On November 21, 1889, the *Star* featured a front-page article that gave its readers everything Weldon could have given them but wouldn't. Mrs. James Finley, the wife of the hotel keeper at Pine Ridge, had just arrived in town with her four-year-old daughter, her husband having judged it unsafe for his wife and child to remain among the Sioux. Although Mrs. Finley recommended shooting Red Cloud and Sitting Bull as a preventative step, she didn't think the army needed to worry about the Indians harming anyone but themselves. The ceremonies at Pine Ridge, at the beginning, were more accessible to whites than the dances at Grand River, and it seemed to Mrs. Finley that the Indians were dancing themselves to such lunacy with "wild and exhausting orgies continuing night and day without food and without cessation" that, left to their own devices, they would dance themselves to death. As for her husband, Mr. Finley "feels sorry for the Indians for they will all be killed. He does not think there will be a great Indian war, but that all the ghost dancers will probably be killed before the matter ends."

The *Star's* reporter was less sanguine. The Indians camped at Wounded Knee Creek were "excited, threatening and boisterous." Soon they would be joined by Sioux from other agencies and resist any attempt to make them stop their dance. The next day's report was that "150 lodges of the Wounded Knee fanatics, including some of the most treacherous redskins in this part of the country, had moved to White river, twenty miles north of here, and had again begun the ghost dance in a wilder manner than has been known thus far. The scouts talked with the leaders, who declared that they would shoot any government officials who attempted to suppress the dance. This is considered by far the most sensational news that has come to General Brooke since his arrival. All these Indians are armed with Winchesters, navy revolvers and knives." Perhaps this was the article Weldon clipped for Sitting Bull. She might have been tempted to seek out Mrs. Finley and talk about the Ghost Dance. Then again, Weldon rarely seemed interested in talking to other whites about the Indians. And James Finley was not highly regarded among the Sioux.

Not even Sitting Bull's supporters spoke well of him. In Chicago, Buffalo Bill expressed the opinion that "Sitting Bull Should Be Sat Down Upon." Of all the Indians, Cody said, "Sitting Bull is worst. . . . He can always be found with the disturbing element, and if there is no disturbance he will ferment one." This from a man who advertised himself as Sitting Bull's friend.

Then the papers went quiet, except for the occasional bit of news or a humor piece about a delegation of Negroes from "two of the lowest neighborhoods of Kansas City" who approached the chief of police with a request to hold a ghost dance of their own to bring about the appearance of a "colored messiah." Weldon was lulled into thinking her friends were safe. But on December 16, she woke to this headline in the *Star:* "SITTING BULL, DECEASED. THE TROUBLE-SOME OLD FELLOW HAS JOINED THE GOOD INDIANS. Shot by the Indian Police While Resisting Arrest—His Son, Crow Foot, and Several Followers Killed—Several of the Government Police Massacred." Although Sitting Bull had in fact been sleeping with his wife when the tribal police broke in, the *Star* reported that the officers had found the Sioux "all ready to depart for the Southwest and instant action was necessary to prevent this movement. The police at once made a rush for Sitting Bull, surrounded him and telling him he was a prisoner started at once on the trail for the agency." The correspondent's fanciful account has the policemen putting Sitting Bull on a horse and leading him toward the agency, at which Crow Foot and a party of his followers "attempted to recapture their chief." Sitting Bull, the reporter claimed, was killed in this heated battle on the road between his camp and the agency.

The *Star's* pastiche of reports provided Weldon with the true but shaded information that the police had taken possession of Sitting Bull's camp "with all women, children and property" and that Sitting Bull's followers, "probably 100, deserted their families and fled west for the Grand river," followed by the judgment that Sitting Bull had been a coward and "even at the Custer battle, with all the force he had, he fled to a place of safety himself and watched the bloody work being performed by his braves." Finally she read the line that sent her running for her pen to write a letter to Thomas Bland: "An enterprising Bismarck merchant this morning offered $1,000 for Sitting Bull's hide."

Over the next few days she read lists of the dead, her friend Hohecikana among them. The paper's tone was mocking. An article describing the chief's burial ended with the sentiment that "Sitting Bull is now enriching the soil of the Dakotas. It is not to be questioned that for fertilizing purposes the old rascal is accomplishing the one good deed for which he was intended."

By December 22, the *Star* had declared "the trouble" at an end, with practically all of Sitting Bull's adherents captured. Weldon must have thought the worst had passed. But the following week, reports of a disturbance at Wounded Knee started reaching Kansas City. "WAR IN EARNEST. The Terrible Hotchkiss Guns Are Turned Loose Upon The Rebellious Redskins With Frightful Slaughter—Women and Children Attacked by Uncle Sam's Merciless Troops, Along with Fighting Bucks, Hardly a Redskin Left." For a while, the *Star* was able to thrill its readers with the prospect of a full-scale war as the Indians retaliated. Then the truth leaked out: the initial "battle" had consisted of Uncle Sam's troops opening fire on Big Foot's dejected refugees, who already had surrendered. (Accounts of what caused the massacre are confusing. While members of the cavalry searched the Indians' camp for guns, one of the braves stooped down, gathered some dirt, and tossed it toward the soldiers. Some soldiers thought this was a signal among the Indians to open fire, but the Indians claimed the man was chanting a Ghost Dance song and tossing dirt in a gesture meant to summon the messiah.) By the time the shooting stopped, at least two hundred of the Indians, including Big Foot, lay dead, among them women, children, and old men; among these dead lay some of the thirty or forty Hunkpapas who had fled Sitting Bull's camp at Grand River after the battle there. Of the cavalry, about thirty soldiers were killed.

Under the command of Kicking Bear, who was furious at Sitting Bull's death and the slaughter of Big Foot's people, the panicked, angry Sioux took potshots at the army. By January 12, however, not even the *Star* could keep up the illusion that the Indians possessed any means to fight back. "My brothers," Kicking Bear told his last holdouts, "this is a hard winter. Our women and children are starving and freezing. If this were summer, I would say we should keep fighting to the end. But this we cannot do. We must make peace." On January 15, 1891, the last Ghost Dancers left the Stronghold, and Kicking Bear surrendered to General Miles.

Weldon had no one in Kansas City to whom she could express her outrage and sorrow at all the killing. She wrote letters to the Blands, the Parkins, the Van Solens, and Willis Fletcher Johnson. They wrote back. But letters only go so far in providing comfort. She sought the church. Not the church her nephew taught at. She didn't get along with her nephew. And her history, if it became known, might cause him to lose his job. The Belgians worshiped at St. Francis, the Italians at the Holy Rosary, the Poles at St. Stanislaus, the Mexicans at Our Lady of Guadalupe. Weldon, I think, sought solace at the Cathedral of the Immaculate Conception around the corner from her rooming house, on Quality Hill. With its stunning copper dome, rich but muted stained glass and serene gold-and-pastel stenciling, this was a church an artist could appreciate. She sat in a pew in the cathedral's cool interior, staring at the mosaic of Mary and the lovely young son dying in her arms.

But Catherine Weldon was not the kind of woman to give in to despair for very long. When I finally found the pamphlet Thomas Bland published in 1891, *A Brief History of the Late Military Invasion of the Home of the Sioux*, it revealed that "Caroline" Weldon had indeed roused herself from her grief and contributed a chapter. The book was published in a hurry, the documents thrown together with barely any commentary or editing from Bland. Fanny Kelly wrote to say that during her captivity she lived with Sitting Bull's family and was treated as a guest. "Sitting Bull was a true nobleman, and great man. He was uniformly [*sic*] gentle, and kind to his wife and children and courteous and considerate in his intercourse with others." But Bland reserved the final chapter for Weldon: "WHAT MRS. WELDON SAYS." As always, he begins by describing Weldon as "a wealthy lady of philanthropic character," although by this time she had lost everything she owned and was living on the largesse of a parochial-school teacher who despised her. Weldon has spent much time among Sitting Bull's people as a teacher and missionary at her own expense, Bland goes on. "When in that country she was always a welcome guest in Sitting Bull's family. This lady holds Sitting Bull in very high esteem." After Sitting Bull died, Weldon sent Bland "a communication" sketching what she knew about the circumstances in which the chief was killed. (Written as it was between the chief's death and the book's publication, this report must have come from Kansas City.) Sitting Bull's death gave Weldon a new mission: to make sure the government didn't portray her friend in such a way that his murder seemed warranted. If she and Sitting Bull ever fought, she wasn't about to reveal their disagreements now. His death restored to her the hero she had traveled west to paint, although she painted him now with words.

Sitting Bull, she writes to Bland, "Was not treacherous, nor cruel. He was not a liar, nor a murderer, as has been charged. He was a man of true nobility of character and generous deeds. As a friend, he was sincere and true, as a patriot devoted and incorruptible. As a husband and father, affectionate and considerate. As a host, courteous and hospitable to the last degree." Weldon had questioned Sitting Bull's wisdom in following the ghost religion, but she praises him now for holding tenaciously to his people's sacred legacy. "He distrusted the innovations sought to be forced upon the Indians. He believed that all the white men cared for was to get the Indian's land from him. He had no faith in Government Commissioners or Christian missionaries. What he saw of white civilization did not impress him favorably. There was too much avarice and too much hypocrisy [*sic*] in it. He never signed a treaty to sell any portion of his people's inheritance, and he refused to acknowledge the right of other Indians to sell his undivided share of the tribal lands. For this he was denounced as an obstructionist, a foe to progress. To those who knew him in his motives, he was a patriot. The great, hope and purpose of his life was to unify the tribes, and bands of the Dakotas, (Sioux) and hold the remaining lands of his people as a sacred inheritance for their children."

Before she left, Weldon says, she learned of a plan to seize the chief set in motion by "agent McGlophlin" (the misspelling of "McLaughlin" is typical of Bland, but he attributes it to Weldon, casting doubt on whether every word is hers). When the plan failed, the agent tried to get Gall to pretend to join the dances, gain the chief's confidence, then grab him and carry him off. "Whether his plot failed for want of approval at Washington," Weldon speculates, "or because Gall refused to act so mean a part is not known to me." She describes the plan that did work—the invasion of Sitting Bull's cabin—but omits to mention that Sitting Bull's friend Catch the Bear fired the first shot.

Her account is notable for details that are mentioned by no one else. This might mean they aren't true. Or they serve as evidence that Weldon reestablished contact with Sitting Bull's family. ("The particulars of this dark tragedy" Weldon gives "on the authority of Sitting Bull's family and others, who were eye-witnesses.") Maybe she traveled to Pine Ridge and spoke with Sitting Bull's survivors. More likely, they wrote to her. However she got the information, Weldon laments that the police weren't content to shoot Sitting Bull through his heart; they also "beat his head to a pulp, then rifled his pockets. Crowfoot, who had hid under the bed, was dragged out and killed though he was unarmed, and begged for his life most piteously. His skull was crushed and four balls fired into his body," an image that must have haunted her, given that Crow Foot was only seventeen, not much older than Christie.

The fight, she says, became general. Sitting Bull's friends were so completely surprised that many of them did not have even a knife with which to defend themselves—here she is lamenting Hohecikana's unarmed death. Sitting Bull's daughter and another girl took refuge in a lodge. This the police set on fire, "and when the girls ran out to save themselves from being burned to death, the policemen pointed their guns at them in wanton cruelty." (The only other mention I could find of the role of women in the battle is from McLaughlin's report of December 24 to the Indian Office, in which he cites a "fact worth mentioning," namely, that during the fight "a number of women of the Sitting Bull faction attacked the police with knives and clubs, and the latter in every instance simply disarmed them and put them in one of the houses under guard until the troops arrived.") The whole affair, Weldon concludes, "was a deliberately planned and cruelly executed assassination."

In July 1998, I flew to Kansas City to find Christie Weldon's grave and try to learn his mother's fate after she lost so much. The air was heavy and dank. Maybe Kansas City was just having a bad summer, but it didn't seem much less depressing than it must have seemed when Weldon looked out her boardinghouse window and prayed for eternal sleep. On Quality Hill, a well-groomed young woman walked a toddler and a Dalmatian along a cobbled street. A tanned young man in cutoffs waxed his SUV. The cathedral's shiny dome, gold now instead of copper, shed its blessing across the hill. But much of the rest of the city seemed abandoned.

Rising beyond the condos was an exceedingly tall pedestal with the sculpture of a fat cow on top. "This monument erected as a tribute to the faith of the pioneers and the determination of the men who have carried on to establish the hereford breed as leader of the beef cattle world. Dedicated Oct 16, 1953, by Dwight D. Eisenhower, President of the United States." I saw a gazebo beyond the pedestal, balanced on a crumbling wall. Far below, in the Bottoms, the Missouri River wound through a Dantesque waste of roofless factories with shattered windows, rusted machines, and empty pens.

A devastating flood in 1951 began the stockyards' decline. The decentralization of the nation's meat-packing industry finished what was left. By the late 1980s, few cows were kept here. The last packing plants closed in the early 1990s. HOLSUM FOODS said the legend on the only factory that still seemed in operation. The gazebo in which I stood—I imagined the young scion of a meat-packing family showing his prospective bride the extent of his family's holdings—was carpeted in trash and pigeon droppings. The howl of a train rose from the Bottoms like the hooting of a drunk blowing across a bottle. A rat lumbered past my shoes. Another rat, as fat as a raccoon, lurked behind a Burger King bag. I left the gazebo to the rats and went to find Christie Weldon's grave.

Kansas City isn't destitute. As is true of most cities, extremes of poverty and wealth coexist in a way that many people take for granted. The Hallmark Company produces eleven million cards a day and ships them from Kansas City to every state in America and one hundred other countries, with an annual gross in excess of $3 billion. The publishing house of the Church of the Nazarene has its headquarters in Kansas City and, as a brochure boasts, "[is] another welcome employer whose presence contributes to the area's beauty and prosperity." Magnificent Union Station, with its beaux arts facade, is being renovated to become a civic center.

Union Hill, to the south, is as quaint as San Francisco, with the highest concentration of artists in the world, most of whom work for Hallmark. (If Joyce Hall had begun his business twenty years earlier, Weldon could have earned her living painting sad-eyed waifs for his cards.) The cottages of Union Hill date back to 1880, with steeply sloping roofs, many-sided bay windows, and richly hued wood. The new condos fit nicely with the picturesque old houses, but they are choking the cemetery. As I stood at the main gate, trying to read the plaques, two workers mixed concrete a yard from where I stood.

The Union Cemetery was incorporated in 1857. Many of the graves had been removed from earlier burying grounds whose capacities were reduced by a cholera epidemic. Among the cemetery's residents are settlers, merchants, missionaries, and heroes. Here lie Elizabeth Potter, taken captive by Indians during the Revolution, kept prisoner all winter, and returned the next spring; George Caleb Bingham, "one of Missouri's most famous artists" and a sworn foe of "vice and dissipation"; Tillman Crabtree, the city's first cop, whose duty it was to lift young belles across the mud; Mina Crain, killed at eighteen while working in an overall factory in 1886; and an unknown number of Chinese immigrants buried beneath four gravestones engraved in Chinese.

My guide to these graves was Rusty Corwin, a retired city worker who organized a group of volunteers to undertake the mammoth job of sorting out "whose grandfather was buried where." A short man with bushy white hair and a bushy white mustache, Corwin thumbed through the files in the sexton's cottage to see if he could find Christie Weldon's records.

"That's interesting," he said. "There are *two* Chris Weldons buried here. Do you know which one you want?"

Two? Why would there be two?

"There's this one." Corwin pointed to a name on a Xeroxed list. "WELDON, CHRYS." The spelling was odd, but the burial date was right—Nov. 17, 1890. The burial fee was $4, and "Chrys" was buried in section 15, lot 1SG, grave 11. The undertaker was "Stine," and, under "miscellaneous," Chrys was listed as a soldier! On the index card filled out by the sexton, the boy's nickname was penciled in as "Christie," his date of death was given as November 14, 1890, which corresponded to the date in Weldon's letters, and he was listed as twelve years old.

"Hope you don't want *this* one," Corwin said. "There isn't anything much about him." This other Chris Weldon was buried on November 10, 1891, for a fee of $6. No location of this Chris Weldon's grave was given, no undertaker, no age, no miscellaneous information. It seemed a strange coincidence that he was buried nearly a year to the day after Catherine's son.

"Ready?" Corwin led me up a hill to an empty patch of ground amid a scattering of modest stones. Twenty-five unmarked coffins lay beneath our feet.

As near as Corwin could tell—the plats had been shuffled around so much, the records so poorly kept—Christie was buried here. His mother must have come to visit often. She stood on this very spot, talking to her son, apologizing for not buying a gravestone; the $25 she had paid the undertaker and the cemetery took the last of what she had. If Christie was really twelve, his mother lied and made him older. "It is a hazardous undertaking," she admitted to McLaughlin, "and my boy is not quite fourteen years old, consequently but of little protection." She feared the agent would disapprove even more if the boy was twelve.

I sat on the grass and thought about that other Chris Weldon, the one who died a year after Catherine's son. Influenced by the will I had found earlier in Brooklyn and the theory I had cooked up that Weldon adopted another boy to replace the one who died, I imagined a scene in which she went to see the priest she mentions in her letter to Sitting Bull. *I am tempted to kill myself, Father, or take vows and become a nun.* The priest senses that the way to save this woman is to give her another cause. *What about all the poor homeless lads you see living on the streets? God has taken your own child, Mrs. Weldon. He means you to help these others.*

Like other readers of the *Star*, Weldon might have seen an advertisement that fall that read: "Female child offered for adoption at female hospital." Or an ad that appeared in the *Star* on December 6: "A beautiful baby girl for adoption. Call afternoon at 906 W. 21st St." Then there were the Sioux orphaned at Wounded Knee. An article in the *Star* on January 2 described the piteous condition of "two tiny Indian babies" who had been found alive in the snow beside their dead mothers' bodies. "The little innocents were brought to the agency and found friends in the wives of some of the Indian scouts," the reporter wrote. Charles Eastman, the agency doctor who became Elaine Goodale's husband, wrote an account of his visit to the battlefield a few days after the massacre. Among the survivors, he said, "were two babies, about three months old, and an old women [*sic*] who is totally blind, also left for dead. Four of them were found out in a field in the storm, which was very severe. . . . A little Indian baby girl about three months old, one of the survivors of the battle of Wounded Knee, who lay for three days beside the dead body of its mother, was adopted by Mrs. Allison Nailor, a wealthy lady of Washington. Major John Burke, manager of Buffalo Bill's Wild West Combination, stood as god-father to the child, and had it christened Maggie C. Nailor, the first name and initial being those of the child's new found benefactress."

Weldon could have read such articles and conceived a plan to adopt the children of her murdered friends. She had heard Fanny Kelly describe her intention to start an orphanage for abandoned mixed-race children. Maybe Weldon listened to the priest, adopted a local boy, and named him in memory of her son. But this second Christie didn't live out the year.

Whoever this second Chris Weldon was, the first was Catherine's son. She took the cable car from town to sit here, on Union Hill, beside her dear boy's grave. She couldn't afford a monument, but that was just as well; the mourners in Kansas City were caught up in a fad that fall for fake marble stumps etched with tributes to the dead. She clawed the ground and cried and shredded her lacy handkerchief. Other times, she sat calmly, telling Christie how much she missed him and laughing about the times he had gone riding with Sitting Bull and learned to shoot with Crow Foot. She brought her pen and inkwell and the black-bordered stationery that showed she was in mourning and wrote letters to Sitting Bull. Flecks of soot settled on the sheets. She brushed them absently and licked her hand. It was December 1, but Sitting Bull had been right and the weather still was mild. Sun glinted from the grass and granite stones. But even from Union Hill on a clear, sunlit day, she couldn't see the river.

"If his body & I were only in Dakota," she wrote her friend, "I would be more content. Although there is always sunshine here & the grass green like in the Spring, I hate this city. The sky is black with the smoke from the factories & one can hardly look across the Missouri. Remember me to all our friends & if you see White Eagle, too, & Hohicikana my brother, & if your heart has not turned from me because I am a white woman, write to me as you have always done. It will be some comfort to me in my great troubles."

But the comfort never came, and two weeks later, she returned to Union Hill to whisper to Christie's grave that their friends were dead, too.

12

Little Rock

Weldon remained in Kansas City long enough to be listed in the 1891 directory—longer than makes sense, considering how much she hated the place and how strained her relations with her nephew and niece. She might have been reluctant to abandon Christie's grave. Maybe she was raising that adopted Christie until he died the next November. She didn't have the wherewithal to buy a ticket east. She thought of going back to Standing Rock or helping the survivors of Wounded Knee. But the Indians might blame her for Sitting Bull's death. And the bureaucracy that ran the reservations was even less receptive to representatives of the NIDA than was true before the war. Even with his high-placed Washington connections, Thomas Bland found it nearly impossible to conduct research for his pamphlet *The Late Military Invasion of the Home of the Sioux.* Since Weldon was contributing her chapter to his book, she must have been aware of the good doctor's difficulties in making contact with their friends.

In June 1891, six months after Wounded Knee, Pine Ridge still bristled with soldiers. Surprised to find himself in accordance with the proposals for reform put forward by the government commission then at the reservation inquiring into the recent unrest, Bland nevertheless complained to Morgan of the hateful attitude toward the Indians among army personnel. In a letter to Morgan dated July 1, 1891, Bland submitted a sample from his diary of the "profane and vicious remarks" he'd had to endure from his military table mates at Finley's Hotel:

"One Lieutenant said, 'Some 35 or 36 years ago, an Indian outbreak occurred in a country over which the Brittish [*sic*] flag waved. At the close of that little disturbance, the leaders of the rebellion were sent to the Happy Hunting Grounds or some other place by being blown from the mouths of cannons. If old Red Cloud and all the other leaders of the Sioux had been hung at the close of the late war, all danger of future rebellion on the part of the Sioux would have been over. If we could have another brush with the reds, here, and I could catch Old Red Cloud, out from home, I would hang him and come in and report that he had committed suicide![']" This sally was greeted with a roar of laughter by the whole party, save Capt. Bailey [Commandant of the Post] who only smiled approval.

"'The d——d Quakers of the East,' said another Lieutenant, 'will visit Wounded Knee, and snivel over the bones of some old buck or squaw who hadent [sic] had a bath for ten years, but they have no tears to shed over the grave of the poor soldier who fell in that fight.[']

"The fourth lieutenant responded, 'If a lot of the d——d sniveling Quakers, who meddle with Indian affairs were hung it would be a good thing for the country.' This was openly approved by the other lieutenants and no one dissented from the sentiment."

After a month's stay at Pine Ridge, Bland moved on to the Rosebud Reservation, where he encountered worse than vicious talk. Approaching the reservation in a mail wagon, he was passed by the agent, George Wright, who was headed in the opposite direction with a military inspector named Captain C. A. Earnest. Immediately upon reaching Valentine, Wright telephoned his clerk at the agency and ordered him to detain and isolate Bland. "Under the circumstances and with Capt. Earnest's strong concurrence," Wright later told Morgan, "it was not considered policy at this time to permit any gentleman with the radical and extreme views on Indian matters held by Dr. Bland, as frequently published in his papers (which have been extensively read here) to mingle and converse with these Indians at this time, and while all Indians were congregated about the Agency to spend July 4th together and waiting to negotiate with the Sioux Commissioners, unless provided with proper authority, that would relieve the authorities at the Agency from the responsibility or consequence of evil results."

Although Wright later claimed that Bland hadn't been arrested, Bland disagreed. "If I was not arrested, and imprisoned I suggest a revision of the dictionaries . . . ," he fumed to Morgan. "I was a prisoner in the stckade [sic] from about 4.30 to 8 P.M., when, the gate being unlocked to allow a party of gentlemen, who had been visiting me in prison to pass out, I passed out with them, and a friend of mine, having engaged another friend, an Indian, to carry me back to Valentine, and his carriage being ready, I took my seat in it and was driven out of the Agency. So far as I know, there was no effort made to recapture me but after I had proceeded a few hundred yards, I discovered a mounted policeman on my trail. He rode up near the carriage and continued to follow it until it crossed the Nebraska line."

The ruckus led to a flurry of charges and countercharges that eventually filled a folder in Washington. When I finally managed to obtain those letters from the National Archives, they bore out my hunch that Bland was much more eloquent in his own defense than he ever was in Weldon's. It seemed impossible that the same person who had scrawled those barely coherent messages to Morgan to convey Sitting Bull's request that Weldon be allowed to set up a school at Grand River later composed and typed page after page of considered rebuttal to Agent Wright's charges, crossing out an awkward phrase here or there to insert a better choice in a careful, artistic hand. America was a free country! Bland reminded the commissioner. A citizen needn't obtain permission to travel anywhere or converse with anyone. Although he granted that Agent Wright was correct in citing a provision of the Sioux treaty of 1868 that prohibited "bad men" from entering a reservation, the intent of the provision was "not to prevent their friends from visiting them for their good." As to the agent's malicious charge that a party of schoolteachers with whom Bland had lunched at a roadside eatery later dismissed him as a "crank," Bland did "not believe that those ladies and gentlemen whom I met and whom I was led to believe from their treatment of me were my friends, were guilty of false statements to my injury."

Bland himself had nothing kind to say about Wright. Conversations with "nearly all the white men, (traders, employees, etc.,)" in his four hours at the Rosebud Agency convinced him that relations between the Indians and the agent were "far from normal" and that Captain Earnest was "exceedingly unpopular" with the Indians, creating a "panicky feeling" among the whites and an "[apprehension] that an outbreak might occur at any moment." The Indians wanted peace, Bland assured Morgan, but they didn't trust Agent Wright and considered Captain Earnest "overbearing and despotic."

Bland himself found Earnest a coarse, offensive, and "very dissipated man. His common headquarters in Valentine is a saloon. He was partially intoxicated when I saw him, and he was in the act of drinking a glass of whiskey." After a strained introduction, Bland asked Earnest to inform him why he had been arrested the day before. "Because I don't want you there," Earnest told the doctor. But *why* didn't he want him there, Bland insisted. "Because you are a Newspaperman, thats enough, I don't want them around," the captain said "in a manner indicating a high degree of wrath," then emptied his glass of whiskey.

Disgusted, Bland boarded the train at Valentine and started his trip back east. Striking up a conversation with "a young man by the name of Cox, who had been on a visit to the Agency, a few days before to form an Indian Base Ball Club to be carried East," Bland learned the truth, namely, that Captain Earnest had ordered Bland arrested for no other reason than "he was a friend of the Indians."

If Bland was visible enough as an NIDA representative to be recognized and arrested the minute he set foot on the Rosebud, Weldon would have had a less than zero chance of getting in. McLaughlin certainly wouldn't have allowed her to return to Standing Rock. The agent at Pine Ridge permitted Bland to stay only after firing off a telegram to Morgan inquiring if "Doctor Bland" was there "by any color of authority or permission from your offices." If Bland gained sufferance to remain at the agency only by virtue of Morgan's reluctant assent, Weldon would surely have been turned away.

She remained in Kansas City, I think, because she was paralyzed by regret, poverty, and indecision. For a year, maybe two, she lived quietly in modest rooms under the name of Caroline. Unknown today, she would have been recognized by anyone who read the papers in her own time. She was "Sitting Bull's white squaw," the crazy widow from New Jersey who helped start an Indian war, the misguided philanthropist who bought Sitting Bull the revolver with which he resisted his arrest, the dizzy dame whose romantic letters to the chief were discovered in his cabin after he was dead. She could have cashed in. She could have offered her own account to counteract the lies in the press. But she was afraid of being vilified and reluctant to make her fortune from the misfortune of her friends. Annie Oakley had used up her savings suing a string of papers that claimed she was thrown in jail for stealing a pair of pants from a Negro used-clothing salesman to finance her cocaine habit. The defendants' lawyers said, What do you expect? She opened herself to scandal by traveling around the world with the notorious Bill Cody and living for seventeen years as the companion of red men. Oakley cleared her name, but Weldon wouldn't have stood a chance.

Every other white who'd had anything to do with Sitting Bull turned a profit from the acquaintance. A Fort Yates photographer named George Scott staged a reenactment of the battle at Sitting Bull's cabin, with the surviving policemen acting out their roles. Three weeks after Wounded Knee, some enterprising citizens of Mandan began agitating to buy the chief's cabin and move it to Chicago for the upcoming World's Fair. Being the "civilized people" living nearest to the great Sioux Reservation, these businessmen claimed, they were "desirous of making a special exhibit of Indian Curios in the proper department from the State of North Dakota" and so asked permission of the secretary of the interior to allow "Hon. P. B. Wickham, A. E. Thorberg and Chris Nordstrom, old settlers

31. Almost immediately after Sitting Bull's death, a Fort Yates photographer named George W. Scott staged a reenactment of the battle in which the chief was arrested and killed. Courtesy of the State Historical Society of North Dakota, A1974.

and residents of such West Missouri country of North Dakota, to procure the log cabin of the late 'Sitting Bull' for exhibition and preservation . . . as such cabin is now unoccupied, and will soon go to ruin from the effects of the weather and of destructive prairie fires that annually sweep over our country."

The businessmen appealed to the secretary to enforce their wishes over McLaughlin's objections. But Secretary Noble declined to overrule his agent.

On February 14, Lyman R. Casey, senator from North Dakota, wrote to Commissioner Morgan on official Senate letterhead. "Sir:-

"I have the honor to suggest to you that the Indian Bureau take the necessary steps to come into possession of as large a part of the personal effects of the late Sitting Bull, the Indian Chief, as shall prove to be practicable, as they cannot fail to be objects of curiosity and interest for many years to come to citizens of the United States. I desire to request further now, that if you succeed in obtaining possession of such effects you will permit the use of them to the State of North Dakota for exhibition at the World's Fair. . . ."

The agent's neatly penned response suggests that Sitting Bull was not possessed of much property "other than his Winchester Rifle, Red Stone Pipe, Riding Saddle, a few articles of clothing, and possibly two horses that were usually rode or driven by him. . . ." Tactfully McLaughlin questions if it is advisable "that the friendly and well disposed Indians should see such prominence given to the memory of one who, during his life time, was a fomenter of mischief and a disaffected leader." Many of Sitting Bull's possessions already have been bought "by persons who procured them through curiosity." If the commissioner insists, McLaughlin could obtain "for a reasonable consideration" any of Sitting Bull's effects yet in possession of his family, "including his log cabin if deemed advisable, but if this cabin should be desired by the World's Fair, I would suggest that it be purchased and exhibited not because it was Sitting Bull's house, but because it was at this building that the Indian police as Officers of law and order made such a gallant and determined stand in upholding the government against their own race and kindred on the morning of Dec 15, 1890."

Despite the subservient language, McLaughlin stonewalled. The entrepreneurs went back to the secretary, maintaining that the cabin was going to waste because Sitting Bull's family were too superstitious to "enter or live in it . . . so it has little value for them." Finally the commissioner put the screws to McLaughlin, which resulted in the agent grudgingly allowing Sitting Bull's heirs to sell the house.

Edward Forte, a carpenter at Yates, supervised the dismantling of Sitting Bull's cabin into numbered logs, which P. B. Wickham and his friends carted to Chicago. There the cabin was rebuilt so that visitors could note the exact number and location of the bullet holes. Forte visited the fair, where he saw the cabin on the Midway "almost opposite the Ferris Wheel," a prime location since this was the first Ferris wheel in the world. An early biographer of Buffalo Bill claims that Cody displayed the cabin at his show outside the gates, but its presence on the Midway is well documented. Maybe Cody bought it later. "I was told that from Chicago it was taken to Coney Island," wrote Frank Fiske, the historian who stole Sitting Bull's bone. "Too bad that no one made an attempt to keep an eye on it."

The entire presence of Indians at the fair was problematic, although more for whites than Indians. After the massacre at Wounded Knee, General Miles jailed thirty leaders of the Ghost Dance, the most prominent among them Kicking Bear. At the same time, Cody was asking the commissioner to let him hire seventy-five Sioux for his next European tour. Morgan granted his permission. No law forbade Indians from accepting any job they chose. And Cody promised to select those Indians whose presence on the reservation the following spring might create the most trouble—not a bad move, since the Indians who had taken part in the recent war would draw the largest crowds. On his way to the reservation, Cody stopped in Chicago to visit his old friend General Miles. Remarkably, Miles asked Cody to hire the prisoners. "It would give them occupation for a year and a half without expense to the Government; they would be away from the Sioux country during that time; their experiences would be valuable to them as they would see the extent, power and numbers of the white race, and when they eventually return, would be entirely different men from what they were when they left the reservation."

The Indians were given the choice of staying in jail for two years or going to Europe. Most preferred the tour. Kicking Bear, who had surrendered in the full belief that he would be hanged immediately or imprisoned in the white man's jail for life, was stunned at the prospect of a trip with Sitting Bull's friend Bill Cody. "For six weeks I have been a dead man," Kicking Bear told Cody. "Now that I see you, I am alive again."

The missionaries were furious. Mary Collins started a campaign to stop Cody from taking the Ghost Dancers to Europe. Traveling with Cody had ruined Sitting Bull, she said. The chief received such a bad impression of white civilization that he became opposed to it forever. His ego was puffed up. All this incited him to lead the Ghost Dance. And how were missionaries supposed to convince the young progressives to stay on the reservation when the Indians who traveled with the shows got to ride horses around a ring, whooping and pretending to murder white people, in return for which they were paid more money than the Indians who stayed at home? When Collins asked the Indians what they thought, a few told her what she wanted to hear. Some Indians probably did object to displaying themselves for an audience's jeers. A few were mistreated, though not in Cody's shows. But most of the performers preferred traveling around the world earning their living as Indians rather than starving at home and trying to act like whites. The government's rules about how Indians in shows must be treated were more protective than the rules dictating their treatment on reservations. Not to mention that their wages rivaled their agents' salaries.

Collins was apoplectic at the idea of rewarding the leaders of the Ghost Dance for "treason, thieving, and possibly murder" by sending them on a nice, profitable excursion to Europe. But when Collins presented her objections to the secretary of the interior, Noble scolded her for making her charges public. "I want you to understand, Madam, that I cannot be driven!"

Besides, Cody's performers had already sailed for Europe. Collins gave up trying to stop the show and switched to demanding that the representation of Indians at the coming World's Fair celebrate their "proper image." The Ghost Dancers, for their part, grew weary of being away from their families and began agitating to go home. Kicking Bear and Short Bull wanted to make sure their followers wouldn't relinquish all hope of the messiah. Cody's manager, Nate Salsbury, who tended to speak in favor of the Indians, reported to the government that Kicking Bear, after eleven months with the troupe, was still "turbulent and lawless. Has no fear of consequences and will promote trouble on the Reservation sure. The war spirit is evidently on him at present. . . ." When the performers sailed back to New York, most of the prisoners were allowed to return to their reservations. Several were held a while longer in Chicago, but by late October, even Kicking Bear, who hadn't seen his wife and children in two years, took the train home.

Then the following spring, all of them came back—along with twenty-seven million other Americans—to see the World's Fair. The Columbian Exposition, celebrating four centuries of white progress, opened in Chicago's Jackson Park on May 1, 1893, with boats hooting from Lake Michigan and a choir belting out the "Hallelujah Chorus" as President Grover Cleveland threw the switch that brought alive the fair's machinery. Just as the miracle of electricity transformed these machines, Cleveland said, so the awakening forces of enlightenment would transform American society. The depression in Kansas City had foreshadowed a depression countrywide, and Americans elsewhere had begun to question their faith in progress. But here at the fair, progress was the electricity that powered each event. And you couldn't celebrate the progress of white civilization without contrasting it to the savagery it had replaced.

Ethnologists from Harvard and the Smithsonian planned to introduce the crowds to the theory that humankind had evolved in stages and scientists could learn about our own civilization by studying savages like the Sioux. The ethnologists set up exhibits at which fair goers could observe such primitive cultures. Think of the dioramas of your youth—the miniature tipis, the Indian women squatting over their cooking fires, the elders weaving baskets, the bare-bottomed children playing games with stones, except that these dioramas were peopled by living Indians. The Bureau of Indian Affairs had a different idea. What good were all its projects if Indians were forever primitive? The Indians did not represent our past. They represented us. Or they could, with some coaching. The BIA wanted whites to see Indians as the products of dollars well spent. The bureau's exhibit was a fake schoolhouse in which real Indian children would be brought from reservations, taught for two weeks with tourists peering in the windows, then sent home and replaced by another class.

Cody wanted to present a third image of Indians—not as primitives caught in time, nor as imitation whites, but as heroes of a race that had achieved its own nobility, vanishing but not yet vanished. The managers of the fair banned

Cody's show as vulgar and not in keeping with the educational intent of most exhibits. Undaunted, Cody leased a tract outside the entrance, at precisely the spot where the trains disgorged their loads. Most fair goers thought Cody's show was the main event. He brought his usual complement of performers from Pine Ridge. And to show up the puny basket-weaving exhibits of the anthropologists, he paid the way of an extra hundred Sioux from Pine Ridge, Standing Rock, and Rosebud. On opening day, he finagled permission to take a group that included Kicking Bear, Short Bull, and Red Cloud's son, Jack, to the top of the administration building, where they watched the parade of flags and listened to a chorus of "My Country 'Tis of Thee." When the crowd looked up, there stood the Indians, a reporter said, "flaunting crests of feathers and flaming blankets which stood out against the gleaming white of the staff dome like a rainbow cleft into remembrances of a lost primitive glory."

Two million people saw the Wild West show. Millions more strolled past the encampments on the Midway, some sponsored by the Smithsonian, most not—among the latter was "Sitting Bull's Death Cabin," sponsored by P. B. Wickham and his fellow entrepreneurs from North Dakota, who hired nine Oglalas to stand around pretending to be Hunkpapas, since no real Hunkpapas would go near the place. Kicking Bear couldn't very well condemn these Indians, given that he had been in Cody's show. But he was not a forgiving man. I imagine him stopping on the Midway and glaring at the cabin. The last time he had been there, that white she-devil Weldon was speaking poison to his uncle. Kicking Bear had had to lie on his back and kick his feet to show he wasn't going, and what did that old white witch do but laugh! Look at those cowardly Oglalas, pretending to be Hunkpapas and showing the whites the bullet holes that pierced the cabin. They made heroes of the police who killed their own leader. Kicking Bear wasn't sorry that he had allowed the white man Cody to bring him to this place. He had seen what needed seeing. Sitting Bull was right—the whites spent their money on foolishness like a giant wheel that lifted them in the air while their own children went hungry. What good was this *electricity* they kept showing him? Did any of these toys bring a person meat? Could the electricity move things as quickly as the earth's own wind? Didn't *Tunkashila's* own fire bring light? If only this entire hideous White City could be smothered beneath the mud the messiah had promised he would bring!

But most of the Indians enjoyed the fair. In his excellent account of the experiences of Native Americans in Wild West shows, L. G. Moses says that Cody's performers at the fair made good money. They toured Chicago and rode the pleasure boats on the lake, ate themselves sick on peanuts and popcorn, bought coconut-fiber hats, stuck them on their heads, and rode the carousel. "One evening in the high summer of Chicago's White City, fifteen Lakota led by Rocky Bear and No Neck mounted the painted ponies. As the carousel picked up speed, No Neck, holding the reins in both hands, gave a full-throated yell. Others in his party joined him. . . . In all, about twenty-seven million people, a few hundred Indians among them, visited the fair. Most, Indians and non-Indians alike, probably had a glorious time."

Was Weldon among the throngs? Everyone went. If she was still wandering around the West, she must have stopped in Chicago. All the trains crossed there. No one as enthralled by electricity as Catherine Weldon—witness her demonstration of that battery to the Hunkpapas—would miss this World's Fair. She probably disapproved of the exhibits. But, like most of her contemporaries, she found it impossible to stay away. I can see her striding down the congested Midway, not allowing herself to linger at the tackiest attractions. No, it wasn't like this. Real Lakota warriors would never act that way. She promised herself a ride on the Ferris wheel. But first she would stop at the cabin she used to live in—or rather, the cabin in which her friend Sitting Bull lived. And look at that! How very unexpected. How did that get here?, astonished to see her portrait of Sitting Bull on the wall, the canvas rent, the painting in a plain wood frame instead of the lovely gilt one she bought for it in Brooklyn. What happened to the old frame? Who tore the canvas? And, of course, the portrait had hung in the smaller of the cabins. How had it gotten here? Wasn't it hers, if Sitting Bull's family didn't want it?

She listened as the barker shouted out the tale of Lieutenant Matthew Steele saving the portrait of Sitting Bull from the tribal policeman's rage. The revolver she gave the chief was a prop in the gruesome battle the fake Hunkpapas acted out, a few of them pretending to be policemen, one of them Sitting Bull, a younger actor as Crow Foot. Weldon stood in that crowd, fingers curling into fists as the traitorous police were praised. Her own name was mentioned. *Here's the very bed in which the old libertine slept with his two Indian wives. Yes, that's right, he married sisters. Not something most of you gentlemen would care to attempt, I'd wager. And then here comes a third wife, a beautiful rich white woman from New York, buying their husband gifts. Why, when they found out she was carrying his child, those Sioux wives were so jealous, they chased Catherine Weldon around the camp waving their butcher knives to scalp her.* What a trial to stand by quietly. But she knew what would happen if she spoke up. *Damned old fool. Meddler. Busybody. Crank. Sure you did, sweetheart!*

She skipped the Ferris wheel and went straight to Cody's tents. She needed to speak to someone who had known Sitting Bull. She would introduce herself to Annie Oakley, who had been Sitting Bull's friend. But Oakley was busy, practicing for the show, as was Cody himself. He had bought back the chief's old gray circus horse and was riding him in the parade. *Sitting Bull Should Be Sat Down Upon*, Buffalo Bill had said. Yet here Cody was, making a fortune by sitting on the chief's old horse. Of course, one couldn't trust anything the papers said. For all she knew, Bill Cody had never uttered any such thing. And he had been the one who'd given Sitting Bull the horse in the first place. But that misguided stunt, taking Kicking Bear to Europe . . . If any other Indian wanted to join the show, he had every right, despite what that stick-in-the-mud Mary Collins thought. But for that miscreant Kicking Bear to get an all-paid trip to London and represent his people to the crowned heads of Europe . . . and for Cody to arrange to bring Kicking Bear to this fair . . . She only hoped she wouldn't run into him. Too bad there weren't any Hunkpapas for her to visit. She didn't know these Oglalas, although they would provide a chance for her to practice her Lakota. Not that there was any reason to keep up her fluency. She had no more opportunity to practice her Lakota than she had to use her French. She ought to start a war and get sent to Paris as her punishment. That was the only way she could ever afford to go.

If Weldon was settled back in Brooklyn by the time the Wild West show visited that city in 1907, she might have seen the cabin there. Perhaps Cody took possession of the cabin after the World's Fair was done. He dismantled and rebuilt it, moving it from town to town, then got tired of transporting it and sold it to a businessman at Coney Island, where Weldon came upon it on the boardwalk, shabby, in disarray. *One thin dime to see the cabin in which the terrifying Sioux chief Sitting Bull was killed!* Her portrait wouldn't have been there. Who knew where it had gone?

Weldon didn't want her private life exposed, but she wanted her paintings seen. I was certain that the portrait hidden for a century in Little Rock must be the one she deeded to the Van Solens. That was why the owners wanted to stay unknown: it wasn't theirs. The scandal about President Clinton's affair with Monica Lewinsky was at its most scandalous that summer, and I joked to my friends that I was going to find evidence linking Weldon with Bill Clinton. I hatched a scheme that involved calling Mrs. J. H. Cobb, the Colonial Dame who had supervised the inventory of American paintings in Little Rock, and baiting her into revealing the owner's name. But I found a listing for a Mr. J. H. Cobb, with no Mrs. listed, and I figured that Mrs. Cobb had died. I pleaded my case to the Smithsonian again. This was a painting for which another museum had the deed! But the curators wouldn't relent. If I wrote a letter to the owner, they would forward it, but the owner could refuse to answer. Kenneth Brooks, the historian whose letters I had found in the files in North Dakota, had taken that advice in 1986, waited three months, and gotten no reply. He begged the Smithsonian to act as an intermediary in one final attempt to elicit biographical information about Weldon while protecting the owner's anonymity. The museum refused.

On a long shot, I asked the Smithsonian to send me an illustration of this second Weldon painting, with whatever data they could release. People tend to be overwhelmed by information. They skim records but rarely study them. If you read bureaucratic files closely enough, clues begin to pop up that weren't visible at first.

Sure enough, when the envelope arrived, it included a fuzzy Xerox of a portrait of Sitting Bull hanging above what seemed to be a bench in a law office. Another sheet provided the details that Sitting Bull was dressed in a gold suede suit with a red blanket draped over his shoulder, a red-and-gold necklace around his neck, and a red-tipped feather in his hair. Under PRESENT OWNER (RELATIONSHIP TO SITTER) the words "no relationship" were typed, which made me doubt that the owner was a descendant of the Van Solens, since the Van Solens were related to Sitting Bull. The owner's address was whited out, but the city, state, and zip code weren't. "Little Rock, AR 72207." So now I was looking for a lawyer in the 72207 postal zone of Little Rock.

Below this, a question asked the owner if he/she wished his/her name to be held in confidence. The box was checked, which made me think the owner wouldn't have asked for anonymity if it hadn't been offered. Aristocratic southerners don't enjoy publicity. It might have been reflex, checking off that box.

Then I found my best clue. Whoever had been told to blot the owner's name had neglected to look farther than the first space marked OWNER. At the bottom of the page was a space for the signature of "owner or other person supplying information." And there, in a spidery scrawl, was the name "Mary Delia Carrigan Prather." Who could this woman be if not the owner? With all those names, she must be someone with enough history to own a portrait of Sitting Bull. Another possibility came to mind. In books about Sitting Bull, the name of the teacher Jack Carignan usually gets written "Carrigan." If anyone was a good suspect for "acquiring" a painting of Sitting Bull, that person was Jack Carignan. He taught school a mile and a half from Sitting Bull's camp. Crow Foot was his pupil. He knew Weldon well enough to tell McLaughlin that Sitting Bull had lost all confidence in whites since she left Grand River. He ignored warnings about the Ghost Dance and stayed at his post, sending reports to his boss. He was rewarded with a stint as agent and eventually ran the largest trading post in Sioux country. He retired to Kansas City. He could have bought the portrait at Yates, or he might have run into Weldon in Kansas City and bought the painting then.

Then there was the "Prather" part of the owner's name. A trooper called W. A. Prather had been the regimental poet with the Ninth Cavalry at Wounded Knee. ("The rest have gone home / And to meet the blizzard's wintry blast, / The Ninth, the willing Ninth, / Is camped here till the last. . . . In warm barracks / Our recent comrades take their ease, / While we, poor devils, / And the Sioux are left to freeze.") Maybe Weldon traveled to Pine Ridge after Wounded Knee and got to know this poet. Or Prather bought the portrait from one of Sitting Bull's survivors.

I used the Internet to do a search for all the Prathers in Little Rock. And yes, there was Mary D., in the 72207 zip code. The woman who returned my call told me that her family did indeed own a portrait of Sitting Bull, but the person I should speak to was her mother, whose name also was Mary Delia. The woman to whom I spoke told me that her great-great-grandfather had been a senator from Arkansas and the chairman of some committee on Indian affairs. Family legend had it that the person who owned the painting no longer wanted it and gave it to the Senator. "It hung in my grandmother's house for years," Mary Delia said. "It scared me half to death."

I called the elder Mary Delia Prather, fearing she would abuse me for disregarding her privacy. But she was nothing if not cordial. In a cultivated southern accent she apologized for being groggy; I had woken her from a nap. Why yes, she said. She did own a painting by C. S. Weldon. She was going to go inside right now and take a look at it, as if she feared Sitting Bull might have gotten it in his head to run away since she had last noticed. "Why, yes, here it is. The signature in the corner says 'C. S. Weldon, 1890.' It's signed in red."

She didn't know much about the painting or its origins, except that her great-grandfather, James Kimbrough Jones, had been a U.S. senator who'd had something to do with Indian affairs. It was just a word-of-mouth story that had come down through the family, but Mary Delia's impression was that the painter wanted to receive some money for the painting, or the painting was supposed to hang in a capitol somewhere and that didn't materialize, so the painter gave it to the Senator.

A capitol. That made sense. After Lucille Van Solen died, the portrait was to go to the people of North Dakota to hang in their museum, or maybe in their capitol. But the people of North Dakota didn't want a picture of Sitting Bull; witness their resistance to his monument being replaced with anything but a slab. The Prathers didn't come by the portrait illegally. The state gave it back to Weldon, and she gave it to the Senator.

Like many good theories, this one turned out to be false. But deciding that the Prathers had come by the portrait honestly helped me speak politely to Mary

Delia. Did she know anything about the painter? I asked. Did her family own anything else related to Weldon?

No, she said slowly. Once, in New York City, she had gone into the public library to try to find out something about the painter C. S. Weldon. All she had been able to learn was that "C. S." was a woman. That surprised her, to find out the painter was a woman. But that was all she knew. The painting had come down to her father because the Senator, James Senior, had given it his son, James Junior, who didn't have a living son, so he passed the painting along to his nephew, Stephen Carrigan, who was Mary Delia's father. The portrait of Sitting Bull hung over the piano in Mary Delia's house while she was growing up. Whenever she practiced, there was Sitting Bull looking down at her. "I didn't look at him, but he looked at me. I believe this is the kind of painting that seems to look at you wherever you are standing. Thank goodness it was eventually replaced by a portrait of my great-grandfather, just looking off in the distance."

I liked Mary Delia. She told a good story. Her comedic timing was impeccable. She had a devilish laugh. I asked if the portrait might have ever hung in a law office.

"Well," she said, "Senator Jones, after he lost the race for the Senate—he had three terms, I believe—he and his son lived in Washington, D.C., and they had a practice there. My own father was a lawyer in Hope."

"Hope?" I said. "Hope, Arkansas? Your father was a lawyer in Hope?"

"Why, yes. I grew up there."

"You grew up in Hope? Did you know the president?"

She laughed pointedly. "Oh, you know, I am nearly double the president's age."

What about his parents?

"Even his mother is younger than I am." And, what she didn't say, that the Carrigans and Clintons would have moved in different circles. Mary Delia Carrigan was descended from a senator. Her father was a lawyer.

Mary Delia was born in Hope in 1917. She taught school for three years before a position opened in Little Rock, and she moved there and got married. She and Roy Prather lived in Little Rock for fifty years. Her husband was an accountant from Alabama—no relation to any regimental poets, as far as she knew. When her mother passed on—this was 1971—Mary Delia and her sister moved their mother's possessions to their own homes. "I had just come back from our mother's house, and my sister called and said, 'Did you bring Sitting Bull?' and I said, 'Yes, Sitting is with us.'"

I held my breath and asked if Mary Delia would mind if I came to Little Rock to see the portrait. Not at all, she said. She would be happy to meet me.

I could tell her all I knew about the painting and C. S. Weldon. "By the way," she asked, "how did you come to learn I had it?"

"The Smithsonian," I said carefully. "I found it in their records, as part of their bicentennial inventory by the Colonial Dames."

A lengthy pause. "Of course. The Smithsonian. The Colonial Dames." Another long silence. "I didn't have any idea how important this painting was!"

～

To discover why Weldon bestowed one of Sitting Bull's portraits on Mary Delia's ancestor, I read everything I could find about James Kimbrough Jones. The seminal—and only—biography of the Senator turned out to be *The Plumed Knight of Arkansas*, published in 1913 by Farrar Newberry "with materials provided by the widow of the late senator and his son," who also revised and "corrected" the manuscript. The photo of Senator Jones showed yet another bald white man with whiskers. His brow protruded strongly, as if to signal his rationality. An appendix titled "The Phrenological Character of James K Jones" gives some idea of where the future politician found his calling. On a trip to New York just before the Civil War, Jones visited a famous phrenologist and got a "chart of characterization of himself, that he might better know how to improve upon the weaker traits in his make-up." The bumps on that impressive brow told the phrenologist Jones was "sharp, wide-awake, intense" and would make a good lawyer. If he went into politics, he would make a good party leader. "You cannot talk in so wordy a style as many, but you talk to the point. You are capable of ardent love and great fondness for children, pets and whatever is helpless and pretty." Maybe the prophecy came true because Jones was the sort of man the prophecy described. Or he purposely turned himself into such a man. Regardless, by the time his widow gave the phrenologist's report to his biographer—Jones had kept it locked up, from modesty—everyone could see how well it fit.

Given how few people outside Arkansas—or even inside Arkansas—remember James K. Jones, his biographer's praise seems a bit hyperbolic. "Like Launcelot brave, like Galahad clean," the senator was a combination of Socrates, Regulus, William the Silent, Plato, Marcus Aurelius, George Washington, and the Plumed Prince Henry of Navarre ("his party's banner ever in the forefront of the line"). The man had only one flaw. No one was more typically Arkansan than James K. Jones, but he did not come from Arkansas. In those days, no one came *from* Arkansas. One came *to* Arkansas. It was a humble place. But then, Newberry reminds us, so was Nazareth.

"James Kimbrough Jones was not born on Arkansas soil. No, the proud State of Mississippi claims the distinction of having first rocked the infant form of

Arkansas widest known political chieftain upon her breast." This was an accident. "His mother simply happened to be visiting relatives at Love, in Marshall County, in that State, and on that visit she prematurely gave birth to a boy." The boy's family came from Wales, as is true of most of the Joneses in this story; the story is so full of Joneses it seems like an Abbott and Costello routine. In 1836, Nat Jones, the Senator's father, married Caroline Jane Jones, no relation, and "James K. Jones was born of this happy union, September 29, 1839." James's mother died. His father moved to Arkansas. Nat Jones remarried, but his second wife died, too. The boy was sent to Tulip for schooling, Tulip being noted for its "moral atmosphere." Both of the Senator's future wives were classmates in his Sunday school. But they probably didn't think much of him romantically. "The sallow complexion, the high cheekbones, the scarcity of flesh upon his face, combined to give him the unmistakable appearance of a consumptive." At twenty-two, he was six feet tall and weighed one hundred pounds. People doubted he would live. He could have stayed home from the war. But he enlisted. Soon enough, he got pneumonia and was sent to Texas to dry out. He recovered, saw service in Mississippi and Tennessee, then fell so sick the doctors sent him home again. After he got over being delirious from illness he got delirious from love and proposed to one of those Sunday-school sweethearts, Sue Rust Eaton. He went back to war and made it to colonel before his health gave out again. His wife gave him two daughters before she died. Then he married his other Sunday-school sweetheart, who was also named Sue. The war left him bankrupt, so he and this second Sue went to live on the family farm in Hampstead. The pure water, fresh air, and outdoor work agreed with young James. He and his wife were happy there. They named the farm "Sunshine."

This is where it gets hard to figure out if James Kimbrough Jones, the eventual owner of Weldon's portrait, was a good guy or a bad guy. If we wish him well on that farm, we have to remember that he was rebuilding it during Reconstruction. "It was on this farm that Mr. Jones had his first experience with freed negroes," his biographer tells us. He had been accustomed to slaves whom he could drive at will, "saying to one, 'Go,' and he goeth, and to another, 'Come,' and he cometh. After the war the situation was materially changed." Jones had no patience for managing free negroes, so he recalled the phrenologist's advice and studied law.

In this pursuit, Jones approached a boyhood friend named Daniel Webster Jones, no relation, who coached him for the exam. James K. passed the bar and entered into partnership with a friend of Dan Webster Jones named Robert Carrigan. Within a few months his services were in demand "for beating and driving from that section forever the influence and power of the Republican carpet-baggers." The Republicans had been in power for a decade, and the Democrats hoped they might finally drive the scalawags out if only they could find the right candidate. They held a nominating convention but couldn't come up with anyone. Then they met in the back of a drugstore, and someone said, Well, why not Jim Jones?

Jones was so stony, cold, and gaunt, with such deep-set eyes and such a black, satanic beard, most people thought the nomination was a joke. But Jones took it seriously. He hated to leave his wife amid so many "unruly negroes," but off he went, learning to tell stories, shake hands, and talk to the folks. "To the utter astonishment of some, and the surprise of many," he was elected. And elected again. Through various ins and outs of his career, James Kimbrough Jones was sent to Washington three times. He put on weight—literal and political. He was the most powerful Democrat at the crazy convention in Chicago in 1896. All that summer, the delegates shouted at one another about silver versus gold. And there sat Jones of Arkansas, through the floods of oratory and the tedious roll calls, "with head thrown back against the standard pole of his State, and eyes half closed, vest open and loose, soft shirt bosom catching every breeze that sweeps through the great hall." When the convention paused to consider what to do next, "the huge bulk of Senator Jones would rise in the aisle . . . shove back the hard bottom chair in which he had been sitting, make a speaking trumpet of his hands, and turn loose his great voice in two words. 'Mr. Chairman!'" He saw everything. He was on guard against all dangers "of any foolish procedure in the silver ranks, or crafty move by the gold-bugs." The leaders of the various delegations crowded around him; "all wish to know the next step in the program. Jones, of Arkansas, tells them."

Jones helped William Jennings Bryan, "the boy orator of the Platte," give his famous "cross of gold" speech and win the nomination. Bryan appointed Jones his campaign manager. "The four men most talked about in the United States at the time were Bryan and McKinley, Mark Hanna and James K. Jones. Their names were to be found in almost every newspaper column in the country; their pictures abounded in the magazines; they were heralded far and wide 'in lithograph, cartoon and song.'" After Bryan lost his first campaign, Jones went home to Hope for a rest and was met by a crowd of well-wishers who escorted him to his daughter's house in a carriage decorated by white chrysanthemums and drawn by white steeds.

As I read, I tried to turn Jones into the kind of hero who would earn Weldon's gift. But I couldn't turn him into a hero any more than I could paint him as a villain. Here was a man whose calling came from his frustration in managing free Negroes and whose greatest triumphs consisted of leading currency fights so tedious I couldn't keep reading long enough to figure out whose side I was on.

Maybe Jones was particularly forward thinking about Indians. I studied his record. He approved of educating the Indians . . . but faulted the government for spending too much money doing it. He hoped Indian country would be a state . . . but believed every acre in the nation ought to be open to homesteaders, no matter if that land was on a reservation. Nonetheless, the treatment of the Indians who brought complaints to his committee made Jones "heartsick and disgusted." He opposed bills to induce the Indians to give up their tribal lands. He helped block the removal of the Lower Brule from their reservation.

In 1901, the leasing arrangements at Standing Rock came into dispute. A few mixed-bloods and whites married to Indians had signed leases with white ranchers to pasture their herds on reservation land. The Indian Commissioner—whose name also was Jones—believed the Sioux would profit more if they leased the land as a tribe. The leases weren't small; the Lemmon ranch would have eaten up 800,000 acres of the reservation and the Walker ranch 450,000 acres. But the IRA raised an outcry (the NIDA no longer existed) and tried to get the leases rewritten so the white ranchers would be required to fence their herds and the Indians' cows wouldn't "accidentally" become tangled up with theirs. (When the cattle mixed freely, one wag put it, "it appeared that the Indians' cows never had calves while the ranchers' cows always had twins.") The IRA got help from Mary Collins, of all people, and from Senator James Kimbrough Jones, who used his influence to elicit testimony on the leases. With the Senator's help, the IRA brought the leases to the attention of Teddy Roosevelt, who declared that he was "not altogether easy" about their fairness. The president was even less easy when the IRA showed him proof that the Sioux had voted unanimously against the leases. Commissioner Jones—not the Senator—took a trip to Standing Rock and became so incensed by the mischief he uncovered there that he canceled the Walker lease; the Lemmon lease was too far along, but he managed to have it modified so the ranchers were required to fence their herds.

Weldon, then, was still involved in reservation politics. The Blands lived in Washington. Thomas had become a celebrated proponent of the theory that the dead might speak to us from the world celestial. If the man she respected most could put her in contact with Sitting Bull and Christie, she might have wanted to go and see him. Visiting the Capitol, she got the idea that a portrait of Sitting Bull should hang in the rotunda. But the government wouldn't buy the idea . . . or the painting. This couldn't have been the portrait she deeded the Van Solens. Senator Jones died in 1908. Weldon must have given him the portrait earlier than that. The Van Solens' portrait remained in North Dakota until 1914. If this wasn't the portrait that was hanging in Sitting Bull's cabin when he died or the painting that Weldon deeded to the Van Solens, it could only be one of the two portraits that were in Weldon's trunks when they were stolen. Which meant the trunks eventually turned up. It was a staggering realization. A fourth portrait might exist. Along with Weldon's diaries. And the letters that Sitting Bull wrote to her.

Weldon gave her portrait of Sitting Bull to Senator Jones around 1901. He hung it in his office. It was the worst period in his life. His friend Dan Webster Jones had just lost his campaign for governor to a demagogue named Jeff Davis. Davis's ally, James Clarke, set out to topple Jones from the Senate seat he had occupied for three terms. Like Davis, Clarke set himself up as the "spokesman for the rednecks." Few Arkansas politicians thought Jones could be defeated. "Alas, they did not reck the uncertainties of the public fortune-wheel, nor consider the fatality of political chicanery!" In other words, Jones lost. He had saved nothing from his salary. He was "bewildered and humiliated" over how to support his family. His constituents in Arkansas expected him to come back home. But Jones visited Hope and couldn't see enough legal business there to justify his return. He was an old man, he said, and he no longer could stand the rigors of building up a practice. Everyone in Washington knew and respected him. He had opportunities to earn a living there, and, despite the aggrieved mutterings of Hope, that was where he stayed.

Taking James Junior as a partner, James Senior founded a legal firm that specialized in acquiring oil leases on Indian land for companies like Standard Oil. On his last return to Hope, in 1908, he received a premonition that he would die. He visited his father's grave, then wrote a letter to his wife. "The sun is approaching the west in plain view . . . the night cometh. I have tried to live for a clear sunset and a quiet night after I am gone—I can't do much more. God bless you and keep you in the hollow of his hand." He made it back to Washington, where, as Newberry puts it, "The great heart ceased to beat, and the pure spirit, freed from the cares of a worn-out physique, fled to the further shore of the Vast Unknown." He left Weldon's painting to his son, who would have left it to his son, but the boy died of scarlet fever, so he left it to his nephew, Mary Delia's father.

As I drove south from Kansas City through the Ozarks, past one roadside "flea sale" after another, the wind got hotter and more oppressive. "Think Its Hot Now Have You Been Saved?" read the sign on one of the jackleg churches I kept passing, each with advice about how to save my soul ("If you plant thorns you can't expect to harvest roses"). Like many northern Jews, I felt ill at ease in the South. On the outskirts of Little Rock, the dinky Pentecostal churches with hand-lettered placards gave way to enormous Pentecostal churches with flashing neon signs. "ROCK! SOLID! PREACHING!" "HAVE YOU BEEN SAVED HAVE YOU BEEN SAVED HAVE YOU BEEN SAVED."

I listened to the radio—Monica was testifying about her relationship to Bill, Bill was swearing to tell the truth about his relationship with Monica, the FBI was testing Monica's stained dress, and Hillary was finishing a tour to promote the preservation of America's Treasures. Until now, the occupants of the White House might have belonged to another species from anyone I knew. But Bill. I knew men like Bill from Yale. And I couldn't condemn Monica. I knew many women like her, convinced that being the lover of a powerful man was somehow the same as being powerful yourself. That was how reporters in Catherine Weldon's day saw her. But Monica was just the opposite of Catherine Weldon. Monica wouldn't have been ashamed to be outed in the press if not for the chance that she might be sent to jail. Weldon was outraged at the charge that she had slept with Sitting Bull. She was his lobbyist, not his lover.

The historical district of downtown Little Rock is so gentrified that I could have been in Faneul Hall in Boston. Mary Delia Carrigan Prather's neighborhood could have been a nice development in any state. But Mary Delia herself was a southern lady. Neat, trim, petite, with a helmet of silver hair, she wore a tailored navy dress with white polka dots and a red handkerchief folded in the pocket. She had prepared cheese straws and lemonade, which she served on a silver tray. "Aren't you glad the hot spell broke?" she kidded. "Would you like to meet Sitting Bull now?"

Yes, I said, I sure would. I had come a long way to meet him. She led me to the den. He was hanging above a desk whose top, I saw now, I had mistaken for a bench in a legal office. I had reached the right conclusion—that Sitting Bull had come to rest in a family of lawyers—by following mistaken clues. The painting was so dark that I needed to climb on top of the desk to see the details. The pigment had gone bad, or it always had been this murky. Weldon painted it at night, in a cabin that was lit by a kerosene lamp. This portrait wasn't copied from any photo. I could tell. She painted it at Grand River, in Sitting Bull's house. The background was dark. Sitting Bull's hair was parted down the middle and braided on either side, the ends wrapped with cloth or fur; a single white feather with a black-and-red tip stood straight up from the back. He wore a beautiful gold suede shirt with a white bone necklace at his throat and a luxurious red shawl thrown carelessly around one shoulder.

I liked this portrait better than the one I had seen in Bismarck. Sitting Bull's features were more subtle and distinct. His mouth rippled in an enigmatic expression that hinted he might be about to speak. He looked old, but the

32. Oil portrait of Sitting Bull signed "C. S. Weldon," dated 1890, oil on canvas, twenty-six inches high by twenty-one inches wide. Photo by Dana Simmons, Arkansas Territorial Restoration, courtesy of Mary Delia Carrigan Prather.

younger man was visible beneath the flesh. The painting was the work of an amateur, but a talented amateur who was invested in her subject. The paint was cracking. And Sitting Bull's gaze was focused so dully that he seemed hypnotized or drugged. But this was the way Weldon saw him in his cabin late at night, staring off at a world no longer there. She wasn't unreasonable to think this portrait of Sitting Bull ought to hang in the nation's Capitol. It was the only portrait of Sitting Bull anyone had painted from life.

I asked Mary Delia what she had known growing up in Hope about Sitting Bull. Did her family talk about the painting?

I thought he was a medicine man, she said. He was the leader of his tribe. My daddy would bring in people who were interested in history and they talked about the painting.

She had invited Bill Worthen, the director of the Arkansas Territorial Restoration Project, to be present when we spoke, and he tried to help her out. "This was a family with a real awareness of history," Worthen told me. What the painting represented was the connection of the Senator to the nation's great events. The Senator had been a really great man. The only reason he was beaten for that fourth term was that Joe Clarke was aligned with Jeff Davis, a rabble-rouser who appealed to the people's basest instincts.

Had Davis been as bad as Huey Long? I asked.

Worse! Worthen laughed.

Mary Delia perked up. Huey Long? She had once heard Huey Long speak. "He was helping some woman get elected to the Arkansas senate. This new invention—a car with a bullhorn—came through town ten days before the election." She made a speaking trumpet of her hands—I had to laugh, remembering Newberry's description of Mary Delia's great-grandfather making a trumpet of his hands and addressing the chairman of the Democratic Convention—and imitated the politician driving through her town. "Huey Long will be speaking this afternoon at the school at two P.M.! He will be speaking at two P.M.!" Then Mary Delia launched into a fast-talking imitation of Huey Long that got me laughing so hard I couldn't write it down. When I had sobered up, I tested the hypothesis that Weldon had given Senator Jones the painting as a reward for helping the Sioux at Standing Rock.

Yes, Mary Delia said, that definitely rang a bell. The painting was a thank-you. The painter wanted the U.S. government to buy the portrait and hang it in the Capitol, but they couldn't agree on a price, so she gave it to the Senator. That's how Mary Delia had grown up with Sitting Bull over her piano. "I felt he gritted his teeth whenever I hit a wrong note," she said. Thankfully, Sitting Bull had been moved to a less conspicuous spot to make room for a portrait of the Senator painted by Mary Delia's aunt. Somber and dark, it hung in her living room. "The Senator at least was indifferent to my playing. I much preferred this painting to the other."

"They both scared me," her daughter grumbled. The younger Mary Delia seemed less comfortable than her mother with the Jones genealogy. She didn't want anyone to think she was putting on airs. A great-great-grandfather who had been a senator was ancient history. It was who you were now that mattered. Why, sometimes it seemed her family claimed connection to every Jones there was. Next thing, she would find out she was related to John Paul Jones, or Davy Jones, or who knew what Jones. And who was going to go through all those boxes in the basement? What was she going to do with all that stuff?

Worthen looked shocked. "If not for people who kept a lot of boxes in their basements, we wouldn't know much about the past," he said. I sympathized with the younger Mary Delia, but I had to agree with Worthen. What if the Prathers had put out their old painting of Sitting Bull at a flea sale? I took another cheese straw, then realized with a start that I had gone from being someone who thought I had nothing to do with Arkansas history to someone who would give anything to go down in Mary Delia's basement and sort through all her boxes of family stuff myself.

13

Three Valentines

Weldon gave her portrait of Sitting Bull to James Kimbrough Jones around 1901. In 1912, when she wrote the deed for the portrait she sent Louise Van Solen, she was living in Brooklyn. I had the will of a Catherine Weldon who died in Brooklyn in 1939. If the woman who wrote that will was the right Catherine Weldon, it would be easy to find her grave. But I was beginning to doubt she was. How could my Catherine Weldon have left so many heirs? My Weldon gave birth to one son, who was buried in Kansas City. Even if she adopted that second Christie, he died a year later. She might have traveled back to Brooklyn and adopted more children there, but that hardly seemed plausible. If I had the wrong will, I might need days to find the right one. New York was smothering beneath a heat wave. The prospect of searching every cemetery in the greater metropolitan area didn't enthrall me. Derek Walcott always portrayed his Catherine Weldon walking through the snow. But when I closed my eyes, I saw her walking through the shimmery Dakota heat. On each of my trips to find her—to Grand River, Kansas City, Little Rock, and Brooklyn—the temperature had been in the nineties.

This trip was no cooler. I was waiting for a bus when an elderly black woman in a cream suit and straw hat dropped her groceries and collapsed. Someone used a cell phone to call an ambulance. She had revived by the time it came, but the attendants lifted her to a gurney and drove her to the hospital. How many elderly people were in the high-rise above my head, dazed by the heat, afraid to go out shopping? Was the heat in Weldon's flat worse than the heat she endured at Grand River? Did anyone stop by to make sure she was alive?

My first destination was the basement of the Surrogate Court, where I went to check the signature on the will whose final page my friend hadn't had enough quarters to copy. What I hadn't foreseen was that the woman who signed the will was so infirm she could barely hold the pen; the signature was so shaky it could have been my name. From the little I could make out, my Catherine wrote her *C* with a florid curlicue at the top, while this Catherine's *C* had a modest loop at the bottom. My Catherine wrote the *e* in Weldon as a capital; this woman, lowercase.

I spent the rest of the afternoon searching Brooklyn and Manhattan directories for the early 1900s. Some years I found no Catherine Weldons. Other years I found so many Catherine Weldons that I felt the victim of a prank. Gradually I figured out that the Catherine Weldon who wrote the will was the widow of an engineer named John who died in the teens or twenties and left her with four heirs. My Catherine was the widow of a man named Richard who died in the 1880s and left her with a son she buried in Kansas City in 1889. The only way these two Weldons could have been the same person was if my Catherine returned from Kansas City and married her husband's brother. I would have dismissed this notion as absurd, but the Catherine Weldon who wrote this will was eighty-six when she died, which meant that she would have been thirty-seven when she lived with Sitting Bull—exactly the age Little Soldier gave Vestal. And the Weldon in the will left a son named Christopher. What was the chance of that? Maybe she married Richard's brother and they named their son Christie in memory of the boy who died in his mother's arms.

The only other Weldon who might have been mine was a "Weldon, C., wid." who, in 1900, was listed as living on Pacific Street in Brooklyn, then never showed up again. I had no other leads. But I had one more day in Brooklyn and a grave at Holy Cross in which someone named Catherine Weldon lay. I hired a taxi and went out there, hoping that John and Richard Weldon might be resting on either side of the wife they shared in life. Maybe the stone would read: CATHERINE S. WELDON, FRIEND OF SITTING BULL.

I wandered Holy Cross, an oasis of trees and grass in the middle of a concrete desert, searching for plot 1199. I found 1198. Then an empty patch of ground. Then the stone for plot 1200. The Catherine Weldon buried here was too poor to buy a monument. Never mind. She wasn't mine. My Catherine Weldon had covered her tracks so thoroughly I had nowhere left to look. I already had searched the census lists for Hoboken, Brooklyn, and Manhattan for the late 1800s and early 1900s. Every ten years, census takers dipped their pens in ink and traced the names of every resident of every city in the United States in an elegant script that today would be seen only on computer fonts. The ink grew fainter with each column, then darker as the writer dipped his pen in his well. But nowhere, not among the faintest of names, had I found my Catherine Weldon. Men in suits and hats trekked up and down the stairwells of New Jersey and New York while Catherine Weldon moved stealthily just ahead in her rustling black dress. After Christie's death, she didn't want to be seen. She was lost to us because of the misogyny and lies of men like James McLaughlin, the carelessness of Captain Talbot, and the indifference of Thomas Bland. But she also was lost because she wanted to be lost. She wanted nothing to survive but her reports about the government's mistreatment of the Sioux and her portraits of Sitting Bull.

But dying makes us visible in ways we can't prevent. She must be buried somewhere. In my years following Weldon's trail, I had come to rely more heavily on intuition. But I still held faith in logic. Most people aren't special. They obey the law of averages. Weldon had been special when she lived with Sitting Bull. But after he died, she slipped back into the anonymous flow of life in Brooklyn, New York, in the early 1900s. Where would most people who died in Brooklyn be buried?

Green-Wood, I thought. She's buried out in Green-Wood. The dispatcher for the cab I had taken to Holy Cross had told me that his parents were buried inside its gates. "But they're the only ones. Everyone else is out at Green-Wood, see? That actor, what's his name, Montgomery Clift? Or is it Cliff? And that conductor, Lennie Bernstein. And the guy who played the wizard in the *Wizard of Oz*. They got more than half a million stiffs buried out at Green-Wood." If half a million Brooklynites were buried out at Green-Wood, the odds were pretty good that Catherine Weldon was buried at Green-Wood, too.

I found a phone and called.

"We don't have a Catherine," the clerk informed me. "Would a Caroline do?"

My heart thudded. There had been half a dozen Catherine Weldons in the directories, but not a single Caroline. And Caroline was the name Weldon had signed to the Van Solens' deed in 1912.

Half an hour later I was standing in the blissfully air-conditioned office of Green-Wood Cemetery, waiting for the clerk to bring me Caroline Weldon's file.

"She has three Valentines in there with her."

I thought she meant that someone had sent Caroline Weldon three valentines after she was dead and the cards were still in her file.

"No, she's buried in a plot with three people named Valentine."

I had no idea who these Valentines might be. But the clerk handed me the file, and I knew I had found my Catherine. "Birthplace: Switzerland," it said. The article I had found in Bismarck about Louise Van Solen's portrait of Sitting Bull mentioned that the artist had been of Swiss birth. Thomas Bland repeatedly referred to Weldon as "Scandinavian," which might be stretched to include someone Swiss. How many Caroline Weldons living in Brooklyn in the early 1900s could have been of Swiss birth?

According to the file, Caroline Weldon had been a widow of eighty-three living in a room at 384 Baltic Street in Brooklyn. The date of death was given as March 15, 1921. She died at Holy Family Hospital. She was buried two days later. The cause of death was "burns."

Burns? She burned to death? I couldn't think about that now. Green-Wood was one of the largest cemeteries in the world. I needed all my concentration to find the right plot. I started in the kiosk beneath the hundred-foot-tall Gothic Revival spires, with their friezes of Christ's life. An interactive computer printed out a map. I took a long drink of water, then set out in the noonday heat to find Caroline Weldon's grave.

I had visited cemeteries all over America and Europe, but I had never seen a cemetery as beautiful as this. The rolling hills were shaded by every species of tree I knew and many trees I didn't. The graves spread for hundreds of acres in each direction. I rested beneath a willow and thumbed a brochure that listed Green-Wood's most famous residents—Samuel F. B. Morse, Horace Greeley, Elias Howe—as well as its most infamous—Lola Montez, Boss Tweed, and Joey Gallo. There was Charles Ebbets, who owned the Dodgers. Henry Ward Beecher, the minister of Plymouth Church succeeded by Lyman Abbott. A Sac princess named Do-Hum-Nee, who came east with her father, fell in love with a local Indian, married him, was feted by New York society, and died of the excitement. There were Currier and Ives, Charles and Louis Tiffany, and the painter George Catlin, who gained his fame the way Catherine Weldon wished she could have gained hers, by painting scenes of Indian life. The monuments ranged from book-size stones whose inscriptions had eroded to the gaudy mausoleum of a girl named Charlotte Canda, "who lost her life on the evening of the 3rd February 1845, being thrown out of her carriage while returning from a party— the day being the seventeenth of her birth." The oldest grave went back to 1838. The most recent was being filled a few yards from where I sat. The diggers tamped the dirt with spades, then bulldozed the many wreaths into a pile for hauling off.

The heat was so soporific I almost took a nap, but I forced myself to travel up and over the next hill. Happily, Weldon's grave lay in a peaceful, shaded spot beside a bucolic green lake. A graceful white crane tiptoed through the shallows.

Lot 13387 was marked with a modest granite obelisk in memory of the Valentines—Carl H., who died in 1882, Maria Barbara, who died in 1887, and Carl Valentine's unnamed child from a previous marriage. A blank expanse of grass yawned beside the stone. I knelt and spread my palms. Yes, this was her. I knew that as clearly as I knew that I was the first person to visit this grave since Weldon was laid to rest here.

But kneeling by that grave, I didn't sense her ghosts were happy ones. Caroline Weldon's last public act was to offer her government a portrait of Sitting Bull, which the government refused. She gave the painting to a senator who was beaten in his next election and spent the rest of his life leasing Indian land for Standard Oil. She died without knowing that she eventually would be vindicated in her belief that the Indians should be permitted to retain their customs and tribal land, that living with Sitting Bull would earn her a place of honor in an epic poem by a Nobel laureate, that her trip to the Dakotas would stand as proof that not every white person allowed the massacres and land thefts and treaty violations to go on as if they were impossible to stop. Maybe someday it would be as difficult to think of the treatment of the Indians in the late 1800s without bringing Catherine Weldon to mind as it would be to imagine the years of slavery without John Brown's raid on Harper's Ferry. A gesture of defiance needn't produce results. The person who makes that gesture needn't be faultless. If only those with perfect hearts are allowed to make such gestures, the rest of us have the perfect excuse to stay home.

I went back to the Green-Wood office to find out who all those Valentines were. As near as I could tell, the woman I had come to know as Catherine Weldon had been born in Switzerland in 1838 as Caroline Schlotter to a father whose first name was unknown and a mother whose given names were Maria Barbara, maiden name unknown. Mr. Schlotter had died, whether in Switzerland or here, and his widow married Carl H. Valentine (or Valentiny, as he was called before he Americanized his name). Valentine was born in Dortmund, Prussia, to German parents. He immigrated to America around 1852, nineteen years before Weldon and her mother. He made his living as a physician. At the time of his death on May 29, 1882, he was living on Pacific Street, so the "C. Weldon" I had found living on Pacific in 1900 must indeed have been my Catherine, although her stepfather was dead by then. Weldon's mother survived her second husband until April 8, 1887, when she died at seventy-nine. Catherine lived with her widowed mother for several years, then kept her apartment.

Catherine also had a sister. In May 1890, just before or just after she went to live in South Dakota for what she hoped would be forever, Weldon acquired a plot of land that would allow her, if she wished, to be buried beside her mother. Michael C. Gross, acting as trustee for the late "Maria Valentiny," deeded her daughter "Caroline Weldon (formerly Schlotter)" a section in the family plot; she also deeded sections to Anna, Fritz, and Wilhelmina Schleicher. Fritz Schleicher was the nephew with whom Weldon lived in Kansas City, so his mother must have been a Schlotter who married a Schleicher. If Fritz's mother—Catherine's sister—still had been alive in the late 1880s, Maria Barbara would have bequeathed her a plot as well.

Fritz himself died young, sometime between 1895, when he moved to San Antonio, and Weldon's death in 1921. There was a telegram in the file at Green-Wood sent from San Antonio to a Mrs. A. Sauerland in care of Peter Doran, who owned the small funeral home to which Weldon's body was taken. The telegram authorized Mrs. Sauerland to "CLAIM THE BODY OF MY AUNT C WELDEN" and was signed "M Schmidthorst." Weldon's nephew was dead by then. His widow had remarried and was giving her permission to dispose of an aunt whose name she couldn't spell. If Weldon's closest relative was the widow of a nephew who disliked her, she truly died alone. A note across the bottom attests that the decedent, Caroline Weldon, "who was formerly Caroline Schlotter, was a part owner of lot 13387 and that she and Caroline Welden on Cemetery records are one and the same person," with Mrs. Sauerland's signature and her address in Mt. Vernon. Maybe Mrs. Sauerland was Weldon's only friend. Or she was a clerk at the funeral home, desperate to find someone who could tell her what to do with Caroline Weldon's corpse.

A date squeezed between the lines on another note insinuates that Weldon's niece Wilhelmina died in 1890, while Weldon was at Standing Rock. There is no mention of the other niece, Anna Schleicher; she never claimed her plot. A German named Henry Mehrens, who died on Christmas Eve, 1861, was buried in the plot that later became the Valentines' but was moved to another grave in 1887, to make room for Maria Barbara and for Carl Valentine's child from an earlier marriage. The Michael C. Gross who handled these transactions was the same Michael C. Gross who, in 1912, drew up the deed for Weldon's gift to the Van Solens. This proved beyond a doubt that I had found the right Weldon: all those years later, she was still using her mother's lawyer.

I spent the next morning at the Melvillean city archives in lower Manhattan, where I was able to turn up Caroline Weldon's death certificate. At the time of her death, Weldon had been living in New York for roughly fifty years. Which meant that she had immigrated to America in 1871, not as a little girl, but as a woman of thirty-three. It came to me suddenly that I had found the missing key, the fact that explained why Weldon traveled to South Dakota and moved in with Sitting Bull when no other white woman of her time and place would have undertaken such a trip. But I was too harried to sit and think. I needed to gather every clue possible before the archives closed and I had to fly back home.

Weldon's father's surname was given wrongly as Valentine; that was her stepfather's name. Her mother's maiden name and birthplace were unknown. Caroline Weldon's occupation at the time of her death was given as "housework," which didn't, as I feared, mean that she cleaned other people's houses but that she stayed home and cleaned her own. The undertaker was Harry Quayle, an employee of the Doran Funeral Home at 210 Hoyt Street in Brooklyn. The cause of death was "3 degree burns of face & body accidental clothes caught fire from candle at 384 Baltic St. Mar 14/21."

No time to dwell on that either. With Weldon's maiden name, I could finally search for evidence of her marriage and Christie's birth. I sped through thirty rolls of film but found nothing I could use. My only other discovery was a minuscule obituary in the *Brooklyn Daily Eagle.* "Suddenly, on March 15, 1921, CAROLINE WELDON. Funeral will take place from 210 Hoyt st., Thursday morning, March 17, at 10 oclock. Interment Green-Wood Cemetery." No "beloved wife," no "dearest mother." Just the shortest, barest notice any stranger might have penned.

After the archives closed, I sat on a splintered bench and tried to make sense of the fact that Caroline Schlotter had lived in Europe for the first three decades of her life. No wonder she was good at foreign languages; they weren't foreign to her. She must have grown up in a German-speaking canton but acquired some facility with Italian and French. That she wrote such fluent English—it was her third or fourth tongue—is a testament to her talent as a linguist, the quality of her education, and her interest in America. What was Lakota but one more language to add to those she knew? With all the letters I had read, it never once occurred to me that she might not be a native speaker. I assumed that she was too rushed or too far from a dictionary to check the spellings of many words. I attributed the run-on sentences to her volatility. That might have been the case. Or she might never have learned to punctuate English correctly. She would have spoken with an accent and florid turns of phrase that marked her as a foreigner. Only on the Plains could Caroline Schlotter Weldon be taken for a New Yorker.

No wonder she preferred to live there. Among the aristocrats of Switzerland, the Schlotters were looked down on as barely middle-class. In Manhattan and Brooklyn Heights, ladies like Abby Abbott scorned Caroline Weldon as an adventuress who could barely support herself on a pittance from her ne'er-do-well dead husband and her "dealings" in foreign art. By their reckoning, she must be on the lookout for a wealthy husband. But the soldiers' wives at Fort Yates, half-breed women like Marie McLaughlin, and self-made men like

Thomas Bland would have taken her fancy clothes and elaborate, polished manners as proof that she was "rich."

At first, I was disappointed to learn that Weldon wasn't a true American. Then I understood that she was the truest American of all—a foreigner who helped remake her new country in the image she brought with her, although this image changed shape as it mingled with the dreams of those already here, white, Indian, and black. She seemed to represent the entire Euro-American fascination with Native American history, myth, and art, a Romantic power so fierce that its hold on Weldon's psyche propelled her to give up everything else she loved. That she spent her first thirty-three years in Switzerland explained why she moved so often. She already had given up the land she loved, the friends she cherished, her native scenes. Why not move again? After her mother's death she was no more tied to Brooklyn than to anywhere else. She could take a cheaper room in Newark or seek the company of the German-speaking radicals and bohemians for which Hoboken was then renowned (among them Ottilie Assing, the half-Jewish German journalist who was Frederick Douglass's white mistress). Like my acquaintance Sam the Cabby, the first time Weldon traveled west she had little idea how expansive this country really was compared to her tiny homeland. But when she saw what was out there, she couldn't help but go back. The dusty buttes of South Dakota weren't replicas of the Alps, but they resembled the Alps more closely than did the skyscrapers of New York.

A girl growing up in Switzerland wouldn't have acquired the same bias against the Indians as a girl growing up in South Dakota, or even in New York. It's easier to be shocked by another country's treatment of its underclass than the treatment of your own. The Swiss revered the Noble Savage. The country's most famous son was Jean-Jacques Rousseau, who preached that humankind was at its happiest in its most primitive state, free of the very institutions the whites were foisting on the Sioux. Weldon escaped being brainwashed into the social code that governed what an American white woman could do. Sophisticated Europeans weren't as conventional as their American counterparts. Although Swiss women didn't get the vote until a century after Caroline Schlotter left, in other ways Swiss women lived on fairly equal terms with their men. Girls as well as boys were required to go to school until their midteens. Swiss universities enrolled women long before this was true in the United States. The Schlotters were middle-class—Weldon's widowed mother was able to marry a physician—so Caroline probably went to college; several reporters of her day comment on what an educated woman she was. The higher classes of Swiss women were notably conversant in politics, literature, music, art, and science. Caroline Schlotter couldn't have graduated from a Swiss university in 1859 thinking that

Native peoples ought to be exterminated. Nor would she have thought that women must stay at home. Girls and boys mingled at school, while young Swiss men and women were allowed to meet at taverns to enjoy the music and dance.

Add to that the Swiss zest for education. The Rousseau who wrote *Emile* passed on his inheritance to an educational reformer named Johann Heinrich Pestalozzi, who gave intellectual birth to a long line of theorists leading to Piaget. Children were born unspoiled, the Swiss believed, and their education must shield them from the corrupting influence of civilization until they were old enough to withstand it. Even the aristocracy sent their sons and daughters to public schools, where they sat beside children so poor they needed to be given food and clothes to attend. Compulsory schooling was decreed a federal law in 1874, but each canton retained control of its local program. A canton taught its own language but encouraged the study of other tongues. The Swiss curriculum was practical: the boys were taught to make things, the girls to cook and sew. Little wonder that the most highly prized governesses in Europe were Swiss or that Caroline Schlotter Weldon felt a calling to teach the Sioux. She thought it natural that every tribe be allowed to keep its language while also learning English. As to her request to start a school of domestic science for the Indian girls, that also makes sense, given that she had studied such subjects in school herself.

Although Switzerland wasn't known for producing great artists, it had a long tradition of appreciating art. The Swiss esteemed those craftsmen who manufactured the splendid textiles, embroidery, and lace for which the nation was renowned. Even the herdsman's crude carvings were taken seriously. Weldon might have studied art in college, perhaps with the renowned Swiss critic, Jakob Burckhardt. "It's a very European portrait," Mark Halvorson had said about Weldon's portrait of Sitting Bull. And now I saw why.

I also understood why Weldon was so generous. No people on earth has a more vibrant history of philanthropy than the Swiss. The founder of the International Red Cross, Jean Henri Dunant, was born in Geneva ten years before Weldon. In 1859, on a business trip foolishly undertaken in the middle of the Franco-Austrian War, Dunant stumbled onto the battlefield of Solferino. Unable to bear the suffering of so many wounded men, he pitched in and tried to nurse them. Then he wrote a book describing the misery he had seen and suggesting the formation of a neutral society that would give succor to the wounded of any war. The book was so popular that Weldon surely saw it. She was still living in Switzerland in 1864, when delegates from around the world met in Geneva to establish the organization that took its name from the red cross on a field of white that is the reverse of Switzerland's flag. If nothing else, the establishment of the Red Cross gave Weldon a common topic to discuss with Cora Bland, who, with Clara Barton, helped to found the American branch.

The Swiss, like the Indians, loved the outdoors. Weldon preferred living in the middle of nowhere to living in any town. Most easterners think the Plains are monotonous and flat, but the rivers, hills, and fields around Sitting Bull's camp are beautiful enough to make any heart swell, and the dramatic buttes of the Badlands, even the valleys along the road from Standing Rock to Mandan, are as sublime as any view a Swiss native could crave. Coming from a country whose spirit and mythology hovered above the Alps, Weldon could understand why Sitting Bull revered the Black Hills. Both Switzerland and the Dakotas are landscapes of extremes—high and low, hot and cold. Hiking in the Alps, you ran the risk of being buried beneath an avalanche of rock or snow. If there wasn't a flood, there was a drought. Lightning kindled summer fields to flame. Plagues of biting flies caused the Swiss to regret that their ancestors had destroyed most of their native birds. Sitting Bull's cabins at Grand River weren't any less comfortable than the huts of Swiss herdsmen who took their flocks to graze in alpine meadows every spring and stayed there half the year. And, like many Swiss, Weldon was accomplished on horseback.

She also could appreciate what it was like for a people to take pride in their tribal past. The Raetians and Helvitii were conveniently dead, so the Swiss could safely mythologize them. Farming the rocky soil was such backbreaking work that most Swiss peasants had given it up in favor of raising cows. Although Switzerland was never exactly a hotbed of Communism, the farmers pastured their cattle in alpine fields the village held in common. The herdsmen's movements from lowland town to highland fields resembled the nomadic life the Sioux had so loved and the seminomadic life they still might lead as ranchers. Weldon didn't need to be a prophet to come up with her schemes for the Sioux. They could herd cows for their main livelihood and add money to their income by selling their crafts to whites and entertaining tourists like the excursionists on Captain Talbot's boat. Raising cows, selling crafts, and entertaining tourists were the three main industries of Switzerland.

The fourth industry was war. Switzerland proclaimed its neutrality, but this didn't make the Swiss pacifists. The government stayed neutral so it could hire out its troops to monarchs in need of soldiers for their own conflicts. Before banking and technology, rocky, landlocked Switzerland couldn't support its sons. Many families left. Others sent their boys to fight for foreign kings and mail their paychecks home. From the Middle Ages on, the Swiss were the most coveted mercenaries in Europe. In the War of Spanish Succession, the French hired twenty thousand Swiss troops, while the Dutch hired thirteen thousand, with various other principalities hiring a few thousand each. In total, forty-two thousand Swiss soldiers fought on either side, this from a country whose population was little more than one million. Like the Sioux, the Swiss wore their fanciest regalia into war (think of the natty Swiss Guard arrayed around the pope). Swiss soldiers marched on their employers' enemies wielding axes, spears, and hammers, along with the terrifying halberd, a six-foot-long staff with an ax and pick on top.

Then there was the crossbow. The story of William Tell was later proved a myth, but Weldon thought it fact. How could she resist telling Sitting Bull the story of this rugged mountaineer who refused to genuflect to a feathered cap that had been set on a pole by a pompous invader, as Sitting Bull refused to bow to the cross Mary Collins had set up so near his home? *The foreigner was angry at Tell for refusing to bow to his hat. He put an apple on the head of Tell's only son and ordered the father to shoot it off.* Weldon mimed Tell's ordeal, with Christie acting the part of Tell's son, a potato from Sitting Bull's farm balanced on his head. *Tell was such an excellent marksman, he cored the apple without harming a single hair on his son's head.* At which Sitting Bull harrumphed that instead of aiming his bow at Crow Foot, he would aim at the man who ordered him to do such a thing. And Weldon laughed. *Exactly! That's exactly what Tell told Gessler! "If that arrow had hurt my son, the next arrow was meant for you!"*

Weldon's habit of reading stories about Napoleon to Sitting Bull no longer seems surprising, given that Napoleon's invasion of Switzerland would have been recent history to her. She could have used Napoleon as an example of a general who returned from exile to claim his rightful throne as chief or a villain who invaded the homeland of a confederacy of tribes and imposed a central government that the cantons overthrew to reassert their tribal ways.

Weldon might have appreciated the Lakota reverence for martial valor, but with her memories of her country's civil war between Protestants and Catholics she wasn't eager to see religious differences split the Native tribes. The Constitution of 1874 guaranteed the Swiss liberty of conscience. No state religion was allowed to dominate the schools. Raised a liberal Catholic, Weldon must have believed a moderate dose of religion to be a salutary thing, but the fanatic Christianity of the messiah craze could bring nothing but destruction.

Perhaps, for all that, the Swiss and the Sioux actually had few traits in common beyond a love of smoking pipes and an endemic susceptibility to the ill effects of alcohol. But the Swiss themselves believed they had a kinship with the Sioux. Like the Germans at the Sun Dance, many Swiss in Weldon's day were long-distance devotees of the Indian way of life. In 1866, a Swiss painter named Frank Buscher sailed to America with a commission from Bern. With the recent Northern success in winning the Civil War, this was the height of the Swiss idealization of American freedom and democracy. Buscher was enthralled with the military men who had commanded both sides; he painted President Johnson, William Tecumseh Sherman, William Cullen Bryant, and Robert E. Lee. But he also took two trips to paint the Indians on the Plains. He spent five years roaming around America before heading back to Switzerland—at exactly the same time that Caroline Schlotter was sailing the other way. Buscher hadn't managed to sell many of his portraits in America, but he'd had a fine time, and he was well received in Switzerland, where his paintings were promptly bought by several large museums.

Weldon might have enjoyed greater success if she had traveled to America, then taken her portraits back to Switzerland to sell. As it was, she arrived in New York in 1871, at the very tail end of the greatest wave of Swiss emigration; after 1870, the economy became prosperous enough to allow most Swiss to stay home. She disembarked in New York with her mother and sister—and possibly her father, if he wasn't already dead—as an unmarried woman of thirty-three. In the late 1870s, Caroline/Catherine Schlotter married Richard Weldon and became Catherine Schlotter Weldon—that's what the S stood for, her maiden name. Their son, Christopher, was born in 1878. In 1882, Weldon lost her stepfather, and, five years later, her mother. Her husband must have died between 1878 and 1889, at which she packed her belongings, settled her affairs, and traveled west.

She was older than anyone thought—fifty-two the year she moved in with Sitting Bull. Silently I offered an apology to Stanley Vestal. She *was* nearing menopause, if she hadn't gone through it already. No one could guess her age because she didn't want anyone to guess it. A widow of fifty-two with a twelve-year-old son! She had married late in life and given birth in her early forties. She looked younger than she was. She lied about Christie's age so she wouldn't be criticized for subjecting so young a boy to the rigors of reservation life and because an older son would mean she had married younger than she did. She never mentioned Richard Weldon because she married him so late, lost him so early, and apparently didn't love him. The proposal was a desperate last chance she came to regret accepting. When she lived with Sitting Bull, she was nearly as old as he was. She was older than his wives. No wonder she wasn't interested in marrying again. She had no parents to care for—or to disapprove of what she did. Her son was growing up. She was free in the way that only a single Victorian woman in her fifties could be free. But to be a woman in your fifties and live so far from town, sleeping on a straw pallet on a board and hauling water through the mud . . .

Then again, Weldon's age explained her readiness to give up her life in New York and retire to the Plains. At fifty-two, a Victorian woman had outlived many of her contemporaries. Weldon must have thought she didn't have many years left and wanted to spend them as she wished.

~～の

On my last night in New York, I walked the few blocks from the room I had rented on Atlantic Avenue to Weldon's last residence on Baltic. I was amazed that I had ever felt out of place in Brooklyn. The very act of traveling here, stumbling around its neighborhoods, getting lost and getting found had made me feel at home.

With rent in Brooklyn Heights so high, the neighborhood where Weldon passed her last years would soon go chic. One of the cafés was already advertising goat-cheese terrine. For now, the stores and restaurants remained cheap, the sidewalks crowded with men and women reluctant to climb the stairs to their overheated rooms. The neighborhood hadn't changed much since Weldon lived there. In the 1915 census, the residents of Hoyt and Baltic were listed as immigrants from Italy, Ireland, and Russia. They gave as occupations "iron-worker," "painter," "butcher," "cooper," "clerk." Weldon wasn't living at 384 Baltic then. Did she keep moving because she was looking for cheaper flats or because she was still trying to hide? It's comforting to think that anyone as strong as Catherine Weldon would stay strong until she died. But that doesn't seem the case. She didn't adopt those orphans. That was a fantasy I concocted to provide a happy ending for her grief. She lived alone and died poor.

The last night of her life, as I imagine it, she was reading by herself in a dingy one-room flat. She tried to save a few cents by using a candle instead of switching on the electric light. She sat at a rickety table in her kitchen, reading the *Brooklyn Eagle*. The local clergy were waging a campaign against risqué movies. The charges were being dropped against the White Sox seven. The Japanese had built new cruisers to rival those of the American navy. And the commissioner of the courts in Queens said he didn't object to calling women for jury duty, he just preferred using men.

She folded the paper to save for kindling, then took out a box of cheap stationery, sharpened a pencil with a knife, and started to write a letter. She didn't have a single living relative. Thomas Bland was dead. If Cora had taken the advice her husband dispensed in his self-help guide, she would have been eighty-seven. More likely, both Blands were in the spirit world happily conversing with Plato, Aristophanes, and Alfred Meacham. Alma Parkin was dead. Her sister, Louise Van Solen, had died the year before, peacefully, after a long illness, with her daughter Lucille by her bed. Louise had been blessed with exactly the sort of funeral Catherine wished for herself—tribal services at Standing Rock, a Catholic mass at the fort, and final burial at the ranch beside her mother.

Dear Lucille, she might have started, *It is hard to believe that it is already one year and one week since your beloved mother passed. I can remember how bereft I felt at the loss of my own poor mother so many years ago. It is difficult to be an orphan at any age, even more difficult to be a woman alone, without a husband to look after her, not to mention a woman with the responsibility of managing a ranch. I so wish I had the financial resources to help you. Or even to come and visit and perhaps ease your heart with fond remembrances of your mother and your aunt, and the good times we all had when you were a little girl and Chaske was still with us on the ranch and my beloved Christie was alive and happy on this earth.*

But I have neither money nor strength to undertake such an arduous journey and would only be a burden to you, with my age and the probability that I still would not be welcome among many of the older white people, who would falsely blame me for the Ghost Dance uprising years ago, or the older Hunkpapas, who might blame me for the death of my friend Sitting Bull.

I wish I could visit your mother's grave, and your aunt's grave, and the grave of Sitting Bull, but I am sure that seeing an unfenced stone in the middle of a field of grazing army nags would only break my heart. I can do nothing but send my love and my fondest wishes that you remain strong and somehow, perhaps through your teaching music at Yates, find the means to hold on to the ranch, as I am certain you will be happy nowhere else. . . .

The thought of poor Lucille losing the beautiful homestead that her ancestors worked so hard to establish amid the wilderness, the only place in the Dakotas where both Indian and white might find welcome, made Catherine bear too heavily on her pencil and snap the point. She wanted to ask Lucille for news of their friends at Cannonball and find out how many of them had held on to their farms, even though she knew it did her no good to think of any of this. Every time she read about the movement to grant the Indians their citizenship and abolish the BIA, her heart pounded so wildly she had to lie down. At least when that miserable Dawes Act passed, the government had the sense not to deed the Indians their allotments outright, but to hold the land in trust until the Indians should have the competency to farm it and learn to read and write and pay their taxes so they wouldn't immediately be defrauded of what they owned. But the twenty-five years stipulated in the act had passed, and what did the Indians' "friends" in Washington say but, *Your time is up, you are citizens, the land is yours, you own it outright, you are not children any longer, you must support your families, we will abolish the BIA and end the government's handouts and leave you to run your own lives,* which would have been an excellent idea, abolishing that nest of incompetents and thieves, except that many of the Indians still could not read or write and were so destitute and despairing that they would sell their land to any white who might offer a dollar to buy it. If only the tribes had been able to retain their land in common, the stronger leading the weak, they wouldn't have now required the government's concern. They certainly wouldn't need the BIA.

Perhaps she ought to be grateful that the Major—excuse me, the *Inspector*—was making sure that each Indian whom the agents claimed was ready to assume his deed was actually competent to do so. Poor man, he was nearly as old as she was, yet he traveled around the country interviewing every farmer whose name had been put forward for citizenship by his agent. The Major—the *Inspector*—had turned down far more applications than any other inspector would have done. But still, he granted too many. Most of the Indians to whom he issued deeds immediately sold their land for the price of an automobile or even a case of liquor. A reporter had questioned the Inspector on this, and what did he answer? That even if an Indian did lose his farm, being destitute would force him to sober up and support his family and be a man. As if it were possible for any man to support a family without a job or a piece of land.

When the Indians *were* men, the Major beat them down and tried to turn them into children. When they had a man to lead them, the Major ordered him killed. She will never, never forgive him for his outrages against her and Sitting Bull. She will never forgive him for killing so many of her friends. All because of a silly dance. As if the Major himself didn't believe the messiah would come back to earth. As if he didn't love rituals himself. Why, look at that ridiculous citizenship ceremony he devised. She had seen a bit of it on a newsreel and heard the rest from Lucille. Any Indian whom the Major decreed fit to become a citizen was given a bow and arrow and ordered to shoot the arrow in the air and promise that this was the last arrow he would ever shoot, because now he was a white man, and he must kiss the flag and put his hand to the plow and denounce his Indian ways. To watch the older men denounce everything that meant so much to them made her weep. Then again, some of the younger men didn't even know which way to hold the bow, and *that* brought her to laughter. She sat there in a crowd of Brooklyn moviegoers who had never met a real Indian and had no idea who she was, weeping and laughing until she began to hiccup and had to leave the theater.

Well, the Major would get little chance for his ceremony now. The policy of granting deeds was at an end. The new commissioner—for the life of her, she could not remember the man's name, not that it mattered, they came and went so quickly—decided not to grant any more certificates of citizenship since even with the Major's competency hearings, far too many Indians were losing their farms to whites. Now all the talk in Washington and at Standing Rock was of making good on the Indians' claims of their losses at Wounded Knee.

Imagine so many years going by and the government suddenly deciding to take the blame. And for General Miles to be the one pressing for the government to make restitution. She had thought when she was young that she understood the world, but she did not, and she was not likely to understand it before she died. She wanted to write to One Bull and ask if he would press his claim, but she hated to mention those evil times. True, the messiah had never come, and the dances brought only the destruction she predicted. Sitting Bull got killed. But secretly One Bull might still suspect that she played McLaughlin's spy. So it was best not to mention anything but the happy times they shared before that dreadful fall.

As if she didn't lose as much as they. Perhaps she should put in a claim. Let them compensate her for her good name, and her broken heart, and her lost savings, and her son. Perhaps God has a sense of justice, or only a sense of humor, because, in the end, the Ghost Dance affair nearly killed the Major. He spent this past winter traveling around Standing Rock and Pine Ridge, investigating the Indians' claims for what they lost at Wounded Knee. The claims were groundless, he told the government. The Indians themselves were at fault for everything they lost, though they might be paid a modest sum in the interest of finally laying the episode to rest. But it was the Major himself who nearly got laid to rest—traveling around the reservation, he got caught in an icy downpour and nearly died.

Nearly, but he survived. Lucille mentioned in this last letter that everyone was excited about the preparations for the Major's fiftieth jubilee. Imagine, fifty years in the Indian service and he still doesn't understand the first thing about the Sioux, and, what is worse, doesn't know what he doesn't know. Jokingly, in her last letter, Lucille proposed that her aunt Caroline travel out to the ranch in time to surprise the Inspector at his celebration. How tempting to accept . . . although she wouldn't survive the journey, and, if she were to travel anywhere, it would be to Kansas City to visit Christie's grave.

She signed and folded the letter, painfully, because of the arthritis in her hands—she can no longer hold a brush—and addressed the envelope to Miss Lucille Van Solen, Parkin Ranch, North Dakota. Just as well she had no one else to write to—she couldn't afford the stamp. The only other people with whom she wished to communicate were in the spirit world. She shook her head and waved her veiny hands above the candle, murmuring the sort of nonsensical incantation she had heard her friend Thomas use to raise the dead. The candle flickered, and, for a moment, she sensed wavering shapes beyond the flame.

But no. She wasn't able to believe in the spirit world even with Thomas there, explaining why it was scientifically and spiritually correct to believe so, and she couldn't believe it now, not with everyone she had ever loved on the other side. Well, if not now, perhaps after she died. But lately she hadn't even been able to trust in that. Fine for Thomas to fall asleep and be granted a tour of Paradise and receive the assurance of an angel that his life hadn't been for naught. Her life *had* been for naught. First she lost her homeland. Then she lost her parents. She married late and not so well, and even so, she lost the husband who might have provided company and a means of sustenance in these lonely last years. She could barely give away her paintings. She'd had a son she loved dearly, and she lost him through neglect. She lost her Indian friends because she couldn't see what they saw. She couldn't believe in heaven. She wanted to believe that she would be rewarded for her losses and her good intentions here on earth. But a person couldn't believe what she couldn't believe.

In thirty years, she hadn't even been able to conjure up a single dream of Christie, or her father, or Sitting Bull. Only once was she visited in her dreams by anyone she cared to see, and that was, strangely enough, Hohecikana. Not that many years ago, she dreamed that she was lying on a bed, paralyzed, if not dying. She was wearing, well, she had the impression that she wasn't wearing much. A gown, perhaps. A shroud. Hohecikana stood above her, towering like an Alp. His head had a halo of clouds around it. And he spoke to her, in English or maybe French, in the richly rolling tones of the elocution teacher who had tutored her in Berne. *In another time and place, perhaps it could have been.* That was all he said. But his voice, his mere presence, suffused her with such calm she wasn't scared to die.

To think, she had dreamed of Hohecikana, whom she had only known those few years, and not a single dream of Christie. How old would he be now? Forty-three or forty-four—with all her lies, she sometimes had difficulty remembering his actual birth date. He would have been a married man, with children, even grandchildren. Let the BIA compensate her for the son and daughter-in-law and grandchildren and great-grandchildren she never would have because she tried to follow her conscience and do what she considered right. As it was, she was left with nothing. She had already written her will—she had little enough to give away, and no one but Lucille to give it to. What reason had she to live, unless to visit Christie's grave? It wasn't even marked. No one would take him flowers or remember he ever lived. And she wouldn't have minded being able to return to Switzerland to see the village where she was born. But that was even more unlikely than visiting Kansas City. At one time, she considered going back there to live, but Sitting Bull said that only a monster would give up living in the land where his parents' bones were buried. And her parents are buried here. Once a week, she walks or takes the streetcar to visit her sainted mother. It's a beautiful spot, in Green-Wood. If she cannot lie beside her boy on Union Hill or beside Sitting Bull at Grand River, she doesn't mind the prospect of lying for eternity beside her mother near Sylvan Lake.

Not that anyone will visit her, any more than they will visit Christie. None of her friends are left. Her neighbors think her a queer, foreign old lady. Just yesterday, when the neighbor's boy—he was barely Christie's age, though quite a bit taller, the children today are so much better fed—helped her carry up her bag, she rewarded him with an arrowhead that once belonged to Sitting Bull, and what did the child say but that he hadn't believed Sitting Bull was real. The child thought him a made-up villain from a dime-store Western or a character in a Wild West show, not a flesh-and-blood man who engineered the only major defeat of the U.S. Army and nearly saved his people from extinction.

Maybe the time had finally come, what with the movement to dismantle the BIA and reevaluate the events leading up to Wounded Knee. Perhaps if a white person told the story, the Indians would be believed and find it easier to receive their claims.

She sharpened the pencil. Where was that paper bag the groceries had come in? Yes, but where to start. Her arrival in New York? Her first interest in the Indians? No one cared about that. The less said about her, the better. She would start with her arrival at the Cannonball that spring, coming ashore and finding Alma waiting to tell her that Sitting Bull was dying from pneumonia.

She began to scratch some words on a bit of the paper bag, but the penciled scrawl was too faint to read. She leaned closer to the candle. It was nearly spring, but the air was still cold and damp, and coal was so expensive. She never thought she would long for the Dakota heat. She pulled the shawl around her, and the long, lacy sleeve, brittle from age, caught fire. Her clothes went up. Her hair. She screamed and beat the flames, then fell to the floor and lay moaning. Would no one ever come? She cried weakly for help, and finally someone heard. *Wait! I'll get my mother!* Another long wait. Then the cooper and the butcher battered down her door. No one had a phone, so the landlord told his boy to run to the drugstore to call an ambulance.

The medics took her to Holy Family, where she suffered all that night, muttering in pain. She kept asking for Sitting Bull, and Christie, and Hohecikana, but no one could make out a word. For a while, her mind cleared. *The painting,* she told a nurse. *You mustn't throw it out.*

Because that's where it had gone. The fourth painting of Sitting Bull. She had kept it for herself. It must have been the best, the one that looked most like him. She had hung it above her bed, and for nearly thirty years no one but her had seen it, but now she wanted to make sure that after she was dead, it would go to a museum, along with the buffalo robe that had been a gift from Circling Bear and her letters from Sitting Bull. *The painting,* she said again. *Please, save Sitting Bull.* But her lips were cracked and dry. Her cheeks pained her when she spoke. Red as any Indian, she thought. I'm burned red as any Lakota squaw.

As I walked along Hoyt, elderly men in crushed hats, middle-aged women in flowered shorts, and teenage boys in baggy jeans lazed languidly on beach chairs, squatted by the curb, or leaned against car hoods while ribs sizzled on hibachis and a van with open doors throbbed salsa through the night. The small brick building that had housed the Doran Funeral Home at 210 Hoyt was intact but boarded up. Around the corner, 384 Baltic was an empty lot beside an auto-body shop. A mural behind the fence proclaimed the loving memory of Nicholas Naquan Heyward, Jr., who had been born in 1981 and died at thirteen. The mural was called PARADISE LOST AND RESURRECTED. In his choir robe, young Nicholas rose joyfully toward heaven, doves fluttering beside his shoulders like wings. Off to one side, the artist had inscribed the sentiment, "We must all rise above the few cultural differences that separate us and try our best to educate one another," and beneath Nicholas's feet a quote from Martin Luther King, Jr.: "Progress comes through the tireless efforts of people willing to be coworkers with God."

The mural seemed a tribute not only to Catherine Weldon, but to all those dead boys: Nicholas Heyward, Jr., Christopher Weldon, Crow Foot, and Chase Wounded. The night before, John F. Kennedy, Jr., had gone down in a plane not far from the spot where Don McNeil had drowned. I offered up a prayer that Don's brother, Ronald, would live a long life and that he and people like Jimmy McLaughlin, Jr., would help their tribe create fulfilling lives for themselves. And I promised that I would go home the next day and hold my son. I was glad that I had spent so much time on Weldon's trail. If nothing else, I learned that a vision must be followed. I had never felt more comfortable in the world than I did now, more connected to America. But my calling for the next few years was to stay home and raise my child.

I sent up a last prayer for Weldon. Had her building burned that night? More likely, it stood until some other tragedy consumed it. She was carried down the stairs on a gurney like the one I saw earlier that week. She died at Holy Family, and her body was sent to the funeral home around the corner, where Mrs. Sauerland sat behind her desk, desperately making phone calls until she turned up the address of that niece in Texas and sent a telegram to ask what she ought to do with her aunt's remains. A few people—not many—showed up to say good-bye. An examiner from the court stopped by the charred apartment to ascertain if Mrs. Weldon had left a will. "She kept to herself," the neighbors said. "She seemed a nice old lady." "She hadn't lived here long." "She gave my son an arrowhead for carrying up her bags." The examiner found a certificate proving that the deceased owned a plot at Green-Wood. She had just enough insurance to pay the fifteen-dollar burial fee and buy a plain wood box, but not enough to buy a monument.

No relatives or friends responded to the ad to claim her things. There were only two trunks, with nothing much inside but a bundle of faded letters; a child's dark, brittle curls wrapped in wrinkled paper; a moth-eaten robe with faded designs on what seemed to be the hide of a buffalo or cow; and some diaries that began in 1853 in German, then switched to English in the '80s, then stopped in '91. She left a closet of dusty clothes, outlandishly outdated. And a painting of an Indian. It wasn't very good. The frame was cheap, the canvas signed by the old lady herself. How much could it be worth? The landlord kept an old-fashioned bonnet for his wife and a pair of white kid gloves. Then he told his son to put everything else inside the trunks—these were cracked with age, so mildewed that no one would want to keep them—and carry them to the curb for the trashman's cart the next day.

Acknowledgments

I am deeply grateful to James Alan McPherson, who first told me about Catherine Weldon and suggested that "someone" write a book about her. I also owe debts I can never repay to Marcie Hershman, Charles Baxter, Suzanne Berne, Maxine Rodburg, Therese Stanton, Nicholas Delbanco, and Maria Massie, whose patience, encouragement, and wisdom informed my journey from start to end, and to David Holtby, without whom *Woman Walking Ahead* might never have been published.

To Ina and Ron McNeil, Isaac Dog Eagle, and their friends and relatives, I render my sincerest appreciation for your time and cooperation and my deepest regrets for any inconvenience or discomfort I might have caused. In your honor, and in memory of Sitting Bull and Catherine Weldon, a quarter of the royalties of this book will be donated to Sitting Bull College.

Thanks also to James McLaughlin, Jr., Mary Delia Carrigan Prather, Mary Delia Prather, Harold Parkin, and Rusty Corwin, guides along the journey; Bill Worthen and Dana Simmons of the Arkansas Territorial Restoration Project; colleagues and fellow searchers Joseph Silinonte, David Gurevitch, David Nicholson, Betty Bell, Linda Gregerson, Terri Tinkle, Bruce and Barbara Limpitlaw, Roberta and Dag Egede-Nissen, and Lincoln Faller; my students, especially Alex Ralph, Mikola de Roo, and Fritz Swanson; Arlene Keizer, Carol Bardenstein, and my other colleagues at the Institute for the Humanities; my parents and siblings; and Noah and Tom, who allowed me to go traipsing around the country in search of Catherine Weldon.

I would not have had the resources to write this book without generous grants from the Rona Jaffe Foundation and the University of Michigan, especially the Department of English, the Institute for the Humanities, and the Office of the Vice President for Research.

Many of the materials quoted in this book were provided through the inter-library loan service of the University of Michigan. Other materials were found in the following archives: the Brooklyn Historical Society; the Brooklyn Public Library; the Surrogate Court of Brooklyn, Supreme Court Building; the Huntington Free Library; the New York City Department of Records and Information Services, Municipal Archives; the New York Public Library; the Smithsonian Museum of Natural History; the Smithsonian Institution National Anthropological Archives; the Library of the National Museum of American Art and the National Portrait Gallery; the Library of Congress; the National Archives and Records Administration in Washington, D.C.; the Historical Society of Washington, D.C.; the State Historical Society of North Dakota; the South Dakota Historical Society; the Kansas City Public Library; the University of Oklahoma Library, Western History Collections, Norman, Oklahoma; the Holy Cross Cemetery of Brooklyn, New York; Union Cemetery Historical Society of Kansas City; and the Green-Wood Cemetery of Brooklyn. My thanks to the librarians and curators at these institutions, especially Mark Halvorson, Susan Dingle, Sharon Silengo, Jerry Newborg, and Chris Dill at the State Historical Society of North Dakota; Bradley Gernand and Laura Carter at the University of Oklahoma Library, Western History Collections; and Therese La Bianca at Green-Wood Cemetery. Special thanks to Gail P. Johnsen for allowing me to use photographs of her ancestor Elaine Goodale Eastman.

This book could not have been written without the earlier efforts of Stanley Vestal, a.k.a. Walter Campbell; I have drawn heavily on the materials about Catherine Weldon in his books about Sitting Bull and the Sioux and his mas-sive collection of papers at the University of Oklahoma in Norman. However, I often gave precedence to the scholarship of Robert Utley, as put forward in his superb biography, *The Lance and the Shield: The Life and Times of Sitting Bull.*

Among the other special collections upon which I relied: at the State Historical Society of North Dakota in Bismarck, *The Microfilm Edition of the Major James McLaughlin Papers*, edited by Louis Pfaller, the Fiske Photographic Collection, the Lucille Van Solen Photographic Collection, and the unpublished notes of Robert C. Hollow, late curator of the museum's archives; the collections of the State Historical Society of South Dakota in Pierre, especially the Riggs Family Papers and the Mary Clementine Collins Family Papers; the collections of the Brooklyn Historical Society and the Kansas City Public Library; the James K. Jones Papers in the Southern Historical Collection of the Library of the University of North

Carolina at Chapel Hill; the files of the U.S. National Archives and Records Administration in Washington, D.C., especially Record Group 75, Records of the Bureau of Indian Affairs, Special Case 188, relating to the Ghost Dance; the 1885 New Jersey State Census and census data for Brooklyn, New York, in 1915; city directories for Brooklyn, Manhattan, and Kansas City, Missouri; the eleven volumes of *The Council Fire and Arbitrator,* 1878–89 (called *The Council Fire* from 1878–81, *The Council Fire and Arbitrator* from 1882–85, *The Council Fire* from 1886–89; edited by Alfred Meacham from 1878–82, edited by Thomas A. and M. Cora Bland 1882–89, published in Philadelphia in 1878 and in Washington, D.C., 1878–89).

Notes

~~⌒⌒~~

Most of the information cited in *Woman Walking Ahead* is documented informally in the text. Additional sources are given below.

CHAPTER ONE
Leaving Brooklyn

pp. 3–4   The quote comes from Vestal, *Sitting Bull*, 264. The documents that formed my earliest impression of Weldon are to be found in Vestal's *New Sources of Indian History, 1850–1891 (NS)*, 92–117.

p. 4   "SHE LOVES SITTING BULL," *Bismarck Daily Tribune*, July 2, 1889.

p. 6   "Poor mis-guided beings . . . ," from Weldon's letter to McLaughlin, October 24, 1890, in *NS*, 102–3.

p. 7   The address "16 Liberty Street" is to be found on Weldon's letter to McLaughlin dated April 5, 1890, *NS*, 98–100.

pp. 12–13   For information about the "fruit streets" of Brooklyn see "Everybody Slept Here," by Rachel Shteir, *New York Times Book Review*, November 10, 1996; for the history of Cadman Plaza, see the *Encyclopedia of New York City*, edited by Kenneth Jackson, and *Old Brooklyn Heights*, by Clay Lancaster. The descriptions of life in Brooklyn in Weldon's day come from Robert Smith's *Brooklyn at Play, 1890–1898*.

CHAPTER TWO
A Strange Apparition

p. 16   The probable identification of the white woman in the photo as Sallie Battles comes from the Sitting Bull Archives of the Historical Society of South Dakota (HSSD). A note written on Smithsonian letterhead describes photograph 3194c, then in possession of the Bureau of American Ethnology. According to this description, the photo shows Sitting Bull seated outside his tipi at Fort Randall with a white woman "identified by Stanley Vestal as probably Miss Sallie Battles," as well as "an Indian woman with twin papooses" identified by Vestal as Sitting Bull's wife, the younger sister of Gray Eagle (this would have been Four Robes), and two older children. The photo is copyrighted by Bailey, Dix, and Mead and dated 1882. A description of Sallie Battles as "the niece of Colonel Andrews" is to be found in *NS*, 272–73.

p. 18   My knowledge of Vestal's divorce comes from Tassin's biography, *Stanley Vestal*, 216–17; Little Soldier's testimony is to be found in the W. S. Campbell Collection, Box 104 f6, in the Western History Collections at the University of Oklahoma in Norman.

Victorian reporters seem to have been notorious for misjudging women's ages, perhaps because asking a lady's birth date was impolite. When the anthropologist Alice Fletcher went to live among the Omahas in 1881, a reporter for the Sioux City *Journal* described her to his readers as "a brunette, solidly built, about twenty-five years old, rather good looking," although Fletcher, at the time, was forty-three (Mark, *Stranger in Her Native Land*, 65).

p. 19   To protect the Indian homesteaders from unscrupulous whites offering ready cash for land, the government held the deed to each 160-acre allotment for twenty-five years, after which the Indian head of the household would own the land outright.

p. 22   McLaughlin mentions his opposition to the first (1888) proposal to divide the reservation in his autobiography, *My Friend the Indian*, 274–75.

p. 24   Weldon's letter to Red Cloud is dated "Yankton Indian Agency, July 3, 1889," and is to be found, in its entirety, in *NS*, 92–96. The *Yankton Daily Press and Dakotan* published its account of Sitting Bull's illness on June 10, 1889.

p. 26   Weldon's encounter with McLaughlin at the settlement on the Cannonball is documented in her letter to Red Cloud; all dialogue comes directly from that letter or is suggested by its contents.

p. 27   Other information relating to Bland's "interference" in the commissioners' work comes from the *Yankton Daily Press*, June 10, 1889; Red Cloud's opposition to the cession is noted in the *Yankton Daily Press* of June 4, 1889.

p. 27   "Sitting Bull was now healthy enough to be interviewed . . . ," from the *Yankton Daily Press*, June 18, 1889. The same issue discusses Red Cloud's opposition to the cession.

pp. 28–29   As noted, this description of Weldon's first meeting with Sitting Bull is derived almost entirely from my imagination.

pp. 29–37   This synopsis of Sitting Bull's youth and middle age comes primarily from Vestal, *Sitting Bull*, and Utley, *The Lance and the Shield*, with precedence given to Utley's version of events.

pp. 37–38   Mary Collins offers most of this version of her first meeting with Sitting Bull in the "Short Autobiography" to be found in *NS*, 61–63. Other information related to Collins comes from Olsen's article, "Mary Clementine Collins," in *North Dakota History*, and Anderson's *Sitting Bull and the Paradox of Lakota Nationhood*, 146–48. Anderson's book provides Sitting Bull's response to the crucifixes erected by Collins and the other missionaries.

p. 40   An example of the hate mail Sitting Bull received can be found in *NS*, 76.

p. 40   Gates's quote from Prucha's *American Indian Policy*, 154.

pp. 41–42   Accounts of Sitting Bull's time with Cody's show can be found in Utley, *The Lance and the Shield*, and Moses's *Wild West Shows.*

p. 43   Vestal's speculations about Sitting Bull sweeping Weldon off her feet can be found in *Sitting Bull*, 264–65.

pp. 44–46   The facts on these pages come from Weldon's letter to Red Cloud. The conversations between Weldon and McLaughlin are given verbatim or suggested by Weldon's account and by McLaughlin's description of the argument in *My Friend the Indian* and his reports to the Commissioner of Indian Affairs (CIA).

p. 47   McLaughlin's reply to Dr. Wilder, dated July 10, 1889, is documented on Roll 20 of the microfilm edition of his correspondence at the State Historical Society of North Dakota (SHSND).

pp. 47–48   Sitting Bull's response to McLaughlin's denial of his pass, Faribault's threats, and Weldon's anger on Sitting Bull's behalf come from Weldon's letter to Red Cloud. The trip to the ferry in Sitting Bull's wagon definitely took place, but the details are invented.

pp. 50–51   The commissioners' activities at Standing Rock and Sitting Bull's response to their tactics are described by Vestal, *Sitting Bull*, and Utley, *The Lance and the Shield*, and by McLaughlin in *My Friend the Indian*. Sitting Bull's statement that there were no Indians left but women comes from the *Yankton Daily Press*, August 8, 1889, although the reporter has Sitting Bull call his warriors "squaws."

CHAPTER THREE
In the World Celestial

pp. 53–55   Collins's calling is described in Olsen's article, "Mary Clementine Collins," in *North Dakota History*, while the details of Goodale's early life come from her memoir, *Sister to the Sioux*, edited by Kay Graber. According to McLaughlin's reports to the CIA (from Roll 21 of his correspondence), Goodale inspected the schools at Standing Rock during the last two weeks of September 1890 and the first two weeks of October. This would have put her at the agency at roughly the same time that Weldon was visiting the Ghost Dancers at Grand River and delivering her sermon against Kicking Bear.

pp. 56–57   Goodale to Collier from Moses, *Wild West Shows*, 339. For Helen Pierce Grey's battle on behalf of the Crows, see Hoxie, *Parading*, 238–40; for Fletcher's change of heart about allotment, see Mark, *Stranger*, 267–68; for a detailed description of Fletcher's relationship to Francis La Flesche, see Mark, *Stranger*; for Jackson's relationship to Anna Leonowens, see Banning, *HHJ*.

p. 57   Cowger concludes in "Dr. Thomas Bland," *American Indian Culture*, 90, that "Bland stood almost alone as an opponent against the overwhelming popularity of assimilation. Nevertheless, he persistently fought against the IRA and the views expressed at the Lake Mohonk conferences. Bland believed that during the Indians' gradual transition into the dominant society, the tribal unit and the reservation should be retained. His aims, in direct contrast with those of the mainline reformers, opposed rather than encouraged forced allotment on the theory that the Indians had a right to determine their own affairs."

pp. 60–65   Anyone interested in the life of Alfred Meacham should consult Thomas Bland's wonderful *Life of Alfred B. Meacham*. The scene in the San Francisco bar comes from Bland's chapter on Meacham in *Pioneers of Progress*, 189–90. Meacham's ordeal in the

Lava Beds is best recounted by Meacham himself in his lecture "Tragedy of the Lava Beds," which Bland reprints in his *Life*. The material related to the Blands' association with Meacham comes from that same book.

pp. 65–66 "After years of repeated importunities . . . ," *Council Fire* (*CF*), January 1878; letter from McLaughlin in *CF*, April 18, 1878.

pp. 66–67 Letter from "Wigwam Writer" in *CF*, April 1879; McLaughlin's raillery against the "squaw men" from his letter to the CIA, October 7, 1881, Roll 32 of the microfilm edition of the McLaughlin correspondence; McLaughlin's first letter to Meacham from *CF*, March 1, 1880. McLaughlin's donation of $5 for a portrait of Meacham is noted in a letter to Mrs. M. Cora Bland dated May 25, 1880, on Roll 19 of microfilm edition of McLaughlin's correspondence. Contribution of $14 noted in *CF*, February 1881.

p. 67 Cora Bland's report on her trip was published under the title "From Savage Life to Civilization," in *CF*, September 1879. The few details I could gather about Cora Bland's life come from the *Records of the Columbia Historical Society, Washington, D.C.*, vol. 21, 306, published by the Columbia Historical Society of Washington, D.C., in 1918, and Gloria Moldow's *Woman Doctors in Gilded-Age Washington*, 19, published in 1987 by the University of Illinois Press in Urbana, Illinois. The charge that Cora Bland's presence on the editorial board of the *Council Fire* made it a refuge for sentimental and womanish ideas comes from Hagan's book *The Indian Rights Association*, 21.

pp. 67-70 Fanny Kelly relates her adventures and misfortunes in her *Narrative of My Captivity*; a more objective survey of her life comes from the prologue and epilogue to that story, written by Clark and Mary Lee Spence. The scene in which Sitting Bull rescues Kelly from Brings Plenty is provided in Vestal, *Sitting Bull*, 65–67. Kelly's injunction to the Sioux to avoid whiskey and her plan to establish a foster home for mixed-race children come from *CF*, September 1878. Her marriage notice is to be found in *CF*, June 1880.

pp. 70–71 "Interview with Sitting Bull's Sioux," *CF*, August 1881.

p. 71 Reprint of interview with Sitting Bull, "The Chieftain Tells a Little of His History," *CF*, October 1881.

pp. 71–72 "Agent McGillicuddy is an epicurean . . . ," *CF*, December 1882. McLaughlin's campaign to stop the army from cutting timber on the reservation is applauded in the May 1882 issue of *CF*. Evidence of Red Cloud's relationship to Fanny Kelly and the Blands from *CF*, October 1878 and January 1883.

pp. 72–75 Bland relates the details of his trip to Pine Ridge in *CF* July/August 1884; he recounts his meeting with Sitting Bull in Washington in *CF*, July 1885. The shift in Bland's thinking from protecting the Indians' property to championing their right to live as Indians is documented in *CF*, October 1885. Lyman Abbott rages against Bland's policies in the same issue. According to Cowger, "Dr. Thomas Bland," 83–84, Bland wanted the government to bestow absolute title to the various reservations to the tribes who lived there. "Bland's suggestions offered a strikingly different, even radical, alternative to other reformers' ideas. Except where a treaty or law gave a tribe fee title to its land, Indians held their reservations with only a right of occupancy, and the fee and the disposition of such lands rested solely with the government. If the tribes were to enjoy the full right and jurisdiction over reservation lands as Bland advocated, then tribal members, and not reformers, could determine when a tribe was prepared to allot the land to individuals. Bland maintained that gradual education of the Indians could also precede and not follow the dissolution of tribal lands as advocated by other reformers."

pp. 75–80   Bland's defense of the Indians' right to own and occupy their land in common is to be found in *CF,* February 1886. Painter's repugnance at the idea of the IRA joining the NIDA is documented in Prucha, *American Indian Policy,* 166. Dawes's denunciation of Bland comes from Hagan, *The Indian Rights Association.* Bishop Hare's accusation is recounted by Cowger, "Dr. Thomas Bland," 85. Abbott's assertion that "no student of the Indian question" supported the NIDA and Bland's response to that attack are printed in *CF,* February 1887. Bland describes his difficulty speaking to Sitting Bull in Washington in *CF,* January 1889. Bland's allusions to Weldon's activities on behalf of the Sioux, her residency in Hoboken, and her illness are to be found in the following editions of the *CF:* February 1889, April 1889, May 1889, September 1889.

pp. 81–83   Most of the information related to Bland's biography comes from the preface to *Pioneers of Progress.*

CHAPTER FOUR
On the Cannonball

pp. 87–89   Weldon's letter to McLaughlin is to be found in its entirety in *NS,* 98–100; Collins's attack on Bland is from Cowger, "Dr. Thomas Bland," 88.

pp. 89–90   For a more thorough description of the conventions of Victorian female life see Plante, *Women at Home,* and Donnelly, *The American Victorian Woman.* My knowledge of train travel in Weldon's time comes from Douglas, *All Aboard!*

pp. 90–95   My account of Weldon's train trip west is pure invention. Details of travel from Mandan to Standing Rock are drawn from Roll 36 of McLaughlin's correspondence and various articles of the day. The material in Miller's article about Weldon appears in similar form in his earlier book, *Ghost Dance.* Although Miller claims in that book to have drawn his facts about the Ghost Dance entirely from interviews with Indian witnesses, he credits no source for his version of Weldon's activities at Grand River or on the Parkin Ranch. The wording of the Weldon material in *Ghost Dance* strongly suggests Vestal as Miller's primary source, although Miller doesn't mention Vestal in any way.

p. 95   "It is a hazardous undertaking . . . ," from Weldon's letter to McLaughlin, *NS,* 100.

pp. 96-99   I owe my knowledge of the lives of Eagle Woman and her family to a series of splendid articles by John S. Gray in *Montana,* spring and summer 1986. The anecdote about Chaska Parkin selling the fillings from his teeth comes from Hinton's *South of the Cannon Ball,* 244. My description of the Parkin Ranch owes much to the same source.

CHAPTER FIVE
My Dakotas!

p. 100   The term *Sioux* is used by white speakers to describe three groups of Native American tribes. The eastern tribes (Mdewankantons, Wahpetons, Wahpekutes, and Sisetons) call themselves *Dakotas* and speak the dialect of the same name.

The middle tribes (Yanktons, Yanktonais, and Assiniboines) speak a dialect called *Nakota*, while the Western, or Teton, Sioux collectively refer to themselves as *Lakotas* and speak that dialect. (The Lakotas further divide themselves into the following tribes: Oglala, Brule, Miniconjou, Two Kettle, Sans Arc, Sihasapa, and Hunkpapa.) The title of this chapter is technically incorrect but derives from Weldon's frequent references to the Hunkpapas—and all Sioux—as "her" Dakotas. Vestal's remark about Weldon's "work for civilization" comes from *Sitting Bull*, 266–67.

p. 101   The rumors about Weldon and her relationship to Sitting Bull and his wives come from Vestal, *Sitting Bull*, 267, and various newspaper accounts of the day. Kelly's conversation with the white captive girl is recounted in her memoir, *Narrative*, 115. Bland's speech about Kelly and Meeker can be found in *CF*, January 1883.

p. 101   Robert Higheagle's testimony from *NS*, 56.

p. 102   After Sitting Bull arrived on the reservation, the local bishop tried to persuade him to give up one of his wives. Oh, I couldn't do that, Sitting Bull protested. I like both my wives equally. How would I decide which woman to divorce? I wouldn't want to hurt either one. Well, the bishop pushed, isn't it true that you promised you would try to live like a white man? All right, Sitting Bull agreed. I will live just like a white man. You give me one white wife and you can have both my Indian wives.

  Like Sitting Bull's joke to the reporter when he landed in Bismarck, this story confirms that he knew how fearfully the whites regarded interracial sex. He wanted to remain married to the two Indian women he loved, and the best way to do this was to remind his white keepers that an Indian content with his own wives was unlikely to cast his eye on theirs. That the chief is reported to have uttered this comment "with a twinkle in his eye and a slight grin of sarcasm" makes this reading more plausible than using the joke to prove he preferred Weldon because she was white (from McLaughlin, *My Friend the Indian*, 65–66, and Burdick, *Last Days*, 21).

pp. 102, 104   Photos of Red Cloud's cabin can be found in Jensen, *Eyewitness*, 74, 146; a photo of American Horse's cabin appears in *Eyewitness*, 147. Anyone interested in viewing photographs of the places and people involved in the Ghost Dance religion and the massacre at Wounded Knee should consult this invaluable resource.

p. 104–5   All descriptions of Rachel Calof's experiences in North Dakota come from her journal, *Rachel Calof's Story*, translated from the Yiddish by Jacob Calof and Molly Shaw and edited by Sanford J. Rikoon.

p. 105   A copy of Collins's response to the eastern ladies is on file in Folder 13, Box 1, among her papers at the HSSD. An Indian named Running Antelope was running a store at Grand River as early as 1884 (see Utley, *The Lance and the Shield*, 254), which leads me to surmise that a similar store was still there six years later.

p. 106   Goodale's quotation comes from Graber, *Sister to the Sioux*, 54.

p. 107   Evan Connell gives evidence of Sitting Bull's limited facility with English in his wonderful book on Custer, *Son of the Morning Star*. Not long before Sitting Bull's death, a telephone was hooked up between Alma Parkin's ranch and the agency. The chief was shown how to place a call to his relative. Though she spoke fluent Lakota, "Sitting Bull reasoned that the telephone understood only English, so when Mrs. Parkin answered the call he exclaimed, 'Hello, hello! You bet, you bet!' which exhausted most of his English. And when he realized that he could speak Dakota with this woman such a long way off he, like his contemporaries, was gravely shocked."

p. 107 Scraps of Weldon's translations were discovered in Sitting Bull's cabin after he was killed. Vestal reprints these in *NS*, 116–17.

p. 107 Luther Standing Bear's testimony comes from his memoir, *My People the Sioux*, 67. A description of the shoddy goods rationed to the Sioux can be found in Hagan's paper "The Reservation Policy: Too Little and Too Late," in *Indian-White Relations*, edited by Smith and Kvasnicka.

p. 107 The story about the Indians' encounter with the battery can be found in abbreviated form in Connell, *Son of the Morning Star*, 218, and in its entirety in Johnson's *Red Record of the Sioux*, 219–22.

pp. 109–10 Goodale's impressions of Sioux modesty can be found in her memoir, *Sister to The Sioux*.

pp. 110–12 Evidence for Weldon's attempt to mount the wild pony comes from a letter she wrote to Sitting Bull from Kansas City on December 1, 1890. The text, which can be found in *NS*, 110, runs as follows: "If I spoke against the dances & war it was because I am your true friend, have seen more of the world & knew what the result would be. A true friend will warn, & point out the dangers. Did you let me ride my wild horse when I wanted to? No. You forcibly detained me for my own good. Oh, my friend, may the Good God who used to watch over both of us, open your eyes to the truth."

The quotations from Weldon's diary are reprinted in *NS*, 116. Sitting Bull's opinions about white women can be found in Utley, *The Lance and the Shield*, 264, 269. Sitting Bull's mercy killing of the Crow woman is described in Vestal, *Sitting Bull*, 24–25. The chief's joke about the way white men treat their women comes from Anderson, *Sitting Bull and the Paradox*, 148.

Evidence that Sitting Bull proposed to Weldon comes from a fragment of her journal (reprinted in *NS*, 115–16), "You had no business to tell me of Chaska. Is that the Reward for so many years of faithful friendship which I have proved to you?" and Vestal's gloss on that fragment: "The reference to Chaska was her reply to Sitting Bull when he asked her to marry him, and reminded her that Chaska (another Sioux) had married a white woman." My conjecture that Chaska was the nickname of Charles DeRockbraine is supported by the testimony of John Loneman, *NS*, 48.

p. 112 "The gift of myself to a Sioux . . . ," from Goodale's memoir, *Sister to The Sioux*," 169); "Poor lady . . . ," from Vestal, *Sitting Bull*, 267.

p. 113 "I think myself just as great . . . ," from *NS*, 117. That "Hankake" might be Weldon's translation of "sisters-in-law" was suggested to me by Smith's *Moon of Popping Trees*, 109, footnote.

p. 113 The most complete and accurate account of Wovoka's activities around this time is provided by Hittman in *Wovoka and the Ghost Dance*; Wovoka's description of what he saw in his vision of heaven from Hittman, 15–17.

p. 114 Collins on Sitting Bull's ability to predict the weather, *NS*, 64.

pp. 114–16 For the evolution of Wovoka's doctrines among the Sioux, see Kehoe, *The Ghost Dance*, and Hittman, *Wovoka and the Ghost Dance*. Kicking Bear's speech comes to us via One Bull, as told to McLaughlin, who recounted it in his autobiography, *My Friend the Indian*, 182–89.

p. 118 Although the messianic elements in Wovoka's sermons might have derived in part from his upbringing in the home of a religious white farmer, David Wilson, contemporary scholars such as Kehoe and Hittman see the movement as largely Indian in its origins and nature. The quote from Mary Crow Dog about her husband's revival of the Ghost Dance in 1973 comes from Crow Dog and Erdoes, *Crow Dog*, 153.

pp. 118–20   Weldon's account of her "mission to the camp of Sitting Bull" and her dispute with Kicking Bear can be found in chapter XXIII of Johnson's *Red Record*. My knowledge of Johnson's life comes from the *Dictionary of American Biography*, vol. V, part I, ff. 134–35, and the *New York Herald Tribune*, March 29, 1931.

pp. 121–24   The text of McLaughlin's letter to the CIA, dated October 17, 1890, can be found among the microfilm publications of the U.S. National Archives and Records Administration, Record Group 75, Records of the Bureau of Indian Affairs, Special Case 188, relating to the Ghost Dance, as well as in the microfilm edition of McLaughlin's correspondence, Roll 35. A print copy can be found in Burdick's *Last Days*, 89–94. The chief's comparison of McLaughlin to his divorced wife Snow on Her comes from Vestal, *Sitting Bull*, 256. The story of Weldon's arrival at the Ghost Dancers' camp comes from her testimony to Johnson in *Red Record*.

pp. 124–28   Weldon's remarkable speech to the Ghost Dancers is given in its entirety in *NS*, 111–15. The story about Nosey Cohen comes from the *New York Herald*, November 28, 1890, while Weldon's note about the Mormons is to be found in *NS*, 115. Morgan's theory of mental atavism from Gonzalez, "The Hidden Power," 45–46; Miles's accusation from Smoak, "The Mormons and the Ghost Dance," 269. For a much fuller discussion of the Mormons' relation to the Ghost Dance see Barney, *Mormons, Indians, and the Ghost Dance* and Smoak, "The Mormons and the Ghost Dance."

pp. 129–30   The most extensive account of Kicking Bear's life is to be found in Miller's *Ghost Dance*. Although Miller is far from reliable on many matters, he appears to have based his narrative of Kicking Bear's visits to Wovoka on interviews with Native witnesses and survivors of the Ghost Dance, most notably Kicking Bear's son, Frank, who was seven when his father made his first pilgrimage to Nevada. According to Miller, Frank Kicking Bear was the prophet's only surviving child. He married Sitting Bull's granddaughter, Nancy, and settled at his father's old camp ten miles downstream from the site of the Wounded Knee Massacre, in what is now Manderson, South Dakota, where he still was living in the 1950s when Miller spoke with him. My attempts to find a descendant of Frank and Nancy Kicking Bear proved unsuccessful.

p. 133   Weldon's notes to McLaughlin, from *NS*, 100–103.

pp. 133–34   Collins's version of her visits to the Ghost Dancers' camp is to be found in *NS*, 66–68. Her dismissal of Sitting Bull as "hopelessly bad" is from the *New York Tribune*, November 26, 1890. Weldon's note to McLaughlin about "Miss Carrigan" from *NS*, 101.

pp. 135–36   "Not that I distrusted . . . ," from Johnson, *Red Record*, 327. McLaughlin's gift of a wagon to Gall, from Roll 34 of the McLaughlin correspondence. Gall's visit to Sitting Bull's camp, from Johnson, Red Record, 327. Biographical facts about Gall from *NS*, 223. Gall's troubles of the heart, from Connell, *Son of the Morning Star*, 376–77.

pp. 137–38   Weldon's note to McLaughlin from the Cannonball, dated October 24, 1890, from *NS*, 102–3.

pp. 139–41	The story of the vote of confidence by the New York Indian Association comes from the *New York Herald*, November 28, 1890, while the *New York Tribune* of November 19, 1890, printed the story about the Baptist Pastors' Conference. The figure of thirty thousand Sioux appeared in the *Tribune* on November 16, 1890; the seven thousand figure appeared on November 19. For copies of Royer's panicky telegrams to Washington see Roll 35 of the microfilm edition of McLaughlin's papers; the same source provides the plea from the frightened white settlers. Bland's discussion of Weldon's reports in the *New York Herald*, November 17 and 18, 1890.
p. 141	Miller's version of Christie's accident is to be found in *Ghost Dance*, 133.

CHAPTER SIX
Sitting Bull's Heart

pp. 143–44	McLaughlin recounts his visit with Primeau to Sitting Bull's camp in a letter to the CIA dated November 19, 1890; other versions are given in McLaughlin's autobiography, *My Friend the Indian*, 201–8, and Burdick, *Last Days*, 94–97.
p. 144	" . . . savages from either direction . . . ," *New York Herald*, November 24, 1890.
p. 146	Carignan's report to McLaughlin from *NS*, 10.
pp. 146–47	My version of Cody's aborted attempt to capture Sitting Bull comes from McLaughlin's account of those events in *My Friend the Indian*, 210–11 and on Roll 35 of the microfilm edition of his correspondence, as well as Vestal's description of Cody's drunkenness in *Sitting Bull*, 280–81.
pp. 147–48	In his biography, *Sitting Bull*, 283–84, Vestal provides the original letter that Andrew Fox wrote to McLaughlin and a more accurate translation of the chief's message. McLaughlin also discusses the letter in *My Friend the Indian*, 215.
pp. 149–52	John Loneman's testimony, *NS*, 45–55. My narrative of Sitting Bull's arrest and murder is derived largely from Vestal, *Sitting Bull*, and Utley, *The Lance and the Shield*.
p. 152	In the battle at Sitting Bull's camp, Shave Head was shot in the stomach. Carted back to the agency in a wagon, he lay in terrible pain. As Utley *(The Lance and the Shield*, 305–6) tells it, he asked McLaughlin if he had done well, and McLaughlin, choked by grief, could only nod. "Then I will die in the faith of the white man and to which my five children already belong, and be with them. Send for my wife, that we may be married by the Black Gown before I die." But Shave Head's wife lived eighteen miles from the agency, and by the time she reached her husband, he was dead.
pp. 152–56	President Harrison's remark on the death of Sitting Bull, from the *New York Tribune*, December 16, 1890. Reverend Murray's testimonial, *NS*, 91. "WHERE'S BULL'S BODY" from the *Bismarck Daily Tribune*, December 20, 1890. Bland's letter to Commissioner Morgan, dated December 27, 1890, and forwarded to McLaughlin on January 12, 1891, can be found on Roll 35 of the microfilm edition of McLaughlin's correspondence. McLaughlin speaks of his defense of Wi-ne-ma in *My Friend the Indian*, 214. One source (Jensen, *Eyewitness*, 56, 61) put the number of Sitting Bull's followers who fled to Big Foot's camp at Cheyenne River at forty, with another ten joining the hostile camp of Ghost Dancers at Pine Ridge. One Bull describes his family's losses in Vestal, *Sitting Bull*, 313.
pp. 156–57	Mention is made of the revolver Weldon supposedly gave to Sitting Bull in the

December 19, 1890, edition of the *New York Herald*, as well as the *Bismarck Daily Tribune* of that same day.

p. 157   Steele's account of the attack on Weldon's portrait of Sitting Bull and Steele's own rescue of the painting comes from a narrative he dictated in May 1939 as part of a Historical Data Project carried out by the SHSND, as well as a letter written by Steele to his mother on February 15, 1891, to be found in the Steele archives at the SHSND.

CHAPTER SEVEN
"I Am Informed That She Is an Adventuress"

pp. 158-59   These stanzas come from Walcott, *Omeros*, chapter XLII, 212.

pp. 159-60   The reference to Weldon working for Cody's circus is from Walcott, *Omeros*, 179. The other quotes appear on pages 213–18 of the poem. "Life is fragile . . . ," *Omeros*, 178. The quote from Walcott's unpublished play about Weldon and Sitting Bull can be found in Hamner's *Epic of the Dispossessed*, 28.

pp. 160-61   Correspondence and phone conversations with Mary Davis, librarian, Huntington Free Library, Bronx, New York, September 1996.

pp. 162-68   Background about Brooklyn in the 1890s from Smith, *Brooklyn at Play*. Description of activities of various women's groups working to help the Indians from LaPotin's *Native American Voluntary Organizations*, 119–20 and Prucha's *American Indian Policy*, 135–38; for a fuller account, see Wanken's *"Women's Sphere" and Indian Reform*. Most of the facts of Lyman Abbott's life come from his biography by Ira Brown, *Lyman Abbott*.

CHAPTER EIGHT
Prairie Knights

p. 181   Data related to alcohol use at Standing Rock from Bordewich, *Killing the White Man's Indian*, 248.

pp. 182-84   My scanty knowledge of Lakota comes from *Lakota: A Language Course for Beginners*, prepared by Oglala Lakota College and published in 1989 by Audio-Forum, a division of Jeffrey Norton Publishers, Inc., Guilford, Connecticut.

pp. 183-84   Goodale's travel experiences from Graber, *Sister to the Sioux*.

pp. 188-90   The original of the deed by which Weldon bestowed a portrait of Sitting Bull to Louise Van Solen is held in the files of the SHSND. Letter from Mrs. J. R. Harmon to SHSND, dated June 17, 1984, and answer to that letter from Robert C. Hollow, then Curator of Collections, dated June 25, 1984; both on file at the SHSND. Letter from John Baker, Ridgewood, New Jersey, dated April 16, 1977, to James Sperry, then Superintendent of the SHSND, and letter from Kenneth Brooks to Lynea Geinert, then registrar, SHSND, both on file at the Historical Society.

p. 192   Facts about early life on the Cannonball can also be found in *North Dakota Place Names*, compiled by Douglas Wick and published by Hedemarken Collectibles, Bismarck, North Dakota, 1988, and Hinton's *South of the Cannon Ball*.

pp. 198-200   Unpublished lecture by Robert C. Hollow, "Sitting Bull: Artifact and Artifake," on file at SHSND. Letter from Matthew Forney Steele to his mother, dated February 15, 1891, on file at SHSND.

pp. 201-2   Census information from Hinton's *South of the Cannon Ball*. Handleman's article was published in *The West*, October 1964.

p. 202   Pfaller's defense of McLaughlin occurs in the preface to *James McLaughlin: Man with an Indian Heart*, xi.

pp. 203-4   McLaughlin's letter to the bishop, Pfaller, *James McLaughlin*, 28; the agent's appeal to the "great chiefs" to "bury the hatchet," Pfaller, *James McLaughlin*, 67; the last buffalo hunt, Pfaller, *James McLaughlin*, 70–71.

pp. 204-5   McLaughlin's diatribe against ranching as the new Indian way of life from Pfaller, *James McLaughlin*, 74–75; the statistics documenting McLaughlin's years as agent in charge of Standing Rock, from various of his reports to the CIA and Pfaller, *James McLaughlin*, 86; " . . . had he cooperated . . . ," Pfaller, *James McLaughlin*, 93; Sitting Bull's trip to visit the Crow Indians in Montana, see Pfaller, *James McLaughlin*, 107–8, and Hoxie, *Parading*, 148–49. Hoxie gives a particularly revealing description of Sitting Bull's journey with a hundred followers to the Little Big Horn Valley, where they camped for two weeks and took a tour of the new monument to Custer and his fallen Seventh. Sitting Bull taunted his old enemies, the Crows, by telling them, "Look at that monument. That marks the work of our people." Because the Sioux had resisted the whites, he said, the whites treated the Sioux better than the Crows. "We get one and one half pounds of beef per ration, while you receive but one half pound. You are kept at home and made to work like slaves, while we do no labor and are permitted to ride from agency to agency and enjoy ourselves." The rest of the time, Sitting Bull preached against breaking up tribal lands and accepting allotments. He and his fellow chiefs had opposed the policy, he said, and their agent had given in. Real tribal leaders didn't cooperate with the government or its agents, he told the Crows. When the Crows' agent heard this, he wrote a furious letter to McLaughlin, complaining that "several of the Crow chiefs who had never before uttered one word against the allotments . . . came forward and took the same stand that Sitting Bull said *he* had taken at *his* agency."

pp. 205-9   All the letters described in these pages are part of the microfilm edition of McLaughlin's correspondence; McLaughlin's letter to Weldon to the effect that he had no vacancies at the school at Grand River is dated July 11, 1890, and is to be found on Roll 21 of his correspondence; the agent's hiring of Lucy Arnold as Matron of Domestic Economy is noted in Pfaller, *James McLaughlin*, 78. Discussions of the role of Victorian white women in inculcating the values of domesticity among the Indians may be found in Mathes, *HHJ*, 814, and Gonzalez, "The Hidden Power."

Sitting Bull's anxieties on behalf of the women of his tribe and their place in reservation life are documented by Mark in her biography of Alice Fletcher, *Stranger*. In 1881, touring Sioux country with Thomas Tibbles and Bright Eyes, Fletcher visited Sitting Bull, then a prisoner of war at Fort Randall. Now that the buffalo were extinct, Sitting Bull told Fletcher, the Indians had no choice but to accept white ways of earning their living. "For us, he said, glancing around at the middle-aged chiefs and headmen who sat in a circle inside his large tent, it is too late, but the young men can easily learn to plow and cultivate the land as the white men do. As he was speaking, one of his wives came in with wood for the fire. She threw the sticks on the flames and then dropped to the ground beside the fire, leaning on her elbow and looking intently at Fletcher. Fletcher noted her handsome face, sparkling eyes, and the gleam of brass bangles on her arms.

"Sitting Bull watched his young wife silently for several moments and then he turned to Fletcher. Through the translator, he began to speak slowly. 'You are a woman,' he said. 'You have come to me as a friend. Pity my women. We men owe what we have to them. They have worked for us . . . but in the new life their work is taken away. For my men I see a future; for my women I see nothing. Pity them; help them, if you can.' He took a ring from his finger and gave it to Alice Fletcher to remind her of his request" (60–62).

p. 210   For a description of the gala at the Parkin Ranch in honor of McLaughlin's promotion, see the *Bismarck Daily Tribune*, February 22, 1895. The details of McLaughlin's family life come from Pfaller, *James McLaughlin*, 193.

p. 211   See also Lass, *A History of Steamboating.*

pp. 213-15   Kelly's assessment of the beauty of the Cannonball Valley occurs in her *Narrative*, 154. The origin of the name "Cannonball" from the Federal Writers' Project guide to North Dakota, 297; directions to the Holy Hill of the Mandans, pp. 297–98 of the same guide; "a good place to observe the Sioux," 298; version of the legend of Standing Rock, Federal Writers' Project guide, 299–300.

p. 216   Description of Winona in its boom years, from the Federal Writers' Project guide, 300–301, and Hinton's *South of the Cannon Ball*, 55.

pp. 219-21   Some of the details of Sitting Bull's burial and the subsequent disturbances of his grave come from Vestal, *Sitting Bull*, and Utley, *The Lance and the Shield*, but most of the material on these pages is to be found in "The History of Sitting Bull's Remains," an unpublished essay written by Robert C. Hollow, then Curator of Collections at the SHSND, and dated August 2, 1985. Mossman's letter to Russell Reid, then superintendent of the Historical Society, is dated July 2, 1931, and can be found in the files of the Historical Society.

p. 222   Vestal's reluctance to award the beauty prize to McLaughlin's granddaughter is noted in Tassin, *Stanley Vestal*, 267.

CHAPTER NINE
Grand River

Passim,   The purpose of this chapter is not to give a complete description of a Sun
Chapter 9   Dance, nor to provide new information about the ritual. My intention was only to visit the site of the most important events in Weldon's life and try to gain insights into her position as a white observer of the Ghost Dance a century earlier. Although I had permission to observe the Sun Dance and was not told beforehand of any restrictions on what I could write, I was asked afterward by Isaac Dog Eagle not to focus on the details of the dance, which the Lakota people regard as intensely sacred and private, but rather on my own investigations regarding Weldon. In deference to this request, I include here only what seems essential to conveying my experiences at Grand River. Everything I have noted here about the Sun Dance already has been revealed in other sources. See, for example, Mails's *Sundancing at Rosebud and Pine Ridge*, especially notable for its photographs and drawings, and Walker's *Lakota Belief and Ritual*, which gives excellent descriptions of the *hunka* ceremony and the role of the *heyoka* in Lakota society.

pp. 243-44	Fiske's account of the schoolteacher, Jack Carignan, taking a Chicago reporter named Sam Clover to the Ghost Dancers' camp disguised as his cousin can be found in Fiske's biography of Sitting Bull, *Life and Death of Sitting Bull*, 35 (although Fiske calls the reporter "Culver"). Clover's own account, which he published on November 5, 1932, in angry response to Vestal's *Sitting Bull*, can be viewed on Roll 15 of the microfilm edition of McLaughlin's correspondence. The incident in which the Indians at Pine Ridge smashed a photographer's camera was first described in Johnson's *Red Record*, 342–45, and is revisited in Jensen's *Eyewitness*, 7. Much of my information about the German obsession with Native American culture comes from an article titled "Taking Reservations," by A. P. reporter Jeff Barnard, reprinted in the *Ann Arbor News* on March 8, 1998.
pp. 247-48	Riggs's burial of Sitting Bull's followers is described in an unsourced article on Roll 20 of the microfilm edition of the McLaughlin correspondence.

CHAPTER TEN
Pierre

pp. 260-61	For a complete account of the events surrounding the construction of the Oahe Dam, see Lawson, *South Dakota History*, 203–28.
p. 262	"Chief Sitting Bull, My Friend . . . ," from *NS*, 103–4. Background on steamboating from Lass, *A History of Steamboating*, and Poole, *Among the Sioux*, 25–27.
pp. 263-66	The history of Dick Talbot and the *Abner O'Neal* can be pieced together from the following editions of the *Bismarck Tribune*: April 1, May 9, July 13, August 5, August 12, October 25, November 9, and November 19, 1890. The excursion to Standing Rock is described in the *Bismarck Tribune*, August 19, 1890.
pp. 266-67	Weldon's letter to Sitting Bull from Kansas City, dated December 1, 1890, can be read in its entirety in *NS*, 109. These passages from her account to Johnson appear in *Red Record*, 330.
pp. 268-69	My information about the drowning of Donald Jackson and Alex Montalvo comes from the following articles in *Newsday*: July 21, 1997, "Wave Riders Missing/Craft Found, Brooklyn Men Gone," by Errol Crockfeld, Jr.; July 24, 1997, "Body of Boater Found/Friend Still Missing," by Olivia Winslow; August 4, 1997, "Sad Relief for Missing Man's Kin," by Emi Endo.

CHAPTER ELEVEN
Kansas City

pp. 270-74	For the complete text of Weldon's letter to Sitting Bull dated November 20, 1890, see *NS*, 103–5; for her letter dated November 23, see *NS*, 105–7; for her last letter, dated December 1, see *NS*, 107–10.
pp. 275-77	My impression of life in Kansas City, 1890–91, is drawn from a series of articles under the general title "Rowdy Times," written by Rick Montgomery and published in the *Kansas City Star* on November 2 and November 23, 1997, as well as Haskell's *City of the Future* and Schirmer and McKinzie's *At the River's Edge*.
pp. 279-80	Cody's remark about Sitting Bull from the *Kansas City Star*, November 24, 1890; report of the Negroes' request to hold a "ghost dance" from *New York Herald*, December 16, 1890, and *Washington Post*, December 17, 1890; remark about Sitting

Bull's body enriching the soil of the Dakotas from *Kansas City Star*, December 18, 1890; "WAR IN EARNEST" from *Kansas City Star*, December 30, 1890.

p. 280   The soldiers buried 147 Indians in a mass grave near the site, but estimates of the total Indian dead at Wounded Knee run as high as 250.

p. 284   The undertaker for "Chrys" Weldon, E. Stine and Sons, still operates in Kansas City, although it is now the Stine and McClure Funeral Home. I called and spoke to "Tammy" in customer service. The funeral home kept records back to its beginnings, she said in a cheerful drawl, but the only records for a Christopher Weldon are for a boy buried on November 17, 1890. He is listed as twelve years old. Whoever buried him paid Stine and Sons $21 for the service.

p. 285   "Female child offered for adoption," *Kansas City Star*, November 24, 1890; Eastman's testimony from Johnson, *Red Record*, 455; for a more factual account of the fate of one of the babies supposedly orphaned at Wounded Knee, see Jensen, *Eyewitness*, 135.

p. 286   "If his body & I were only in Dakota . . . ," from Weldon's letter to Sitting Bull dated December 1, 1890, *NS*, 110.

CHAPTER TWELVE
Little Rock

pp. 287-90   Correspondence concerning Bland's visits to Pine Ridge and Rosebud from NARA Record Group 75, letters received 1881–1907, letters 21019, 27528, 27758, 28442, 30469.

p. 290   Annie Oakley's efforts to clear her name in Riley, *Life and Legacy*, 76.

pp. 290-92   Scott reenactment from Jensen, *Eyewitness*, 96, with photo. Letters related to procurement of Sitting Bull's cabin and effects all from McLaughlin correspondence, as follows: Hansborough and Johnson to Secretary of the Interior, January 21, 1891; Casey to Morgan, February 14, 1891; Hansborough to Morgan, March 9, 1891; McLaughlin to Morgan, March 6, 1891; Johnson to Noble, March 13, 1891; Johnson to Noble, May 31, 1891; Shandler to Commissioner of Indian Affairs, May 13, 1891; testimony of Edward Forte, first sergeant Group "D," Seventh Cavalry, and civilian carpenter at Standing Rock, in Fiske, *Life and Death of Sitting Bull*, 55; quote from Fiske about possibility that Sitting Bull's cabin ended up at Coney Island from Fiske's letter dated September 27, 1950, sent from Fort Yates to Allan Eastman at the *Bismarck Daily Tribune*, in the files of the SHSND.

pp. 292-97   My account of the Indians' experiences at the World's Fair draws heavily on Moses, *Wild West Shows*, 106–9.

According to Miller (*Ghost Dance*, 274–75), to the end of his life Kicking Bear lived apart from whites. In 1899, the new agent at Pine Ridge tried to force Kicking Bear to send his children to a boarding school at the agency. When Kicking Bear refused, a tribal policeman showed up at his camp to bring the children in. Kicking Bear stood them off with a rifle, and the agent gave up. In 1903, a year before his death, Kicking Bear was still enough of a disciple of the Ghost Dance that he traveled again to Nevada to visit Wovoka and later taught the religion to an Assiniboine named Fred Robinson (Kehoe, *The Ghost Dance*, 44). Kicking Bear's thoughts upon seeing Sitting Bull's cabin, as well as the material related to Weldon's possible visit to the fair, are entirely my invention.

p. 299   Prather's poetry from Jensen, *Eyewitness*, 176.

pp. 301-5   Most of my knowledge of James K. Jones's life comes from Newberry's biography, *James K. Jones*; for a more objective discussion of his political career, see Niswonger's "Arkansas and the Election of 1896," *Arkansas Historical Quarterly*, spring 1975; for Jones's work on behalf of the Indians, see Hagan, *The Indian Rights Association*, 137, 245; documents related to Senator Jones's activities after he left office are to be found in the Manuscripts Department of the Library of the University of North Carolina at Chapel Hill, as part of the Southern Historical Collection.

CHAPTER THIRTEEN
Three Valentines

pp. 313-16   Information related to Weldon's death and burial from the files of Green-Wood Cemetery, 500—25th Street, Brooklyn, New York; information about Green-Wood from Vogel, "Green-Wood: Brooklyn's 'Garden City of the Dead,'" and various brochures available from the cemetery office. Weldon's death certificate, number 5238, on file in the Municipal Archives of the State of New York; death notice for Weldon's stepfather, Carl H. Valentiny, M.D., in *Brooklyn Daily Eagle*, May 29, 1882; death notice for Weldon's mother, Maria Barbara Valentiny, in *Brooklyn Daily Eagle*, April 9, 1887.

pp. 317-21   My discussion of Swiss culture and history comes largely from Herold, *The Swiss without Halos*; Luck, *A History of Switzerland*; Sorell, *The Swiss*; Story, *Swiss Life*; and Thürer, *Free and Swiss*.

pp. 322-29   My impression of Weldon's last days is simply that.

Sources

⁓

Newspapers

Bismarck Daily Tribune, June 20, July 2, 1889; April 1, 3, 19, May 8, 9, July 13, Aug. 5, 12, 14, 19, Oct. 25, 28, 30, Nov. 1, 9, 11, 18, 19, 20, 23, 25, Dec. 18, 19, 20, 25, 1890; February 22, 1895; March 9, 1920.

Bismarck Weekly Tribune, May 31, June 7, 15, 21, 25, July 5, 29, 30, 1889.

Brooklyn Daily Eagle, Nov. 7, 20, 23, 29, 1890; Dec. 2, 17, 20, 1890; March 16, 1921; Feb. 11, 12, 1939.

Kansas City Star, Nov. 21, 22, 24, 1890, Dec. 6, 16, 17, 18, 20, 22, 29, 30, 1890; Jan. 2, 10, 12, 17, 1891.

Kansas City Times, Nov. 26, Dec. 14, 30, 1890.

Newsday, July 21, 24, 25, Aug. 3, 4, 1997.

New York Herald, Oct. 29, Nov. 16, 17, 18, 19, 22, 24, 26, 28, Dec. 7, 16, 19, 23, 28, 1890.

New York Tribune, Oct. 28, Nov. 16, 17, 18, 19, 20, 21, 22, 23, 24, 25, 26, Dec. 4, 6, 16, 1890.

Pierre Daily Capital Journal, Aug. 15, 1889–Feb. 12, 1890; Feb. 13–Dec. 31, 1890.

Pierre Daily Free Press, Nov. 13, 1890.

Sioux City Journal, June–July 1889; May–Dec. 1890.

Washington Post, Nov. 14, 15, 16, 17, 18, 19, 25, 28, Dec. 17, 1890.

Yankton Daily Press and Dakotan, May 25, 1889–April 3, 1890 (esp. June 4, 10, 11, 13, 18, 26, 28, July 3, 10, Aug. 7, 8, 1889).

Books, Monographs, and Articles

Adams, Alexander B. *Sitting Bull.* New York: Putnam, 1973.

Anderson, Gary Clayton. *Sitting Bull and the Paradox of Lakota Nationhood.* New York: HarperCollins, 1996.

Banning, Evelyn I. *Helen Hunt Jackson.* New York: Vanguard Press, 1973.

Barney, Garold D. *Mormons, Indians and the Ghost Dance Religion of 1890.* Lanham, Md.: University Press of America, 1986.

Behrens, Jo Lea Wetherilt. "In Defense of 'Poor Lo': National Indian Defense Association and *Council Fire*'s Advocacy for Sioux Land Rights." *South Dakota History* 24 (fall/winter 1994): 153–73.

Bland, Thomas A. *A Brief History of the Late Military Invasion of the Home of the Sioux.* Washington, D.C.: National Indian Defence Association, 1891.

————. *Esau; or, The Banker's Victim.* Washington, D.C.: published by the author, 1892.

————. *Farming as a Profession, or, How Charles Loving Made It Pay.* Boston: Loring, 1870.

————. *How to Get Well and How to Keep Well: A Family Physician and Guide To Health.* Boston: Plymouth Publishing Co., 1894.

————. *How to Grow Rich: Illustrated by Brief Sketches of Famous Men of Ancient and Modern Times.* Washington, D.C.: Rufus H. Darby, 1881.

————. *In the World Celestial.* New York: Alliance Publishing; Chicago: Plymouth Publishing Co., 1901.

————. *Life of Alfred B. Meacham, Together with His Lecture "The Tragedy of the Lava Beds."* Washington, D.C.: T. A. & M. C. Bland, Publishers, 1883.

————. *Pioneers of Progress.* Chicago: T. A. Bland & Co., 1906.

Bordewich, Fergus M. *Killing the White Man's Indian: Reinventing Native Americans at the End of the Twentieth Century.* New York: Doubleday, 1996.

Brown, Dee. *Bury My Heart at Wounded Knee.* New York: Pocket Books/Washington Square Press, 1981.

Brown, Ira. *Lyman Abbott: Christian Evolutionist, A Study in Religious Liberalism.* Cambridge: Harvard University Press, 1953.

Bruchac, Joseph. *Native American Sweat Lodges: History and Legends.* Freedom, Calif.: Crossing Press, 1993.

Burdick, Usher L. *The Last Days of Sitting Bull, Sioux Medicine Chief.* Baltimore: Wirth Bros., 1941.

Carroll, John M., ed. *The Arrest and Killing of Sitting Bull: A Documentary.* Glendale, Calif.: Arthur H. Clark Co., 1986.

Connell, Evan S. *Son of the Morning Star.* New York: HarperPerennial, 1991.

Cook-Lynn, Elizabeth. *Why I Can't Read Wallace Stegner and Other Essays: A Tribal Voice.* Madison: University of Wisconsin Press, 1996.

Cowger, Thomas W. "Dr. Thomas Bland, Critic of Forced Assimilation." *American Indian Culture and Research Journal* 16:4 (1992): 77–97.

Crow Dog, Leonard, and Richard Erdoes. *Crow Dog: Four Generations of Sioux Medicine Men.* New York: HarperCollins, 1995.

DeBarthe, Joe. *Life and Adventures of Frank Grouard.* Edited by Edgar I. Stewart. Norman: University of Oklahoma Press, 1957.

DeLoria, Philip J. *Playing Indian.* New Haven: Yale University Press, 1998.

DeLoria, Vine, Jr. *Custer Died for Your Sins.* Toronto: Macmillan Co., 1969.

DeLoria, Vine V., Sr. "The Standing Rock Reservation: A Personal Reminiscence." *South Dakota Review* 9 (summer 1971): 169–95.

DeMallie, Raymond J., and Douglas H. Parks, eds. *Sioux Indian Religion.* Norman: University of Oklahoma Press, 1987.

Densmore, Frances. *Teton Sioux Music.* Bureau of American Ethnology Bulletin 61. Washington, D.C.: Government Printing Office, 1918.

Donnelly, Mabel Collins. *The American Victorian Woman: The Myth and the Reality.* Westport, Conn.: Greenwood Press, 1986.

Dorris, Michael. *The Broken Cord.* New York: HarperPerennial, 1990.

Douglas, George H. *All Aboard!: The Railroad in American Life.* New York: Marlowe & Co., 1995.

Dykshorn, Jan, ed. "Sitting Bull Collection." *South Dakota History* 5 (summer 1975): 245–65.

Eastman, Charles Alexander. *The Soul of the Indian: An Interpretation.* Lincoln and London: University of Nebraska Press, 1980.

Eastman, Elaine Goodale. "The Ghost Dance War and Wounded Knee Massacre of 1890–91." *Nebraska History* 26 (January–March 1945): 26–42.

Fechet, Edmond G. "The Capture of Sitting Bull." *South Dakota Historical Collections* 4 (1908): 185–93.

Federal Writers' Project, Works Progress Administration. *North Dakota: A Guide to the Northern Prairie State.* New York: Oxford University Press, 1950.

Federal Writers' Project, Works Progress Administration. *South Dakota: A Guide to the State.* 2d ed. New York: Hastings House Publishers, 1952.

Fiske, Frank Bennett. *Life and Death of Sitting Bull.* Fort Yates, N.Dak.: Pioneer-Arrow, 1933.

Gay, E. Jane. *With the Nez Perces: Alice Fletcher in the Field, 1889–92.* Lincoln: University of Nebraska Press, 1981.

Gidmark, Jill B., and Anthony Hunt. "Catherine Weldon: Derek Walcott's Visionary Telling of History." *CEA Critic* 59 (fall 1996): 8–20.

Gonzalez, John. "The Hidden Power: Domesticity and National Allegory in Helen Hunt Jackson's *Ramona.*" Unpublished paper, 2001.

Graber, Kay, ed. *Sister to the Sioux: The Memoirs of Elaine Goodale Eastman, 1885–1891.* Lincoln: Bison Books/University of Nebraska Press, 1985.

Gray, John S. "The Story of Mrs. Picotte-Galpin, a Sioux Heroine." *Montana: The Magazine of Western History* 36 (spring 1986): 2–21; (summer 1986): 2–21.

Grobsmith, Elizabeth S. *Lakota of the Rosebud: A Contemporary Ethnography.* New York: Harcourt Brace Jovanovich, 1981.

Hagan, William T. *The Indian Rights Association: The Herbert Welsh Years, 1882–1904.* Tucson: University of Arizona Press, 1985.

Hamner, Robert D. *Epic of the Dispossessed: Derek Walcott's Omeros.* Columbia and London: University of Missouri Press, 1997.

Handleman, Charles. "Was Mrs. Weldon Sitting Bull's White Squaw?" *The West* (October 1964): 8–11, 66–67.

Haskell, Henry C., Jr., Richard B. Fowler, and Frank Glenn. *City of the Future: A Narrative History of Kansas City, 1850–1950.* Kansas City, Mo.: F. Glenn Publishing Co., 1950.

Hassrick, Royal B. *The Sioux: Life and Customs of a Warrior Society.* 5th ed. Norman: University of Oklahoma Press, 1977.

Herold, J. Christopher. *The Swiss without Halos.* New York: Columbia University Press, 1958.

Hinton, May E. *South of the Cannon Ball: A History of Sioux, the War Bonnet County.* North Dakota: n.p., 1984.

Hittman, Michael, and Don Lynch. *Wovoka and the Ghost Dance.* Lincoln: University of Nebraska Press, 1990.

Hollow, Robert C. "Sitting Bull: Artifact and Artifake." Address delivered at Eighth Annual Plains Indian Seminar, Buffalo Bill Historical Center, Cody, Wyo., Sept. 29, 1984; unpublished manuscript in archives at the State Historical Society of North Dakota, Bismarck.

———. "The History of Sitting Bull's Remains." Unpublished manuscript. Bismarck: State Historical Society of North Dakota.

Holmes, Steven A. "Bringing Hope and Education to the Reservation: Tribal Colleges Grapple with Challenges of Success." *New York Times,* August 3, 1997.

Hoover, Herbert T. *The Sioux: A Critical Bibliography.* Bloomington: Indiana University Press, 1979.

Hoover, Herbert T., and Robert C. Hollow. *Last Years of Sitting Bull.* Bismarck: State Historical Society of North Dakota, 1984.

Hoover, Herbert T., and Karen P. Zimmerman. *The Sioux and Other Native American Cultures of the Dakotas: An Annotated Bibliography.* Westport, Conn.: Greenwood Press, 1993.

Hoxie, Frederick E. *Parading through History: The Making of the Crow Nation in America, 1805–1935.* Cambridge, England: Cambridge University Press, 1995.

Hyde, George E. *Red Cloud's Folks: A History of the Oglala Sioux Indians.* Norman: University of Oklahoma Press, 1957.

Jackson, Kenneth, ed. *Encyclopedia of New York City.* New Haven: Yale University Press, 1995.

Jensen, Richard E., R. Eli Paul, and John E. Carter, eds. *Eyewitness at Wounded Knee.* Lincoln and London: University of Nebraska Press, 1991.

Johnson, W. Fletcher. *The Red Record of the Sioux: Life of Sitting Bull and History of the Indian War of 1890-'91.* n.p.: Edgewood Publishing Company, 1891.

Kasper, Shirl. *Annie Oakley.* Norman: University of Oklahoma Press, 1992.

Kehoe, Alice Beck. *The Ghost Dance: Ethnohistory and Revitalization.* New York: Holt, Rinehart and Winston, 1989.

Kelly, Fanny. *Narrative of My Captivity among the Sioux Indians.* Edited by Clark and Mary Lee Spence. Chicago: Lakeside Press/R. R. Donnelley & Sons, 1990.

Kolbenschlag, George R. *A Whirlwind Passes: Newspaper Correspondents and the Sioux Indian Disturbances of 1890–1891.* Vermillion, S.Dak.: University of South Dakota Press, 1990.

Lancaster, Clay. *Old Brooklyn Heights.* Rutland, Vt.: Charles E. Tuttle, Co., 1961.

Landon, Margaret. *Anna and the King of Siam.* Garden City, N.Y.: Garden City Publishing Co., 1944.

LaPotin, Armand S., ed. *Native American Voluntary Organizations.* Westport, Conn.: Greenwood Press, 1987.

Lass, William E. *A History of Steamboating on the Upper Missouri River.* Lincoln: University of Nebraska Press, 1962.

Lawson, Michael L. "The Oahe Dam and the Standing Rock Sioux." *South Dakota History* 6 (spring 1976): 203–28.

Leonowens, Anna Harriette. *The English Governess at the Siamese Court.* Boston: Fields, Osgood and Company, 1870.

Lounsberry, Colonel Clement A. *Early History of North Dakota: Essential Outlines of American History.* Washington, D.C.: Liberty Press, 1919.

Luck, James Murray. *A History of Switzerland.* Palo Alto: Society for the Promotion of Science and Scholarship, Inc., 1985.

Mails, Thomas E. *Sundancing at Rosebud and Pine Ridge.* Sioux Falls, S.Dak.: Center for Western Studies, Augustana College, 1978.

Mardock, Robert Winston. *The Reformers and the American Indian.* Columbia: University of Missouri Press, 1971.

Mark, Joan. *A Stranger in Her Native Land: Alice Fletcher and the American Indians.* Lincoln: University of Nebraska Press, 1988.

Marken, Jack W., and Herbert T. Hoover. *Bibliography of the Sioux.* Metuchen, N.J.: Scarecrow Press, 1980.

Mathes, Valerie Sherer. *Helen Hunt Jackson and Her Indian Reform Legacy.* Austin: University of Texas Press, 1990.

Mathes, Valerie Sherer, ed. *The Indian Reform Letters of Helen Hunt Jackson, 1879–1885.* Norman: University of Oklahoma Press, 1998.

McConn, Thomas. "Guest of the Railroad: Sitting Bull in Bismarck, September, 1883." Unpublished manuscript, State Historical Society of North Dakota, 1993.

McLaughlin, James. *My Friend the Indian.* Cambridge: Riverside Press/Houghton Mifflin Co., 1910.

Meier, Heinz K. *The United States and Switzerland in the Nineteenth Century.* The Hague: Mouton & Co., 1963.

Mihesuah, Devon A., ed. *Natives and Academics: Researching and Writing about American Indians.* Lincoln and London: University of Nebraska Press, 1998.

Miller, David Humphreys. *Ghost Dance.* New York: Duell, Sloan and Pearce, 1959.

———. "Sitting Bull's White Squaw." *Montana: The Magazine of Western History* 14 (April 1964): 55–71.

Montgomery, Rick. "Rowdy Times." *Kansas City Star,* November 2, 1997, and November 23, 1997.

Mooney, James. *The Ghost-Dance Religion and the Sioux Outbreak of 1890.* Abridged, with an introduction by Anthony F. C. Wallace. Chicago: University of Chicago Press, 1965.

Moses, L. G. *Wild West Shows and the Images of American Indians, 1883–1933.* Albuquerque: University of New Mexico Press, 1996.

Neihardt, John G. *Black Elk Speaks.* New York: William Morrow & Co., 1932.

Newberry, Farrar. *James K. Jones: The Plumed Knight of Arkansas.* n.p.: Siftings Herald Co., 1913.

Niswonger, Richard. "Arkansas and the Election of 1896." *Arkansas Historical Quarterly* 34 (spring 1975): 41–78.

Odell, Ruth. *Helen Hunt Jackson.* New York: D. Appleton-Century Company, 1939.

Olsen, Louise P. "Mary Clementine Collins." *North Dakota History* 19 (January 1952): 59–81.

Pfaller, Louis L. *James McLaughlin: The Man with an Indian Heart.* Richardton, N.Dak.: Assumption Abbey Press, 1992.

Plante, Ellen M. *Women at Home in Victorian America: A Social History.* New York: Facts on File, Inc., 1997.

Poole, D. C. *Among the Sioux of Dakota: Eighteen Months' Experience as an Indian Agent, 1869–70.* St. Paul: Minnesota Historical Society Press, 1988.

Prucha, Francis Paul. *American Indian Policy in Crisis: Christian Reformers and the Indian, 1865–1900.* Norman: University of Oklahoma Press, 1976.

Riggs, Stephen R. *Mary and I: Forty Years with the Sioux.* Minneapolis: Ross and Haines, 1969.

Riggs, Thomas L., as told to Mary K. Howard. "Sunset to Sunset: A Lifetime with My Brothers the Sioux." *South Dakota Historical Collections* 24 (1958): 258–69.

Rikoon, J. Sanford, ed. *Rachel Calof's Story.* Bloomington: Indiana University Press, 1995.

Riley, Glenda. *Life and Legacy of Annie Oakley.* Norman: University of Oklahoma Press, 1994.

Robinson, Doane. "Some Sidelights on the Character of Sitting Bull." *Collections of the Nebraska State Historical Society* 16 (1911): 187–92.

Rose, Wendy. "The Great Pretenders, Further Reflections on Whiteshamanism." *The State of Native American Genocide, Colonization, and Resistance.* Edited by M. Annette Jaimes. Boston: South End Press, 1992.

Schirmer, Sherry Lamb, and Richard McKinzie. *At the River's Edge: An Illustrated History of Kansas City.* Woodland Hills, Calif.: Windsor Publications, 1982.

Seymour, Flora Warren. *Indian Agents of the Old Frontier.* n.p.: Appleton Century, 1941.

Shteir, Rachel. "Everybody Slept Here." *New York Times Book Review,* November 10, 1996.

Smith, Jane F., and Robert M. Kvasnicka, eds. *Indian-White Relations: A Persistent Paradox.* Washington, D.C.: Howard University Press, 1976.

Smith, Rex Alan. *Moon of Popping Trees.* New York: Reader's Digest Press, 1975.

Smith, Robert P. *Brooklyn at Play: The Illusion and the Reality, 1890–1898.* New York: Revisionist Press, 1977.

Smoak, Gregory E. "The Mormons and the Ghost Dance of 1890." *South Dakota History* 16 (fall 1986): 269–94.

Sorell, Walter. *The Swiss: A Cultural Panorama of Switzerland*. New York: Bobbs-Merrill Company, 1972.

Standing Bear, Luther. *My People the Sioux*. Edited by E. A. Brininstool. Lincoln: University of Nebraska Press, 1975.

Steele, Mathew Forney. Letter to his mother, February 15, 1891. State Historical Society of North Dakota, Bismarck.

Story, Alfred T. *Swiss Life in Town and Country*. New York: G. P. Putnam's Sons, 1902.

Tassin, Ray. *Stanley Vestal: Champion of the Old West*. Glendale, Calif.: Arthur H. Clark Company, 1973.

Thürer, Georg. *Free and Swiss*. London: Oswald Wolf, 1970.

Turner, Harold W. *Bibliography of New Religious Movements in Primal Societies*. Vol. II, *North America*. Boston: G. K. Hall & Co., 1978.

Twofeathers, Manny. *The Road to the Sundance: My Journey into Native Spirituality*. New York: Hyperion, 1994.

Utley, Robert M. *The Lance and the Shield: The Life and Times of Sitting Bull*. New York: Ballantine Books, 1993.

——. *The Last Days of the Sioux Nation*. New Haven: Yale University Press, 1963.

Vestal, Stanley. *New Sources of Indian History, 1850–1891*. Norman: University of Oklahoma Press, 1934.

——. *Sitting Bull, Champion of the Sioux: A Biography*. 2d ed. Norman: University of Oklahoma Press, 1957.

——. *Warpath: The True Story of the Fighting Sioux Told in a Biography of Chief White Bull*. Edited by Raymond DeMallie. Lincoln: University of Nebraska Press, 1984.

——. "White Bull and One Bull—An Appreciation." *Westerners Brand Book* (Chicago) 4 (October 1947): 46–48.

Vogel, Frederick G. "Green-Wood: Brooklyn's 'Garden City of the Dead.'" *American Cemetery Magazine* (January–April 1985).

Walcott, Derek. *Omeros*. New York: The Noonday Press/Farrar, Straus and Giroux, 1990.

Walker, James R. *Lakota Belief and Ritual*. Edited by Raymond J. DeMallie and Elaine A. Jahner. Lincoln and London: University of Nebraska Press, 1991.

——. *Lakota Society*. Edited by Raymond J. DeMallie. Lincoln and London: University of Nebraska Press, 1992.

Wanken, Helen M. *"Women's Sphere" and Indian Reform: The Women's National Indian Association, 1879–1901*. Ph.D. diss., Marquette University, 1981.

Worthen, William B. "Arkansas and the Toothpick State Image." *Arkansas Historical Quarterly* 53 (summer 1994): 161–90.

Yellowtail, as told to Michael Oren Fitzgerald. *Yellowtail: Crow Medicine Man and Sun Dance Chief, An Autobiography*. Norman: University of Oklahoma Press, 1991.

Index

⁓